Thomas Dolby

Dictionary of Shakespearean Quotations.

Exhibiting the Most Forcible Passages...

Thomas Dolby

Dictionary of Shakespearean Quotations.
Exhibiting the Most Forcible Passages...

ISBN/EAN: 9783337275235

Printed in Europe, USA, Canada, Australia, Japan

Cover: Foto ©Andreas Hilbeck / pixelio.de

More available books at **www.hansebooks.com**

DICTIONARY

OF

Shakespearian Quotations.

EXHIBITING

THE MOST FORCIBLE PASSAGES

ILLUSTRATIVE OF THE VARIOUS

PASSIONS, AFFECTIONS AND EMOTIONS

OF THE HUMAN MIND.

SELECTED AND ARRANGED

IN ALPHABETIC ORDER,

FROM THE WRITINGS OF

The Eminent Dramatic Poet.

PHILADELPHIA:
CLAXTON, REMSEN & HAFFELFINGER,
624, 626 & 628 Market Street.
1877.

Explanation

OF THE ABBREVIATED REFERENCE TO THE CONTEXT, APPENDED TO EACH EXTRACT OR QUOTATION.

A. C.   Antony and Cleopatra.
A. W.   All's Well that Ends Well.
A. Y.   As You Like It.
C.   Coriolanus.
C. E.   Comedy of Errors.
Cym.   Cymbeline.
H.   Hamlet.
H. IV. PT. I.   Henry Fourth, Part First.
H. IV. PT. II.   Henry Fourth, Part Second.
H. VI. PT. I.   Henry Sixth, Part First.
H. VI. PT. II.   Henry Sixth, Part Second.
H. VI. PT. III.   Henry Sixth, Part Third.
J. C.   Julius Cæsar.
H. V.   Henry Fifth.
H. VIII.   Henry Eighth.
K. J.   King John.

K. L.   King Lear.
R. II.   Richard the Second.
R. III.   Richard the Third.
L. L.   Love's Labour Lost.
M.   Macbeth.
M. A.   Much Ado about Nothing.
M. M.   Measure for Measure.
M. N.   Midsummer Night's Dream.
M. V.   Merchant of Venice.
M. W.   Merry Wives of Windsor.
O.   Othello.
P. P.   Pericles, Prince of Tyre.
R. J.   Romeo and Juliet.
T.   Tempest.
T. A.   Timon of Athens.
Tit. And.   Titus Andronicus.
T. C.   Troilus and Cressida.
T. G.   Two Gentlemen of Verona.
T. N.   Twelfth Night.
T. S.   Taming of the Shrew.
W. T.   Winter's Tale.

*** The *Act* is expressed by Roman numerals; the *Scene* by Arabic figures.

EXAMPLE: *A. C.* iv. 7, signifies, Antony and Cleopatra, Act the Fourth, Scene the Seventh.

Preface.

The matchless genius of Shakespeare has furnished occupation for authors, from the very age in which he wrote, down to the present day; so that, independent of the innumerable editions of his plays, from the original authentic copies, to the modern mutilations represented under his name upon the stage, we have more than two hundred works of which Shakespeare and his writings are the subject.

Such being the case, it may be thought necessary, for one who ventures to add to the number, to offer some apology to the public for so doing. That tendered for the present compilation is founded on the belief, that among all these works, there does not exist one which effectively occupies the ground here taken, and very few which even attempt to connect Shakespeare's felicitous expressions —exhibiting, as they do, a matchless insight into human nature— with the various casualties, motives, and objects of ordinary life. Such a task, if performed with judgment and faithfulness, could hardly fail to prove both pleasing and useful. In support of the opinion that this task yet remained to be accomplished, it will be necessary to submit a few observations concerning the works which profess to have the same object, upon the comparative merits of which with the SHAKESPEARIAN DICTIONARY, its pretensions to public favour must be founded.

Ayscough's "Index to Shakespeare," is a work of great labour, and, as a verbal compilation, is doubtless of utility; but it is a dictionary of the poet's *words*, rather than of his *expressions*, giving only so much of the context as was necessary to elucidate the peculiar sense wherein each word is to be understood, and connecting this with remarkable speeches only by means of references. From almost any arrangement of the words of such an author, occasional scintillations will necessarily flash out; but in

Preface.

this case, the pleasing effect, which thus occurs, is destroyed when we arrive at the next word in the catalogue. We may learn to number the occasions wherein each word recurs throughout the author's writings, but what have the imagination or the feelings to do with such a calculation? We may, indeed, retain the consciousness we bring with us of treading on hallowed ground, but feel not the inspiring influence of the divinity.

Certain smaller compilations, put forth under the captivating title of "Beauties of Shakespeare," contain only the more remarkable speeches, and, for the most part, are confined to such as are clothed in verse; omitting altogether the thousands of expressions strewed profusely throughout the prose speeches and colloquies, wherein are to be found all those most surprising flashes of description, alternating from the grotesque to the sublime, which peculiarly distinguish the Bard of Avon from all other writers, either ancient or modern.

In this class of compilations must be included a work, published about ten years since, "by the author of the Peerage and Baronetage Chart," and called "A Dictionary of Quotations from Shakespeare;" but the same objection that attends the "Beauties," must be made against the "Dictionary." The quotations are given exclusively from the measured poetry of the author, while the prose speeches and colloquies are wholly neglected. Fearful of being suspected of speaking unfairly, concerning a work which comes, perhaps, the nearest in collision with the present, a specimen is here introduced, whence the reader may form some opinion of the editorial discrimination which has been exhibited. Under the head of *Drunkenness*, the description of Danish regal ceremonies is introduced from Hamlet:—

> " Give me the cups;
> And let the kettle to the trumpet speak,
> The trumpet to the cannoneer without,
> The cannons to the heavens, the heavens to earth,
> Now the king drinks to Hamlet."

Under the same head we find inserted the pledge of returning amity between Brutus and Cassius, taken from the play of Julius Cæsar:—

> "Give me a bowl of wine;
> In this I bury all unkindness, Cassius."

Preface.

As another illustration of the same subject, we have the expression of Richard, endeavouring to rally his downcast spirits against the pressure of a guilty conscience:—

"Give me a bowl of wine;
I have not that alacrity of spirit
Nor cheer of mind that I was wont to have."

Now it is difficult to conceive how these different quotations relate to drunkenness, save only as they refer to the act of drinking; without which, that wretched state or propensity which we express by the word drunkenness, cannot indeed have existence.

"The Aphorisms of Shakespeare," edited by Mr. Capel Lofft, and printed and published at Bury St. Edmunds about twenty years ago, formed a collection worthy of that highly gifted gentleman. Mr. Lofft extracted sentences from Shakespeare, beginning with the play of *Hamlet*. To each extract he prefixed a synonym, or concisely descriptive sentence. Where he conceived the author to be obscure, from having used terms that have become obsolete, or encumbered by expletives, he took the liberty of altering the text, and of reducing any extract according to his own pleasure, into an aphoristic compass. The result proved, as might have been expected from so competent an editor, and such rich materials, one of the most choice collections of aphoristic wisdom that ever issued from the press. The defects of Mr. Lofft's book were, that he arranged each play separately, without any classification of subjects, or alphabetical order: hence its inconvenience as a work of reference. Suppose it were required to be known what Shakespeare had said on the subject of *Grief, Man, Pride*, or any other matter, a person would probably require to look for these in as many different places, as Shakespeare wrote plays. As a Dictionary of Shakespearian Quotations, it could not, for obvious reasons, be of any use.

In the compilation now submitted to the public, each extract will be found classed under its appropriate head; and where the import could be expressed in a single word, it is so expressed; but where such brevity was found impracticable, the drift or spirit of the extract is expressed in the fewest words possible. In certain cases it has been found impracticable to express the import of an extract literally, either by a single word, or by a short sentence. In such cases the compiler has endeavoured to catch the spirit, and to prefix such a term as would best convey it to the reader's comprehension.

Preface.

If he has not in all such cases been successful, the candid will not hastily condemn, but refer for a better term to the context. Whatever the compiler's demerits may be, the charge of altering the language of Shakespeare cannot be sustained, for the text is in no instance meddled with, except with the view to reconcile slight variations which occur in the most authentic editions. The whole collection has been finally revised, and collated with the edition of *Heminge* and *Condell*, folio, Lond. 1632.

As a table-book, it is presumed this work will be found no less pleasing, than as a book of reference it will be useful. Expressions, long and short, grave and gay, when read consecutively, will ever produce a pleasing effect; and the devoted admirer of Shakespeare will not, it is hoped, be displeased at occasionally meeting beauties which had long been familiar to him, suddenly presenting themselves from behind coverts where he had not expected to see them.

The DICTIONARY OF SHAKESPEARIAN QUOTATIONS, being the result of some thought, as well as labour, is respectfully offered as a book of utility to foreigners, young persons, and others, engaged in enquiries into the structure of our language; the synonym and the extract being mutually illustrative, according to Locke's idea of a *definition*.

BRIEF CRITICISMS

ON THE

Works of Shakespeare.

There have been men of learning and talent in the world, whose merits, real or supposed, have ensured to their names and memories honours more glorious and more lasting than the highest titles which any merely hereditary or heraldic claims could boast. We have "the *learned* John Selden;" "the *judicious* Hooker;" "the *ever-memorable* John Hales;" "the *admirable* Crichton;" "the *leviathan in literature*, Dr. Samuel Johnson," and many others; but not one of all this phalanx of merit has more justly deserved his honorary distinction, than "the Immortal Shakespeare." Had this man lived in the ancient days of Greece or Rome, he had now occupied no contemptible place in the mythological records of those times. But Shakespeare was born to higher honours than any to be derived from a Pagan apotheosis. He lives in the heart of every man of correct taste—he dwells on the lip of eloquence—he gives life, and soul, and energy to every feeling expression—he lends his powerful aid to the moralist, and is not despised even by the true religionist —nay, his very enemies, the saints of modern date, "praise him in the gate"—and often, unwittingly, it is granted, do homage to his memory by borrowing his language to aid their own crude conceptions; nor have instances been wanting, within the observation of the writer, of persons, even in the pulpit, quoting the "bard of Avon," at a time when they themselves imagined they were borrowing from some of our best divines.

Alas! how difficult a task it is to write of Shakespeare and his works in terms adequate to their claims on our wonder, admiration, and esteem! Yet nearly one hundred different works have already been successively published on the writings and genius of this truly immortal bard.

Of the life of our author nothing new can be said: his biography has been exhausted, yet would it be a gross injustice to him to print his works without prefixing whatever has been authentically handed down to us. But his *mind* lives for ever; and will for ever furnish some new topic of admiration, or some fresh subject of literary criticism.

A contemporary writer on Ecclesiastical History, speaking of that best of books, the Bible, thus expresses himself: "One little book, which I can carry in my bosom, and refer to in every exigence of moment to my soul's peace, is worth all the mighty tomes of the Vatican; superior, in my estimation, to all that ever bishops wrote, or canonists have quarrelled about." There is nothing profane in the observation, that what the Sacred Volume is to the devout Christian, the works of Shakespeare are to the man of taste; for there is scarcely a subject of the slightest interest, that has not received some illustration from the writings of this author, in whose mind appear to have been embodied all the forms and fashions, all the great, and all the minute shades of human character. Shakespeare was great upon all subjects, which is more than can, with truth, be asserted of any other writer, in any age or any country. His writings may be referred to on almost all occasions; and the man whose mind is stored with the language of our bard, need never be at a loss for topics of conversation, or subjects of important reflection.

Shakespeare was not only what Ben Jonson denominates him, the

"——————— soul of the age,
The applause, delight, and wonder of the stage;"

but is to this hour the constant companion of the contemplative, as well as the gay associate of the playful and the happy.

"Thus while I wond'ring pause o'er Shakespeare's page,
I mark in visions of delight the sage;
High o'er the wrecks of man, who stands sublime,
A column in the melancholy waste,
(Its glory humbled and its glories past,)
Majestic 'mid the solitude of time."

Criticisms on the Works of Shakespeare.

On this head it would be unpardonable to omit noticing what Schlegel has said of our poet, in his German "Lectures on the Drama," which, translated into English, is as follows:—Never, perhaps, was there so comprehensive a talent for characterization as Shakespeare's. It not only grasps the diversities of rank, sex, and age, down to the dawnings of infancy; not only do the king and the beggar, the hero and the pickpocket, the wise and the idiot, speak and act with equal truth—not only does he transport himself to distant ages and to foreign nations, and pourtray in the most accurate manner, with only a few apparent violations of costume, the spirit of the ancient Romans—of the French in their wars with the English—of the English themselves during a great part of their history—of the Southern Europeans (in the serious parts of many of his comedies,) the cultivated society of that time, and the former rude and barbarqus state of the north; his human characters have not only such depth and precision that they cannot be arranged under classes, and are inexhaustible, even in conception; no, this Prometheus not merely forms men, but opens the gates of the magical world of spirits; calls up the midnight ghost; exhibits before us his witches amidst their unhallowed mysteries; peoples the air with sportive fairies and sylphs; and these beings, existing only in imagination, possess such truth and consistency, that even when they are deformed monsters, like Caliban, he extorts the assenting conviction that, if there should be such beings, they would so conduct themselves. In a word, as he carries with him the most fruitful and daring fancy into the kingdom of nature, on the other hand he carries nature into the regions of fancy, lying beyond the confines of reality. We are lost in astonishment at seeing the extraordinary, the wonderful, and the unheard, in such intimate nearness.

Again: if Shakespeare deserves our admiration for his characters, he is equally deserving of it for the exhibition of passion—taking this word in its widest signification, as including every mental condition, every tone of indifference, or familiar mirth, to the wildest rage and despair. He gives us the history of minds; he lays open to us, in a single word, a whole series of preceding conditions. His passions do not at first stand displayed to us in all their height, as is the case with so many tragic poets, who, in the language of Lessing, are thorough masters of the legal style of love. He paints, in a most inimitable manner, the gradual progress from the first origin. "He gives," as Lessing says, "a living picture of

Criticisms on the Works of Shakespeare.

all the most minute and secret artifices by which a feeling steals into our souls; of all the imperceptible advantages which it there gains; of all the stratagems by which every other passion is made subservient to it, till it becomes the sole tyrant of our desires and aversions. Of all poets, perhaps, he alone has pourtrayed the mental diseases—melancholy, delirium, lunacy,—with such inexpressible, and in every respect, definite truth, that the physician may enrich his observations from them in the same manner as from real cases.

And yet Johnson has objected to Shakespeare, that his pathos is not always natural and free from affectation. There are, it is true, passages, though, comparatively speaking, very few, where his poetry exceeds the bounds of true dialogue; where a too soaring imagination, a too luxuriant wit, rendered the complete dramatic forgetfulness of himself impossible. Hence an idea has been formed of simple and natural pathos, which consists in exclamations destitute of imagery, and nowise elevated above every-day life. But energetical passions electrify the whole of the mental powers, and consequently they will, in highly-favoured natures, express themselves in an ingenious and figurative manner. Besides, to use the observation of Mrs. Montagu—" Heaven-born genius acts from something superior to rules, and antecedent to rules, and has a right of appeal to Nature herself." In accordance with this sentiment, it is remarked by the German critic, that the rights of the poetical form have not been duly weighed. Shakespeare, who was always sure of his object, to move in a sufficiently powerful manner when he wished to do so, has occasionally, by indulging in a freer play, purposely moderated the impressions when too painful, and immediately introduced a musical alleviation of our sympathy. He had not those rude ideas of his wit which many moderns seem to have, as if the poet, like the clown in the proverb, must strike twice in the same place.

THE LIFE

OF

William Shakespeare.

WILLIAM SHAKESPEARE, the most illustrious name in the history of English dramatic poetry, was born at Stratford-upon-Avon, on the 23d of April, 1564. His father, who sprang from a good family, was a considerable dealer in wool, and had been an officer and bailiff of Stratford, where he for some time acted as justice of the peace. His mother was of the ancient family of Arden, in the same county, one of undoubted gentility. William, who was the eldest of ten children, received the common education of a country free-school, where, it is probable, he acquired what little Latin he was master of. At an early age, he was taken by his father to assist in his own business, and thus deprived of attaining any proficiency in classical literature; but whether a better acquaintance with ancient authors might not have restrained some of that fire, impetuosity, and even beautiful extravagance, which we admire in Shakespeare, may well admit of a dispute. Be this as it may, he seems to have adopted the mode of life which his father proposed to him; and we find that in his eighteenth year he married Ann Hathaway, the daughter of a substantial yeoman in the neighbourhood, who was eight years older than himself. Of his domestic establishment, or professional occupation, at this time nothing determinate is recorded; but it appears that he was wild and irregular, from the fact of his connexion with a party who made a practice of stealing the deer of Sir Thomas Lucy, of Charlecote, near Stratford. This imprudence brought upon him a

Life of William Shakespeare.

prosecution, which he rendered more severe by a lampoon upon that gentleman, in the form of a ballad which he had affixed to his park gates. He also indulges in a vein of splenetic drollery upon the same magistrate, in the character of *Justice Shallow*, in the opening scene of "The Merry Wives of Windsor;" which continued hostility, as he was indisputably a kind-hearted man, we may presume was occasioned by an excess of rigour and pertinacity on the part of Sir Thomas.

The consequence of this youthful imprudence drove him to London for shelter; and it is some proof that he had already imbibed a taste for the drama, that his first application was to the players, among whom, in one Thomas Green, a popular comedian of the day, he met a townsman and acquaintance. This removal has been thought to have taken place in 1586, when he was in his twenty-second year. If tradition may be depended upon, he was necessitated, in the first instance to become the prompter's call-boy or attendant, while another less probable story describes him as holding the horses of those who attended the play without servants, a prevalent custom at that period.

As an actor, the top of his performance is said to have been the *Ghost* in his own *Hamlet*. "I should have been much more pleased," says Mr. Rowe in his remarks on the genius and writings of Shakespeare, "to have learned, from certain authority, which was the first play he wrote; it would be without doubt a pleasure to any man, curious in things of this kind, to see and know what was the first essay of a fancy like Shakespeare's. Perhaps we are not to look for his beginnings, like those of other authors, among their least perfect writings; art had so little, and nature so large a share in what he did, that, for aught I know, the performances of his youth, as they were the most vigorous, and had the most fire and strength of imagination in them, were the best. I would not be thought by this to mean, that his fancy was so loose and extravagant, as to be independent of the rule and government of judgment; but that what he thought was commonly so great, so justly and rightly conceived in itself, that it wanted little or no correction, and was immediately approved by an impartial judgment at the first sight. But, though the order of time in which the several pieces were written, be generally uncertain, yet there are passages in some few of them which seem to fix their dates. So the *Chorus* at the end of the fourth act of *Henry the Fifth*, by a compliment

Life of William Shakespeare.

very handsomely turned to the Earl of Essex, shows the play to have been written when that lord was general for the queen in Ireland; and his eulogy upon Queen Elizabeth, and her successor King James, in the latter end of his *Henry the Eighth*, is a proof of that play's being written after the accession of the latter of these two princes to the crown of England. Whatever the particular times of his writings were, the people of his age, who began to grow wonderfully fond of diversions of this kind, could not but be highly pleased to see a genius arise amongst them of so pleasurable, so rich a vein, and so plentifully capable of furnishing their favourite entertainments. Besides the advantages of his wit, he was in himself a good natured man, of great sweetness in his manners, and a most agreeable companion; so that it is no wonder, if, with so many good qualities, he made himself acquainted with the best conversations of those times. Queen Elizabeth had several of his plays acted before her; and, without a doubt, gave him many gracious marks of her favour: it is that maiden princess plainly whom he intends by

"—— a fair vestal, throned by the west."
A Midsummer Night's Dream.

And that whole passage is a compliment very properly brought in, and very handsomely applied to her. She was so well pleased with the admirable character of *Falstaff*, in the Two Parts of *Henry the Fourth*, that she commanded him to continue it for one play more, and to show him in love. This is said to be the occasion of his writing *The Merry Wives of Windsor*. How well she was obeyed, the play itself is an admirable proof. Upon this occasion, it may not be improper to observe, that this part of Falstaff is said to have been written originally under the name of *Oldcastle:* some of that family being then remaining, the Queen was pleased to command him to alter it; upon which he made use of Falstaff. The present offence was indeed avoided; but I do not know whether the author may not have been somewhat to blame in his second choice, since it is certain that Sir John Falstaff, who was a knight of the garter, and a lieutenant-general, was a name of distinguished merit in the wars in France in Henry the Fifth's and Henry the Sixth's times. What grace soever the Queen conferred upon him, it was not to her only he owed the fortune which the reputation of his wit made.

Life of William Shakespeare.

He had the honour to meet with many great and uncommon marks of favour and friendship from the Earl of Southampton, famous in the histories of that time for his friendship to the unfortunate Earl of Essex. It was to that noble lord that he dedicated his poem of *Venus and Adonis*. There is one instance so singular in the magnificence of this patron of Shakespeare's, that if I had not been assured that the story was handed down by Sir William D'Avenant, who was probably very well acquainted with his affairs, I should not have ventured to have asserted it; that my lord Southampton at one time gave him a thousand pounds, to enable him to go through with a purchase which he heard he had a mind to. A bounty very great, and very rare at any time, and almost equal to that profuse generosity the present age has shown to French dancers and Italian singers.

"What particular habitude or friendships he contracted with private men, I have not been able to learn, more than that every one, who had a true taste of merit, and could distinguish men, had generally a just value and esteem for him. His exceeding candour and good nature must certainly have inclined all the gentler part of the world to love him, as the power of his wit obliged the men of the most delicate knowledge and polite learning to admire him.

"His acquaintance with Ben Jonson began with a remarkable piece of humanity and good nature: Mr. Jonson, who was at that time altogether unknown to the world, had offered one of his plays to the players, in order to have it acted; and the persons into whose hands it was put, after having turned it carelessly and superciliously over, were just about returning it to him with an ill-natured answer, that it would be of no use to their company; when Shakespeare luckily cast his eye on it, and found something so well in it, as to engage him first to read it through, and afterwards to recommend Mr. Jonson and his writings to the public. Jonson was certainly a very good scholar, and in that had the advantage of Shakespeare; though at the same time I believe it must be allowed, that what nature gave the latter, was more than a balance for what books had given the former; and the judgment of a great man upon this occasion was, I think, very just and proper. In a conversation between Sir John Suckling, Sir William d'Avenant, Endymion Porter, Mr. Hales, of Eton, and Ben Jonson; Sir John Suckling, who was a professed admirer of Shakespeare, had undertaken his defence against Ben Jonson with some warmth; Mr. Hales, who

Life of William Shakespeare.

had sat still for some time, told them, *That if Mr. Shakespeare had not read the ancients, he had likewise not stolen anything from them; and that, if he would produce any one topic finely treated by any one of them, he would undertake to show something upon the same subject at least as well written by Shakespeare."*

The latter part of his life was spent, as all men of good sense will wish theirs may be, in ease, retirement, and the conversation of his friends. His pleasurable wit and good nature engaged him in the acquaintance, and entitled him to the friendship, of the gentlemen of the neighbourhood. Amongst them, it is a story, still remembered in that country, that he had a particular intimacy with Mr. Combe, an old gentleman noted thereabouts for his wealth and his usury: it happened, that in a pleasant conversation amongst their common friends, Mr. Combe told Shakespeare, in a laughing manner, that he fancied he intended to write his epitaph, if he happened to outlive him; and since he could not know what might be said of him when he was dead, he desired it might be done immediately: upon which Shakespeare gave him these four verses:

> *" Ten in the hundred* lies here ingraved,
> 'Tis a hundred to ten his soul is not saved;
> If any man ask, Who lies in this tomb?
> Oh! ho! quoth the devil, 'tis my John-a-Combe."

For some years before his death, he resided at Stratford, in a house which he bought from the Clopton family, and which continued in the possession of his descendants until the Restoration, when it was repurchased by a member of the same family, the representative of which, Sir Hugh Clopton, entertained Garrick, Macklin, and others, in 1742, under the mulberry tree, planted by Shakespeare. His executor sold the house to a clergyman of the name of Gastrel, who being rated for the poor higher than he conceived he had a right to pay, peevishly declared that the house should never pay again; and in spite to the inhabitants of Stratford, who were benefitted by the company it brought to the town, he pulled it down, and sold the materials. He had previously cut down the mulberry tree for fuel, but an honest silversmith purchased the whole of it, which he profitably manufactured into memorials of the poet. Such was the fate of a residence in which Shakespeare exhibited so little solicitude for fame, or consciousness of his own merits, that a similar example of modesty is scarcely to be found.

Life of William Shakespeare.

He died on his birth-day, April 23, 1616, having exactly completed his fifty-second year. He was interred on the north side of the chancel of the great church of Stratford, where a monument is placed on the wall, in which he is represented under an arch in a sitting posture, a cushion spread before him, with a pen in his right hand, and his left resting on a scroll of paper. The following Latin distich is engraved under the cushion:—

> "Judicio Pylium, genio Socratem, arte Maronem,
> Terra tegit, populus mœret, Olympus habet."

To this Latin inscription may be added the lines to be found underneath it:—

> "Stay, passenger, why dost thou go so fast?
> Read, if thou canst, what envious death hath placed
> Within this monument; Shakespeare, with whom
> Quick nature died; whose name doth deck the tomb
> Far more than cost; since all that he hath writ
> Leaves living art but page unto his wit."

This monument was erected within seven years of his death; but on his grave-stone beneath are written the following lines, which seem to have been engraven in an uncouth mixture of large and small letters, at the time of his interment:—

> "Good Friend for Iesus SAKE forbeare
> To digg T-E Dust EncloAsed HERe
> Blest be T-E Man Y-T spares T-Es Stones
> And curst be He Y-T moves my Bones"

It is uncertain whether this request and imprecation were written by Shakespeare, or by one of his friends. They probably allude to the custom of removing skeletons after a certain time, and depositing them in charnel houses; and similar execrations are found in many Latin epitaphs. Shakespeare's remains, however, have been ever carefully protected from injury.

His family consisted of two daughters, and a son named Hamnet, who died in his twelfth year. Susannah, the eldest daughter, and her father's favourite, was married June 5, 1607, to Dr. John Hall, a physician, who died November, 1635, aged 60. Mrs. Hall died July 11, 1649, aged 66. They left only one child, Elizabeth, born

Life of William Shakespeare.

1607-8, and married April 22, 1626, to Thomas Nashe, Esq., who died in 1647, and afterwards to Sir John Barnard, of Abington, in Northamptonshire; but died without issue by either husband. Judith, Shakespeare's youngest daughter, was married, February 10, 1615-16, to a Mr. Thomas Quiney, and died, February, 1661-62, in her 77th year. By Mr. Quiney she had three sons, Shakespeare, Richard and Thomas, who all died unmarried, and here the descendants of our poet became extinct.

In the year 1741, a monument was erected to the memory of the "immortal bard" in Westminster Abbey, by the direction of the Earl of Burlington, Dr. Mead, Mr. Pope, and Mr. Martyn. It was the work of Schoemaker, (who received £300 for it,) after a design of Kent, and was opened in January of that year, one hundred and twenty-five years after the death of him whom it commemorates, and whose genius appears to have been forgotten during almost the whole of that long period. The performers of each of the London theatres gave a benefit to defray the expenses, and the Dean and Chapter of Westminster took nothing for the ground. The money received by the performance at Drury-lane theatre amounted to above £200, but the receipts at Covent-garden did not exceed £100.

From these imperfect notices, which are all we have been able to collect from the labours of his biographers and commentators, the reader will perceive that less is known of Shakespeare than of almost any writer who has been considered as an object of laudable curiosity. Nothing could be more highly gratifying than an account of the early studies of this wonderful man, the progress of his pen, his moral and social qualities, his friendships, his failings, and whatever else constitutes personal history. But on all these topics his contemporaries and his immediate successors have been equally silent, and if aught can be hereafter discovered, it must be by exploring sources which have hitherto escaped the anxious researches of those who have devoted their whole lives, and their most vigorous talents, to revive his memory, and illustrate his writings.

Dr. Johnson, in his elaborate and just review of Shakespeare, observes, "He has scenes of undoubted and perpetual excellence, but perhaps not one play, which, if it were now exhibited as the work of a contemporary writer, would be heard to the conclusion. I am indeed, (says he,) far from thinking that his works were wrought to his own ideas of perfection; when they were such as

Life of William Shakespeare.

would satisfy the audience, they satisfied the writer. It is seldom that authors, though more studious of fame than Shakespeare, rise much above the standard of their own age; to add a little to what is best will always be sufficient for present praise, and those who find themselves exalted into fame, are willing to credit their encomiasts, and to spare the labour of contending with themselves."

The dramatic reputation of Shakespeare, although great in his own days, became partially obsolete during the period when French taste prevailed, and French models were studied, under the second Charles; and rising again as it did on its own intrinsic pretension, until his productions established a national taste, the fact is still more honorable to his genius. That much of the admiration entertained for him is national and conventional, may be freely allowed; but giving all due weight to the cold hints of this nature, which pervade criticism of a certain tone, a fair appeal may be made on the ground of positive qualification, and a knowledge of the human heart, which, in its diversity at least, has never been surpassed. To this faculty must be added, that of an imagination powerful, poetical, and so felicitously creative, that presuming the existence of the vivid offspring of his fancy, the adopted feelings and manners seem to belong to them alone.

Voltaire observes that Shakespeare has been the favourite of the English nation for more than a century; and that that which has engrossed national admiration for a hundred years, will by prescription insure it for ever. But though there may be some truth in this remark, the obvious and undeniable fact is, that great native strength of genius can alone establish the prepossession.

DICTIONARY

OF

Shakespearian Quotations.

A.

ABILITY, INNATE.
There's in him stuff that puts him to these ends:
For, being not propp'd by ancestry, whose grace
Chalks successors their way; nor call'd upon
For high feats done to the crown; neither allied
To eminent assistants; but spider-like,
Out of his self-drawing web, he gives us note;
The force of his own merit makes his way;
A gift that heaven gives for him, which buys
A place next to the king.   *H. VIII.* i. 1.

* ABSENCE.
I have this while with leaden thoughts been press'd;
But I shall, in a more continuate time,
Strike off this score of absence.   *O.* iii. 4.

————— LOVERS'.
What! keep a week away? seven days and nights?
Eight score eight hours,—and lovers' absent hours,—
More tedious than the dial eight score times?
O weary reckoning!   *O.* iii. 4.
O thou that dost inhabit in my breast,
Leave not the mansion so long tenantless;
Lest growing ruinous the building fall,
And leave no memory of what it was.   *T. G.* v. 4

ABUSE, AND BAD ENGLISH (See also VITUPERATION).
Have I lived to stand at the taunt of one that makes fritters of English? *M. W.* v. 5.

Here will be an old abusing of God's patience and the king's English. *M. W.* i. 4.

Let them keep their limbs whole, and hack our English.
M. W. iii. 4.

ACCUSATION.
To vouch this is no proof,
Without more certain and more overt test,
Than these thin habits, and poor likelihoods
Of modern seeming do prefer against him. *O.* i. 3.

ACHIEVEMENT.
A very good piece of work, I assure you, and a merry.
M. N. D. i. 1.

Let it be booked with the rest of this day's deeds; or I swear I will have it in a particular ballad, with mine own picture on the top of it. *H. IV.* PT. II. iv. 1

ACQUITTAL.
Now doth thy honour stand,
In him that was of late an heretic,
As firm as faith. *M. W.* iv. 4.

ACTION, DRAMATIC.
Let your own discretion be your tutor: suit the action to the word, and the word to the action; with this special observance, that you o'erstep not the modesty of nature: for any thing so overdone is from the purpose of playing, whose end, both at the first, and now, was, and is, to hold, as 'twere, the mirror up to nature; to show virtue her own feature, scorn her own image, and the very age and body of the time his form and pressure: * * * O, there be players, that I have seen play,—and heard others praise, and that highly,—not to speak it profanely, that, neither having the accent of Christians, nor the gait of Christian, Pagan, nor man, have so strutted, and bellowed, that I have thought some of nature's journeymen had made men, and not made them well, they imitated humanity so abominably. *H.* iii. 2.

ADOPTION.
'Tis often seen
Adoption strives with nature; and choice breeds
A native slip to us from foreign seeds. *A. W.* i. 3.

ADORATION, A LOVER'S.
What you do,

ADORATION,—*continued.*
. Still betters what is done. When you speak, sweet,
I'd have you do it ever: when you sing,
I'd have you buy and sell so; so give alms;
Pray so; and, for the order of your affairs,
To sing them too: When you do dance, I wish you
A wave o' the sea, that you might ever do
Nothing but that; move still, still so, and own
No other function: Each your doing,
So singular in each particular,
Crowns what you are doing in the present deeds,
That all your acts are queens. *W. T.* iv. 4.

ADVERSITY (See also MISFORTUNE).
A man I am, cross'd with adversity. *T. G.* iv. 1.

                    But myself,
Who had the world as my confectionary;.
The mouths, the tongues, the eyes, the hearts of men
At duty, more than I could frame employment;
That numberless upon me stuck, as leaves
Do on the oak, have with one winter's brush
Fell from their boughs, and left me open, bare,
For every storm that blows; I, to bear this,
That never knew but better, is some burden. *T. A.* iv. 3

Such a house broke!
So noble a master fallen! All gone! and not
One friend to take his fortune by the arm,
And go along with him! *T. A.* iv. 2.

—————— FOLLY OF REPINING AT.
        What think'st
That the bleak air, thy boisterous chamberlain,
Will put thy shirt on warm? Will these moist trees,
That have out-lived the eagle, page thy heels,
And skip when thou point'st out? will the cold brook,
Candied with ice, caudle thy morning taste,
To cure thy o'er-night's surfeit? Call the creatures;
Whose naked natures live in all the spight
Of wreakful heaven; whose bare unhoused trunks,
To the conflicting elements expos'd,
Answer mere nature,—bid them flatter thee. *T. A.* iv. 3.

——————— ITS USES.
Sweet are the uses of adversity,
Which, like the toad, ugly and venomous,
Wears yet a precious jewel in its head. *A. Y.* ii. 1.

'Tis good for men to love their present pains,
Upon example; so the spirit is eas'd:

ADVERSITY,—*continued.*
And, when the mind is quicken'd, out of doubt,
The organs, though defunct and dead before,
Break up their drowsy grave, and newly move
With casted slough, and fresh legerity. *H. V.* iii. 1.
In poison there is physic; and these news
Having been well, that would have made me sick;
Being sick, have in some measure made me well.
And as the wretch whose fever-weaken'd joints,
Like strengthless hinges, buckle under life,
Impatient of his fit, breaks like a fire.
Out of his keeper's arms; even so my limbs,
Weaken'd with grief, being now enrag'd with grief,
Are thrice themselves. *H. IV.* PT. II. 1. 1.

ADVICE (See also CAUTION).
Fasten your ear to my advisings. *M. M.* iii 1.

Obey thy parents; keep thy word justly; swear not; commit not with man's sworn spouse; set not thy sweet heart on proud array. *K. L.* iii. 4.

Take heed, be wary how you place your words.
H. VI. PT. I. iii. 2.

Let go thy hold, when a great wheel runs down a hill, lest it break thy neck with following it; but the great one that goes up the hill, let him draw thee after. When a wise man gives thee better counsel, give me mine again.
K. L. ii. 4.

Pray be counsel'd:
I have a heart as little apt as yours,
But yet a brain, that leads my use of anger
To better 'vantage. *C.* iii. 2.

       Love all, trust a few,
Do wrong to none: be able for thine enemy
Rather in power than use; and keep thy friend
Under thy own life's key: be check'd for silence,
But never tax'd for speech. *A. W.* i. 1

Keep thy pen from lenders' books, and defy the foul fiend. *K. L.* iii. 4.

Let not the creaking of shoes, nor the rustling of silks, betray thy poor heart to women. *K. L.* iii. 4.

———————— TO A YOUNG WOMAN.
        Fear it, my dear sister;
And keep you in the rear of your affection,
Out of the shot and danger of desire.
The chariest maid is prodigal enough,
If she unmask her beauty to the moon;

ADVICE,—*continued.*
Virtue itself 'scapes not calumnious strokes:
The canker galls the infants of the spring,
Too oft before their buttons be disclos'd;
And in the morn and liquid dew of youth
Contagious blastments are most imminent.
Be wary then; best safety lies in fear;
Youth to itself rebels, though none else near. *H.* i. 3.

——————— TO A YOUNG MAN.
    Give thy thoughts no tongue,
Nor any unproportion'd thought his act.
Be thou familiar but by no means vulgar.
The friends thou hast, and their adoption tried,
Grapple them to thy soul with hoops of steel:
But do not dull thy palm with entertainment
Of 'each unhatch'd, unfledged comrade. Beware
Of entrance to a quarrel: but, being in,
Bear it that the opposer may beware of thee.
Give ev'ry man thine ear, but few thy voice:
Take each man's censure, but reserve thy judgment.
Costly thy habit as thy purse can buy,
But not express'd in fancy: rich, not gaudy:
For the apparel oft proclaims the man:—
Neither a borrower nor a lender be:
For loan oft loses both itself and friend;
And borrowing dulls the edge of husbandry.
This above all,—To thine own self be true;
And it must follow, as the night the day,
Thou canst not then be false to any man.
Farewell:—my blessing season this in thee! *H.* i. 3.

——————— TO A STATESMAN.
Mark but my fall, and that that ruin'd me.
Cromwell, I charge thee, fling away ambition;
By that sin fell the angels; how can man then,
The image of his Maker, hope to win by't?
Love thyself last; cherish those hearts that hate thee;
Corruption wins not more than honesty.
Still in thy right hand carry gentle peace,
To silence envious tongues. Be just, and fear not:
Let all the ends thou aim'st at be thy country's,
Thy God's, and truth's; then if thou fall'st, O Cromwell,
Thou fall'st a blessed martyr. *H. VIII.* iii. 2.

ADULATION (See also FLATTERY).
    You shout me forth
In acclamations hyperbolical;
As if I lov'd my little should be dieted
In praises sauc'd with lies. *C.* ..

AFFECTED Speakers.
These new tuners of accents. *R. J.* ii. 4.

AFFECTION (See Parental Affection).

AFFLICTION.
Affliction is enamour'd of thy parts,
And thou art wedded to calamity. *R. J.* iii. 3

AGE.
The silver livery of advised age. *H. VI.* pt. ii. v. 2.

Do you set down your name in the scroll of youth, that are written down old, with all the characters of age? Have you not a moist eye? a dry hand? a yellow cheek? a white beard? a decreasing leg? an increasing belly? Is not your voice broken? your wind short? your chin double? your wit single? and every part about you blasted with antiquity? and will you yet call yourself young? O fye, Sir John. *H. IV.* pt. ii. i. 2.

Youth no less becomes
The light and careless livery that it wears,
Than settled age his sables, and his weeds,
Importing health and graveness. *H.* iv. 7.

Though now this grained face of mine be hid
In sap-consuming winter's drizzled snow,
And all the conduits of my blood froze up;
Yet hath my night of life some memory,
My wasting lamp some fading glimmer left,
My dull deaf ears a little use to hear. *C. E.* v. 1.

I would there were no age between ten and three-and-twenty; or that youth would sleep out the rest; for there is nothing between but wenching, wronging the ancientry, stealing, and fighting. *W. T.* iii. 3.

His silver hairs
Will purchase us a good opinion,
And buy men's voices to commend our deeds:
It shall be said his judgment rul'd our hands;
Our youths, and wildness, shall no whit appear,
But all be buried in his gravity. *J. C.* ii. 1.

As you are old and reverend you should be wise.
K. L. i. 4.

When age is in the wit is out. *M. A.* iii. 5.

Becomes it thee to taunt his valiant age,
And twit with cowardice a man half dead?
H. VI. pt. i. iii. 2.

AGE   Shakespearian Dictionary.   AMA

AGE AND FRAILTY.
    The blood of youth burns not with such excess
As gravity's revolt to wantonness.   *L. L.* v. 2.
    Thou should'st not have been old before thou had'st been wise.   *K. L.* i. 5.

— —— AND GRIEF.
    I am old now,
And these same crosses spoil me.   *K. L.* v. 3.
    O! grief hath chang'd me since you saw me last;
And careful hours, with Time's deformed hand,
Have written strange defeatures in my face.   *C. E.* v. 1.

— —— AND LOQUACITY.
These tedious old fools!   *H.* ii. 2.

AIM.
    Here is the heart of my purpose.   *M. W.* ii. 2.

AIR.
    A bond of air, strong as the axle-tree
On which heaven rides.   *T. C.* i. 3.

ALARM.
    What stir is this? what tumult's in the heavens?
Whence cometh this alarum, and the noise?
    H. VI. PT. I. i. 4

    What's the business,
That such a hideous trumpet calls to parley
The sleepers of the house?   *M.* ii. 3.
    Silence that dreadful bell, it frights the isle
From its propriety.   *O.* ii. 3.

ALLEGIANCE.
    Your highness' part
Is to receive our duties: and our duties
Are to your throne and state, children and servants;
Which do but what they should, by doing every thing
Safe toward your love and honour.   *M.* i. 4.

AMAZEMENT.
    But the changes I perceived in the king and Camillo, were very notes of admiration: they seemed almost, with staring on one another, to tear the cases of their eyes; there was speech in their dumbness, language in their very gesture; they looked, as they had heard of a world ransomed, or one destroyed. A notable passion of wonder appeared in them: but the wisest beholder, that knew no more but seeing, could not say if the importance were joy or sorrow: but in the extremity of one it must be.   *W. T.* v. 2.

AMBITION.

The very substance of the ambitious is merely the shadow
of a dream. *II.* ii. 2.

I hold ambition of so airy and light a quality, that it is
but a shadow's shadow. *II.* ii. 2.

'Tis a common proof
That lowliness is young ambition's ladder,
Whereto the climber upward turns his face;
But when he once attains the upmost round,
He then unto the ladder turns his back,
Looks in the clouds, scorning the base degrees
By which he did ascend. *J. C.* ii. 4.

Ye gods, it doth amaze me,
A man of such a feeble temper should
So get the start of the majestic world,
And bear the palm alone. *J. C.* i. 2.

What see'st thou there? King Henry's diadem,
Enchas'd with all the honours of the world?
If so, gaze on, and grovel on thy face,
Until thy head be circled with the same.
Put forth thy hand, reach at the glorious gold:—
What, is't too short? I'll lengthen it with mine:
And, having both together heav'd it up,
We'll both together lift our heads to heaven;
And never more abase our sight so low,
As to vouchsafe one glance unto the ground,
H. VI. PT. II. i. 2.

That is a step,
On which I must fall down, or else o'erleap,
For in my way it lies. *M.* i. 4.

I have no spur
To prick the sides of my intent, but only
Vaulting ambition, which o'erleaps itself,
And falls on t'other side. *M.* i. 7.

The devil speed him! no man's pie is freed
From his ambitious finger. *H. VIII.* i. 1.

Follow I must, I cannot go before,
While Glo'ster bears this base and humble mind.
Were I a man, a duke, and next of blood,
I would remove these tedious stumbling blocks,
And smooth my way upon their headless necks.
H. VI. PT. II. i. 2.

Two stars keep not their motion in one sphere;
Nor can one England brook a double reign,
Of Harry Percy and the Prince of Wales.
H. IV. PT. II v. 4.

AMBITION,—*continued.*
The noble Brutus
Hath told you Cæsar was ambitious:
If it were so, it was a grievous fault;
And grievously hath Cæsar answered it.   *J. C.* iii. 2.

——— DEFEATED.
People, and senators! be not affrighted;
Fly not; stand still:—ambition's debt is paid.   *J. C.* iii. 1.

ALLOY, UNIVERSAL, IN THIS PROBATIONARY LIFE.
Unruly blasts wait on the tender spring,
  Unwholesome weeds take root with precious flowers;
The adder hisseth where the sweet birds sing;
  What virtue breeds, iniquity devours.   *Poems.*

AMEN.
Let me say, Amen, betimes, lest the devil cross my prayer.
                                            M. V. iii. 1.

AMENDMENT (See also REFORM).
God mend all.   *H. VIII.* i. 3.

ANCESTRY (See also LINEAGE).
  Look in the chronicles, we came in with Richard conqueror.   *T. S.* IND. 1

ANGER (See also FURY—RAGE).
To be in anger is impiety,
But who is man that is not angry.   *T. A.* iii. 5.
Never anger made good guard for itself.   *A. C.* iv. 1.
This tyger-footed rage, when it shall find
The harm of unscann'd swiftness, will, too late,
Tie leaden pounds to his heels.   -   *C.* iii. 1.
               Stay, my lord!
And let your reason with your choler question
What 'tis you go about.   To climb steep hills
Requires slow pace at first.   Anger is like
A full hot horse, who, being allowed his way,
Self mettle tires him.   *H. VIII.* i. 1.
               It were for me
To throw my sceptre at the injurious gods;
To tell them that this world did equal theirs,
Till they had stol'n our jewel,   All's but naught;
Patience is sottish; and impatience does
Become a dog that's mad.   *A. C.* iv. 13.

Why, what a wasp-stung and impatient fool
Art thou, to break into this woman's mood. *H. IV.* PT. L i. 3.
Now, by the ground that I am banish'd from,
Well could I curse away a winter's night,

ANGER,—*continued.*
Though standing naked on a mountain top,
Where biting cold would never let grass grow,
And think it but a minute spent in sport.
H. VI. PT. II. iii. 2.

Away to heaven, respective lenity,
And fire-ey'd fury be my conduct now. *R. J.* iii. 1.

What! drunk with choler? stay, and pause awhile.
H. IV. PT. I. i. 3.

A plague upon them! wherefore should I curse them?
Would curses kill as doth the mandrake's groan,
I would invent as bitter-searching terms,
As curst, as harsh, and horrible to hear,
Delivered strongly through my fixed teeth,
With full as many signs of deadly hate,
As lean-faced Envy in her loathsome cave:
My tongue should stumble in mine earnest words;
Mine eyes should sparkle like the beaten flint;
My hair be fix'd on end, as one distract;
Ay, every joint should seem to curse and ban:
And even now my burdened heart would break,
Should I not curse them. Poison be their drink!
Gall, worse than gall, the daintiest that they taste!
Their sweetest shade, a grove of cypress trees!
Their chiefest prospect, murd'ring basilisks!
Their softest touch, as smart as lizards' stings!
Their music, frightful as the serpent's hiss;
And boding screech-owls make the concert full!
H. VI. PT. II. iii. 2

Be advis'd;
Heat not a furnace for your foes so hot,
That it do singe yourself: we may out-run,
By violent swiftness, that which we run at,
And lose by over-running. Know you not,
The fire that mounts the liquor till't run o'er,
In seeming to augment it, wastes it. Be advis'd.
H. VIII. i. 1.

O, that my tongue were in the thunder's mouth!
Then with a passion would I shake the world. *K. J.* iii. 4.

I am about to weep; but, thinking that
We are a queen, (or long have dream'd so) certain,
The daughter of a king, my drops of tears
I'll turn to sparks of fire. *H. VIII.* ii. 4.

O Cassius, you are yoked with a lamb
That carries anger as the flint bears fire;
Who, much enforced, shows a hasty spark,
And straight is cold again. *J. C.* iv. 3

Shakespearian Dictionary.

ANGER,—*continued.*
Anger's my meat: I sup upon myself,
And so shall starve with feeding.   *C.* iv. 2
But anger has a privilege.   *K. L.* ii. 2
     By the gods
You shall digest the venom of your spleen,
Though it do split you: for, from this day forth,
I'll use you for my mirth, yea, for my laughter,
When you are waspish.   *J. C.* iv. 3.

ANGLING.
The pleasant'st angling is to see the fish
Cut with her golden oars the silver stream,
And greedily devour the treacherous bait.   *M. A.* iii 1.

ANNOYANCE, IMPERTINENT.
The loose encounters of lascivious men.   *T. G.* ii. 3.

ANSWER.
Definitively thus I answer you.   *R. III.* iii. 7.
Your answer, Sir, is enigmatical.   *M. A.* v. 4.

—— ——, GENERAL.
But for me, I have an answer will serve all men.
    A. W. ii. 2.

ANSWERING A LETTER.
Any man, that can write, may answer a letter.   *R. J.* ii. 4.

ANT.
    We'll set thee to school to an ant, to teach thee there's
no labouring in the winter.   *K. L.* ii. 4.

ANTICIPATION.
By the pricking of my thumbs,
Something wicked this way comes.   *M.* iv. 1.
I smell it; upon my life, it will do well.   *H. IV.* PT. I. i. 3.
Excellent! I smell a device.   *T. N.* ii. 3
A man may hear this shower sing in the wind.
    M. W. iii. 2.
Great business must be wrought ere noon;
Upon the corner of the moon
There hangs a vapourous drop profound;
I'll catch it ere it come to ground.   *M.* iii. 5.
I am giddy; expectation whirls me round.
The imaginary relish is so sweet,
That it enchants my sense.   *T. C.* iii. 2.

ANTIQUITIES.
        What's to do?
Shall we go see the reliques of this town?   *T. N.* iii. 3.

APOLOGIST.
I have laboured for the poor gentleman, to the extremest shore of my modesty. *M. M.* iii. 2.

APOLOGY.
What, shall this speech be spoke for our excuse?
Or shall we on without apology. *R. J.* i. 4.

APOPLEXY.
This apoplexy is, as I take it, a kind of lethargy, an't please your lordship; a kind of sleeping in the blood, a whoreson tingling. *H. IV.* pt. ii. i. 2

APOTHECARY.
I do remember an apothecary,—
And hereabouts he dwells,—whom late I noted
In tatter'd weeds, with overwhelming brows,
Culling of simples; meagre were his looks,
Sharp misery had worn him to the bones:
And in his needy shop a tortoise hung,
An alligator stuff'd, and other skins
Of ill-shap'd fishes; and about his shelves
A beggarly account of empty boxes,
Green earthen pots, bladders and musty seeds,
Remnants of packthread, and old cakes of roses,
Were thinly scatter'd to make up a show.
Noting this penury, to myself I said,—
An' if a man did need a poison now,
Whose sale is present death in Mantua.
Here lives a caitiff wretch would sell it him. *R. J.* v. 1

APPARITION (See also GHOSTS, SPIRITS).
I have heard (but not believ'd) the spirits of the dead
May walk again: if such thing be, thy mother
Appear'd to me last night; for ne'er was dream
So like a waking. *W. T.* iii. 3.

APPEAL.
And here I stand:—judge, my masters. *H. IV.* pt. i. ii. 4.

APPELLATIONS OF JUVENILE ENDEARMENT.
Adoptedly; as school-maids change their names
By vain, though apt affection. *M. M.* i. 5.

APPLAUSE, POPULAR (See also POPULARITY, MOB).
And there is such confusion in my powers,
As, after some oration fairly spoke
By a beloved prince, there doth appear
Among the buzzing pleased multitude:
Where every something being blent together,
Turns to a wild of nothing *M. V.* iii. 2

APP   *Shakespearian Dictionary.*   ARM

APPREHENSION.
Heaven! that I had thy head! he has found the meaning.
P. P. i. 1.
——————— OF THE WORTHLESS.
Wisdom and goodness to the vile seem vile;
Filths savour but themselves.   *K. L.* iv. 2.

APTITUDE.
Your spirits shine through you.   *M.* iii. 1.
I cannot draw a cart, nor eat dried oats;
If it be man's work, I will do it.   *K. L.* v. 3.

ARDOUR, MILITARY (See also WAR).
O let the hours be short,
Till fields, and blows, and groans applaud our sport.
H. IV. PT. I. i. 3.

ARITHMETICIAN.
Forsooth, a great arithmetician.   *O.* i. 1.

ARMAMENT, SAILING.
Thus with imagin'd wing our swift scene flies,
In motion of no less celerity
Than that of thought. Suppose that you have seen
The well-appointed King at Hampton pier
Embark his royalty, and his brave fleet
With silken streamers the young Phœbus fanning.
Play with your fancies; and in them behold,
Upon the hempen tackle ship-boys climbing:
Hear the shrill whistle which doth order give
To sounds confus'd; behold the threaden sails,
Borne with the invisible and creeping wind,
Draw the huge bottoms through the furrow'd sea,
Breasting the lofty surge: O do but think,
You stand upon the rivage, and behold
A city on the inconstant billows dancing;
For so appears this fleet majestical,
Holding due course to Harfleur.   *H. V.* ii. *chorus.*

ARMY (See also WAR).
A braver choice of dauntless spirits
Than now the English bottoms have waft o'er,
Did never float upon the swelling tide,
To do offence and scath in Christendom.
The interruption of their churlish drums
Cuts off more circumstance: they are at hand,
To parley, or to fight; therefore prepare.   *K. J.* ii. 1.
England, impatient of your just demands,
Hath put himself in arms; the adverse winds,
Whose leisure I have staid, have given him time

ARMY,—*continued.*
To land his legions all as soon as I
His marches are expedient to this town,
His forces strong, his soldiers confident.   *K. J.* ii. 1.
               Tell the Constable,
We are but warriors for the working day;
Our gayness, and our gilt, are all be-smirch'd
With rainy marching in the painful field.
There's not a piece of feather in our host,
(Good argument I hope we shall not fly,)
And time has worn us into slovenry:
But, by the mass, our hearts are in the trim.   *H. V.* iv. 3.

Within a ken our army lies;
Upon mine honour, all too confident
To give admittance to a thought of fear.
                                    H. IV. PT. II. iv. 1.

All the unsettled humours of the land,—
Rash, inconsiderate, fiery voluntaries,
With ladies' faces, and fierce dragons' spleens,—
Have sold their fortunes at their native homes,
Bearing their birthrights proudly on their backs,
To make a hazard of new fortunes here.   *K. J.* ii. 1

Remember who you are to cope withal;—
A sort of vagabonds, rascals, and run-aways,
A scum of Bretagnes, and base lackey peasants,
Whom their o'er-cloy'd country vomits forth
To desperate ventures, and assur'd destruction.
                                    R. III. v. ?.

          Big Mars seems bankrupt in their beggar'd host,
And faintly through a rusty beaver peeps.
The horsemen sit like fixed candlesticks,
With torch-staves in their hands; and their poor jades
Lob down their heads, drooping the hides and hips;
The gum down-roping from their pale dead eyes;
And in their pale dull mouths the gymold bit
Lies foul with chaw'd grass, still and motionless;
And their executors, the knavish crows,
Fly o'er them all, impatient for their hour.   *H. V.* iv. 2.

His army is a ragged multitude
Of hinds and peasants, rude and merciless.
                                         H. VI. PT. II. iv. 4.

ARRAIGNMENT.
    It shall be done, I will arraign them straight:—
   Come, sit thou here, most learned justicer.   *K. L.* iii. 6.

ARREST.
     If I could speak so wisely under an arrest, I would send

ARREST,—*continued.*
for certain of my creditors: and yet, to say the truth, I had as lief have the foppery of freedom, as the morality of imprisonment. *M. M.* i. 3.

ART AND NATURE.
Nature is made better by no mean,
But nature makes that mean ; so, o'er that art
Which, you say, adds to nature, is an art
That nature makes. *W. T.* iv. 3.
This is an art
Which does mend nature,—change it rather ; but
The art itself is nature. *W. T.* iv. 3.

ARTS, FORBIDDEN.
I therefore apprehend and do attach thee,
For an abuser of the world, a practiser
Of arts inhibited, and out of warrant. *O.* i. 2.

ASPECT, MARTIAL.
Say, what's thy name?
Thou hast a grim appearance, and thy face
Bears a command in't ; though thy tackle's torn
Thou show'st a noble vessel. *C.* iv. 5.

He is able to pierce a corslet with his eye ; talks like a knell, and his hum is a battery. *C.* v. 4.

——— SOUR.
The tartness of his face sours ripe grapes. *C.* iv. 4.

ASPIRANT.
A high hope for a low having : God grant us patience!
L. L. i. 1.
Sir, I lack advancement. *H.* iii. 2.

ASS.
Now, what a thing it is to be an ass! *Tit. And.* iv. 2.

O that he were here to write me down an ass! but, masters, remember that I am an ass ; though it be not written down, yet forget not that I am an ass. *M. A.* iv. 2.

I do begin to perceive that I am made an ass. *M. W.* v. 5.

If thou be'st not an ass, I am youth of fourteen.
A. W. ii. 3.

With the help of a surgeon he might recover, and prove an ass. *M. N.* v. 1.

ASSASSINS.
Kill men i' the dark! where are these bloody thieves?
O. v. 1.

Shakesperian Dictionary.

ASSIMILATION.
The mightiest space in fortune nature brings
To join like likes, and kiss like native things. *A. W.* i. 1.

ASTRONOMERS.
These earthly godfathers of heaven's lights,
That give a name to every fixed star,
Have no more profit of their shining nights
Than those that walk and wot not what they are.
Too much to know; is to know nought but fame,
And every godfather can give a name. *L. L.* i. 1.

ATTACHMENT.
I have professed me thy friend, and I confess me knit to
thy deserving with cables of perdurable toughness.
O. i. 3.

I have forsworn his company hourly, any time this two
and-twenty years, and yet I'm bewitched with the rogue's
company. If the rascal have not given me medicines to
make me love him, I'll be hanged; it could not be else.
H. IV. PT. I. ii. 2

ATTENDANCE.
Creaking my shoes on the plain masonry. *A. W.* ii. 1.

ATTENTION.
Lend thy serious hearing to what I shall unfold. *H.* i. 5.

Season your admiration for a while
With an attent ear; till I may deliver,
Upon the witness of these gentlemen,
This marvel to you. *H.* i. 2.

ATTRACTIONS, PERSONAL.
But I can tell, that in each grace of these
There lurks a still and dumb discoursive devil,
That tempts most cunningly. *T. C.* iv. 4.

AVARICE.
This avarice,
Sticks deeper; grows with more pernicious root
Than summer-seeding lust. *M.* iv. 3.

AVERSION.
I think oxen and wain-ropes cannot hale them together.
T. N. iii. 2.

AUSTERITY.
Be opposite with a kinsman, surly with servants; let thy
tongue tang arguments of state; put thyself into the trick
of singularity. *T. N.* iii. 4.

AUTHENTICITY.
Five justices' hands to it, and authorities more than my
pack will hold. *W.T.* iv. 3.

AUTHOR (See also POET, RHYMSTER).
Nay, do not wonder at it: you are made
Rather to wonder at the things you hear
Than to work any. Will you rhyme upon't,
And vent it for a mockery? *Cym.* v. 3

AUTHORITY (See also OFFICE).
O place! O form!
How often dost thou with thy case, thy habit,
Wrench awe from fools, and tie the wisest souls
To thy false seeming. Blood, thou still art blood:
Let's write good angel on the devil's horn,
Tis not the devil's crest. *M.M.* ii. 4.

Thou hast seen a farmer's dog bark at a beggar,
And the creature run from the cur: There,
thou might'st behold the great image of authority:
A dog's obeyed in office. *K.L.* iv. 6.

Authority, though it err like others,
Hath yet a kind of medicine in itself,
That skins the vice o' the top. *M.M.* ii. 2.

I shall remember:
When Cæsar says,—*Do this*, it is perform'd. *J.C.* i. 2.

Authority bears a credent bulk,
That no particular scandal once can touch
But it confounds the breather. *M.M.* iv. 4.

Who will believe thee, Isabel!
My unsoil'd name, the austereness of my life,
My vouch against you, and my place i' the state,
Will so your accusation overweigh,
That you shall stifle in your own report,
And smell of calumny. *M.M.* ii. 4.

O, he sits high, in all the people's hearts;
And that which would appear offence in us,
His countenance, like richest alchemy,
Will change to virtue and to worthiness. *J.C.* i. 3.

Well, I must be patient, there is no fettering of
authority. *A.W.* ii. 3

And though authority be a stubborn bear, yet he is oft
led by the nose with gold. *W.T.* iv. 3.

Thus can the demi-god, Authority,
Make us pay down for our offence by weight. *M.M.* i. 3

———— INSOLENCE OF.
Could great men thunder,

AUTHORITY,—*continued.*
As Jove himself does, Jove would ne'er be quiet;
For every pelting petty officer
Would use his heaven for thunder; nothing but thunder.
Merciful heaven!
Thou rather, with thy sharp and sulphurous bolt,
Split'st the unwedgeable and gnarled oak,
Than the soft myrtle. O, but man! proud man!
Dress'd in a little brief authority,
Most ignorant of what he's most assur'd,
His glassy essence, like an angry ape,
Plays such fantastic tricks before high heaven
As make the angels weep. *M. M.* ii. 2.

AUTUMN.
Not yet on summer's death, nor on the birth
Of trembling winter. *W. T.* iv. 3.

B.

BABBLER (See also TALKER).
Fie, what a spendthrift he is of his tongue! *T.* ii. 1.

Tut, tut, my lord, we will not stand to prate,
Talkers are no good doers, be assur'd:
We go to use our hands, and not our tongues. *R. III.* i. 3.

BACKING.
Call you that backing your friends? a plague upon such backing! give me them that will face me.
H. IV. PT. I. ii. 4.

BACKWARDNESS (See also FRIENDS COOLING).
Cousin, thou wast not wont to be so dull. *R. III.* iv. 2.

BADNESS.
Damnable, both sides rogue. *A. W.* iv. 3.

Abhorred slave;
Which any print of goodness will not take
Being capable of all ill. *T.* i. 2.
God keep the prince from all the pack of you!
A knot you are of damned blood-suckers. *R. III.* iii. 3.

BALLADS.
I love a ballad but even too well; if it be doleful matter merrily set down; or a very pleasant thing indeed, and sung lamentably. *W. T.* iv. 3.

Traduc'd by odious ballads. *1. W.* ii. 1.

BALLADS,—*continued.*
An I have not ballads made on you all, and sung to filthy tunes, let a cup of sack be my poison.
II. IV. PT. II. ii. 2.
I love a ballad in print a' life; for then we are sure they are true. *W. T.* iv. 3.

BALLAD-MONGERS (See also POETRY, RHYMSTERS).
I had rather be a kitten, and cry,—mew,
Than one of these same metre ballad-mongers:
I had rather hear a brazen can'stick turn'd,
Or a dry wheel grate on an axletree;
And that would set my teeth nothing on edge,
Nothing so much as mincing poetry;
'Tis like the forc'd gait of a shuffling nag.
H. VI. PT. iii. 1.

BALLAD-SINGER, ITINERANT.
O master, if you did but hear the pedlar at the door, you would never dance again after a tabor and pipe; no, the bag-pipe could not move you: he sings several tunes, faster than you'll tell money; he utters them as he had eaten ballads, and all men's ears grow to their tunes. *W. T.* iv. 3.

BANISHMENT.
Banish'd, is banish'd from the world,
And world's exile is death: then banish'd
Is death misterm'd: calling death,—banishment,
Thou cut'st my head off with a golden axe,
And smil'st upon the stroke that murders me. *R. J.* iii. 3.
Then England's ground, farewell; sweet soil, adieu;
My mother, and my nurse, that bears me yet!
Where'er I wander, boast of this I can,—
Though banish'd, yet a true-born Englishman. *R. II.* i. 3.
Banished?
O friar, the damned use that word in hell;
Howlings attend it. *R. J.* iii. 3.
I've stoopt my neck under your injuries,
And sigh'd my English breath in foreign clouds,
Eating the bitter bread of banishment. *R. II.* iii. 1.
Banish me?
Banish your dotage; banish usury,
That makes the senate ugly. *T. A.* iii. 5.

BANTERING.
With that, all laugh'd, and clapp'd him on the shoulder;
Making the bold wag, by their praises, bolder:
One rubb'd his elbow, thus; and fleer'd, and swore,
A better speech was never heard before. *L. L.* v. 2.

BANTERING.—*continued.*
  Close, in the name of jesting!   *T. N.* ii. 5.
  ——————— Girls.
  The tongues of mocking wenches are as keen
   As is the razor's edge invisible,
  Cutting a smaller hair than may be seen;
   Above the sense of sense: so sensible
  Seemeth their conference; their conceits have wings,
   Fleeter than arrows, bullets, wind, thought, swifter things.
             L. L. v. 2.

BASENESS.
  Base and unlustrous as the smoky light
  That's fed with stinking tallow.   *Cym.* i. 7
       You shall mark
  Many a duteous and knee-crooking knave,
  That, doting on his own obsequious bondage,
  Wears out his time, much like his master's ass,
  For nought but provender, and, when he's old, cashier'd;
  Whip me such honest knaves.   *O.* i. 1.
     Some kinds of baseness
  Are nobly undergone; and most poor matters
  Point to rich ends.   *T.* ii. 1.

BASTARD.
  Bastard instructed, bastard in mind, bastard in valour;
  in every thing illegitimate.   *T. C.* v. 8.
      Why bastard? wherefore base?
  When my dimensions are as well compact,
  My mind as generous, and my shape as true,
  As honest madam's issue?   *K. L.* i. 2.

  Ha! Fie, these filthy vices! It were as good
  To pardon him that hath from nature stolen
  A man already made, as to remit
  Their saucy sweetness, that do coin heaven's image
  In stamps that are forbid: 'tis all as easy
  Falsely to take away a life true made,
  As to put mettle in restrained means,
  To make a false one   *M. M.* ii. 4.

     Fine word,—legitimate!
  Well, my legitimate, if this letter speed,
  And my invention thrive, Edmund the base
  Shall top the legitimate. I grow: I prosper:—
  Now, gods, stand up for bastards.   *K. L.* i. 2.

BATCHELOR.
  Because I will not do them the wrong to mistrust any, I

BAT **Shakespearian Dictionary.** BAT

BATCHELOR,—*continued.*
will do myself the right to trust none; and the fine is, for the which I may go the finer, I will live a batchelor.
M. A. i. 1.
Shall I never see a batchelor of three score again?
M. A. i. 1.
————————'s RECANTATION.
When I said I would die a batchelor, I did not think I should live till I were married. *M. A.* ii. 3.

BATTLE (See also WAR).
With boisterous untun'd drums,
And harsh resounding trumpets' dreadful bray,
And grating shock of wrathful iron arms. *R. II.* i. 3.

Being mounted, and both roused in their seats,
Their neighing coursers daring of the spur,
Their armed staves in charge, their beavers down,
Their eyes of fire sparkling through sights of steel,
And the loud trumpet blowing them together.
H. IV. PT. II. iv. 1

Once more unto the breach, dear friends, once more;
Or close the wall up with our English dead!
In peace, there's nothing so becomes a man,
As modest stillness and humility:
But when the blast of war blows in our ears,
Then imitate the action of the tyger;
Stiffen the sinews, summon up the blood,
Disguise fair nature with hard-favour'd rage:
Then lend the eye a terrible aspect:
Let it pry through the portals of the head,
Like the brass cannon'; let the brow o'erwhelm it
As fearfully as doth the galled rock
O'er-hang and jutty his confounded base,
Swill'd with the wild and wasteful ocean.
Now set the teeth and stretch the nostrils wide,
Hold hard the breath, and bend up every spirit
To his full height! On, on, you noble English. *H. V.* ii. 1.

A thousand hearts are great within my bosom:
Advance our standards; set upon our foes!
Our ancient word of courage, fair St. George,
Inspires us with the spleen of fiery dragons!
Upon them! *R. III.* v. 3.

Fight, gentlemen of England; fight boldly, yeomen·
Draw, archers, draw your arrows to the head.
Spur your proud horses hard, and ride in blood:
Amaze the welkin with your broken staves. *R. III.* v. 3.

BAT *Shakespearian Dictionary.* BAT

BATTLE,—*continued.*
This battle fares like to the morning's war,
When dying clouds contend with growing light;
What time the shepherd blowing of his nails,
Can neither call it perfect day, or night.
Now sways it this way like a mighty sea,
Forc'd by the tide to combat with the wind;
Now sways it that way, like the self-same sea,
Forc'd to retire by fury of the wind:
Sometimes the flood prevails; and then the wind:
Now, one the better; then, another best;
Both tugging to be victors, breast to breast,
Yet neither conqueror nor conquered:
So is the equal poize of the fell war. *H. VI.* PT. III. ii. 5.

My uncles both are slain in rescuing me;
And all my followers to the eager foe
Turn back, and fly, like ships before the wind,
Or lambs pursued by hunger-starved wolves.
My sons,—God knows,—what hath bechanced them:
But this I know,—they have demean'd themselves
Like men borne to renown, by life, or death.
Three times did Richard make a lane to me;
And thrice cried,—Courage, father! Fight it out!
And full as oft came Edward to my side
With purple faulchion, painted to the hilt
In blood of those that had encountered him.
And when the hardest warriors did retire,
Richard cried,—*Charge! and give no foot of ground!*
And cried,—*A crown, or else a glorious tomb!*
A sceptre! or an earthly sepulchre!
With this, we charg'd again. *H. VI.* PT. III. i. 4

Never did captive with a freer heart
Cast off his chains of bondage, and embrace
His golden uncontroll'd enfranchisement,
More than my dancing soul doth celebrate
This feast of battle with mine adversary. *R. II.* i. 3

Let each man do his best: and here draw I
A sword, whose temper I intend to stain
With the best blood that I can meet withal,
In the adventure of this perilous day.
Now,—*Esperance!* Percy!—and set on.
Sound all the lofty instruments of war,
And by that music let us all embrace:
For heaven to earth, some of us never shall
A second time do such a courtesy. *H. IV.* PT. I. v. 2

Heaven in thy good cause make thee prosperous!
Be swift like lightning in the execution;

BATTLE,—*continued.*
And let thy blows, doubly redoubled,
Fall like amazing thunder on the casque
Of thy amaz'd pernicious enemy. *R. II.* i. 3.

In single opposition, hand to hand,
He did confound the best part of an hour
In changing hardiment with great Glendower:
Three times they breath'd, and three times did they drink,
Upon agreement, of swift Severn's flood;
Who then affrighted with their bloody looks,
Ran fearfully among the trembling reeds,
And hid his crisp head in the hollow bank,
Blood-stained with these valiant combatants.
H. IV. PT. I. i. 3.

Prepare you, generals:
The enemy comes on in gallant show;
Their bloody sign of battle is hung out,
And something to be done immediately. *I. C.* v. 1.

We few, we happy few, we band of brothers
For he, to-day, that sheds his blood with me.
Shall be my brother; be he ne'er so vile,
This day shall gentle his condition:
And gentlemen in England now abed
Shall think themselves accurs'd, they were not here;
And hold their manhoods cheap, while any speaks,
That fought with us upon St. Crispin's day. *H. V.* iv. 3.

For the love of all the gods,
Let's leave the hermit pity with our mothers;
And when we have our armours buckled on,
The venom'd vengeance ride upon our swords. *T. C.* v. 3.

Let's whip these stragglers o'er the seas again;
Lash hence these over-weening rags of France,
These famish'd beggars, weary of their lives;
Who, but for dreaming on this fond exploit,
For want of means, poor rats, had hang'd themselves.
R. III. v. 3.

I'll lean upon one crutch, and fight with the other,
Ere stay behind this business. *C.* i. 1.

———— OF AGINCOURT, PREPARATIONS FOR THE.
Now entertain conjecture of a time,
When creeping murmur and the poring dark,
Fill the wide vessel of the universe.
From camp to camp, through the foul womb of night,
The hum of either army stilly sounds,
That the fixed sentinels almost receive
The secret whispers of each other's watch:

BAT 𝕾𝖍𝖆𝖐𝖊𝖘𝖕𝖊𝖆𝖗𝖎𝖆𝖓 𝕯𝖎𝖈𝖙𝖎𝖔𝖓𝖆𝖗𝖞. **BEA**

BATTLE,—*continued.*
Fire answers fire ; and through their paly flames,
Each battle sees the other's umbered face :
Steed threatens steed in high and boastful neighs,
Piercing the night's dull ear ; and from the tents,
The armourers accomplishing the knights,
With busy hammers closing rivets up,
Give dreadful note of preparation.
The country cocks do crow ; the clocks do toll,
And the third hour of drowsy morning name.
Proud of their numbers, and secure in soul,
The confident and over-lusty French
Do the low-rated English play at dice ;
And chide the cripple tardy-gaited night,
Who, like a foul and ugly witch, doth limp
So tediously away. The poor condemned English,
Like sacrifices by their watchful fires
Sit patiently, and inly ruminate
The morning's danger ; and their gestures sad,
Investing lank-lean cheeks, and war-worn coats,
Presenteth them unto the gazing moon
So many horrid ghosts. *H. V.* iv. *chor*

BEARD.
He that hath a beard is more than a youth: and he that hath none, is less than a man. *M. A.* ii. 1.

Now, Jove, in his next commodity of hair, send thee a beard ! *T. N.* iii. 1.

BEAU.
This gallant pins the wenches on his sleeve ;
Had he been Adam he had tempted Eve :
He can carve too, and lisp : Why this is he,
That kiss'd away his hand in courtesy ;
This is the ape of form, monsieur the nice,
That when he plays at tables, chides the dice
In honourable terms. *L. L.* v. 2.

BEAUX, SCENTED.
Like many of these lisping hawthorn buds, that come like women in men's apparel, and smell like Bucklersbury in simple-time. *M. W.* iii. 3.

BEAUTY.
Beauty is but a vain and doubtful good,
 A shining gloss that vadeth suddainly,
A flower that dies, when first it 'gins to bud,
 A brittle glass that's broken presently.
A doubtful good, a gloss, a glass, a flower,
Lost, vaded, broken, dead, within an hour. *Poems.*

BEAUTY,—*continued.*

By Jupiter, an angel! or, if not,
An earthly paragon! *Cym.* iii. 6.

A wither'd hermit, five score winters worn,
Might shake off fifty looking in her eye. *L. L.* iv. 3.

    The most peerless piece of earth, I think,
That e'er the sun shone bright on. *W.T.* v. 1.

'Tis beauty truly blent, whose red and white
Nature's own sweet and cunning hand laid on :
Lady, you are the cruellest she alive,
If you will lead these graces to the grave,
And leave the world no copy. *T. N.* i. 5.

There's nothing ill can dwell in such a temple. *T.* i. 2.

            Her sunny locks
Hang on her temples like a golden fleece. *M.V.* i. 1.

As plays the sun upon the glassy streams;
Twinkling another counterfeited beam,
So seems this gorgeous beauty to mine eyes.
H.VI. PT. I. v. 3.

This is such a creature,
Would she begin a sect, might quench the zeal
Of all professors else; make proselytes
Of who she but bid follow. *W.T.* v. 1.

       I saw her once
Hop forty paces through the public street
And having lost her breath, she spoke, and panted,
That she did make defect perfection,
And, breathless, power breathe forth. *A.C.* ii. 2.

    All hearts in love use their own tongues;
Let every eye negociate for itself,
And trust no agent; for beauty is a witch,
Against whose charms faith melteth into blood. *M. A.* ii. 1.

She speaks :—
O speak again, bright angel! for thou art
As glorious to this night, being o'er my head,
As is a winged messenger of heaven
Unto the white-upturned wond'ring eyes
Of mortals, that fall back to gaze on him,
When he bestrides the lazy-pacing clouds,
And sails upon the bosom of the air. *R. J.* ii 2.

O she doth teach the torches to burn bright!
Her beauty hangs upon the cheek of night
Like a rich jewel in an Ethiop's ear;
Beauty too rich for use, for earth too dear. *R. J.* i. 5.

BEAUTY,—continued.

Beauty is bought by judgment of the eye,
Not utter'd by base sale of chapmen's tongues. *L. L.* ii. 1.
She's a most exquisite lady. *O.* ii. 3.
She's beautiful; and therefore to be woo'd:
She is a woman; therefore to be won. *H. VI.* PT. I. v. 3.
   It shall be inventoried; and every particle, and utensil, labelled to my will; as, *item*, two lips, indifferent red; *item*, two grey eyes, with lids to them; *item*, one neck, one chin, and so forth. *T. N.* i. 4.
I know a wench of excellent discourse,
Pretty, and witty; wild, and yet, too, gentle. *C. E.* iii. 1.
Beauty provoketh thieves sooner than gold. *A. Y.* i. 3.
   There was never yet fair woman but she made mouths in a glass. *K. L.* iii. 2.
When in the chronicle of wasted time,
  I see descriptions of the fairest wights,
And beauty making beautiful old rime,
  In praise of ladies dead, and lovely knights,
Then in the blazon of sweet beauty's best,
  Of hand, of foot, of lip, of eye, of brow,
I see their antique pen would have expressed
  Even such a beauty as you master now. *Poems.*

―――― AND DECEIT.

O serpent heart, hid with a flowering face!
Did ever dragon keep so fair a cave?
Beautiful tyrant! fiend angelical!
Dove-feather'd raven! wolvish-ravening lamb!
Despised substance of divinest show!
Just opposite to what thou justly seem'st,
A damned saint, an honourable villain!—
O, nature!—what had'st thou to do in hell,
When thou didst bower the spirit of a fiend
In mortal paradise of such sweet flesh?
Was ever book, containing such vile matter,
So fairly bound? O, that deceit should dwell
In such a gorgeous palace! *R. J.* iii. 2.
O beauty! where's thy faith! *T. C.* v. 2.

―――― AND HONESTY.

   Honesty coupled to beauty, is to have honey sauce to sugar. *A. V.* iii. 3

BEDLAM BEGGARS.

The country gives me proof and precedent
Of Bedlam beggars, who, with roaring voices,
Strike in their numb'd and mortified bare arms,.

BEDLAM Beggars,—*continued*.
Pins, wooden pricks, nails, sprigs of rosemary;
And with this horrible object, from low farms,
Poor pelting villages, sheep cotes, and mills,
Sometimes with lunatic bans, sometimes with prayers,
Inforce their charity.   *K. L.* ii. 3.

BEES.
                So work the honey bees;
Creatures, that by a rule in nature teach
The art of order to a peopled kingdom.
They have a king, and officers of sorts;
Where some, like magistrates, correct at home;
Others, like merchants, venture trade abroad;
Others, like soldiers, armed in their stings,
Make boot upon the summer's velvet buds;
Which pillage they with merry march bring home,
To the tent-royal of their emperor;
Who, busied in his majesty, surveys
The singing masons building roofs of gold;
The civil citizens kneading up the honey;
The poor mechanic porters crowding in
Their heavy burdens at his narrow gate;
The sad-ey'd justice, with his surly hum,
Delivering o'er to executors pale
The lazy yawning drone.   *H. V* i. 2.

BEGGARS.
The adage must be verified,
That beggars mounted, run their horse to death.
                             H. VI. PT. III. i. 4.

Well, whiles I am a beggar, I will rail,
And say,—there is no sin, but to be rich;
And being rich, my virtue then shall be,
To say,—there is no vice but beggary.   *K. J.* ii. 2.

What! a young knave, and beg! Is there not wars? is there not employment? Doth not the king lack subjects? Do not the rebels need soldiers? Though it be a shame to be on any side but one, it is worse shame to beg than to be on the worst side, were it worse than the name of rebellion can tell how to make it.   *H. IV.* PT. II. i. 2.

Speak with me, pity me, open the door,
A beggar begs that never begg'd before.   *R. II.* v. 3.

You taught me first to beg; and now, methinks,
You teach me how a beggar should be answer'd.
                                       M. V. iv 1.

BEGONE.
Rogues, hence, avaunt! vanish like hailstones, go!
Trudge, plod, away, o' th' hoof; seek shelter, pack!
               M.W. i. 3.
Hag-seed, hence!   *T.* i. 2.

BENEDICTION (See also SALUTATION).
The benediction of these covering heavens
Fall on their heads like dew!   *Cym.* v. 5.
      May he live!
Longer than I have time to tell his years!
Ever belov'd, and loving may his rule be!
And when old Time shall lead him to his end,
Goodness and he fill up one monument! *H.VIII.* ii. 1.
Bless thy five wits.   *K. L.* iii. 4

——————— PARENTAL.
And make me die a good old man!
That is the butt end of a mother's blessing;
I marvel that her grace did leave it out. *R. III.* ii. 2

——————— MILITARY.
Now the fair goddess, Fortune,
Fall deep in love with thee; and her great charms
Misguide thy opposers' swords! Bold gentleman,
Prosperity be thy page!   *C.* i. 5.

All the gods go with you! upon your sword
Sit laurell'd victory! and smooth success
Be strew'd before your feet.   *A.C.* 1. 3.

Mars dote on you for his novices. *A.W.* ii. 1.

BEWAILINGS (See also LAMENTATION).
    Where thou didst vent thy groans
As fast as mill-wheels strike.   *T.* i. 2

BILLOWS.
What care these roarers for the name of king? *T.* i. 1

BIOGRAPHY.
        I long
To hear the story of your life, which must
Take the ear strangely.   *T.* v. 1.

BIRDS, ENCAGED.
  Such a pleasure as incaged birds
Conceive, when, after many moody thoughts,
At last, by notes of household harmony,
They quite forget their loss of liberty.
          H.VI. PT. III. iv. 6.

Shakesperian Dictionary.

BLACK.
Black, forsooth, coal black as jet. *H. VI.* PT. II. ii. 1.
Coal black is better than another hue,
In that it scorns to bear another hue. *Tit. And.* iv. 2.
All the water in the ocean
Can never turn a swan's black legs to white,
Although she lave them hourly in the flood. *Tit. And.* iv. 2.
      Black is the badge of hell,
The hue of dungeons, and the scowl of night. *L. L.* iv. 3.

BLAMEABLE.
                You shall not sin,
If you do say, we think him over proud,
And under honest. *T. C.* ii. 3.

BLEMISHES.
In nature, there's no blemish but the mind;
None can be called deformed but the unkind:
Virtue is beauty; but the beauteous-evil
Are empty trunks, o'er-flourished by the devil. *T. N.* iii. 4.
Read not my blemishes in the world's report:
I have not kept my square; but that to come
Shall all be done by the rule. *A. C.* ii. 3.

BLOT (See also STAIN).
Mark'd with a blot, damn'd in the book of heaven.
R. II. iv. 1.

BLUNTNESS.
             This is some fellow,
Who, having been prais'd for bluntness, doth affect
A saucy roughness; and constrains the garb
Quite from his nature. He can't flatter, he!—
An honest man and plain,—he must speak truth:
An they will take it, so; if not, he's plain.
This kind of knaves I know, which in this plainness,
Harbour more craft, and more corrupter ends
Than twenty silly ducking observants,
That stretch their duties nicely. *K. L.* ii. 2

I am no orator as Brutus is:
But, as you know me all, a plain blunt man,
That love my friend; and that they know full well
That gave me public leave to speak of him.
For I have neither wit, nor words, nor worth,
Action, nor utterance, nor the power of speech,
To stir men's blood: I only speak right on. *J. C.* iii. 2.

BLUSHES.
The heart's meteors tilting in the face. *C. E.* iv. 2

BLUSHES,—*continued.*
Now, if you can blush, and cry guilty, cardinal,
You'll show a little honesty.   *H. VIII.* iii. 2
And bid the cheek be ready with a blush,
Modest as morning when she coldly eyes
The youthful Phœbus.   *T. C.* i. 3.
    Come, quench your blushes; and present yourself that which you are, the mistress of the feast.   *W. T.* iv. 3.

BOASTING.
And topping all others in boasting.   *C.* ii. 1.
O, Sir, to such as boasting show their scars,
A mock is due.   *T. C.* iv. 5.
Why, Valentine, what Braggardism is this!   *T. C.* ii. 4.

BOLDNESS.
What I think, I utter; and spend my malice in my breath.
    C. ii. 1.
Think'st thou that duty shall have dread to speak,
When power to flattery bows? To plainness honour's bound,
When majesty stoops to folly.   *K. L.* i. 1.

BOLD EXTERIOR.
We'll have a swashing and a martial outside;
As many other mannish cowards have,
That do outface it with their semblances.   *A. Y.* i 3.

BOMBAST.
These signs have mark'd me extraordinary,
And all the courses of my life do show
I am not in the roll of common men.   *H. IV.* PT. I. iii. 1.

BONDS (See also INFLEXIBILITY).
I'll have my bond; speak not against my bond:
I have sworn an oath, that I will have my bond.
    M. V. iii. 3.

BONES, HUMAN.
    Chapless, and knock'd about the mazzard with a sexton's spade: Here's a fine revolution, an' we had the trick to see't!   *H.* v. 1.

BOOBY.
    Thou art bought and sold, among those of any wit, like a Barbarian slave.   *T. C.* ii. 1.

BOOKS, CONSOLATION OF.
Come, and take choice of all my library,
And so beguile thy sorrow.   *Tit. And.* iv. 1.

BOOK-COVERS.
That book, in many's eyes doth share the glory,
That in gold clasps, locks in the golden story.   *R. J.* i. 3.

BOOK-WORMS.
Small have continual plodders ever won
Save base authority from others' books.   *L. L.* i. 1.

BORROWING.
          Timon is shrunk indeed;
And he, that's once denied, will hardly speed.   *T. A.* iii. 2.

  I can get no remedy against this consumption of the purse; borrowing only lingers and lingers it out, but the disease is incurable.   *H. IV.* PT. II. i. 2.

BOUNTY.
'Tis pity bounty had not eyes behind;
That man might ne'er be wretched for his mind.
                                      T. A. i. 2.

Magic of bounty! all these spirits thy power
Hath conjur'd to attend.   *T. A.* i. 1.
          For his bounty,
There was no winter in't; an autumn 'twas,
That grew the more by reaping,   *A. C.* v. 2.

No villainous bounty yet hath pass'd my heart;
Unwisely, not ignobly, have I given.   *T. A.* ii. 2.

——— ILL-REQUITED.
Even so;
As with a man by his own alms empoison'd,
And with his charity slain.   *C.* v. 5.

BRAGGARTS.
A mad-cap ruffian, and a swearing Jack,
That thinks with oaths to face the matter out.   *T. S.* ii. 1.

                I know them, yea,
And what they weigh, even to the utmost scruple;
Scambling, out-facing, fashion-mong'ring boys,
That lie, and cog, and flout, deprave, and slander,
Go anticly, and show an outward hideousness,
And speak off half a dozen dangerous words,
How they might hurt their enemies if they durst;
And this is all.   *M. A.* v. 1.
He speaks plain cannon, fire, and smoke, and bounce;
He gives the bastinado with his tongue;
Our ears are cudgell'd; not a word of his,
But buffets better than a fist of France;
Zounds! I was never so bethump'd with words.   *K. J.* ii. 2.

BRAGGARTS,—*continued.*
             Who knows himself a braggart,
Let him fear this ; for it will come to pass
That every braggart shall be found an ass.   *A. W.* iv. 3
What cracker is this same, which deafs our ears
With this abundance of superfluous breath?   *K. J.* ii. 1
             Here's a large mouth, indeed,
That spits forth death, and mountains, rocks and seas ;
Talks as familiarly of roaring lions,
As maids of thirteen do of puppy dogs.   *K. J.* ii. 2
             What art thou? Have not I
An arm as big as thine ? a heart as big ?
Thy words, I grant, are bigger ; for I wear not
My dagger in my mouth.   *Cym.* iv. 2.

BRAINS.
                 Not Hercules
Could have knock'd out his brains, for he had none.
                                             Cym. iv. 2.
       Hector shall have a great catch, if he knock out either
of your brains; a' were as good crack a fusty nut with
no kernel.   *T. C.* ii. 1.

BRAWLS.
Swords out, and tilting one at other's breast,
In opposition bloody.   *O.* ii. 3.
       I pray you to serve Got, and keep you out of prawls and
prabbles, and quarrels, and dissentions, and, I warrant you,
it is the petter for you.   •   *H. V.* iv. 8.
             What's the matter,
That you unlace your reputation thus,
And spend your rich opinion for the name
Of a night brawler ?   *O.* ii. 3.
Help, masters !—Here's a goodly watch, indeed. *O.* ii. 3.

BREEDING.
Highly fed, and lowly taught.   *A. W.* ii. 1.

BREVITY.
Therefore,—since brevity is the soul of wit,
And tediousness the limbs and outward flourishes,
I will be brief.   *H.* ii. 2.

BRIBERY.
                 Shall we now
Contaminate our fingers with base bribes ?
And sell the mighty space of our large honours,
For so much trash as may be grasped thus ?

BRIBERY,—*continued.*
I had rather be a dog and bay the moon,
Than such a Roman. *J. C.* iv. 3.
        You yourself
Are much condemn'd to have an itching palm;
To sell and mart your offices for gold,
To undeservers. *J. C.* iv. 3.

BRITAIN (See also ENGLAND).
        Britain is
A world by itself; and we will nothing pay
For wearing our own noses. *Cym.* iii. 1.
        Which stands
As Neptune's park, ribbed and paled in
With rocks unscaleable, and roaring waters. *Cym.* iii. 1.
        I' the world's volume,
Our Britain is as of it, but not in it;
In a great pool, a swan's nest. *Cym.* iii. 4.

BROILS, DOMESTIC.
        Wars are no strife
To the dark house, and the detested wife. *A. W.* ii. 3.

BRUTUS.
This was the noblest Roman of them all;
All the conspirators, save only he,
Did that they did in envy of great Cæsar;
He, only, in a general honest thought,
And common good to all, made one of them.
His life was gentle; and the elements
So mix'd in him, that Nature might stand up
And say to all the world: This was a man! *J.C.* v. 5

BUBBLES.
The earth hath bubbles, as the water hath,
And these are of them. *M.* i. 3
On my life, my lord, a bubble. *A. W.* iii. 6

BUTTON-HOLDER.
        Sometimes he angers me,
With telling me of the mold-warp, and the ant,
Of the dreamer Merlin, and his prophecies;
And of a dragon and a finless fish,
A clip-wing'd griffin, and a moulten raven,
A couching lion, and a rampant cat,
And such a deal of skimble-skamble stuff
As puts me from my faith. I'll tell you what,—
He held me, but last night, at least nine hours,
In reckoning up the several devils' names.

BUTTON-HOLDER,—*continued.*
That were his lackeys: I cried—humph,—and well—go to--
But mark'd him not a word. O he's as tedious
As is a tired horse, a railing wife;
Worse than a smoky house: I had rather live
With cheese and garlick, in a windmill, far,
Than feed on cates, and have him talk to me,
In any summer-house in Christendom. *H. IV.* PT. I. iii. 1.

BUT YET.
I do not like *but yet*, it does allay
The good precedence; fie upon *but yet;*
But yet is as a jailer to bring forth
Some monstrous malefactor. Pr'ythee, friend,
Pour out the pack of matter to mine ear,
The good and bad together. *A. C.* ii. 5.

C.

CALUMNY (See also SLANDER.)
  Back-wounding **calumny**
The whitest virtue strikes. *M. M.* iii. 2.

Be thou as chaste as ice, as pure as snow, thou
Shalt not escape calumny. *H.* iii. 1.

That thou art blam'd, shall not be thy defect,
For slander's mark was ever yet the fair. *Poems.*

CANDOUR.
Speak of me as I am; nothing extenuate,
Nor set down aught in malice. *O.* v. 3

In simple and pure soul I come to you. *O.* i. 1

CANNONADE (See also SIEGE).
By east and west, let France and England mount
Their battering cannon, charged to the mouths;
Till their soul-fearing clamours have brawl'd down
The flinty ribs of this contemptuous city:
I'd play incessantly upon these jades.
Ev'n till unfenced desolation
Leave them as naked as the vulgar air. *K. J.* ii. 2.

CAPACITY.
  The truth is, I am only old in judgment and understanding; and he that will caper with me for a thousand marks, let him lend me the money, and have at him.
  H. IV. PT. II. i. 2.

CAP   **Shakespearian Dictionary.**   CAU

CAPTAIN, THE TITLE OF, PROSTITUTED.
    Captain! thou abominable cheater, art thou not ashamed
to be called captain? If captains were of my mind, they
would truncheon you out, for taking their names upon you
before you have earned them. You a captain, you slave!
for what? A captain! these villains will make the word
captain odious: therefore, captains had need look to it.
                                             H. IV. PT. II. ii. 4.

CAPTIOUSNESS.
    You must needs learn, lord, to amend this fault.
Though sometimes it show greatness, courage, blood,
(And that's the dearest grace it renders you)
Yet oftentimes it doth present harsh rage,
Defect of manners, want of government,
Pride, haughtiness, opinion, and disdain:
The least of which haunting a nobleman,
Loseth men's hearts; and leaves behind a stain
Upon the beauty of all parts besides,
Beguiling them of commendation.   *H. IV.* PT. I. iii. 1.

CARE.
    Care keeps his watch in every old man's eye,
And where care lodges sleep will never lie;
But where unbruised youth with unstuff'd brain
Doth couch his limbs, there golden sleep doth reign.
                                                R. J. ii. 3.

              You lay out too much pains,
For purchasing but trouble.   *Cym.* ii. 3.

CARNAGE.
              Slaying is the word;
It is a deed in fashion.   *J.C.* v. 5.

CAVALIER.
    But he, as loving his own pride and purposes,
Evades them with a bombast circumstance,
Horribly stuff'd with epithets of war;
And, in conclusion, nonsuits
My mediators.   *O.* i. 1

CAVILLER.
                 I'll give thrice so much land
To any well deserving friend;
But in the way of bargain, mark you me,
I'll cavil on the ninth part of a hair.   *H. IV.* PT. I. iii. 1.

CAUSE, COMMON.
    For 'tis a cause that hath no mean dependence
Upon our joint and several dignities.   *T. C.* ii. 2.

CAUSE, DEFECTIVE.
A rotten cause abides no handling. *M. IV.* PT. II. iv. 1.
I cannot fight upon this argument. *T. C.* i. 1.

CAUTION (See also ADVICE).
Too much trust hath damag'd such
As have believ'd men in their loves too much. *Poems.*
Take heed o' the foul fiend! *K. L.* iii. 4.
It is the bright day that brings forth the adder,
And that craves wary walking. *J. C.* ii. 1.

Good, my lord, let's fight with gentle words,
Till time lend friends, and friends their helping swords.
R. II. iii. 3.
Come not between the dragon and his wrath. *K. L.* i. 1.

Hear you me, Jessica:
Lock up my doors; and when you hear the drum,
And the vile squeaking of the wry-neck'd fife,
Clamber not you up to the casement then,
Nor thrust your head into the public street,
To gaze on Christian fools with varnish'd faces;
But stop my house's ears; I mean my casements:
Let not the sound of shallow foppery enter
My sober house. *M. V.* ii. 5.

Think him as a serpent's egg,
Which, hatch'd, would, as his kind, grow mischievous;
And kill him in the shell. *J. C.* ii. 1.

Let me still take away the harms I fear,
Not fear still to be taken. *K. L.* i. 4.
How far your eyes may pierce I cannot tell,
Striving to better, oft we mar what's well. *K. L.* i. 4.

———— EXCESSIVE, OF THE AGED.
But, beshrew my jealousy!
It seems, it is as proper to our age
To cast beyond ourselves in our opinions,
As it is common for the younger sort
To lack discretion. *H.* ii. 1.

CELEBRITY (See also FAME).
Thrice-fam'd beyond all erudition. *T. C.* ii. 3.

CELERITY.
Celerity is never more admir'd.
Then by the negligent. *A. C.* iii. 7
The flighty purpose never is o'ertook,
Unless the deed go with it. *M.* iv. 1.

CENSURE (See also OPINION).
 We, in the world's wide mouth
Live scandaliz'd, and foully spoken of.   *H. IV.* PT. I. i. 3.
Why, who cries out on pride,
That can therein tax any private party?
Doth it not flow as hugely as the sea,
Till that the weary very means do ebb?
What woman in the city do I name,
When that I say, The city woman bears
The cost of princes on unworthy shoulders?
Who can come in and say that I mean her,
When such a one as she, such is her neighbour?
Or what is he of basest function,
That says his bravery is not on my cost,
(Thinking that I mean him,) but therein suits
His folly to the mettle of my speech?
There, then; How, what then? Let me see wherein
My tongue hath wrong'd him; if it do him right,
Then he hath wrong'd himself; if he be free,
Why then, my taxing like a wild-goose flies,
Unclaim'd of any man.   *A. Y.* ii. 7.

CEREMONY (See also REGAL CEREMONIES).
 Was but devis'd at first to set a gloss
On faint deeds, hollow welcomes,
Recanting goodness, sorry ere 'tis shown,
But where there is true friendship, there needs none.
            T. A. i. 2.
      Rebukable
And worthy shameful check it were to stand
On more mechanic compliment.   *A. C.* iv. 4.

CERES, INVOCATION TO.
 Ceres, most bounteous lady, thy rich lees
Of wheat, rye, barley, vetches, oats, and pease;
Thy turfy mountains where live nibbling sheep,
And flat meads thatch'd with stover, them to keep;
Thy banks with peonied and lilied brims,
Which spungy April at thy hest betrims,
To make cold nymphs, chaste crowns; and dark broom
 groves,
Whose shadow the dismissed bachelor loves,
Being lass-lorn; thy pole-clipt vineyard;
And thy sea-marge, sterile, and rocky hard,
Where thou thyself dost air: The queen o' sky,
Whose watery arch, and messenger, am I,
Bids thee leave these; and with her sovereign grace,
Here, on this grass-plot, in this very place,
To come and sport.   *T.* iv. 1.

CHA   *Shakespearian Dictionary.*   CHA

CHALLENGE.

Here's the challenge, read it; I warrant there's vinegar
and pepper in't.   *T. N.* iii. 4.

Nay, answer me: stand, and unfold
Yourself.   *H.* i. 1.

God bless me from a challenge!   *M. A.* v. 1.

Read thou this challenge; mark but the penning of it.
   K. L. iv. 6.

Draw, you rogue; for though it be night, the moon
shines.   *K. L.* ii. 2.

I'll write thee a challenge; or I'll deliver thy indignation
by word of mouth.   *T. N.* ii. 4.

By gar, it is a shallenge: I vill cut his troat in de park.
   M. W. i. 4.

Go, write it in a martial hand; be curst and brief; it is
no matter how witty, so it be eloquent, and full of invention; taunt him with the license of ink.   *T. N.* iii. 2.

             I protest
Maugre thy strength, youth, place, and eminence,
Despite thy victor sword, and fire-new fortune,
Thy valour, and thy heart,—thou art a traitor:
False to thy gods, thy brother, and thy father;
Conspirant 'gainst this high illustrious prince;
And from the extremest upward of thy head,
To the descent and dust beneath thy feet,
A most toad-spotted traitor. Say thou, No,
This sword, this arm, and my best spirits are bent,
To prove upon thy heart, whereto I speak,
Thou liest.   *K. L.* v. 3.

I never in my life
Did hear a challenge urg'd more modestly,
Unless a brother should a brother dare
To gentle exercise and proof of arms.
He gave you all the duties of a man;
Trimm'd up your praises with a princely tongue;
Spoke your deservings like a chronicle;
Making you ever better than his praise,
By still dispraising praise, valued with you:
And, which became him like a prince indeed,
He made a blushing cital of himself;
And chid his truant youth with such a grace,
As if he master'd there a double spirit,
Of teaching and of learning instantly.   *H. IV.* PT. I. v. 2.

CHAMPION.

Like a bold champion, I assume the lists,

CHA   *Shakespearian Dictionary.*   CHA

CHAMPION,—*continued.*
Nor ask advice of any other thought
But faithfulness and courage.   *P. P.* i. 1.

CHANCE (See also FORTUNE).
Full oft 'tis seen,
Our mean secures us; and our mere defects
Prove our commodities.   *K. L.* iv. 1.

CHANGE.
Why, here's a change indeed in the commonwealth!
   M. M. i. 2.
And art thou come to this?   *K. L.* iii. 4.

————, THE NECESSITY OF.
If all the year were playing holidays,
To sport would be as tedious as to work;
But when they seldom come, they wish'd-for come,
And nothing pleaseth but rare accidents.   *H. IV.* PT. I. i. 2.

CHANGELING.
     His humour
Was nothing but mutation; Ay and that
From one bad thing to worse.   *Cym.* iv. 2.

CHARITY.
     My learn'd lord cardinal,
Deliver all with charity.   *H. VIII.* i. 2.

For he is gracious if he be observ'd;
He hath a tear for pity, and a hand
Open as day for melting charity.   *H. IV.* PT. II. iv. 4.

CHARM.
For a charm of powerful trouble
Like a hell-broth boil and bubble.   *M.* iv. 1.

     Then I beat my tabor,
At which, like unback'd colts, they prick'd their ears,
Advanc'd their eyelids, lifted up their noses,
As they smelt music; so I charm'd their ears,
That, calf-like, they my lowing follow'd through
Tooth'd briars, sharp furzes, pricking goss, and thorns,
Which enter'd their frail shins: at last I left them
I'the filthy mantled pool beyond your cell.   *T.* iv. 1

———— DISSOLVING.
     The charm dissolves apace;
And as the morning steals upon the night,
Melting the darkness, so their rising senses
Begin to chase the ignorant fumes that mantle
Their clearer reason.   *T.* v. 1.

CHASTITY.

Chaste as the icicle,
That's curded by the frost from purest snow,
And hangs on Dian's temple. *C. v. 3.*
Of chastity, the ornaments are chaste. *Poems.*
She'll not be hit
With Cupid's arrow; she hath Dian's wit;
And, in strong proof of chastity well arm'd,
From love's weak childish bow she lives unharm'd.
R. J. i. 1.
I thought her
As chaste as unsunn'd snow. *Cym. ii. 6.*
She will not stay the siege of loving terms,
Nor 'bide th' encounter of assailing eyes,
Nor ope her lap to saint-seducing gold. *R. J. i. 1.*

CHEATS (See also KNAVES).

They say, this town is full of cozenage;
As, nimble jugglers, that deceive the eye,
Dark-working sorcerers, that change the mind,
Soul-killing witches, that deform the body;
Disguised cheaters, prating mountebanks,
And many such like libertines of sin. *C. E. i. 2.*

CHECK.

I see this hath a little dash'd your spirits. *O. iii. 3.*

CHEERFULNESS.

Why should a man whose blood is warm within,
Sit like his grandsire cut in alabaster?
Sleep when he wakes, and creep into the jaundice
By being peevish. *M. V. i. 1.*

CHIDING.

But I'll not chide thee;
Let shame come when it will, I do not call it:
I do not bid the thunder-bearer shoot,
Nor tell tales of thee to high-judging Jove:
Mend, when thou can'st; be better at thy leisure:
I can be patient. *K. L. ii. 4.*
O, what a beast was I to chide him! *R. J. iii. 2.*

CHILDREN, UNDUTIFUL (See also FILIAL INGRATITUDE).

I shall see
The winged vengeance overtake such children. *K. L. iii. 7.*

CHIVALRY.

Now thou art seal'd the son of chivalry. *H. VI. PT. I. iv. 6.*
In this glorious and well foughten field,
We kept together in our chivalry. *H. V. iv. 6.*

Shakesperian Dictionary.

CHIVALRY,—continued.
I am to day i' the vein of chivalry. *T. C.* v. 3.
For my part, I may speak it to my shame,
I have a truant been to chivalry. *H. IV.* PT. I. v. 1.

CHOICE.
There's a small choice in rotten apples. *T. S.* i. 1.

CHRISTENING.
You must be seeing christenings! Do you look for ale and cakes here, you rude rascals! *H. VIII.* v. 3.

CHRISTIAN WARS.
I always thought,
It was both impious and unnatural,
That such immanity and bloody strife
Should reign among professors of one faith.
H. VI. PT. I. v. 1.

CHURCHMEN.
Who should be pitiful if you be not?
Or who should study to prefer a peace,
If holy churchmen take delight in broils?
H. VI. PT. I. iii. 1.

Love and meekness, lord,
Become a churchman better than ambition;
Win straying souls with modesty again,
Cast none away. *H. VIII.* v. 2.

I am of the church, and will be glad to do my benevolence, to make atonements and compromises between you.
M. W. i. 1.

If we did think
His contemplations were above the earth,
And fix'd on spiritual objects, he should still
Dwell in his musings: but I am afraid,
His thinkings are below the moon, not worth
His serious considering. *H. VIII.* iii. 2.

CHURCH MILITANT.
What! the sword and the word! do you study them both, master parson? *M. W.* iii. 1.

CHURLISHNESS.
My master is of churlish disposition,
And little recks to find the way to heaven,
By doing deeds of hospitality. *A. Y.* ii. 4.

CIRCUMLOCUTION.
Thou shalt never get such a secret from me, but by a parable. *T. G.* ii. 5.

CIRCUMSPECTION.
Wear your eye,—thus, not jealous nor secure:
I would not have your free and noble nature,
Out of self bounty, be abus'd; look to't.   *O.* iii. 3.

Lay thy finger,—thus, and let thy soul be instructed.
   O. ii. 1.

CLAIM, Antiquated.
'Tis no sinister, nor no aukward claim,
Pick'd from the worm-holes of long vanish'd days,
Nor from the dust of old oblivion rak'd.   *H.V.* ii. 4.

CLEOPATRA, Sailing.
The barge she sat in, like a burnish'd throne,
Burn'd on the water: the poop was beaten gold;
Purple the sails, and so perfumed, that
The winds were love-sick with them: the oars were silver;
Which to the tune of flutes kept stroke, and made
The water, which they beat, to follow faster,
As amorous of their strokes. For her own person,
It beggar'd all description: she did lie
In her pavilion (cloth of gold of tissue)
O'er-picturing that Venus, where we see,
The fancy out-work nature; on each side her,
Stood pretty dimpled boys, like smiling Cupids,
With diverse-colour'd fans, whose wind did seem
To glow the delicate cheeks which they did cool;—
And what they undid, did.
Her gentlewomen, like the Nereides,
So many mermaids, tended her i' the eyes,
And made their bends adornings: at the helm,
A seeming mermaid steers; the silken tackle
Swell with the touches of those flower-soft hands,
That yarely frame the office. From the barge,
A strange invisible perfume hits the sense
Of the adjacent wharfs.   *A.C.* ii. 2.

CLERICAL FUNCTION.
The very opener and intelligencer,
Between the grace, the sanctities of heaven,
And our dull workings.   *IV.* pt. ii. iv. 2.

CLOUDS.
That, which is now a horse, even with a thought,
The rack dislimns; and makes it indistinct,
As water is in water.   *A. C.* iv. 12.

Sometimes we see a cloud that's dragonish;
A vapour, sometimes, like a bear, or lion,
A tower'd citadel, a pendant rock,

CLOUDS,—*continued.*
A forked mountain, or blue promontory,
With trees upon't, that nod unto the world,
And mock our eyes with air: Thou hast seen these signs;
They are black vesper's pageants.   *A.C.* iv. 12.

CLOWN.
A clod of wayward marle.   *M. A.* ii. 1.
It is meat and drink to me to see a clown.   *A.Y.* v. 1.

COAST AT SUN-RISE.
Even till the eastern gate, all fiery red,
Opening on Neptune with fair blessed beams
Turns into yellow gold his salt-green streams.   *M. N.* iii. 2.

COCK, CROWING.
I have heard,
The cock, that is the trumpet of the morn,
Doth with his lofty and shrill-sounding throat
Awake the god of day; and, at his warning,
Whether in sea, or fire, in earth, or air,
The extravagant and erring spirit hies
To his confine.   *H.* i. 1.

COCKATRICES.
This will so fright them both, that they will kill one
another by the look, like cockatrices.   *T.N.* iii. 4.

COLDNESS (See also FRIGIDITY).
Tut, tut, thou art all ice; thy kindness freezes.
   R. III. iv. 2.

COLLECTOR.
A snapper up of unconsidered trifles.   *W. T.* iv. 2.
            And in his brain,
Which is as dry as the remainder biscuit
After a voyage,—he hath strange places cramm'd
With observation, the which he vents
In mangled forms.   *A.Y.* ii. 7.

Every lane's end, every shop, church, session, hanging,
yields a careful man work.   *W.T.* iv. 3.

A poor humour of mine, Sir, to take that that no man
else will.   *A.Y.* v. 4.

COMBAT.
Now they are clapper-clawing one another; I'll go look on
   T.C. v. 4.

COMFORT.
Thoughts tending to content, flatter themselves,—
That they are not the first of fortune's slaves,

COMFORT,—*continued.*
Nor shall not be the last; like silly beggars,
Who, sitting in the stocks, refuge their shame,—
That many have, and others must sit there,
And in this thought they find a kind of ease,
Bearing their own misfortunes on the back
Of such as have before endur'd the like. *R. II.* v. 5

How mightily, sometimes, we make us comforts of our losses.
A. W. iv. 3.

COMMODITY.
Commodity, the bias of the world;
The world, who of itself is poised well,
Made to run even upon even ground;
Till this advantage, this vile drawing bias,
This sway of motion, this commodity,
Makes it take head from all indifferency,
From all direction, purpose, course, intent:
And this same bias, this commodity,
This bawd, this broker, this all-changing word,
Clapp'd on the outward eye of fickle France,
Hath drawn him from his own determin'd aid,
From a resolv'd and honourable war,
To a most base and vile concluded peace. *K. J.* ii. 2.

COMMOTION (See also MOB).
The times are wild; contention, like a horse
Full of high feeding, madly hath broke loose,
And bears down all before him. *H. IV.* PT. II. i. 1.

You have made good work,
You and your apron men; you that stood so much
Upon the voice of occupation, and
The breath of garlic-eaters. *C.* iv. 6.

COMPACT.
A seal'd compáct,
Well ratified by law and heraldry. *H.* i. 1

COMPANIONS, JUVENILE.
We were as twinn'd lambs that did frisk i' the sun,
And bleat the one at the other: what we chang'd
Was innocence for innocence; we knew not
The doctrine of ill-doing, no, nor dream'd
That any did. *W.T.* i. 2

COMPANY.
It is certain, that either wise bearing, or ignorant carriage is caught as men take diseases, one of another; therefore, let men take heed of their company.
H. IV. PT. II. v. 1.

There is a thing, Harry, which thou hast often heard of,

Shakespearian Dictionary.

COMPANY,—*continued.*
and it is known to many in our land by the name of pitch:
this pitch, as ancient writers do report, doth defile; so doth
the company thou keepest. *H. IV.* PT. I. ii. 4.
Well, heaven send the prince a better companion.
H. IV. PT. II. i. 2.

COMPASSION.
Had he been slaughter-man to all my kin,
I should not for my life but weep with him,
To see how inly sorrow gripes his soul. *H. VI.* PT. III. i. 4.

COMPENDIUM.
There are some shrewd contents in yon' same paper.
M. V. iii. 2.

COMPLAINT.
O, that I were
Upon the hill of Basan, to outroar
The horned herd! for I have savage cause;
And to proclaim it civilly, were like
A halter'd neck, which does the hangman thank
For being yare about him. *A. C.* iii. 11.

COMPLIMENT.
'Twas never merry world
Since lowly feigning was call'd compliment. *T. N.* iii. 1.

COMPUNCTION (See also REMORSE).
Art thou afeard
To be the same in thine own act and valour,
As thou art in desire? Would'st thou have that
Which thou esteem'st the ornament of life,
And live a coward in thine own esteem;
Letting I dare not, wait upon I would,
Like the poor cat i' the adage? *M.* i. 7.

We will proceed no further in this business:
He hath honour'd me of late, and I have bought
Golden opinions of all sorts of people. *M.* i. 7.

But wherefore could I not pronounce, Amen?
I had most need of blessing, and Amen
Stuck in my throat. *M.* ii. 2.

COMRADE.
Friend and companion in the front of war. *A. C.* v. 1.

CONCEIT.
So sensible
Seemeth their conference, their conceits have wings
Fleeter than arrows, bullets, wind, thought, swifter things
L. L. v. 2.

CONCEIT,—*continued.*
Conceit in weakest bodies strongest works. *II.* iii. 4.

CONCLUSION.
Indeed, without an oath, I'll make an end on't. *H.* iv. 5

———————— F<small>ALSE</small>.
O most lame and impotent conclusion ! *O.* ii. 1.
But then there is no consonancy in the sequel. *T. N* ii. 5.

CONDESCENSION.
I extend my hand to him thus, quenching my familiar smile with an austere regard of controul. *T. N.* ii. 5.

CONFERENCE, L<small>EARNED</small>.
I'll talk a word with this same learned Theban.
K. L. iii 4.

CONFIDENCE.
As gentle and as jocund as to jest,
Go I to fight: Truth has a quiet breast. *R. II.* i. 3.

———————— U<small>NWARRANTED</small>.
Is not this a strange fellow, my lord ? that so confidently seems to undertake this business, which he knows is not to be done; damns himself to do, and dares better be damn'd than to do it. *A. W.* iii. 6.

CONJUROR.
They brought one Punch: a hungry lean-fac'd villain,
A mere anatomy, a mountebank,
A thread-bare juggler, a fortune-teller ;
A needy, hollow-ey'd, sharp-looking wretch,
A living dead man : this pernicious slave,
Forsooth, took on him as a conjuror ;
And, gazing in mine eyes, feeling my pulse,
And with no face, as 'twere, out-facing me,
Cried out, I was possess'd. *C. E.* v. 1

CONNEXIONS.
Why, this is to have a name in great men's fellowship.
A. C. ii. 7

CONQUEROR (See also W<small>AR</small>).
Before him
He carries noise, and behind him he leaves tears. *C.* ii. 1
A conqueror and afear'd to speak ! *L. L.* v. 2.

CONQUEST.
Truly to speak, Sir, and with no addition,
We go to gain a little patch of ground,
That hath in it no profit but the name. *H.* iv. 4.

Shakespearian Dictionary.

CONSCIENCE (See also SUICIDE).
I'll teach you how you shall arraign your conscience,
And try your penitence, if it be sound,
Or hollowly put on. *M. M.* ii. 3
   Go to your bosom ;
Knock there ; and ask your heart what it doth know.
            M. M. ii. 2.
   Who has a breast so pure,
But some uncleanly apprehensions
Keep leets and law-days, and in sessions sit
With meditations lawful? *O.* iii. 3.

What stronger breast-plate than a heart untainted?
Thrice is he arm'd that hath his quarrel just ;
And he but naked though locked up in steel,
Whose conscience with injustice is corrupted.
         H. VI. PT. II. iii. 2.
   I feel within me
A peace above all earthly dignities,
A still and quiet conscience. *H. VIII.* iii. 2

You shall see, anon ; 'tis a knavish piece of work ; but what of that ? Your majesty, and we that have free souls, it touches us not: Let the gall'd jade wince, our withers are unwrung. *H.* iii. 2.

Why, let the stricken deer go weep,
 The hart ungalled play ;
For some must watch, while some must sleep ;
 Thus runs the world away. *H.* iii. 2.

   I'll observe his looks ;
I'll tent him to the quick ; if he do blench,
I know my course. *H.* ii. 2.

I'll not meddle with it, it is a dangerous thing, it makes a man a coward ; a man cannot steal, but it accuseth him ; a man cannot swear, but it checks him ; a man cannot lie with a neighbour's wife, but it detects him : 'Tis a blushing shame-fac'd spirit, that mutinies in a man's bosom ; it fills one full of obstacles : it made me once restore a purse of gold, that by chance I found ; it beggars any man that keeps it ; it is turned out of all towns and cities for a dangerous thing. *R. III.* i. 4.

─────────── GUILTY.
My conscience hath a thousand several tongues,
And every tongue brings in a several tale ;
And every tale condemns me for a villain. *R. III.* v. 3.
How is't with me when every noise appals me? *M.* ii. 2.

CONSCIENCE, GUILTY,—*continued*.
Suspicion always haunts the guilty mind;
The thief doth fear each bush an officer.
H. VI. PT. III. v. 6.

     How smart
A lash that speech doth give my conscience! *H.* iii. 1.

Thou turn'st mine eyes into my very soul;
And there I see such black and grained spots
As will not leave their tinct. *H.* iii. 4.

Methought the billows spoke and told me of it;
The winds did sing it to me; and the thunder,
That deep and dreadful organ-pipe, pronounc'd
The name of Prosper; it did bass my trespass,
Therefore my son i' th' ooze is bedded. *T.* ii. 2.

    Soft; I did but dream,
O, coward conscience, how dost thou affright me!
 R. III. v. 3.

With clog of conscience and sour melancholy. *R. II.* v. 6.

Not so sick, my lord,
As she is troubled with thick-coming fancies,
That keep her from her rest. *M.* v. 3.

Canst thou not minister to a mind diseas'd;
Pluck from the memory a rooted sorrow;
Raze out the written troubles of the brain;
And with some sweet oblivious antidote,
Cleanse the foul bosom of that perilous stuff,
Which weighs upon the heart? *M.* v. 3.

——————— SEARED.
    If it were a kybe,
'Twould put me to my slipper; but I feel not
This deity in my bosom: twenty consciences,
That stand 'twixt me and Milan, candied be they,
And melt, ere they molest. *T.* ii. 1.

Let not our babbling dreams affright our souls;
Conscience is but a word that cowards use,
Devis'd at first, to keep the strong in awe. *R. III.* v. 3.

CONSPIRACY.
   While you here do snoring lie
   Open-ey'd conspiracy
    His time doth take:
  If of life you keep a care,
  Shake off slumber, and beware:
    Awake! Awake! *T.* ii. 2.

CONSPIRACY,—*continued.*
    O conspiracy!
Sham'st thou to show thy dangerous brow by night,
When evils are most free? O, then, by day,
Where wilt thou find a cavern dark enough
To mask thy monstrous visage? Seek none, conspiracy,
Hide it in smiles and affability:
For if thou path thy native semblance on,
Not Erebus itself were dim enough
To hide thee from prevention.   *J. C.* ii. 1.

—————— Popular.
It is a purpos'd thing, and grows by plot,
To curb the will of the nobility:—
Suffer it, and live with such as cannot rule
And never will be rul'd.   *C.* iii. 1.

CONSTANCY (See also Fidelity).
The fineness of which metal is not found
In fortune's love; for then, the bold and coward,
The wise and fool, the artist and unread,
The hard and soft, seem all affin'd and kin;
But in the wind and tempest of her frown,
Distinction, with a broad and powerful fan,
Puffing at all, winnows the light away;
And what hath mass, or matter, by itself
Lies, rich in virtue, and unmingled.   *T.C.* i. 3.

Master, go on; and I will follow thee,
To the last gasp, with truth and loyalty.   *A.Y.* ii. 3.

    Time, force, and death,
Do to this body what extremes you can;
But the strong base and building of my love
Is as the very centre of the earth,
Drawing all things to it.   *T.C.* iv. 2.

    Now from head to foot,
I am marble constant; now the fleeting moon
No planet is of mine.   *A.C.* v. 2.

But I am constant as the northern star,
Of whose true fix'd, and resting quality,
There is no fellow in the firmament.   *J.C.* iii. 1.

—————— Conjugal.
    Here I kneel.—
If e'er my wish did trespass 'gainst his love,
Either in discourse, in thought, or actual deed;
Or that mine eyes, mine ears, or any sense,
Delighted them in any other form;
Or that I do not yet, and ever did,
And ever will,—though he do shake me off

CONSTANCY, Conjugal,—*continued.*

  To beggarly divorcement,—love him dearly,
  Comfort forswear me! Unkindness may do much;
  And his unkindness may defeat my life,
  But never taint my love.   *O.* iv. 2.

  He counsels a divorce: a loss of her,
  That, like a jewel, has hung twenty years
  About his neck, yet never lost her lustre;
  Of her, that loves him with that excellence
  That angels love good men with; even of her,
  That when the greatest stroke of fortune falls,
  Will bless the king.   *H. VIII.* ii. 2.

      Sir, call to mind,
  That I have been your wife in this obedience,
  Upward of twenty years, and have been bless'd
  With many children by you. If, in the course
  And process of this time, you can report,
  And prove it too, against mine honour aught,
  My bond to wedlock, or my love and duty,
  Against your sacred person, in God's name,
  Turn me away; and let the foul'st contempt
  Shut door upon me, and so give me up
  To the sharpest kind of justice. *H. VIII.* ii. ii.

  O bid me leap, rather than marry Paris,
  From off the battlements of yonder tower;
  Or walk in thievish ways; or bid me lurk
  Where serpents are; chain me with roaring bears;
  Or shut me nightly in a charnel house,
  O'er-cover'd quite with dead men's rattling bones,
  With reeky shanks, and yellow chapless skulls;
  Or bid me go into a new made grave,
  And hide me with a dead man in his shroud;
  Things that, to hear them told, have made me tremble;
  And I will do it without fear or doubt,
  To live an unstain'd wife to my sweet love. *R. J.* iv. 1.

CONSTERNATION.

  Behold, destruction, frenzy, and amazement,
  Like witless antics, one another meet. *T. C.* v. 3.

CONSULTATION.

  Now sit we close about the taper here,
  And call in question our necessities. *J. C.* iv. 3.

CONSUMMATION.

  When the hurly-burly's done,
  When the battle's lost and won. *M.* i. 1

Shakespearian Dictionary.

CONTEMPLATION.
Contemplation makes a rare turkey-cock of him; how he jets
under his advanced plumes!   *T. N.* ii. 5.

CONTEMPTIBLE.
Put on him what forgeries you please; marry, none so rank
As may dishonour him.   *H.* ii. 1.

CONTENT (See also MODERATION).
        Our content
Is our best having.   *H. VIII.* ii. 3.
        Verily,
I swear 'tis better to be lowly born,
And range with humble livers in content,
Than to be perk'd up in a glistering grief,
And wear a golden sorrow.   *H. VIII.* ii. 3.
My crown is in my heart, not on my head;
Not deck'd with diamonds and Indian stones,
Nor to be seen; my crown is call'd content;
A crown it is that seldom kings enjoy.   *H. VI.* PT. III. iii. 1.
        Willing misery
Outlives incertain pomp, is crown'd before:
The one is filling still, never complete;
The other, at high wish.   *T. A.* iv. 3.

CONTENTION.
I pr'ythee take thy fingers from my throat;
For though I am not splenetive and rash,
Yet have I in me something dangerous,
Which let thy wisdom fear.   *H.* v. 1.

CONVERSATION.
These high wild hills and rough uneven ways,
Draw out our miles and make them wearisome;
And yet your fair discourse hath been as sugar,
Making the hard way sweet and délectable.   *R. II.* ii. 3.

    I praise God for you, Sir; your reasons at dinner, have
been sharp and sententious; pleasant without scurrility,
witty without affectation, audacious without impudency,
learned without opinion, and strange without heresy.
                                 L. L. v. 1.

COOKERY.
But his neat cookery! He cut our roots in characters;
And sauc'd our broths as Juno had been sick,
And he her dieter.   *Cym.* iv. 2.

COOLING.
And in the height of this bath, when I was more than
half stew'd in grease, like a Dutch dish, to be thrown into

COOLING,—*continued.*
the Thames, and cooled glowing hot, in that surge, like a horse-shoe, think of that;—hissing hot;—think of that, Master Brook. *M. W.* iii. 5.

CORINTHIAN.
A Corinthian, a lad of mettle. *H.IV.* PT. I. ii. 4

CORIOLANUS.
Thou art left, Marcius:
A carbuncle entire, as big as thou art,
Were not so rich a jewel. Thou wast a soldier
Even to Cato's wish, not fierce and terrible
Only in strokes; but, with thy grim looks, and
The thunder-like percussion of thy sounds,
Thou mad'st thine enemies shake, as if the world
Were feverous and did tremble. *C.* i. 4.

His nature is too noble for the world:
He would not flatter Neptune for his trident,
Or Jove for his power to thunder. His heart's his mouth:
What his breast forges, that his tongue must vent;
And, being angry, does forget that ever
He heard the name of death. *C.* iii. 1.

CORRECTION.
Your purpos'd low correction,
Is such, as basest and contemned'st wretches,
For pilferings and most common trespasses,
Are punished with. *K. L.* ii. 2.

My masters of St. Alban's, have you not beadles in your town, and things called whips? *H.VI.* PT. II. ii. 1.

———— DIFFICULTIES OF.
For full well he knows,
He cannot so precisely weed this land,
As his misdoubts present occasion;
His foes are so enrooted with his friends,
That, plucking to unfix an enemy,
He doth unfasten so, and shake a friend.
So that this land, like an offensive wife,
That hath enrag'd him on to offer strokes,
As he is striking, holds his infant up,
And hangs resolv'd correction in the arm
That was uprear'd to execution. *H. IV.* PT. II. iv. 1

•COVETOUSNESS.
Those that much are of gain so fond,
That oft they have not that which they possess;
They scatter and unloose it from their bond,
And so, by hoping more, they have but less. *Poems*

COUNSEL.
Is this your Christian counsel? out upon ye!
Heaven is above all yet; there sits a judge,
That no king can corrupt.   *H. VIII.* iii. 1.

COUNTENANCE, BENIGN.
Her face, the book of praises, where is read
Nothing but curious pleasures, as from thence
Sorrow were ever raz'd, and testy wrath
Could never be her mild companion.   *P.P.* i. 1.

COURAGE (See also VALOUR).
                 Pr'ythee peace;
I dare do all that may become a man;
Who dares do more, is none.   *M.* i. 7.

Things out of hope are compass't oft with vent'ring. *Poems.*

         Wise men ne'er sit and wail their loss,
But cheerly seek how to redress their harms.
What though the mast be now blown overboard,
The cable broke, the holding anchor lost,
And half our sailors swallow'd in the flood?
Yet lives our pilot still: Is't meet that he
Should leave the helm, and like a fearful lad,
With tearful eyes add water to the sea,
And give more strength to that which hath too much;
Whiles, in his moan, the ship splits on the rock,
Which industry and courage might have sav'd?
                       H. VI. PT. III. v. 4.

By how much unexpected, by so much
We must awake endeavour for defence;
For courage mounteth with occasion.   *K. J.* ii. 1.

                 For this last,
Before and in Corioli, let me say,
I cannot speak him home; he stopp'd the fliers;
And by his rare example, make the coward
Turn terror into sport: as waves before
A vessel under sail, so men obey'd,
And fell below his stern: his sword, death's stamp,
Where it did mark, it took; from face to foot,
He was a thing of blood, whose every motion
Was tim'd with dying cries.   *C.* ii. 2

But wherefore do you droop? why look you sad?
Be great in act, as you have been in thought;
Let not the world see fear and sad distrust
Govern the motion of a kingly eye:
Be stirring as the time; be fire with fire;
Threaten the threatener and outface the brow

COURAGE,—*continued.*
Of bragging horror: so shall inferior eyes,
That borrow their behaviour from the great,
Grow great by your example, and put on
The dauntless spirit of resolution.
Away; and glister like the god of war,
When he intendeth to become the field:
Show boldness and aspiring confidence.
What, shall they seek the lion in his den,
And fright him there? and make him tremble there?
O, let it not be said! Forage, and run
To meet displeasure further from the doors;
And grapple with him ere he come so nigh. *K. J.* v. 1.

He hath borne himself beyond the promise of his age;
doing in the figure of a lamb the feats of a lion. *M. A.* i. 1.

When by and by the din of war 'gan pierce
His ready sense; then straight his doubled spirit
Re-quicken'd what in flesh was fatigate,
And to the battle came he; where he did
Run reeking o'er the lives of men, as if
'Twere a perpetual spoil; and till we call'd
Both field and city ours he never stood
To ease his breath with panting. *C.* ii. 2.

That misbegotten devil, Faulconbridge,
In spite of spite, alone, upholds the day. *K. J.* v. 4.

Alone he enter'd
The mortal gate o' the city, which he painted
With shunless destiny, aidless came off,
And with a sudden reinforcement struck
Corioli, like a plane. *C.* ii. 2.

Safe, Anthony; Brutus is safe enough:
I dare assure thee, that no enemy
Shall ever take alive the noble Brutus:
The gods defend him from so great a shame!
When you do find him, or alive or dead,
He will be found like Brutus, like himself. *J. C.* v. 4.

Our then dictator
Whom without praise I point at, saw him fight,
When with his Amazonian chin he drove
The bristled lips before him: he bestrid
An o'er-press'd Roman, and i' the consul's view,
Slew three opposers. *C.* ii. 2,

Slave, I have set my life upon a cast
And I will stand the hazard of the die. *R. III.* v. 4.

COURT.

Do you take the court for Paris garden? you rude slaves, leave your gaping. *H. VIII.* v. 3.

——— BEAUTY.

Let the court of France show me such another: I see how thine eye would emulate the diamond: thou hast the right arched bent of the brow, that becomes the ship-tire, the tire-valiant, or any tire of Venetian admittance.
M. W. iii. 3.

COURTIER (See also TOOLS, SLAVISHNESS).

I am a courtier. See'st thou not the air of the court in these enfoldings? Hath not my gait in it the measure of the court? Receiveth not thy nose court-odour from me? Reflect I not on thy baseness court-contempt?
W. T. iv. 3.

You shall mark
Many a duteous and knee-crooking knave,
That doting on his own obsequious bondage,
Wears out his time, much like his master's ass,
For nought but provender; and when he's old, cashier'd.
O. i. 1.

But howso'er, no simple man that sees
This jarring discord of nobility,
This shouldering of each other in the court,
This factious bandying of their favorites,
But that it does presage some ill event. *H. IV.* PT. 1. iv. 1.

COURTSHIP (See also LOVE).

That man that hath a tongue, I say is no man,
If with his tongue he cannot win a woman. *T. G.* iii. 1.

Every night he comes
With music of all sorts, and songs compos'd
To her unworthiness. It nothing steads us
To chide him from our eaves; for he persists,
As if his life lay on't. *A. W.* iii. 7.

I will attend her here,
And woo her with some spirit when she comes.
Say, that she rail; why, then I'll tell her plain,
She sings as sweetly as a nightingale:
Say, that she frown; I'll say, she looks as clear
As morning roses newly wash'd with dew:
Say, she be mute, and will not speak a word;
Then I'll commend her volubility,
And say,—she uttereth piercing eloquence:
If she do bid me pack, I'll give her thanks,
As though she bid me stay by her a week;

COURTSHIP,—*continued.*

If she deny to wed, I'll crave the day
When I shall ask the banns, and when be married.
T. S. ii. 1.

I'll make my heaven in a lady's lap,
And deck my body in gay ornaments,
And witch sweet ladies with my words and looks.
H. VI. PT. III. iii. 2.

    My story being done,
She gave me for my pains a world of sighs:
She swore,—In faith, 'twas strange, 'twas passing strange;
'Twas pitiful, 'twas wondrous pitiful:
She wish'd she had not heard it; yet she wish'd
That heaven had made her such a man: she thank'd me;
And bade me, if I had a friend that lov'd her,
I should but teach him how to tell my story,
And that would woo her. Upon this hint I spake:
She lov'd me for the dangers I had pass'd;
And I lov'd her that she did pity them.
O. i. 3.

 King Edward.—What love, think'st thou, I sue so much to get?
 Lady Grey.—My love till death, my humble thanks, my prayers; That love, which virtue begs, and virtue grants.
H. VI. PT. III. iii. 2.

Make me a willow cabin at your gate,
And call upon my soul within the house:
Write loyal cantons of contemned love,
And sing them loud even in the dead of night;
Holla your name to the reverberate hills,
And make the babbling gossip of the air
Cry out, Olivia! O, you should not rest
Between the elements of air and earth,
But you should pity me.
T. N. i. 5.

Take no repulse, whatever she doth say;
For, *get you gone,* she doth not mean, *away.*
Flatter and praise, commend, extol their graces;
Though ne'er so black, say they have angels' faces.
T. G. iii. 1.

  Say, that upon the altar of her beauty
You sacrifice your tears, your sighs, your heart:
Write till your ink be dry; and with your tears
Moist it again, and frame some feeling line,
That may discover such integrity.
T. G. iii. 2.

    I tell you, father,
I am as peremptory as she proud-minded;
And when two raging fires meet together,

COURTSHIP,—*continued.*
They do consume the thing that feeds their fury:
Though little fires grow great with little wind,
Yet extreme gusts will blow out fire and all:
So I to her, and so she yields to me;
For I am rough, and woo not like a babe. *T. S.* ii. 1.

Go then, my mother, to your daughter go;
Make bold her bashful ears with your experience;
Prepare her ears to hear a wooer's tale. *R. III.* iv. 4.

What! I that kill'd her husband, and his father,
To take her in her heart's extremest hate:
With curses in her mouth, tears in her eyes,
The bleeding witness of my hatred by;
With God, her conscience, and these bars against me,
And I no friends to back my suit withal,
But the plain devil and dissembling looks,
And yet to win her,—all the world to nothing! *R. III.* i. 2.

After your dire lamenting elegies,
Visit by night your lady's chamber window,
With some sweet concert; to their instruments
Tune a deploring dump: the night's dead silence
Will well become such sweet complaining grievance.
This, or else nothing, will inherit her. *T. G.* iii. 2.

Frame yourself
To orderly solicits; and be friended
With aptness to the season: make denials
Increase your services: so seem, as if
You were inspir'd to do those duties which
You tender to her; that you in all obey her,
Save when command to your dismission tends,
And therein you are senseless. *Cym.* ii. 3.

Never give her o'er;
For scorn at first, makes after-love the more.
If she do frown, 'tis not in hate of you,
But rather to beget more love in you;
If she do chide, 'tis not to have you gone;
For why, the fools are mad if left alone. *T. G.* iii. 1.

The count he wooes your daughter,
Lays down his wanton siege before her beauty,
Resolves to carry her; let her, in fine, consent,
As we'll direct her how 'tis best to bear it,
Now his important blood will nought deny
That she'll demand. *A. W.* iii. 7.

She is a woman, therefore may be woo'd;
She is a woman, therefore may be won. *Tit. And.* ii. 1.

COURTSHIP,—*continued.*
Men are April when they woo, December when they wed; maids are May when they are maids, but the sky changes when they are wives. *A. Y.* iv. 1.

Was ever woman in this humour woo'd?
Was ever woman in this humour won? *R. III.* i. 2

Henceforth my wooing mind shall be express'd
In russet *yeas*, and honest-meaning *noes*. *L. L.* v. 2.

COWARDS.
His mind is not heroic, and there's the humour of it.
M. W. i. 3.

A coward, a most devout coward; religious in it.
T. N. iii. 4

I know him a notorious liar;
Think him a great way fool, solely a coward:
Yet these fix'd evils sit so fit in him,
That they take place, when virtue's steely bones
Look bleak in the cold wind. *A. W.* i. 1.

You souls of geese,
That bear the shapes of men, how have you run
From slaves that apes would beat! Pluto and hell!
All hurt behind; backs red, and faces pale
With flight and agued fear! Mend, and charge home,
Or, by the fires of heaven, I'll leave the foe,
And make my wars on you: Look to't. *C.* i. 4.

So bees with smoke, and doves with noisome stench,
Are from their hives, and houses, driven away.
They call'd us, for our fierceness, English dogs;
Now, like to whelps, we crying run away.
H. VI. PT. I. 1. 5.

The enemy full-hearted,
Lolling the tongue with slaughtering, having work
More plentiful than tools to do't, struck down
Some mortally, some slightly touch'd, some falling
Merely through fear; that the straight pass was damn'd
With dead men, hurt behind, and cowards living
To die with lengthened shame. *Cym.* v. 3.

To fear the foe, since fear oppresseth strength,
Gives, in your weakness, strength unto your foe,
And so your follies fight against yourself.
Fear and be slain; no worse can come, to fight:
And fight and die, is death destroying death;
Where, fearing dying, pays death servile breath.
R. II. iii. 2.

COWARD,—*continued.*

A coward is worse than a cup of sack with lime in it.
H. IV. PT. I. ii. 4.

Slander'd to death by villains;
That dare as well answer a man, indeed,
As I dare take a serpent by the tongue;
Boys, apes, braggarts, jacks, milksops. *M. A.* v. 1.

Well, for two of them, I know them to be as true bred cowards as ever turned back; and for the third, if he fight longer than he sees reason, I'll forswear arms.
H. IV. PT. I. i. 2.

How many cowards, whose hearts are all as false
As stairs of sand, wear yet upon their chins
The beards of Hercules, and frowning Mars;
Who, inward search'd, have livers white as milk!
And these assume but valour's excrement,
To render them redoubted. *M. V.* iii. 2.

A plague of all cowards, I say, and a vengeance too! marry and amen! *H. IV.* PT. I. ii. 4.

The mouse ne'er shunn'd the cat, as they did budge
From rascals worse than they. *C.* i. 6.

Reproach and everlasting shame
Sit mocking in our plumes. *H. V.* iv. 5.

Did I but suspect a fearful man,
He should have leave to go away betimes;
Lest, in our need, he might infect another,
And make him of like spirit to himself.
If any such be here, as God forbid!
Let him depart before we need his help.
H. VI. PT. III. v. 4.

To say the truth, this fact was infamous,
And ill-beseeming any common man;
Much more a knight, a captain, and a leader.
H. VI. PT. I. iv. 1.

We took him for a coward, but he's the very devil incarnate. *T. N.* v. 1.

Cowards father cowards, and base things sire base:
Nature hath meal, and bran; contempt, and grace.
Cym. iv. 2.

All the contagion of the south light on you!
You shames of Rome! You herd of,—Boils and plagues
Plaster you o'er; that you may be abhorred
Farther than seen, and one infect another
Against the wind a mile! *C.* 1. 4.

COWARD,—*continued.*
　　　　He which hath no stomach to this fight,
Let him depart; his passport shall be made,
And crowns for convoy put into his purse :
We would not die in that man's company,
That fears his fellowship to die with us.　　*H.V.* iv. 3.
Perish the man whose mind is backward now.　*H.V.* iv. 3.

　　He's a great quarreller; and, but that he hath the gift of a coward, to allay the gust he hath in quarrelling, 'tis thought among the prudent, he would quickly have the gift of a grave.　　　　　　　　　　　　　*T.N.* i. 3.

　　In a retreat he outruns any lacquey; marry, in coming on, he has the cramp.　　　　　　　　　　*A.W.* iv. 3.

You are the hare of whom the proverb goes,
Whose valour plucks dead lions by the beard.　*K.J.* ii. 1.

Plenty and peace, breed cowards : hardness ever
Of hardiness is mother.　　　　　　　　　　*Cym.* iii. 6.

I have fled myself; and have instructed cowards
To run, and show their shoulders.　　　　　*A.C.* iii. 9.

Foul-spoken coward ! that thunderest with thy tongue,
And with thy weapon nothing dar'st perform.　*Tit. And.* ii. 1.

　　He excels his brother for a coward, yet his brother is reputed one of the best that is.　　　　　　*A.W.* iv. 3.

Turn head and stop pursuit; for coward dogs
Most spend their mouths, when what they seem to threaten
Runs far before them.　　　　　　　　　　*H.V.* ii. 4

So cowards fight when they can fly no further :
As doves do peck the falcon's piercing talons ;
So desperate thieves, all hopeless of their lives,
Breathe out invectives 'gainst the officers.
　　　　　　　　　　　　　　　　H.VI. pt. iii. i. 4

Cowards die many times before their deaths :
The valiant never taste of death but once.　　*J.C.* ii. 2.

COXCOMB (See also Fribble).
　　Believe me, an absolute gentleman, full of most excellent differences, of very soft society, and great showing : indeed, to speak feelingly of him, he is the card or calendar of gentry, for you shall find in him the continent of what part a gentleman would see.　　　　　　　*H.* v. 2

A man in all the world's new fashion planted,
That hath a mint of phrases in his brain :
One, whom the music of his own vain tongue
Doth ravish like enchanting harmony ;
A man of compliments, whom right and wrong
Have chose as umpire of their mutiny.　　*L.L.* i. 1

COXCOMB,—*continued.*
O murd'rous coxcomb! what should such a fool
Do with so good a wife? *O.* v. 2.
O most profane coxcomb! *L. L.* iv. 3.

Thus has he and many more of the same breed, that, I know, the drossy age dotes on, only got the tune of the time, and outward habit of encounter; a kind of yeasty collection, which carries them through and through the most fond and winnowed opinions; and do but blow them to their trial, the bubbles are out. *H.* v. 2.

A barren-spirited fellow. *T. C.* iv. 1.

COZENERS.
And, indeed, Sir, there are cozeners abroad; therefore it behoves men to be wary. *W. T.* iv. 3.

CRAFT, EXPLODED.
My antient incantations are too weak. *H. VI.* PT. I. v. 3.

CREDULITY.
Thus credulous fools are caught! *O.* iv. 1.

But he that will believe all that they say, shall never be saved by half that they do. *A. C.* v. 2.

CRIMES.
All have not offended:
For those that were, it is not square, to take,
On those that are, revenges: crimes, like lands,
Are not inherited. *T. A.* v. 5.

How oft the sight of means to do ill deeds,
Makes ill deeds done! *K. J.* iv. 2

———— UNPUNISHED.
For we bid this be done,
When evil deeds have their permissive pass,
And not their punishment. *M. M.* i. 4.

CRISIS.
Ha! is it come to this! *K. L.* i. 4.

Before the curing of a strong disease,
Even in the instant of repair and health,
The fit is strongest; evils that take leave,
On their departure most of all show evil. *K. J.* iii. 4.

Things at the worst will cease; or else climb upward
To what they were before. *M.* iv. 2.

CRITICAL.
I am nothing if not critical. *O.* ii. 1.

69

CRO   *Shakesperian Dictionary.*   CRU

CROAKER.
I would croak like a raven; I would bode, I would bode.
                                                                           T.C. v. 2.

CROWN, REGAL (See also KINGS).
O polish'd perturbation! golden care!
That keeps the ports of slumber open wide
To many a watchful night! sleep with it now!
Yet not so sound, and half so deeply sweet
As he, whose brow with homely biggin bound,
Snores out the watch of night.   *H. IV.* PT. II. iv. 4.
A thousand flatteries sit within thy crown,
Whose compass is no bigger than thy head;
And, yet incaged in so small a verge,
The waste is no whit lesser than thy land.   *R. II.* ii. 1.
        Do but think
How sweet a thing it is to wear a crown;
Within whose circuit is Elysium,
And all that poets feign of bliss and joy. *H. IV.* PT. III. i. 2.
        Heaven knows, my son,
By what by-paths, and indirect crook'd ways,
I met this crown; and I myself know well,
How troublesome it sat upon my head. *H. IV.* PT. II. iv. 4
I spake unto the crown as having sense,
And thus upbraided it: *The care on thee depending,
Hath fed upon the body of my father;
Therefore thou, best of gold, art worst of gold;
Other, less fine in carat, is more precious,
Preserving life in med'cine potable;
But thou, most fine, most honour'd, most renown'd,
Hast eat thy bearer up.* Thus, my most royal liege,
Accusing it, I put it on my head;
To try with it, as with an enemy,
That had before my face murder'd my father,—
The quarrel of a true inheritor.   *H. IV.* PT. II. iv. 4.

CRUELTY.
O, be thou damn'd, inexorable dog!
And for thy life let justice be accus'd.
Thou almost mak'st me waver in my faith,
To hold opinion with Pythagoras,
That souls of animals infuse themselves
Into the trunks of men: thy currish spirit,
Govern'd a wolf; who, hang'd for human slaughter,
Even from the gallows did his fell soul fleet,
And whilst thou layest in thy unhallow'd dam,
Infus'd itself in thee; for thy desires
Are wolfish, bloody, starv'd, and ravenous.   *M. V.* iv. 1.

Shakespearian Dictionary.

CRUELTY,—*continued.*

I am sorry for thee; thou art come to answer
A stony adversary, an inhuman wretch,
Uncapable of pity, void and empty
From any dram of mercy.   *M.V.* iv. 1.

See, ruthless queen, a hapless father's tears;
This cloth thou dipp'dst in blood of my sweet boy,
And I with tears do wash the blood away,
Keep thou the napkin, and go boast of this:
And, if thou tell'st the heavy story right,
Upon my soul, the hearers will shed tears;
Yea, even my foes will shed fast-falling tears;
And say,—Alas, it was a piteous deed!   *H.VI.* PT. III. i. 4.

She-wolf of France, but worse than wolves of France,
Whose tongue more poisons than the adder's tooth!
How ill-beseeming is it in thy sex,
To triumph like an Amazonian trull,
Upon their woes whom fortune captivates!
                            H.VI. PT. III. i. 4.

But neither bended knees, pure hands held up,
Sad sighs, deep groans, nor silver-shedding tears,
Could penetrate her uncompassionate sire.   *T.G.* iii. 1.

CRUSADE.
                    Therefore, friends,
As far as to the sepulchre of Christ,
(Whose soldier now, under whose blessed cross
We are impressed and ingag'd to fight,)
Forthwith a power of English shall we levy;
Whose arms were moulded in their mother's womb,
To chase these pagans, in those holy fields,
Over whose acres walk'd those blessed feet,
Which fourteen hundred years ago, were nail'd,
For our advantage, on the bitter cross.   *H.IV.* PT. I. i. 1.

CUCKOLD.
Amaimon sounds well; Lucifer, well; Barbason, well; yet they are devils' additions, the names of fiends; but cuckold! wittol-cuckold! the devil himself hath not such a name.   *M.W.* ii. 2

CUDGEL.
I'll have the cudgel hallow'd and hung o'er the altar: it hath done meritorious service.   *M.W.* iv. 2.

CUPIDS.
Some Cupids kill with arrows, some with traps. *M.A.* iii. 1.

CURIOSITIES.
I pray you, let us satisfy our eyes

CURIOSITIES,—*continued.*
With the memorials and the things of fame,
That do renown this city. *T. N.* iii. 3.

CURRENTS, MARITIME.
Like to the Pontic sea,
Whose icy current, and compulsive course
Ne'er feels retiring ebb, but keeps due on
To the Propontic, and the Hellespont. *O.* iii. 3.

CURS.
O 'tis a foul thing, when a cur cannot keep himself in all companies! I would have, as one should say, one that taketh upon him to be a dog indeed, to be, as it were, a dog at all things. *T.G.* iv. 4.

When a man's servant shall play the cur with him, look you, it goes hard: one that I brought up a puppy; one that I saved from drowning, when three or four of his blind brothers and sisters went to it! I have taught him—even as one would say precisely,—Thus I would teach a dog. *T.G.* iv. 4.

CURSING.
I would the gods had nothing else to do,
But to confirm my curses! *C.* iv. 2.

CUSTOM (See also HABIT).
Custom hath made it in him a property of easiness.
H. v. 1

Custom calls me to't:—
What custom wills in all things should we do't;
The dust on antique time would lie unswept,
And mountainous error be too highly heap'd
For truth to overpeer. *C.* ii.)
Nice customs curt'sey to great kings. *H.V.* v. 2.
Assume a virtue if you have it not,
That monster, custom, who all sense doth eat
Of habit's devil, is angel yet in this. *H.* iii. 4
Thou, nature, art my goddess; to thy law
My services are bound. Wherefore should I
Stand in the plague of custom? *K. L.* i. 2

—————VILE.
Though I am native here,
And to the manner born,—it is a custom
More honour'd in the breach than the observance. *H.* i. 4.

D

DAGGERS.
I will speak daggers to her, but use none. *H.* iii. 2.

DALLIANCE, UNSEASONABLE.
No, when light-wing'd toys
Of feather'd Cupid seel with wanton dullness
My speculative and active instruments,
That my disports corrupt and taint my business,
Let housewives make a skillet of my helm,
And all indign and base adversities
Make head against my estimation. *O.* i. 3.
A woman impudent and mannish grown
Is not more loath'd than an effeminate man
In time of action. I stand condemn'd for this;
They think, my little stomach to the war,
And your great love to me, restrains you thus:
Sweet, rouse yourself; and the weak wanton Cupid
Shall from your neck unloose his amorous fold,
And, like a dew-drop from the lion's mane,
Be shook to air. *T. C.* iii. 3.

DANGER.
There Monitaurs and ugly treason lurk. *H. VI.* PT. I. v. 3.
Smooth runs the water where the brook is deep.
H. VI. PT. II. iii. 1.
France, thou mayest hold a serpent by the tongue,
A cased lion by the mortal paw,
A fasting tyger safer by the tooth
Than keep in peace that hand which thou dost hold.
K. J. iii. 1.
" *The purpose you undertake is dangerous:*"—why, that's
certain; 'tis dangerous to take a cold, to sleep, to drink;—
but I tell you, my lord fool, out of this nettle, danger, we
pluck this flower, safety. *H. IV.* PT. I. ii. 3.
The welfare of us all
Hangs on the cutting short that fraudful man.
H. VI. PT. II. iii. 1.
If you do wrongfully seize Hereford's rights—
You pluck a thousand dangers on your head;
You lose a thousand well-disposed hearts,
And prick my tender patience to those thoughts
Which honour and allegiance cannot think. *R. II.* ii. 1.
Blunt wedges rive hard knots: the seeded pride
That hath to this maturity blown up

DANGER,—*continued.*
In rank Achilles, must or now be cropp'd,
Or, shedding, breed a nursery of like evil,
To overbulk us all. *T. C.* i. 3.
There is more in it than fair visage. *H. VIII.* iii. 2.
——— OLD.
'Tis better playing with a lion's whelp
Than with an old one dying. *A. C.* iii. 11.

DARING.
As full of peril and adventurous spirit
As to o'er-walk a current roaring loud
On the uncertain footing of a spear. *H. IV.* PT. I. i. 3
I'll cross it though it blast me. *H.* i. 1.
I dare damnation: To this point I stand. *H.* iv. 5.

DARKNESS, ITS EFFECT ON THE FACULTY OF HEARING.
Dark night, that from the eye his function takes,
The ear more quick of apprehension makes;
Wherein it doth impair the seeing sense,
It pays the hearing double recompense. *M. N.* iii. 2.
——— MENTAL.
Madam, thou errest: I say, there is no darkness but ignorance; in which thou art more puzzled, than the Egyptians in their fog. *T. N.* iv. 2.

DAUGHTERS.
Fathers, from hence trust not your daughters,
By what you see them act. *O.* i. 1.

DAWN.
The third hour of drowsy morning. *H. V.* iv. *chorus.*
    The silent hour steals on,
And flaky darkness breaks within the east. *R. III.* v. 3.
And yon grey lines that fret the clouds,
Are messengers of day. *J. C.* ii. 1.
This morning, like the spirit of youth
That means to be of note, begins betimes. *A. C.* iv. 4.
Swift, swift, you dragons of the night!—that dawning
May bare the raven's eye. *Cym.* ii. 2.
But, look, the dawn, in russet mantle clad,
Walks o'er the dew of yon high eastern hill. *H.* i. 1.
The glow-worm shows the matin to be near,
And 'gins to pale his ineffectual fire. *H.* i. 5.
    Night's swift dragons cut the clouds full fast;
And yonder shines Aurora's harbinger;

DAW **Shakespearian Dictionary.** DEA

DAWN,—*continued.*

At whose approach, ghosts wand'ring here and there.
Troop home to church-yards: damned spirits all,
That in cross-ways and floods have burial,
Already to their wormy beds are gone. *M. N.* iii. 2.

The wolves have prey'd; and look, the gentle day
Before the wheels of Phœbus, round about
Dapples the drowsy east with spots of grey. *M. A.* v. 3.

The grey-ey'd morn smiles on the frowning night
Checkering the eastern clouds with streaks of light;
And flecked darkness like a drunkard reels
From forth day's path-way made by Titan's wheels.
R. J. ii. 3.

It was the lark, the herald of the morn,
No nightingale: look, love, what envious streaks
Do lace the severing clouds in yonder east:
Night's candles are burnt out, and jocund day
Stands tip-toe on the misty mountain's top. *R. J.* iii. 5.

Look, the unfolding star calls up the shepherd. *M. M.* iv. 2.

DAY.

Even from Hyperion's rising in the east
Until his very downfall in the sea. *Tit. And.* v. 2.

The stirring passage of the day. *C. E.* iii. 1.

As when the golden sun salutes the morn,
And having gilt the ocean with his beams,
Gallops the zodiac in his glistering coach,
And overlooks the highest peering hills. *Tit. And.* ii. 1.

'Tis a lucky day, boy; and we'll do good deeds on't.
W. T. iii. 3

O, such a day,
So fought, so follow'd, and so fairly won,
Came not, till now, to dignify the times,
Since Cæsar's fortunes! *H. IV.* PT. II. i. 1.

DEATH (See also MAN, TIME, MIGHTY DEAD, LIFE, SOLDIER'S
DEATH).

The blind cave of eternal night. *R. III.* v. 3.

Here is my journey's end; here is my butt,
And very sea-mark of my utmost sail. *O.* v. 2.

O ruin'd piece of nature! this great world
Shall so wear out to nought. *K. L.* iv. 6.

Nay, nothing; all is said:
His tongue is now a stringless instrument;
Words, life, and all, old Lancaster hath spent. *R. II.* ii. 1

DEATH,—*continued*.
Dead, for my life.
Even so ;—my tale is told. *L. L.* v. 2.

Have felt the worst of death's destroying wound
And lie full low, grav'd in the hollow ground. *R. II.* iii. 2.

Art thou gone too ? all comfort go with thee!
For none abides with me : my joy is—death ;.
Death, at whose name I oft have been afeard,
Because I wish'd this world's eternity. *H. VI.* PT. II. II. 4

O, I do fear thee, Claudio ; and I quake
Lest thou a feverous life should'st entertain,
And six or seven winters more respect
Than a perpetual honour. *M. M.* iii. 1

I am a tainted wether of the flock,
Meetest for death ; the weakest kind of fruit
Drops earliest to the ground, and so let me. *M. V.* iv. 1

All is but toys : renown, and grace, is dead ;
The wine of life is drawn, and the mere lees
Is left this vault to brag of. *M.* ii. 3

To-day, how many would have given their honours
To have sav'd their carcasses ! took heel to do't,
And yet died too ! I, in mine own woe charm'd,
Could not find death, where I did hear him groan ;
Nor feel him, where he struck. *Cym.* v. 3

It is too late ; the life of all this blood
Is touch'd corruptibly ; and his pure brain
(Which some suppose the soul's frail dwelling house,)
Doth, by the idle comments that it makes,
Foretel the ending of mortality. *K. J.* v. 7

So now prosperity begins to mellow,
And drop into the rotten mouth of death, *R. III.* iv. 4.

Thou know'st 'tis common ; all that live must die,
Passing through nature to eternity. *H.* i. 2.

    This fell serjeant death
Is strict in his arrest. *H.* v. 5.

     Dost fall ?
If thou and nature can so gently part,
The stroke of death is as a lover's pinch
Which hurts and is desir'd. Dost thou lie still ?
If thus thou vanishest, thou tell'st the world
It is not worth leave-taking. *A. C.* v. 2.

    O. our lives' sweetness !
That with the pain of death, we'd hourly die,
Rather than die at once ! *K. L.* v. 3.

Shakespearian Dictionary.

DEATH,—*continued*.

    We must die, Messala:
With meditating that she must die once,
I have the patience to endure it now. *J.C.* iv. 3.

    O amiable, lovely death!
Thou odoriferous stench! sound rottenness!
Arise forth from the couch of lasting night,
Thou hate and terror to prosperity,
And I will kiss thy détestable bones;
And put my eye-balls in thy vaulty brows;
And ring these fingers with thy household worms;
And stop this gap of breath with fulsome dust,
And be a carrion monster like thyself:
Come, grin on me; and I will think thou smil'st;
And buss thee as thy wife? Misery's love,
O, come to me! *K.J.* iii. 4.

    Eyes, look your last!
Arms, take your last embrace! and lips, O you,
The doors of breath, seal with a righteous kiss
A dateless bargain to engrossing death. *R.J.* v. 3.

Stay but a little; for my cloud of dignity
Is held from falling with so weak a wind,
That it will quickly drop. *H. IV.* PT. II. iv. 4.

Thy bones are marrowless, thy blood is cold;
Thou hast no speculation in those eyes
Which thou dost glare with. *M.* iii. 4.

    O, my love! my wife!
Death, that hath suck'd the honey of thy breath,
Hath had no power yet upon thy beauty:
Thou art not conquer'd; beauty's ensign yet
Is crimson in thy lips, and in thy cheeks,
And death's pale flag is not advanced there. *R.J.* v. 3.

By medicine life may be prolong'd, yet death
Will seize the doctor too. *Cym.* v. 5.

That we shall die, we know; 'tis but the time,
And drawing days out, that men stand upon. *J. C.* iii. 1.

Cowards die many times before their deaths;
The valiant never taste of death but once.
Of all the wonders that I yet have heard,
It seems to me most strange that men should fear;
Seeing that death, a necessary end,
Will come when it will come. *J. C.* ii. 2.

Close up his eyes, and draw the curtain close,
And let us all to meditation. *H.VI.* PT. II. iii. 3.

DEATH,—*continued.*
Death remember'd, should be like a mirror,
Who tells us, life's but a breath; to trust it, error.
P. P. i. 1.
Oft have I seen a timely parted ghost,
Of ashy semblance, meagre, pale, and bloodless,
Being all descended to the labouring heart;
Who, in the conflict that it holds with death,
Attracts the same for aidance 'gainst the enemy;
Which, with the heart there cools and ne'er returneth
To blush and beautify the cheek again. *H. VI.* PT. II. iii. 2.
     The sleeping and the dead
Are but as pictures: 'tis the eye of childhood
That fears a painted devil.   *M.* ii. 2.
Finish, good lady, the bright day is done,
And we are for the dark.   *A. C.* v. 2.
     Dar'st thou die?
The sense of death is most in apprehension;
And the poor beetle that we tread upon,
In corporal sufferance feels a pang as great,
As when a giant dies.   *M. M.* iii. 1.
Though death be poor, it ends a mortal woe. *R. II.* ii. 1.
O you mighty gods!
This world I do renounce; and in your sights,
Shake patiently my great affliction off:
If I could bear it longer, and not fall
To quarrel with your great opposeless wills,
My snuff, and loathed part of nature, should
Burn itself out.   *K. L.* iv. 6.

Her blood is settled and these joints are stiff;
Life and these lips have long been separated:
Death lies on her, like an untimely frost
Upon the sweetest flower of all the field. *R. J.* iv. 5
To die, is to be banish'd from myself.   *T. G.* iii. 1
O, death's a great disguiser.   *M. M.* iv. 2
We cannot hold mortality's strong hand.   *K. J.* iv. 2
Ay, but to die, and go we know not where;
To lie in cold obstruction, and to rot:
This sensible warm motion to become
A kneaded clod; and the delighted spirit
To bathe in fiery floods, or to reside
In thrilling regions of thick-ribbed ice:
To be imprison'd in the viewless winds,
And blown with restless violence round about
The pendant world; or to be worse than worst

DEATH,—*continued.*
Of those, that lawless and incertain thoughts
Imagine howling!—'tis too horrible!
The weariest and most loathed worldly life,
That age, ache, penury, and imprisonment
Can lay on nature, is a paradise
To what we fear of death. *M. M.* iii. 1.
Where art thou, death?
Come hither, come! come, come, and take a queen
Worth many babes and beggars. *A. C.* v. 2.
Art thou so bare, and full of wretchedness,
And fear'st to die? Famine is in thy cheeks,
Need and oppression starveth in thy eyes,
Upon thy back hangs ragged misery,
The world is not thy friend nor the world's law. *R. J.* v. 1.
  Receive what cheer you may;
The night is long that never finds a day. *M.* iv. 3.
Just death, kind umpire of men's miseries,
With sweet enlargement doth dismiss me hence.
          H. VI. PT. I. ii. 5.
I am resolv'd for death or dignity. *H. VI.* PT. II. v. 1.
Ah, what a sign it is of evil life,
When death's approach is seen so terrible!
          H. VI. PT. II. iii. 3.
The worst is,—death, and death will have his day.
          R. II. iii. 2.
He has walk'd the way of nature. *H. IV.* PT. II. v. 2.
  Pr'ythee, have done,
And do not play in wench-like words with that
Which is so serious. Let us bury him,
And not protract with admiration, what
Is now due debt. To the grave. *Cym.* iv. 2.

 ———— OF BUCKINGHAM, THE DUKE OF.
All good people,
You that thus far have come to pity me,
Hear what I say, and then go home and lose me.
I have this day receiv'd a traitor's judgment,
And by that name must die; yet, heaven bear witness,
And if I have a conscience let it sink me,
Even as the axe falls, if I be not faithful!
  You few that lov'd me,
And dare be bold to weep for Buckingham,
His noble friends, and fellows, whom to leave
Is only bitter to him, only dying,
Go with me like good angels, to my end;
And as the long divorce of steel falls on me.

DEATH,—*continued.*
Make of your prayers one sweet sacrifice,
And lift my soul to heaven. Lead on, o' God's name.
H.VIII. ii. 1.

———— FALSTAFF.
'A made a finer end, and went away an it had been any christom child; 'a parted just between twelve and one;— e'en at the turning of the tide: for after I saw him fumble with the sheets, and play with flowers, and smile upon his fingers, ends, I knew there was but one way; for his nose was as sharp as a pen, and 'a babbled of green fields. How now, Sir John, quoth I: what, man! be of good cheer. So 'a cried out, God!—three or four times: now I, to comfort him, bid him 'a should not think of God; I hoped there was no need to trouble himself with any such thoughts yet.
H.V. ii. 3.

———— GLOUCESTER, HUMPHREY, DUKE OF.
But, see, his face is black and full of blood;
His eye-balls further out than when he liv'd,
Staring full ghastly like a strangled man;
His hair uprear'd, his nostrils stretch'd with struggling;
His hands abroad display'd, as one that grasp'd
And tugg'd for life, and was by strength subdued.
Look on the sheets, his hair, you see, is sticking;
His well-proportion'd beard made rough and rugged,
Like to the summer's corn by tempests lodg'd.
H.VI. PT. II. iii. 2.

———— KING HENRY IV.
By his gates of breath,
There lies a downy feather, which stirs not:
Did he suspire, that light and weightless down
Perforce must move.—My gracious lord! my father!
This sleep is sound indeed; this is a sleep,
That from this golden rigol hath divorc'd
So many English kings. *H.IV.* PT. II. iv. 4.

———— KING HENRY VI.
I'll hear no more.—Die, prophet, in thy speech;
For this among the rest was I ordain'd.—
What, will the aspiring blood of Lancaster
Sink in the ground? I thought it would have mounted
See, how my sword weeps for the poor king's death!
O, may such purple tears be always shed
From those that wish the downfall of our house!
If any spark of life be yet remaining,
Down, down, to hell; and say,—I sent thee thither.
H.VI. PT. III. v. 6.

DEATH,—*continued.*
——— KING JOHN.
Aye, marry, now my soul hath elbow room ;
It would not out at windows nor at doors.
There is so hot a summer in my bosom,
That all my bowels crumble up to dust :
I am a scribbled form, drawn with a pen,
Upon a parchment ; and against this fire
Do I shrink up.
    Prince Henry.—How fares your Majesty?
    King John.—Poison'd,—ill fare ;—dead, forsook, cast off:
And none of you will bid the winter come,
And thrust his icy fingers in my maw ;
Nor let my kingdom's rivers take their course
Through my burn'd bosom ; nor entreat the north
To make his break winds kiss my parched lips,
And comfort me with cold : I do not ask you much,
I beg cold comfort.
                         [*Enter Falconbridge.*
O cousin, thou art come to set mine eye :
The tackle of my heart is crack'd and burn'd ;
And all the shrouds wherewith my life should sail,
Are turned to one thread, one little hair :
My heart hath one poor string to stay it by,
Which holds but till thy news be utter'd ;
And then all this thou see'st is but a clod,
And module of confounded royalty.   *K. J.* v. 7.
——— JULIUS CÆSAR.
Et tu Brute?—Then fall, Cæsar.   *J. C.* iii. 1.

    How many ages hence,
Shall this our lofty scene be acted over,
In states unborn and accents yet unknown!   *J. C.* iii. 1.
——— KING RICHARD II.
How now ? what means death in this rude assault ?
Villain, thy own hand yields thy death's instrument.
Go thou and fill another room in hell.
That hand shall burn in never-quenching fire,
That staggers thus my person. Exton, thy fierce hand
Hath, with the king's blood, stain'd the king's own land.
Mount, mount, my soul! thy seat is up on high ;
Whilst my gross flesh sinks downward here to lie.
                                    R. II. v. 5
——— WARWICK, EARL OF.
Ah, who is nigh ? come to me, friend or foe.
And tell me who is victor, York or Warwick ?
Why ask I that ? my mangled body shows,
My blood, my want of strength, my sick heart shows,

DEATH,—*continued*.
   That I must yield my body to the earth,
   And, by my fall, the conquest to my foe.
         Thus yields the cedar to the axe's edge,
   Whose arms gave shelter to the princely eagle,
   Under whose shade the ramping lion slept:
   Whose top-branch overpeer'd Jove's spreading tree,
   And kept low shrubs from winter's powerful wind.
   These eyes that now are dimm'd with death's black veil,
   Have been as piercing as the mid-day sun,
   To search the secret treasons of the world:
   The wrinkles in my brows now fill'd with blood,
   Were liken'd oft to kingly sepulchres;
   For who liv'd king but I could dig his grave.
         Lo, now my glory, smear'd in dust and blood!
   My parks, my walks, my manors that I had,
   Even now forsake me; and, of all my lands,
   Is nothing left me but my body's length!
   Why, what is pomp, rule, reign, but earth and dust?
   And, live we how we can, yet, die we must.
                              H. VI. PT. III. v. 2.

———— Wolsey, Cardinal.
   At last, with easy roads, he came to Leicester,
   Lodg'd in the abbey; where the reverend abbot,
   With all his convent, honourably receiv'd him;
   To whom he gave these words,—*O, father abbot,*
   An old man, broken with the storms of state,
   Is come to lay his weary bones among ye;
   Give him a little earth for charity!
   So went to bed: where eagerly his sickness
   Pursued him still; and, three days after this,
   About the hour of eight (which he himself
   Foretold should be his last,) full of repentance,
   Continual meditations, tears, and sorrows,
   He gave his honours to the world again,
   His blessed part to heaven,—and slept in peace.
                              H. VIII. iv. 2.

———— of the Illustrious, by vile hands.
   Great men oft die by vile bezonians:
   A Roman sworder and banditti slave,
   Murder'd sweet Tully; Brutus' bastard hand
   Stabb'd Julius Cæsar; savage islanders
   Pompey the great: and Suffolk dies by pirates.
                              H. VI. PT. II. iv. 1

———— Contempt of.
   There spake my brother; there my father's grave
   Did utter forth a voice! Yes, thou must die:

DEA   **Shakesperian Dictionary.**   DEA

DEATH,—*continued.*
Thou art too noble to conserve a life
In base appliances.   *M. M.* iii. 1.

———— LEVELS DISTINCTIONS.
Thersites' body is as good as Ajax'
When neither are alive.   *Cym.* iv. 2.

———— ABIDES WITH THE LUXURIOUS.
          Being an ugly monster,
'Tis strange he hides him in fresh cups, soft beds,
Sweet words; or hath more ministers than we
That draw his knives i' the war.   *Cym.* v. 3.

———— RELIEVES AND PREVENTS MISERIES.
Which shackles accidents, and bolts up change.   *A.C.* v. 2.
          Duncan is in his grave;
After life's fitful fever, he sleeps well;
Treason has done his worst: nor steel, nor poison,
Malice domestic, foreign levy, nothing,
Can touch him further.   *M.* iii. 2.

Had I but died an hour before this chance,
I had liv'd a blessed time, for, from this instant,
There's nothing serious in mortality.   *M.* ii. 3.

Give me your hand, Bassanio; fare you well?
Grieve not that I am fallen to this for you;
For herein Fortune shows herself more kind
Than is her custom: it is still her use,
To let the wretched man outlive his wealth,
To view with hollow eye and wrinkled brow,
An age of poverty; from which ling'ring penance
Of such a misery doth she cut me off.   *M.V.* iv. 1.

Why, he that cuts off twenty years of life,
Cuts off as many years of fearing death.   *J.C.* iii. 1.

———— UNTIMELY.
Cut off even in the blossoms of my sin,
Unhousel'd, disappointed, unanel'd;
No reckoning made, but sent to my account
With all my imperfections on my head.   *H.* i. 5.

DEATH BED INJUNCTION.
O, but they say, the tongues of dying men
Enforce attention like deep harmony:
Where words are scarce, they're seldom spent in vain:
For they breathe truth, that breathe their words in pain.
He, that no more may say, is listen'd more
    Than they whom youth and ease have taught to gloze;
More are men's ends mark'd than their lives before:

DEATH BED INJUNCTION,—*continued.*
The setting sun, and music at the close,
As the last taste of sweets, is sweetest last;
Writ in remembrance, more than things long past:
Though Richard my life's counsel would not hear,
My death's sad tale may yet undeaf his ear. *R. II.* ii. 1.

DEBT.
They have e'en put my breath from me, the slaves;
Creditors!—devils. *T. A.* iii. 4.

DEBTS, DESPERATE.
These debts may well be call'd desperate ones, for a madman owes 'em. *T. A.* iii. 4.

DECAY.
My way of life
Is fall'n into the sear, the yellow leaf. *M.* v. 3.

DECEIT.
You are abus'd, and, by some putter on
That will be damn'd for't;—would I knew the villain.
W. T. ii. 1
Who builds his hope in air of your fair looks,
Lives like a drunken sailor on a mast. *R. III.* iii. 4.

DECREPITUDE.
You see me here, you gods, a poor old man,
As full of grief as age; wretched in both. *K. L.* ii. 4.
I am old now,
And these same crosses spoil me. *K. L.* v. 3.
Pray do not mock me:
I am a very foolish fond old man,
Fourscore and upward; and to deal plainly,
I fear I am not in my perfect mind. *K. L.* iv. 7.
But on us both did haggish age steal on,
And wore us out of act. *A. W.* i. 2.

DEFEATED.
Thou art not vanquish'd.
But cozen'd and beguil'd. *K. L.* v. 3.

DEFIANCE.
Defiance, traitors, hurl we in your teeth. *J. C.* v. 1.
Marry,
Thou, thou dost wrong me; thou dissembler, thou:—
Nay, never lay thy hand upon thy sword,
I fear thee not. *M. A.* v. 1.
What man dare, I dare:
Approach thou like the rugged Russian bear,

DEFIANCE,—*continued.*
The arm'd rhinoceros, or the Hyrcan tyger,
Take any shape but that, and my firm nerves
Shall never tremble: Or, be alive again,
And dare me to the desert with thy sword;
If trembling I inhibit thee, protest me
The baby of a girl.   *M.* iii. 4.

And spur thee on, with full as many lies
As may be holla'd in thy treacherous ear
From sun to sun.   *R. II.* iv. 1.

Stand back, lord Salisbury, stand back, I say;
By heaven, I think my sword as sharp as yours:
I would not have you, lord, forget yourself,
Nor tempt the danger of my true defence;
Lest I, by marking of your rage, forget
Your worth, your greatness, and nobility.   *K. J.* iv. 3.

Who sets me else? by heaven, I'll throw at all:
I have a thousand spirits in one breast,
To answer twenty thousand such as you.   *R. II.* iv. 1.

Health to you, valiant Sir,
During all the question of the gentle truce;
But when I meet you arm'd, as black defiance,
As heart can think, or courage execute.   *T. C.* iv. 1.

Win me and wear me,—let him answer me,—
Come, follow me, boy; come, boy, follow me:
Sir boy, I'll whip you from your foining fence;
Nay, as I am a gentleman, I will.   *M. A.* v. 1.

            What I did, I did in honour,
Led by the impartial conduct of my soul;
And never shall you see that I will beg
A ragged and forestall'd remission.   *H. IV.* PT. II. v. 2.

There is my gage, the manual seal of death,
That marks thee out for hell: I say, thou liest,
And will maintain what thou hast said, is false,
In thy heart blood, though being all too base
To stain the temper of my knightly sword.   *R. II.* iv 1.

If that thy valour stand on sympathies,
There is my gage, Aumerle, in gage to thine:
By that fair sun which shows me where thou stand'st,
I heard thee say, and vauntingly thou spak'st it,
That thou wert cause of noble Glo'ster's death.
If thou deny'st it, twenty times thou liest;
And I will turn thy falsehood to thy heart,
Where it was forged, with my rapier's point.   *R. II.* iv. 1.

Shall I be flouted thus with dunghill grooms!
                                         H. VI. PT. I. i. 3.

DEFIANCE,—continued.

 Scorn, and defiance; slight regard, contempt,
And any thing that may not misbecome
The mighty sender, doth he prize you at.   *H. V.* ii. 4.
  Though I am not splenetive and rash,
Yet have I in me something dangerous,
Which let thy wisdom fear.   *H.* v. 1.
I had rather chop this hand off at a blow,
And with the other fling it at thy face,
Than bear so low a sail to strike to thee.
          H.VI. FT. III. v. 1.
   I will fight with him upon this theme,
Until my eye-lids will no longer wag.   *H.* v. 1.
Let them pronounce the steep Tarpeian death,
Vagabond exile, flaying; pent to linger
But with a grain a day, I would not buy
Their mercy at the price of one fair word.   *C.* iii. 3.
    You fools! I and my fellows
Are ministers of fate; the elements
Of whom your swords are temper'd, may as well
Wound the loud winds, or with bemock'd-at stabs
Kill the still-closing waters, as diminish
One dowle that's in my plume.   *T.* iii 3.
    Thou injurious tribune!
Within thine eyes sat twenty thousand deaths,
In thy hands clutch'd as many millions, in
Thy lying tongue both numbers, I would say,
Thou liest, unto thee, with voice as free
As I do pray the gods.   *C.* iii. 3.
     Let them come;
They come like sacrifices in their trim,
And to the fire-ey'd maid of smoky war,
All hot and bleeding will we offer them;
The mailed Mars shall on his altar sit
Up to the ears in blood.   *H. IV.* PT. I. iv. 1.
I do defy him, and I spit at him;
Call him a slanderous coward, and a villain.   *R. II.* i. 1.
      Gentle heaven,
Cut off all intermission; front to front,
Bring thou this fiend of Scotland, and myself;
Within my sword's length set him; if he 'scape,
Heaven forgive him too!   *M.* iv. 3.
Let him do his spite:
My services, which I have done the signiory
Shall out-tongue his complaints.   *O.* i. 2.

DEFORMITY.

Why, love forswore me in my mother's womb:
And, for I should not deal in her soft laws,
She did corrupt frail nature with a bribe
To shrink mine arm up like a wither'd shrub;
To make an envious mountain on my back,
Where sits deformity to mock my body;
To shape my legs of an unequal size;
To disproportion me in every part;
Like to a chaos, or an unlick'd bear-whelp,
That carries no impression like the dam.
And am I then a man to be belov'd?
O, monstrous fault to harbour such a thought!
H. VI. PT. III. iii. **2.**

But I,—that am not shap'd for sportive tricks,
Nor made to court an amorous looking glass;
I that am rudely stampt, and want love's majesty,
To strut before a wanton ambling nymph;
I, that am curtail'd of this fair proportion,
Cheated of feature by dissembling nature,
Deform'd, unfinish'd, sent before my time
Into this breathing world, scarce half made up,
And that so lamely and unfashionable,
That dogs bark at me as I halt by them:—
Why I, in this weak piping time of peace,
Have no delight to pass away the time,
Unless to spy my shadow in the sun,
And descant on mine own deformity. *R. III.* i. **1.**

But, O, how vile an idol proves this god!.
Thou hast, Sebastian, done good feature shame.
In nature there's no blemish but the mind;
None can be call'd deform'd but the unkind:
Virtue is beauty; but the beauteous evil
Are empty trunks, o'er-flourish'd by the devil. *T. N.* iii. **4.**

DEGENERACY.

But, woe the while! our fathers' minds are dead,
And we are govern'd by our mothers' spirits;
Our yoke and sufferance show us womanish. *J. C.* i. **3.**

O, that a mighty man of such descent,
Of such possessions, and so high esteem,
Should be infused with so foul a spirit! *T. S.* IND. **2.**

What a falling off was there! *H.* i. **5.**

But now 'tis odds beyond arithmetic;
And manhood is call'd foolery, when it stands
Against a falling fabric. *C.* iii. **1**

DEG   **Shakespearian Dictionary.**   DEL

DEGENERACY,—*continued.*
For in the fatness of these pursy times,
Virtue itself of vice must pardon beg.   *H.* iii. 4.

'Twas never merry world, since, of two usuries, the merriest was put down, and the worser allowed, by order of law, a furred gown to keep him warm ; and furred with fox and lambskins too, to signify that craft, being richer than innocency, stands for the facing.   *M.M.* iii. 2.

Shall it, for shame, be spoken in these days,
Or fill up chronicles in time to come,
That men of your nobility and power,
Did 'gage them both in an unjust behalf,—
As both of you, God pardon it! have done?
                                            H.IV. PT. I. i. 3

       The world is grown so bad,
That wrens may prey where eagles dare not perch;
Since every Jack became a gentleman,
There's many a gentle person made a Jack.   *R. III.* i. 3.

DEGRADATION.
       Now I must
To the young man send humble treaties, dodge
And palter in the shifts of lowness.   *A.C.* iii. 9.

DEGREES.
So man and man should be ;
But clay and clay differs in dignity
Whose dust is both alike.   *Cym.* iv. 2.

DELAY (See also IRRESOLUTION, OPPORTUNITY).
Omission to do what is necessary
Seals a commission to a blank of danger ;
And danger, like an ague, subtly taints
Ev'n then when we sit idly in the sun.   *T.C.* iii. 3.

Sir, in delay
We waste our lights in vain, like lamps by day.   *R.J.* i. 4.

Come,—I have learn'd that fearful commenting
Is leaden servitor to dull delay ;
Delay leads impotent and snail-pac'd beggary.
                                            R.III. iv. 3.

    Let's be revenged on him ; let's appoint him a meeting ; give him a show of comfort in his suit ; and lead him on with a fine-baited delay.   *M.W.* ii. 1.

O, my good lord, that comfort comes too late ;
'Tis like a pardon after execution ;
That gentle physic, given in time, had cur'd me ;
But now I'm past all comfort here, but prayers.
                                            H.VIII. iv. 2.

DELICACY OF IDLENESS.
The hand of little employment hath the daintier sense.
H. v. 1.

DELIGHTS.
All delights are vain; but that most vain,
Which, with pain purchas'd, doth inherit pain. *L. L.* i. 1.
These violent delights have violent ends,
And in their triumph die; like fire and powder,
Which, as they kiss, consume; the sweetest honey
Is loathsome in its own deliciousness,
And in the taste confounds the appetite:
Therefore, love moderately; long love doth so;
Too swift arrives as tardy as too slow. *R. J.* ii. 6.

DELIRIUM OF THE DYING.
O vanity of sickness! fierce extremes,
In their continuance will not feel themselves.
Death, having prey'd upon the outward parts,
Leaves them insensible; and his siege is now
Against the mind, the which he pricks and wounds
With many legions of strange fantasies;
Which, in their throng and press to that last hold,
Confound themselves. 'Tis strange that death should sing.
I am the cygnet to this pale-fac'd swan,
Who chaunts a doleful hymn to his own death;
And, from the organ-pipe of frailty, sings
His soul and body to their lasting rest. *K. J.* v. 7.

DELUSION (See also ILLUSION).
'Twas but a bolt of nothing, shot at nothing,
Which the brain makes of fumes: our very eyes
Are sometimes like our judgments, blind. *Cym.* iv. 2.

Oftentimes, to win us to our harm,
The instruments of darkness tell us truths;
Win us with honest trifles, to betray us
In deepest consequence. *M.* i. 3.

And be these juggling fiends no more believ'd,
That palter with us in a double sense;
That keep the word of promise to our ear,
And break it to our hope. *M.* v. 7.

Why, thou hast put him in such a dream, that, when the
image of it leaves him, he must run mad. *T. N.* ii. 5

Thus may poor fools believe false teachers. *Cym.* iii. 4.

This is the very coinage of your brain;
This bodiless creation extacy
Is very cunning in. *H.* iii. 4.

DELUSION,—*continued.*
Alas, how is't with you?
That you do bend your eyes on vacancy,
And with the incorporal air do hold discourse? *H.* iii. 4.
It will but skin and film the ulcerous place;
Whiles rank corruption, mining all within,
Infects unseen. *H.* iii. 4
Indeed, it is a strange disposed time:
But men may construe things after their fashion,
Clean from the purpose of the things themselves.
J.C. i. 3.

DENIAL OF JUSTICE (See also JUDGMENT, JUSTICE).
And is this all?
Then, oh, you blessed ministers above,
Keep me in patience; and, with ripen'd time,
Unfold the evil which is here wrapp'd up
In countenance! *M.M.* v. 1.

DEPRAVITY, YOUTHFUL.
You're a fair viol, and your sense the strings;
Who, finger'd to make man his lawful music,
Would draw heaven down, and all the gods to hearken;
But, being play'd upon before your time,
Hell only danceth at so harsh a chime. *P.P.* i. 1.

DEPRIVATION OF THINGS DISCLOSES THEIR VALUE.
What our contempts do often hurl from us,
We wish it ours again. *A.C.* i. 2.

DEPUTY.
A substitute shines brightly as a king,
Until a king be by; and then his state
Empties itself, as doth an inland brook
Into the main of waters. *M.V.* v. 1.
In our remove, be thou at full ourself;
Mortality and mercy in Vienna
Live in thy tongue and heart. *M.M.* i. 1.

DERANGEMENT, MENTAL (See also DESPONDENCY, MADNESS).
A sight most pitiful in the meanest wretch;
Past speaking of in a king. *K.L.* iv. 6.

DESCRIPTION.
I have cried her almost to the number of her hairs; I have drawn her picture with my voice. *P.P.* iv. 3.
O, he hath drawn my picture in his letter! *L.L.* v. 2.

DESDEMONA.
A maid
That paragons description, and wild fame;

DESDEMONA,—*continued.*
One that excels the quirks of blazoning pens,
And in the essential vesture of creation,
Does bear all excellency. *O.* ii. 1.
Tempests themselves, high seas, and howling winds,
The gutter'd rocks, and congregated sands,—
Traitors ensteep'd to clog the guiltless keel,—
As having sense of beauty, do omit
Their mortal natures, letting go safely by
The divine Desdemona. *O.* ii. 1.

DESERT.
Use every man according to his desert, and who shall escape whipping? use them after your own honour and dignity: the less they deserve, the more merit is in your bounty. *H.* ii. 2.
O, your desert speaks loud; and I should wrong it,
To lock it in the wards of covert bosom,
When it deserves, with characters of brass,
A forted residence, 'gainst the tooth of time,
And razure of oblivion. *M. M.* v. 1.
But let desert in pure election shine. *Tit. And.* i. 1.

DESERTION.
Him did you leave,
Second to none, unseconded by you. *H. IV.* PT. II. ii. 2.

DESIGNATION.
We call a nettle but a nettle; and
The faults of fools but folly. *C.* ii. 1.

DESIRE.
The cloyed will
(That satiate yet unsatisfied desire,
That tub both fill'd and running) ravening first
The lamb, longs after for the garbage. *Cym.* i. 7.
Happy! but most miserable
Is the desire that's glorious. Blessed be those,
How mean soe'er, that have their honest wills
Which seasons comfort. *Cym.* 1. 7.

DESOLATION.
I, an old turtle,
Will wing me to some wither'd bough; and there
My mate, that's never to be found again,
Lament till I am lost. *W. T.* v. 3.
Then was I as a tree
Whose boughs did bend with fruit; but in one night,
A storm, or robbery, call it what you will,

DESOLATION,—*continued.*
Shook down my mellow hangings, nay, my leaves,
And left me bare to wither. *Cym.* iii. 3.

Shipwreck'd upon a kingdom, where no pity,
No friends, no hope ; no kindred weep for me,
Almost no grave allow'd me ;—like the lily,
That once was mistress of the field, and flourish'd,
I'll hang my head and perish. *H. VIII.* iii. 1.

Alack, and what shall good old York there see,
But empty lodgings and unfurnish'd walls,
Unpeopled offices, untrodden stones ?
And what cheer there for welcome but my groans ?
Therefore commend me, let him not come there,
To reek out sorrow that dwells every where :
Desolate, desolate, will I hence and die ;
The last leave of thee takes my weeping eye. *R. II.* i. 2

DESPAIR.

There's nothing in this world can make me joy ;
Life is as tedious as a twice told tale,
Vexing the dull ear of a drowsy man. *K. J.* iii. 4.

I will despair, and be at enmity
With cozening hope ; he is a flatterer,
A parasite, a keeper back of death,
Who gently would dissolve the bands of life,
Which false hope lingers in extremity. *R. II.* ii. 2.

Now let not Nature's hand
Keep the wild flood confin'd ! Let order die !
And let this world no longer be a stage,
To feed contention in a lingering act ;
But let one spirit of the first-born Cain
Reign in all bosoms, that, each heart being set
On bloody courses, the rude scene may end,
And darkness be the burier of the dead. *H. IV.* PT. II. i. 1.

O sovereign mistress of true melancholy,
The poisonous damp of night disponge upon me ;
That life, a very rebel to my will,
May hang no longer on me ; throw my heart
Against the flint and hardness of my fault ;
Which, being dried with grief, will break to powder,
And finish all foul thoughts. *A. C.* iv. 9.

I pull in resolution ; and begin
To doubt the equivocation of the fiend,
That lies like truth. *M.* v. 5.

O, I am fortune's fool ! *R. J.* iii. 1.

DESPAIR,—*continued.*
I shall despair.—There is no creature loves me;
And, if I die, no soul will pity me;—
Nay, wherefore should they? since that I myself
Find in myself no pity to myself.   *R. III.* v. 3.

For now I stand as one upon a rock,
Environ'd with a wilderness of sea;
Who marks the waxing tide grow wave by wave,
Expecting ever when some envious surge
Will, in his brinish bowels, swallow him.   *Tit. And.* iii. 1.

They have tied me to the stake, I cannot fly,
But, bear-like, I must fight the course.   *M.* v. 7.

        Take the hint
Which my despair proclaims; let that be left
Which leaves itself.   *A. C.* iii. 9.

I 'gin to be a-weary of the sun,
And wish the estate of the world were now undone. *M.* v. 5.

Your enemies, with nodding of their plumes,
Fan you into despair.   *C.* iii. 3.

My very hairs do mutiny; for the white
Reprove the brown for rashness; and they them
For fear and doting.   *A. C.* iii. 9.

DESPATCH.
If it were done, when 'tis done, then 'twere well
It were done quickly.   *M.* i. 7.

   Come, to the forge with it then; shape it; I would not
have things cool.   *M. W.* iv. 2.

It makes us, or it mars us; think on that,
And fix most firm thy resolution.   *O.* v. 1.

Briefness, and fortune, work.   *K. L.* ii. 1.

We must do something, and i' the heat.   *K. L.* i. 1.

DESPERATION.
Some say he's mad; others, that lesser hate him,
Do call it valiant fury; but for certain,
He cannot buckle his distemper'd cause
Within the belt of rule.   *M.* v. 2.

        Fortune knows,
We scorn her most when most she offers blows. *A. C.* iii. 9.

        Whip me, ye devils,
From the possession of this heavenly sight!
Blow me about in winds! roast me in sulphur!
Wash me in steep-down gulfs of liquid fire!
O Desdemona!   *O.* v. 2

DESPERATION,—continued.

Our enemies have beat us to the pit:
It is more worthy to leap in ourselves,
Than tarry till they push us.   *J. C.* v. 5.

Yet I will try the last: Before my body
I throw my warlike shield; lay on, Macduff;
And damn'd be he that first cries "Hold! Enough!"
   M. v. 7.

Ring the alarum bell: Blow wind, come wrack!
At least we'll die with harness on our back.   *M.* v. 5.

The time and my intents are savage wild;
More fierce and more inexorable far
Than empty tigers, on the roaring sea.   *R. J.* v. 3.

　　　　　Now could I drink hot blood,
And do such business as the bitter day
Would quake to look on.   *H.* iii. 2.

No, I defy all counsel, all redress,
But that which ends all counsel, true redress,
Death, death.   *K. J.* iii. 4.

O all you host of heaven! O earth!—what else?
And shall I couple hell?—O fie!—Hold, hold, my heart;
And you, my sinews, grow not instant old,
But bear me stiffly up.   *H.* i. 5.

Ah, women, women! come; we have no friend
But resolution and the briefest end.   *A. C.* iv. 13.

DESPONDENCY (See also DERANGEMENT, MADNESS).

I am not mad; I would to heaven I were!
For then, 'tis like I should forget myself:
O, if I could, what grief should I forget!   *K. J.* iii. 4.

Preach some philosophy to make me mad,
And thou shalt be canonized, cardinal;
For, being not mad, but sensible of grief,
My reasonable part produces reason
How I may be deliver'd of these woes,
And teaches me to kill or hang myself.   *K. J.* iii. 4.

I am sick of this false world; and will love nought
But even the mere necessities upon it.
Then, Timon, presently prepare thy grave;
Lie, where the light foam of the sea may beat
Thy grave-stone daily.   *T. A.* iv. 3.

　　　　　How stiff is my vile sense,
That I stand up and have ingenious feeling
Of my huge sorrows! better I were distract;
So should my thoughts be sever'd from my griefs;

DES   **Shakespearian Dictionary.**   DET

DESPONDENCY,—*continued.*
And woes, by wrong imaginations, lose
The knowledge of themselves.   *K. L.* iv. 6.
O, that this too, too solid flesh would melt,
Thaw, and resolve itself into a dew!
Or, that the everlasting had not fix'd
His canon 'gainst self-slaughter! O God! O God!
How weary, stale, flat, and unprofitable,
Seem to me all the uses of this world!
Fie on't! fie on't! 'tis an unweeded garden,
That grows to seed; things rank, and gross in nature,
Possess it merely.   *H.* i. 2.
Even here I will put off my hope, and keep it
No longer for my flatterer.   *T.* iii. 3.
I have not that alacrity of spirit
Nor cheer of mind that I was wont to have.   *R. III.* v. 3.
              Nothing I'll bear from thee
But nakedness, thou détestable town!
Timon will to the woods; where he shall find
The unkindest beast more kinder than mankind.
   T. A. iv. 1.
What say you now? what comfort have we now?
By heaven, I'll hate him everlastingly,
That bids me be of comfort any more.   *R. II.* iii. 2.

DESTINY.
All unavoided is the doom of destiny.   *R. III.* iv. 4.
         The lottery of my destiny
Bars me the right of voluntary choosing   *M. V.* ii. 1.
The antient saying is no heresy:—
Hanging and wiving go by destiny.   *M. V.* ii. 9.
'Tis destiny unshunnable, like death.   *O.* iii. 3.

DESTITUTION.
Who gives any thing to poor Tom?   *K. L.* iii. 4.

DETERIORATION.
When nobles are their tailors' tutors.   *K. L.* iii. 2.
The man was noble,
But with his last attempt he wip'd it out.   *O.* v. 3.

DETERMINATION (See also RESOLUTION).
       I have given suck; and know
How tender 'tis, to love the babe that milks me:
I would, while it was smiling in my face,
Have pluck'd my nipple from his boneless gums,
And dash'd the brains out, had I so sworn as
You have done to this.   *M.* i. 7.

DETERMINATION,—*continued.*
I'll speak to it, though hell itself should gape,
And bid me hold my peace. *H.* i. 2.
Cannot, is false; and that I dare not, falser;
I will not come to-day: tell them so, Decius. *J.C.* ii. 2.
Shall I stay here to do't; no, no, although
The air of paradise did fan the house,
And angels offic'd all: I will be gone. *A.W.* iii. 2.
    It was my will and grant;
And for this once, my will shall stand for law.
         H.VI. pt. iii. iv. 1.
Then all too late comes counsel to be heard,
Where will doth mutiny with wit's regard. *R.II.* ii. 1.
My resolution, and my hands I'll trust;
None about Cæsar. *A.C.* iv. 13.
I am fire and air; my other elements
I give to baser life. *A.C.* v. 2.

DETRACTION.
Ay, an you had any eye behind you, you might see more detraction at your heels than fortunes before you.
         T.N. ii. 5.
Happy are they that hear their detractions, and put them to mending. *M.A.* ii. 3.

DEVICE.
What a slave art thou to hack thy sword as thou hast done; and then say, it was in fight! *H.IV.* pt. i. ii. 4.

DEVIL.
Heaven prosper our sport! No one means evil but the devil, and we shall know him by his horns. *M.W.* v. 1
A devil, a born devil, on whose nature
Nurture can never stick; on whom my pains,
Humanely taken, all, all, quite lost;
And as, with age, his body uglier grows,
So his mind cankers. *T.* iv. 1

DEVOTION.
    My heart's subdued
Even to the very quality of my lord:
I saw Othello's visage in his mind;
And to his honour and his valiant parts,
Did I my soul and fortunes consecrate. *O.* i. 3.
My best attires:—I am again for Cydnus,
To meet Marc Antony. *A.C.* v. 2.
Yours in the ranks of death. *K.L.* iv. 2.

DEVOTION,—*continued.*
A true devoted pilgrim is not weary
To measure kingdoms with his feeble steps. *T. G.* ii. 7.
Vouchsafe to show the sunshine of your face,
That we, like savages, may worship it. *L. L.* v. 2.
From the four corners of the earth they come,
To kiss this shrine, this mortal breathing saint.
M. V. ii. 7.

———— Pious.
        With modest paces
Came to the altar, where she kneel'd, and saint-like
Cast her fair eyes to heaven, and pray'd devoutly.
H. VIII. iv. 1.

DEW.
And that same dew which sometime on the buds
Was wont to swell, like round and orient pearls,
Stood now within the pretty flow'ret's eyes,
Like tears that did their own disgrace bewail. *M. N.* iv. 1.
I must go seek some dew-drops here,
And hang a pearl on every cowslip's ear. *M. N.* ii. 1.
As fresh as morning dew distill'd on flowers.
Tit. And. ii. 4.

DIFFIDENCE.
        A tardiness in nature,
Which often leaves the history unspoke,
That it intends to do. *K. L.* i. 1.

DIGNITY.
        Master Robert Shallow, choose what office thou wilt in the land, 'tis thine.—Pistol, I will double charge thee with dignities. *H. IV.* pt. ii. v. 3.
        Nothing but death,
Shall e'er divorce my dignities. *H. VIII.* iii. 1.

DIGRESSION.
        Shifted out of thy tale, into telling me of the fashion.
M. A. iii. 3.

DILIGENCE.
        He'll watch the horologe a double set. *O.* ii. 3.

DINNER.
        He had not din'd:
The veins unfill'd, the blood is cold, and then
We pout upon the morning, are unapt
To give or to forgive; but when we have stuff'd
These pipes and these conveyances of our blood

DINNER,—*continued.*
With wine and feeding, we have suppler souls
Than in our priest-like fasts; therefore I'll watch him
Till he be dieted to my request,
And then I'll set upon him. *C.* v. 1.

DIRGE.
I cannot sing: I'll weep, and word it with thee;
For notes of sorrow, out of tune, are worse
Than priests and fancs that lie. *Cym.* iv. 2.

DISASTERS.
                Checks and disasters
Grow in the veins of actions highest rear'd;
As knots, by the conflúx of meeting sap,
Infect the sound pine, and divert his grain
Tortive and errant from his course and growth. *T.C.* i. 3.
                Why then, you princes,
Do you with cheeks abash'd behold our works;
And think them shames, which are, indeed, nought else,
But the protractive trials of great Jove. *T.C.* i. 3.

DISCLOSURE.
. You shall see, anon; 'tis a knavish piece of work.
                                          H. iii. 2.

DISCONTENT.
What's more miserable than discontent?
                                    H.VI. PT. II. iii. 1.
Happiness courts thee in her best array;
But like a misbehav'd and sullen wench,
Thou pout'st upon thy fortune and thy love:
Take heed, take heed, for such die miserable. *R.J.* iii. 3.
With what a majesty he bears himself;
How insolent of late he is become,
How proud, peremptory, and unlike himself!
                                       H.VI. PT. II. iii. 1.

—————————— POPULAR.
              And the pretence for this
Is nam'd, your wars in France: this makes bold mouths;
Tongues spit their duties out, and cold hearts freeze
Allegiance in them; their curses now,
Live where their prayers did; and it's come to pass,
That tractable obedience is a slave
To each incensed will. *H.VIII.* i. 2.

DISCRETION.
For 'tis not good that children should know any wickedness: old folks, you know, have discretion, as they say, and know the world. *M.W.* ii. 2.

DISGUISE.
Disguise, I see thou art a wickedness,
Wherein the pregnant enemy does much. *T. N.* ii. 2.

DISINTERESTEDNESS.
O, good old man, how well in thee appears
The constant service of the antique world,
When service sweat for duty, not for meed!
Thou art not for the fashion of these times,
Where none will sweat but for promotion;
And having that, do choke their service up,
Even with the having. *A. Y.* ii. 3.

DISLIKE.
Alas, I had rather be set quick i' the earth,
And bowl'd to death with turnips. *M. W.* iii. 4.

DISMAY (See also FEAR, TERROR).
Thou tremblest, and the whiteness in thy cheek
Is apter than thy tongue to tell thy errand.
Even such a man, so faint, so spiritless,
So dull, so dead in look, so woe-begone,
Drew Priam's curtain in the dead of night,
And would have told him half his Troy was burn'd.
But Priam found the fire, ere he his tongue.
  H. IV. PT. II i. 1.

His death (whose spirit lent a fire
Even to the dullest peasant in his camp,)
Being bruited once, took fire and heat away
From the best temper'd courage in his troops;
For from his metal was his party steel'd;
Which once in him abated, all the rest
Turn'd on themselves, like dull and heavy lead.
And as the thing that's heavy in itself,
Upon enforcement, flies with greater speed;
So did our men, heavy in Hotspur's loss,
Lend to this weight such lightness with their fear,
That arrows fled not swifter toward their aim,
Than did our soldiers, aiming at their safety,
Fly from the field. *H. IV.* PT. II. i. 1.

DISMISSAL.
Cassio, I love thee;
But never more be officer of mine. *O.* ii. 3.
How! what does his cashier'd worship mutter?
  T. A. iii. 4.

——— SILENT.
Dismiss'd me
Thus, with his speechless hand. *C* v. 1.

DISORDER.
>But they did no more adhere and keep place together,
than the hundredth psalm to the tune of Green Sleeves.
M. W. ii. 1.
>For night owls shriek, where mounting larks should sing.
R. II. iii. 3.

DISPERSION.
>Our army is dispers'd already;
Like youthful steers unyok'd, they take their courses
East, west, north, south; or, like a school broke up,
Each hurries towards his home and sporting place.
H. IV. pt. ii. iv. 2.

DISPLEASURE, Rash.
>Our rash faults
Make trivial price of serious things we have,
Not knowing them until we know their grave.
Oft our displeasures, to ourselves unjust,
Destroy our friends, and after, weep their dust:
Our own love waking cries to see what's done,
While shameful hate sleeps out the afternoon. *A. W.* v. 3.

DISPROPORTION.
>O, the more angel she,
And you the blacker devil. *O.* v. 2.

DISQUIET.
>Look where he comes! Not poppy, nor mandragora,
Nor all the drowsy syrups of the world,
Shall ever med'cine thee to that sweet sleep
Which thou ow'dst yesterday. *O.* iii. 3.
>Indeed, indeed, Sirs, but this troubles me. *H.* i. 2.

DISSIMULATION (See Hypocrisy, Quoting Scripture).
>We are oft to blame in this;—
'Tis too much prov'd,—that with devotion's visage,
And pious action, we do sugar o'er
The devil himself. *H.* iii. 1.
>Divinity of hell!
When devils will their blackest sins put on,
They do suggest at first with heavenly shows. *O.* ii. 3.
>If I do not put on a sober habit,
Talk with respect, and swear but now and then,
Wear prayer-books in my pocket, look demurely;
Nay more, while grace is saying, hood mine eyes
Thus—with hat, and sigh, and say, amen;
Use all the observance of civility,
Like one well studied in a sad ostent
To please his grandam, never trust me more. *M. V.* ii. 2.

DISSIMULATION,—*continued.*
Why, I can smile, and murder while I smile;
And cry content to that which grieves my heart;
And wet my cheeks with artificial tears,
And frame my face to all occasions. *H. VI.* PT. III. iii. 2.

Though I do hate him as I do hell pains,
Yet, for necessity of present life,
I must show out a flag and sign of love,
Which is indeed but sign. *O.* i. 1.

     Where we are
There's daggers in men's smiles; the near in blood,
The nearer bloody. *M.* ii. 3.

In following him I follow but myself;
Heaven is my judge, not I for love or duty,
But seeming so, for my peculiar end:
For when my outward action doth demonstrate
The native act and figure of my heart
In compliment extern, 'tis not long after,
But I will wear my heart upon my sleeve,
For daws to peck at. I am not what I am. *O.* i. 1.

    To beguile the time,
Look like the time; bear welcome in your eye,
Your hand, your tongue: look like the innocent flower,
But be the serpent under it. *M.* i. 5.

Away, and mock the time with fairest show,
False face must hide what the false heart doth know. *M.* i. 7.

     Good now, play one scene,
Of excellent dissembling; and let it look
Like perfect honour. *A. C.* i. 3.
Hide not thy poison with such sugar'd words.
H. VI. PT. II. iii. 2.

   And with a countenance as clear
As friendship wears at feasts. *W. T.* i. 2.

You vow, and swear, and super-praise my parts,
When I am sure you hate me in your hearts. *M. N.* iii. 2.

As I, perchance, hereafter shall think meet
To put an antic disposition on. *H.* i. 5.

DISTINCTION.
     Art thou officer,
Or art thou base, common, and popular? *H. V.* iv. 1

——————— UNBECOMING.
It lies as sightly on the back of him,
As great Alcides' shoes upon an ass. *K. J.* ii. 1

Shakesperian Dictionary.

DISTRACTION.
 Contending with the fretful elements;
Bids the winds blow the earth into the sea,
Or swell the curled waters 'bove the main,
That things might change or cease: tears his white hair;
Which the impetuous blasts, with eyeless rage,
Catch in their fury and make nothing of:
Strives in his little world of man to outscorn
The to-an-fro-conflicting wind and rain. *K.L.* iii. 1.

DISTRESS.
     The thorny point
Of bare distress hath ta'en from me the show
Of smooth civility. *A.Y.* ii. 7.

DISTURBERS.
    Who rather had,
Though they themselves did suffer by't, behold
Dissentious numbers pestering streets, than see
Our tradesmen singing in their shops, and going
About their functions freely. *C.* v. 6

DISUNION.
 When that the general is not like the hive,
To whom the foragers shall all repair,
What honey is expected? *T.C.* i. 3.
    How, in one house,
Should many people, under two commands,
Hold amity? 'Tis hard, almost impossible. *K. L.* ii. 4.

DOOM.
    Away! By Jupiter,
This shall not be revok'd. *K.L.* i. 1.

DOTARD.
 The brains of my Cupid's knock'd out; and I begin to love, as an old man loves money, with no stomach.
 A.W. iii. 2

DOVER Cliffs.
     How fearful
And dizzy 'tis to cast one's eyes below!
The crows, and choughs, that wing the midway air,
Show scarce so gross as beetles: Half way down
Hangs one that gathers samphire; dreadful trade!
Methinks he seems no bigger than his head:
The fishermen, that walk upon the beach,
Appear like mice; and yon tall anchoring bark,
Diminish'd to her cock; her cock, a buoy,
Almost too small for sight: The murm'ring surge,
That on the unnumber'd idle pebbles chafes,

DOVER CLIFFS,—*continued.*
    Cannot be heard so high : I'll look no more ;
    Lest my brain turn, and the deficient sight
    Topple down headlong.   *K. L.* iv. 6.

DRAMAS.
    The best of this kind are but shadows ; and the worst
    are no worse, if imagination amend them.   *M. N.* v. 1.

DREAMS.
                      I talk of dreams ;
Which are the children of an idle brain,
Begot of nothing but vain fantasy ;
Which is as thin of substance as the air ;
And more inconstant than the wind, which wooes
Even now the frozen bosom of the north,
And, being anger'd, puffs away from thence,
Turning his face to the dew-dropping south.   *R. J.* i. 4.

    I have had a most rare vision. I have had a dream ;—past the wit of man to say what dream it was. Man is but an ass if he go about to expound this dream.
                                                       M. N. iv. 1.

'Tis still a dream ; or else such stuff as madmen
Tongue and brain out ; either both, or nothing ;
Or senseless speaking, or a speaking such
As sense cannot untie. Be what it is,
The action of my life is like it, which
I'll keep, if but for sympathy.   *Cym.* v. 4.

By the apostle Paul, shadows to-night
Have struck more terror to the soul of Richard,
Than can the substance of ten thousand soldiers,
Armed in proof, led on by shallow Richmond. *R. III.* v. 3.

                        Poor wretches, that depend
On greatness' favour, dream as I have done,
Awake, and find nothing.   *Cym.* v. 4.

This is the rarest dream that e'er dull sleep
Did mock sad fools withal.   *P. P.* v. 1.

In thy faint slumbers, I by thee have watch'd,
And heard thee murmur tales of iron wars :
Speak terms of manage to thy bounding steed ;
Cry, *Courage!—to the field!* And thou hast talk'd
Of sallies, and retires ; of trenches, tents,
Of palisadoes, frontiers, parapets ;
Of basilisks, of cannon, culverin ;
Of prisoners' ransom, and of soldiers slain,
And all the currents of a heady fight.   *H. IV.* PT I. ii. 3.

Thy spirit within thee hath been so at war,

DREAMS,—*continued.*
And thus hath so bestirr'd thee in thy sleep,
That beads of sweat have stood upon thy brow,
Like bubbles on a late disturbed stream:
And in thy face strange motions have appear'd,
Such as we see when men restrain their breath
On some great sudden haste. *H. IV.* PT. I. ii. 3.

There is some ill a-brewing toward my rest,
For I did dream of money bags to-night. *M.V.* ii. 5.

Let not our babbling dreams affright our souls. *R. III.* v. 3.

There are a kind of men so loose of soul,
That in their sleeps will mutter their affairs. *O.* iii. 3.

DRESS (See also ADVICE TO A YOUNG MAN).
For 'tis the mind that makes the body rich;
And as the sun breaks through the darkest clouds,
So honour peereth in the meanest habit. *T. S.* iv. 3.

What, is the jay more precious than the lark,
Because his feathers are more beautiful?
Or is the adder better than the eel,
Because his painted skin contents the eye? *T. S.* iv. 3.

                And now, my honey love,
We will return unto thy father's house;
And revel it as bravely as the best;
With silken coats, and caps, and golden rings,
With ruffs, and cuffs, and farthingales, and things:
With scarfs, and fans, and double change of bravery,
And amber bracelets, beads, and all this knavery.
                The tailor stays thy leisure,
To deck thy body with his rustling treasure. *T. S.* iv. 3

My dukedom to a beggarly denier,
I do mistake my person all this while:
Upon my life, she finds, although I cannot,
Myself to be a marvellous proper man.
I'll be at charges for a looking-glass;
And entertain a score or two of tailors,
To study fashions to adorn my body.
Since I am crept in favour with myself,
I will maintain it with some little cost. *R. III.* i. 2.

The gown? why, ay;—Come, tailor, let us see't.
O mercy, God! what masking stuff is here?
What's this? a sleeve? 'tis like a demi-cannon:
What! up and down, carv'd like an apple-tart?
Here's snip, and nip, and cut, and slish, and slash,
Like to a censer in a barber's shop:—
Why, what, o' devil's name, tailor, call'st thou this?
                                        T. S. iv. 3.

DRESS,—*continued.*
Cloten.—Thou villain base,
Know'st thou not me by my cloaths?
Guiderius.—No, nor thy tailor, rascal,
Who is thy grandfather: he made those cloaths,
Which, as it seems, make thee. *Cym.* iv. 2.

I will never trust a man again for keeping his sword clean; nor believe he can have every thing in him for keeping his apparel neatly. *A. W.* iv. 3.

DROWNING.
Lord! methought what pain it was to drown!
What dreadful noise of water in my ears!
What sights of ugly death within mine eyes!
Methought I saw a thousand fearful wrecks;
A thousand men that fishes gnaw'd upon. *R. III.* i. 4.

Often did I strive
To yield the ghost; but still the envious flood
Kept in my soul, and would not let it forth
To seek the empty, vast, and wand'ring air:
But smother'd it within my panting bulk,
Which almost burst to belch it in the sea. *R. III.* i. 4.

A pox of drowning thyself! it is clean out of the way.
O. i. 3.

DRUMS.
Strike up the drums: and let the tongue of war
Plead for our interest. *K. J.* v. 2.

Do but stir
An echo with the clamour of thy drum,
And even at hand a drum is ready brac'd,
That shall reverberate all as loud as thine;
Sound but another, and another shall,
As loud as thine, rattle the welkin's ear,
And mock the deep mouth'd thunder. *K. J.* v. 2.

He's a good drum, my lord, but a naughty orator.
A. W. v. 3.

I'll no more drumming; a plague of all drums.
A. W. iv. 3.

DRUNKARD (See WINE).
A howling monster: a drunken monster. *T.* iii. 2.

· O that men should put an enemy into their mouths, to steal away their brains!—that we should, with joy, revel, pleasure, and applause, transform ourselves into beasts! *O.* ii. 3.

DRUNKARD,—*continued.*
O monstrous beast!—how like a swine he lies!
T. S. IND. 1.
When he is best, he is little worse than a man; and when he is worst, he is little better than a beast.
M. W. i. 2.
Every inordinate cup is unblessed, and the ingredient is a devil. *O.* ii. 3.
Like a drowned man, a fool, and a madman; one draught above heat makes him a fool; the second mads him; and a third drowns him. *T. N.* i. 4.
You see this fellow that is gone before;—
He is a soldier fit to stand by Cæsar
And give direction: and do but see his vice;
'Tis to his virtue a just equinox,
The one as long as th' other. *O.* ii. 3.
I will ask him for my place again; he shall tell me, I am a drunkard! Had I as many mouths as Hydra, such an answer would stop them all. To be now a sensible man, by and by a fool, and presently a beast. *O.* ii. 3.
One drunkard loves another of the name. *L. L.* iv. 3.
He'll be as full of quarrel and offence
As my young mistress' dog. *O.* ii. 3.
I will, like a true drunkard, utter all to thee. *M. A.* iii. 3.
    And now, in madness,
Being full of supper, and distempering draughts,
Upon malicious bravery dost thou come,
To start my quiet. *O.* i. 1.
They were red hot with drinking;
So full of valour that they smote the air
For breathing in their faces; beat the ground
For kissing of their feet. *T.* iv. 1.
Do not think, gentlemen, I am drunk;—this is my antient;—this is my right hand, and this my left hand:—I am not drunk:—I can stand well enough; and speak well enough: Why, very well then; you must not think then that I am drunk. *O.* ii. 3.

———— ————, PIOUS.
I'll ne'er be drunk whilst I live again, but in honest, civil, godly company, for this trick; if I be drunk, I'll be drunk with those that have the fear of God, and not with drunken knaves. *M. W.* i. 1.

DUELLIST.
Room for the incensed worthies. *L. L.* v. 2.

DUELLIST,—*continued.*
Thou art one of those fellows, that, when he enters the confines of a tavern, claps me his sword upon the table, and says, *God send me no need of thee!* and, by the operation of the second cup, draws it on the drawer, when, indeed, there is no need.   *R. J.* iii. 1.

If wrongs be evils, and enforce us kill,
What folly 'tis to hazard life for ill.   *T. A.* iii. 5.

Your words have took such pains, as if they labour'd
To bring manslaughter into form, set quarrelling
Upon the head of valour; which, indeed,
Is valour misbegot, and came into the world
When sects and factions were but newly born.   *T. A.* iii. 5.

He is a devil in a private brawl: souls and bodies hath he divorced three; and his incensement at this moment is so implacable, that satisfaction can be none but by pangs of death and sepulchre; hob, nob, is his word; give't, or take't.   *T. N.* iii. 4.

DUEL PREVENTED.
Boys of art, I have deceived you both; I have directed you to wrong places: your hearts are mighty, and your skins are whole, and let burnt sack be the issue.
M. W. iii. 1.

DULNESS.
Cudgel your brains no more about it; for your dull ass will never mend his pace with beating.   *H.* v. 1.

DUNS.
They answer, in a joint and corporate voice,
That now they are at fall, want treasure, cannot
Do what they would; are sorry—you are honourable,—
But yet they could have wish'd—they knew not—but
Something hath been amiss—a noble nature
May catch a wrench—would all were well—'tis pity—
And so, intending other serious matters,
After distasteful looks, and these hard fractions,
With certain half caps, and cold moving nods,
They froze me into silence.   *T. A.* ii. 2.

DUPE.
Whose nature is so far from doing harms,
That he suspects none; on whose foolish honesty
My practices ride easy.   *K. L.* i. 2.

E.

EAGERNESS.
                 My desire,
More sharp than filed steel, did spur me forth.   *T. N.* iii. 3.

EARTHQUAKES.
Diseased nature oftentimes breaks forth
In strange eruptions: and the teeming earth
Is with a kind of cholic pinch'd and vex'd
By the imprisoning of unruly wind
Within her womb; which, for enlargement striving,
Shakes the old beldame earth, and topples down
Steeples and moss-grown towers.   *H. IV.* pt. i. iii. 1.

ECHO.
                 Let us sit,
And, whilst the babbling echo mocks the hounds,
Replying shrilly to the well-tun'd horns,
As if a double hunt were heard at once.   *Tit. And.* ii. 3.

My hounds shall make the welkin answer them,
And fetch shrill echoes from the hollow earth.   *T. S.* Ind. 2.
The reverberate hills.   *T. N.* i. 5.
The babbling gossip of the air.   *T. N.* i. 5.

EFFORTS, Abortive.
   How my achievements mock me!   *T. C.* iv. 2.

EGOTISM.
    There's not one wise man among twenty that will praise himself.   *M. A.* v. 4.

ELEPHANT.
    The Elephant hath joints, but none for courtesy: his legs are legs for necessity, not for flexure.   *T. C.* ii. 3.

ELEVATION of Soul.
                 I have
Immortal longings in me.   *A. C.* v. 2.

ELOQUENCE.
               Some there are
Who on the tip of their persuasive tongue
  Carry all arguments and questions deep;
And replication prompt, and reason strong,
  To make the weeper smile, the laugher weep.
They have the dialect and different skill,
Catching all passions in their craft of will.

ELOQUENCE,—*continued.*
That in the general bosom they do reign
Of young and old, and either sex enchain. *Poems.*

When rank Thersites opes his mastiff jaws
We shall hear music, wit and oracle. *T. C.* i. 3

ELVES (See also Faries, Spirits).
Ye elves of hills, brooks, standing lakes, and groves;
And ye, that on the sands with printless foot
Do chace the ebbing Neptune, and do fly him,
When he comes back; you demi-puppets, that
By moonshine do the green-sour ringlets make,
Whereof the ewe not bites; and you, whose pastime
Is to make midnight mushrooms; that rejoice
To hear the solemn curfew; by whose aid
(Weak masters though you be) I have be-dimm'd
The noontide sun, call'd forth the mutinous winds,
And twixt the green sea and the azur'd vault
Set roaring war: to the dread rattling thunder
Have I given fire, and rifted Jove's stout oak
With his own bolt: the strong bas'd promontory
Have I made shake; and by the spurs pluck'd up
The pine and cedar: graves at my command,
Have wak'd their sleepers; ope'd and let them forth
By my so potent art: but this rough magic
I here abjure: and, when I have requir'd
Some heav'nly music (which even now I do)
To work mine end upon their senses, that
This airy charm is for, I'll break my staff,
Bury it certain fathoms in the earth,
And deeper than did ever plummet sound,
I'll drown my book. *T.* v. 1

EMBLEM (See Roses of York and Lancaster).

EMOTION (See also Passions).

——————— Alternating.
I have felt so many quirks of joy, and grief,
That the first face of neither, on the start,
Can woman me unto't. *A. W.* iii: 2.

——————— Conflicting.
You have seen
Sunshine and rain at once. Those happy smiles
That play'd on her ripe lip, seem'd not to know
What guests were in her eyes; which parted thence
As pearls from diamonds dropp'd. *K. L.* iv. 3.

But, O, the noble combat, that, 'twixt joy and sorrow

EMOTIONS, Conflicting,—*continued*.
was fought in Paulina! She had one eye declined for the loss of her husband; another elevated that the oracle was fulfilled; she lifted the princes from the earth; and so locks her in embracing, as if she would pin her to her heart. *W.T.* v. 2.

———— Silent.
He has strangled
His language in his tears. *H.VIII.* v. 1.

Silence is the perfectest herald of joy. I were but little happy if I could say how much. *M.A.* ii. 1.

EMULATION.
For honour travels in a strait so narrow,
Where one but goes abreast; keep then the path;
For emulation hath a thousand sons,
That one by one pursue: If you give way,
Or hedge aside from the direct forthright,
Like to an entered tide, they all rush by,
And leave you hindmost:—
Or, like a gallant horse fallen in first rank,
Lies there for pavement to the abject rear,
O'er-run and trampled on: Then what they do in present,
Though less than yours in past, must o'er-top yours.
T.C. iii. 3.

END.
The long day's task is done,
And we must sleep. *A.C.* iv. 12.

———— (the) Crowns the Means.
Near, or far off, well won is still well shot. *K.J.* i. 1.

The end crowns all;
And that old common arbitrator, Time,
Will one day end it. *T.C.* iv. 5.

ENDLESS.
What! will the line stretch out to the crack of doom?
M. iv. 1.

ENEMIES.
You have many enemies, that know not
Why they are so; but, like to village curs,
Bark when their fellows do. *H.VIII.* ii. 4.

If the enemy is an ass, and a fool, and a prating coxcomb, is it meet, think you, that we should also, look you, be an ass, and a fool, and a prating coxcomb?
H.V. iv. 1.

Shakespearian Dictionary.

ENGLAND (See also BRITAIN).
This royal throne of kings, this scepter'd isle,
This earth of majesty, this seat of Mars,
This other Eden, demi-paradise;
This fortress built by nature for herself,
Against infection and the hand of war;
This happy breed of men, this little world;
This precious stone set in the silver sea,
Which serves it in the office of a wall,
Or as a moat defensive to a house,
Against the envy of less happy lands;
This blessed plot, this earth, this realm, this England,
This nurse, this teeming womb of royal kings,
Fear'd by their breed, and famous by their birth,
Renowned for their deeds as far from home,
(For Christian service, and true chivalry,)
As is the sepulchre in stubborn Jewry,
Of the world's ransom, blessed Mary's son:
This land of such dear souls, this dear dear land,
Dear for her reputation through the world,
Is now leas'd out (I die pronouncing it,)
Like to a tenement, or pelting farm:
England, bound in with the triumphant sea,
Whose rocky shore beats back the envious siege
Of watery Neptune, is now bound in with shame,
With inky blots, and rotten parchment bonds;
That England that was wont to conquer others,
Has made a shameful conquest of itself. *R. II.* ii. 1.

Our sea-wall'd garden, the whole land,
Is full of weeds, her fairest flowers choak'd up,
Her fruit-trees all un-prun'd, her hedges ruin'd,
Her knots disorder'd, and her wholesome herbs
Swarming with caterpillars. *R. II.* iii. 4.

I will no more return,
Till Angiers, and the right thou hast in France,
Together with that pale, that white-fac'd shore,
Whose foot spurns back the ocean's roaring tides,
And coops from other lands her islanders;
Even till that England, hedg'd in with the main,
That water-walled bulwark, still secure
And confident from foreign purposes,
Even till that utmost corner of the west
Salute thee for her king. *K. J.* ii. 1.

This England never did, (nor never shall)
Lie at the proud foot of a conqueror,
But when it first did help to wound itse'f.

ENGLAND,—*continued.*
    *   *   *   *   Nought shall make us rue
If England to herself do rest but true.   *K. J.* v. 7.
O England, model to thy inward greatness,
Like little body with a mighty heart,—
What might'st thou do, that honour would thee do,
Were all thy children kind and natural!
But see thy fault!   *H. V.* ii. *chorus.*
               O nation, that thou could'st remove!
That Neptune's arms, who clippeth thee about,
Would bear thee from the knowledge of thyself,
And grapple thee unto a pagan shore.   *K. J.* v. 2.

——————'s DEFENCE.
Let us be back'd with God, and with the seas,
Which he hath given for fence impregnable,
And with their helps, only, defend ourselves;
In them, and in ourselves, our safety lies.
    H. VI. PT. III. iv. 1.

ENGLISH, THE.
Would I had never trod this English earth,
Or felt the flatteries that grow upon it!
Ye have angels' faces, but heaven knows your hearts!
    H. VIII. iii. 1.
    The men do sympathize with the mastiffs, in robustious and rough coming on, leaving their wits with their wives; and then give them great meals of beef, and iron, and steel, they will eat like wolves, and fight like devils.
    H. V. iii. 7.

——————WRANGLERS.
    Be friends, you English fools, be friends; we have French quarrels enough, if you could tell how to reckon.
    H. V. iv. 1.

ENJOYMENT, FREQUENCY OF, DIMINISHES PLEASURE.
The nightingale in summer's front doth sing,
And stops his pipe in growth of riper days;
Not that the summer is more pleasant now
   Then when his mournful hymns did hush the night,
But that wild music burdens every bough,
   And sweets grown common lose their dear delight.
    Poems.

ENLARGEMENT.
Ay, marry, now my soul hath elbow room.   *K. J.* v. 7.

ENMITY.
If I had a thunderbolt in mine eye, I can tell who should down.   *A. Y.* i. 2.

Shakespearian Dictionary.

·ENTERPRISE.
Impossible be strange attempts, to those
That weigh their pains in sense; and do suppose
What hath been cannot be.   *A.W.* i. 1.
Of all exploits since first I follow'd arms,
Ne'er heard I of a warlike enterprise
More venturous or desperate than this.   *H.VI.* PT. I. ii. 1.

ENVY.
Know you not, master, to some kind of men
Their graces serve them but as enemies?
No more do yours; your virtues, gentle master,
Are sanctified and holy traitors to you.
O, what a world is this, when what is comely
Envenoms him that bears it!   *A.Y.* ii. 3.
Lean-fac'd Envy in her loathsome cave.
                              H.VI. PT. II. iii. 2.
               Now I feel
Of what coarse metal ye are moulded,—envy.
How eagerly ye follow my disgraces,
As if it fed ye! and how sleek and wanton
Ye appear in every thing may bring my ruin!
Follow your envious courses, men of malice;
You have Christian warrant for them, and, no doubt,
In time will find their fit rewards.   *H.VIII.* iii. 2.
My heart laments, that virtue cannot live
Out of the teeth of emulation.   *J.C.* ii. 3.
            Men, that make
Envy, and crooked malice, nourishment,
Dare bite the best.   *H.VIII.* v. 2.

EPITHETS.
Truly, master Holofernes, the epithets are sweetly varied,
like a scholar at the least.   *L.L.* iv. 2.

——— FOND.
             A world
Of pretty, fond, adoptious Christendoms,
That blinking Cupid gossips.   *A.W.* i. 1.

EQUANIMITY.
Nobly he yokes
A smiling with a sigh: as if the sigh.
Was that it was, for not being such a smile;
The smile, mocking the sigh, that it would fly
From so divine a temple, to commix
With winds, that sailors rail at.   *Cym.* iv. 2.
Thus ready for the way of life or death,
I wait the sharpest blow.   *P.P.* i. 1.

EQUIVOCATION.
'Faith, here's an equivocator, that could swear in both the scales against either scale; who committed treason enough for God's sake, yet could not equivocate to heaven.
M. ii. 3.

How absolute the knave is! we must speak by the card, or equivocation will undo us. *H.* v. 1.

ERROR.
O hateful error, melancholy's child!
Why dost thou show to the apt thoughts of men
The things that are not? O error, soon conceiv'd,
Thou never com'st unto a happy birth,
But kill'st the mother that engender'd thee. *J.C.* v. 3.

But we worldly men
Have miserable, mad, mistaking eyes. *Tit. And.* v. 2.

O, what men dare do! what men may do! what men daily do! not knowing what they do! *M.A.* iv. 1.

When from things true, the heart and eyes have err'd,
To a false plague they often are transferr'd. *Poems.*

In your affairs, my lord,
If ever I were wilful-negligent,
It was my folly; if industriously
I play'd the fool, it was my negligence,
Not weighing well the end; if ever fearful
To do a thing, where I the issue doubted,
Whereof the execution did cry out
Against the non-performance, 'twas a fear
Which oft affects the wisest: these, my lord,
Are such allow'd infirmities, that honesty
Is never free of. *W.T.* i. 2.

—— Popular.
'Tis the time's plague, when madmen lead the blind.
K.L. iv. 1.

ESCAPE.
You may thank the unquiet time for your quiet o'er-posting that action. *H. IV.* pt. ii. i. 2.

I have been in such a pickle since I saw you last, that, I fear me, will never out of my bones: I shall not fear fly-blowing. *T.* v. 1.

ESPOUSALS (See also Wife).
Let still the woman take
An elder than herself, so wears she to him,
So sways she level in her husband's heart.
For, boy, however we do praise ourselves,
Our fancies are more giddy and unfirm,

ESPOUSALS,—*continued.*
More longing, wavering, sooner lost and won,
Than women's are. *T. N.* ii. 4

Then let thy love be younger than thyself,
Or thy affection cannot hold the bent:
For women are as roses, whose fair flower,
Being once display'd, doth fall that very hour. *T. N.* ii. 4.

EVASION.
What trick, what device, what starting hole, canst thou now find out, to hide thee from this open and apparent shame. *H. IV.* PT. I. ii. 4.

For, well you know, we of th' offending side
Must keep aloof from strict arbitrament:
And stop all sight-holes; every loop, from whence
The eye of reason may pry in upon us. *H. IV.* PT. I. iv. 1.

— ——— WORN-OUT.
I ne'er had worse luck in my life, in my,— *O Lord, Sir:*
I see, things may serve long, but not serve ever.
A. W. ii. 2.

EVENING.
Light thickens; and the crow
Makes wing to the rooky wood. *M.* iii. 2.

The west yet glimmers with some streaks of day:
Now spurs the lated traveller apace,
To gain the timely inn. *M.* iii. 3.

Good things of day begin to droop and drowze. *M.* iii. 2

EVIL.
There is some soul of goodness in things evil
Would men observingly distil it out:
For our bad neighbour makes us early stirrers,
Which is both healthful, and good husbandry;
Besides, they are our outward consciences,
And preachers to us all; admonishing,
That we should dress us fairly for our end.
Thus may we gather honey from the weed,
And make a moral of the devil himself. *H. V.* iv. 1.

EXALTATION.
Now climbeth Tamora Olympus' top;
Safe out of fortune's shot: and sits aloft,
Secure of thunder's crack, or lightning's flash;
Advanc'd above pale Envy's threat'ning reach.
Tit. And. ii. 1

EXAMINATION.
      Peace; sit you down,
And let me wring your heart; for so I shall,
If it be made of penetrable stuff;
If damned custom have not braz'd it so,
That it be proof and bulwark against sense. *H.* iii. 4.
You go not, till I set you up a glass,
Where you may see the inmost part of you. *H.* iii. 4.

EXAMPLE.
Thieves for their robbery have authority
When judges steal themselves. *M. M.* ii. 2.
 More authority, dear boy, name more; and, sweet my child, let them be even of good repute and carriage.
            L. L. i. 1.

EXASPERATION.
Why, look you, I am whipp'd and scourg'd with rods,
Nettled, and stung with pismires, when I hear
Of this vile politician, Bolingbroke. *H. IV.* PT. I. i. 3.

EXCELLENCE.
     They are worthy
To inlay heaven with stars. *Cym.* v. 5.
   The top of admiration; worth
What's dearest to the world. *T.* iii. 1.
     But you, O you,
So perfect and so peerless, are created
Of every creature's best. *T.* iii. 1.

EXCESS.
As surfeit is the father of much fast,
So every scope by the immoderate use
Turns to restraint: our natures do pursue
(Like rats, that ravin down their proper bane)
A thirsty evil; and when we drink, we die. *M. M.* i. 3.
Allow not nature more than nature needs. *K. L.* ii. 4.

EXCITEMENT.
And thereof came it that the man was mad. *C. E.* v. 1.

EXCUSES SOMETIMES IMPROPER.
When workmen strive to do better than well,
They do confound their skill in covetousness:
And, oftentimes, excusing of a fault,
Doth make the fault the worse by the excuse;
As patches set upon a little breach,
Discredit more in hiding of the fault,
Than did the fault before it was so patch'd. *K. J.* iv. 2.

EXPECTATION.
Oft expectation fails, and most oft tnere
Where most it promises; and oft it hits,
Where hope is coldest, and despair most sits.   *A. W.* ii. 1.
For now sits Expectation in the air.   *H. V.* ii. *chorus*.
         So tedious is this day,
As is the night before some festival
To an impatient child, that hath new robes,
And may not wear them.   *R. J.* iii. 2.
Now expectation, tickling skittish spirits,
On one and other side, Trojan and Greek
Sets all on hazard.   *T. C. Prologue.*
The town is empty; on the brow o' the sea
Stand ranks of people, and they cry,—a sail.   *O.* ii. 1.
For every minute is expectancy
Of more arrivance.   *O.* ii. 1.
         It is a high-wrought flood;
I cannot, 'twixt the heaven and the main,
Descry a sail.   *O.* ii. 1.
Even till we make the main, and the aërial blue
An indistinct regard.   *O.* ii. 1.

EXPEDIENCY.
Construe the times to their necessities.   *H. IV.* PT. II. iv. 1.

EXPERIENCE.
Experience is by industry achiev'd,
And perfected by the swift course of time.   *T. G.* i. 3.
Experience, O, thou disprov'st report!   *Cym.* v. 2.

EXPIRING.
Vex not his ghost; O let him pass, he hates him,
That would upon the rack of this tough world
Stretch him out longer.   *K. L.* v. 3.

EXPLANATION.
To my unfolding lend a gracious ear;
And let me find a charter in your voice,
To assist my simpleness.   *O.* i. 3.

EXPLOSION.
         It shall go hard,
But I will delve one yard below their mines,
And blow them to the moon.   *H.* iii. 4.

EXPOSURE.
         Come, come;
Lend me a light. Know we this face, or no?   *O.* v. 1.

EXPRESSION, LASCIVIOUS.
Fie, fie upon her!
There's language in her eye, her cheek, her lip;
Nay, her foot speaks; her wanton spirits look out,
At every joint and motion of her body.
O, these encounterers, so glib of tongue,
That give a coasting welcome ere it comes,
And wide unclasp the tables of their thoughts
. To every ticklish reader! set them down
For sluttish spoils of opportunity,
And daughters of the game. *T.C.* iv. 5.

EXPULSION.
I cannot tell, good Sir, for which of his virtues it was, but he was certainly whipped out of the court. *W.T.* iv. 2.

EXTACY.
O Helicanus, strike me, honor'd Sir;
Give me a gash, put me to present pain;
Lest this great sea of joys rushing upon me,
O'erbear the shores of my mortality,
And drown me with their sweetness. *P.P.* v. 1.

EXTENUATION.
I would, I could
Quit all offences with as clear excuse,
As well as, I am doubtless, I can purge
Myself of many I am charg'd withal:
Yet such extenuation let me beg,
As, in reproof of many tales devis'd,—
Which oft the ear of greatness needs must hear,—
By smiling pick-thanks and base newsmongers,
I may, for some things true, wherein my youth
Hath faulty wander'd and irregular,
Find pardon on my true submission. *H. IV.* PT. I. iii. 2.

EXTERIOR, PLAUSIBLE.
There is a fair behaviour in thee, captain;
And though that nature, with a beauteous wall,
Doth oft close in pollution, yet of thee
I will believe, thou hast a mind that suits
With this thy fair and outward character. *T. N* i. 2.

EYE.
Men's eyes were made to look, and let them gaze.
R. J. iii. 1.
The eye sees not itself,
But by reflection, by some other things. *J.C.* i. 2.
Let every eye negociate for itself, and trust no agent.
M. A. ii. 1.

EYE,—*continued*.
An eye like Mars, to threaten and command. *H.* iii. 4.
What an eye she hath! methinks it sounds a parley of
provocation. *O.* ii. 3.
    For his ordinary, pays his heart,
For what his eyes eat only. *A. C.* ii. 2.
    From women's eyes this doctrine I derive:
They sparkle still the right Promethean fire;
They are the books, the arts, the academies,
That show, contain, and nourish all the world;
Else, none at all in aught proves excellent. *L. L.* iv. 3.

Thou tell'st me there is murder in mine eye:
'Tis pretty, sure, and very probable;
That eyes,—that are the frail'st and softest things,
Who shut their coward gates on atomies,—
Should be call'd tyrants, butchers, murderers!
Now I do frown on thee with all my heart;
And, if mine eyes can wound, now let them kill thee;
Now counterfeit to swoon; why now fall down;
Or, if thou can'st not, O, for shame, for shame,
Lie not, to say mine eyes are murderers.
Now show the wound mine eyes have made in thee:
Scratch thee but with a pin, and there remains
Some scar of it; lean but upon a rush,
The cicatrice and capable impressure
Thy palm some moment keeps: but now mines eyes,
Which I have darted at thee, hurt thee not;
Nor, I am sure, there is no force in eyes,
That can do hurt. *A. Y.* iii. 5.

She speaks, yet she says nothing;—what of that?
Her eye discourses, I will answer it.
I am too bold, 'tis not to me she speaks:
Two of the fairest stars in all the heaven,
Having some business, do entreat her eyes
To twinkle in their spheres till they return. *R. J.* ii. 2.

          I perceive, these lords,
At this encounter, do so much admire,
That they devour their reason; and scarce think
Their eyes do offices of truth, their words
Are natural breath. *T.* v. i.

The beauty that is borne here in the face
The bearer knows not, but commends itself
To others' eyes: nor doth the eye itself
(That most pure spirit of sense) behold itself,
Not going from itself; but eye to eye oppos'd
Salute each other with each other's form. *T. C.* iii. 3.

EYE-Brows.
Your brows are blacker; yet black brows, they say,
Become some women best; so that there be not
Too much hair there, but in a semi-circle,
Or half moon made with a pen. *W.T.* ii. 1

—— AND EARS.
My will enkindled by mine eyes and ears,
Two traded pilots 'twixt the dangerous shores
Of will and judgment. *T.C.* ii. 2.

F.

FACE.
If he be not one that truly loves you,
That errs in ignorance and not in cunning,
I have no judgment in an honest face. *O.* iii. 3.
Your face, my thane, is as a book, where men
May read strange matters. *M.* i. 5.

FACILITY.
'Tis as easy as lying. *H.* iii. 2.

FAIRIES (See also ELVES, QUEEN MAB.)
Where the bee sucks, there suck I,
In a cowslip's bell I lie:
There I couch when owls do cry.
On the bat's back I do fly,
After summer merrily:
Merrily, merrily shall I live now,
Under the blossom that hangs on the bough. *T.* v. 1.

Fairies, black, grey, green, and white,
You moon-shine revellers, and shades of night,
You orphan-heirs of fixed destiny,
Attend your office, and your quality. *M.W.* v. 5.

Elves, list your names; silence, you airy toys.
Cricket, to Windsor chimneys shalt thou leap:
Where fires thou find'st unrak'd, and hearths unswept,
There pinch the maids as blue as bilberry:
Our radiant queen hates sluts and sluttery. *W.M.* v. 5

But that it eats our victuals, I should think
Here were a fairy. *Cym.* iii. 6

Come, now a roundel, and a fairy song;
Then, for the third part of a minute, hence;
Some, to kill cankers in the musk-rose buds;
Some, war with rear-mice for their leathern wings,
To make my small elves coats; and some, keep back

FAIRIES,—*continued.*

The clamorous owl, that nightly hoots, and wonders
At our quaint spirits.   *M. N.* ii. 3

Where's Pede?—Go you, and where you find a maid,
That, ere she sleep, has thrice her prayers said,
Raise up the organs of her fantasy,
Sleep she as sound as careless infancy;
But those that sleep, and think not on their sins,
Pinch them, arms, legs, back, shoulders, sides, and shins.
                                                    M. W. v. 5

About, about;
Search Windsor-Castle, elves, within and out:
Strew good luck, ouphes, in every sacred room:
That it may stand till the perpetual doom,
In state as wholesome as in state 'tis fit;
Worthy the owner, and the owner it.
The several chairs of order look you scour
With juice of balm, and every precious flower:
Each fair instalment, coat, and several crest,
With loyal blazon, evermore be blest!
And nightly, meadow-fairies, look, you sing,
Like to the Garter's compass, in a ring:
The expressure that it bears, green let it be,
More fertile-fresh than all the field to see;
And *Hony soit qui mal y pense,* write
In emerald tufts, flowers purple, blue, and white;
Like sapphire, pearl, and rich embroidery,
Buckled below fair knighthood's bending knee:
Fairies use flowers for their charactery.
Away; disperse.   *M. W.* v. 5.

Then, my queen, in silence sad,
Trip we after the night's shade:
We the globe can compass soon,
Swifter than the wand'ring moon.   *M. N.* iv. 1.

Pray you, lock hand in hand: yourselves in order set:
And twenty glow-worms shall our lanterns be,
To guide our measure round about the tree.   *M. W.* v. 5.

Be kind and courteous to this gentleman;
Hop in his walks, and gambol in his eyes;
Feed him with apricocks and dewberries,
With purple grapes, green figs, and mulberries;
The honey bags steal from the humble bees,
And, for night-tapers, crop their waxen thighs,
And light them at the fiery glow-worm's eyes,
To have my love to bed, and to arise;
And pluck the wings from painted butterflies.

FAIRIES,—*continued.*
To fan the moon-beams from his sleeping eyes:
Nod to him, elves, and do him courtesies. *M. N.* iii. 1.
——— EMPLOYMENT.
To tread the ooze of the salt deep;
To run upon the sharp wind of the north;
To do me business in the veins o' the earth,
When it is bak'd with frost. *T.* i. 2.

FAITH.
Well, if ever thou dost fall from this faith, thou wilt
prove a notable argument. *M. A.* i. 1.

FALLEN GREATNESS (See also LIFE, DEATH, MIGHTY DEAD.)
'Tis a sufferance, panging
As soul and body's severing. *H. VIII.* ii. 3.
Farewell, a long farewell, to all my greatness!
This is the state of man: To-day he puts forth
The tender leaves of hope; to-morrow blossoms,
And bears his blushing honours thick upon him;
The third day comes a frost, a killing frost;
And when he thinks, good easy man, full surely
His greatness is a ripening,—nips his root,
And then he falls, as I do. I have ventur'd,
Like little wanton boys that swim on bladders,
This many summers in a sea of glory;
But far beyond my depth: my high-blown pride
At length broke under me; and now has left me,
Weary, and old with service, to the mercy
Of a rude stream, that must for ever hide me.
Vain pomp, and glory of this world, I hate ye;
I feel my heart new opened: O, how wretched
Is that poor man, that hangs on princes' favours!
There is, betwixt that smile we would aspire to,
That sweet aspect of princes, and their ruin,
More pangs and fears than wars and women have;
And when he falls, he falls like Lucifer,
Never to hope again. *H. VIII.* iii. 2.
But yesterday, the word of Cæsar might
Have stood against the world: now lies he there,
And none so poor to do him reverence. *J. C.* iii. 2.
O sun, thy uprise shall I see no more:
Fortune and Antony part here; even here
Do we shake hands.—All come to this? The hearts
That spaniel'd me at heels, to whom I gave
Their wishes, do discandy, melt their sweets
On blossoming Cæsar; and this pine is bark'd
That over-topp'd them all. *A. C.* iv. 10.

FALLEN Greatness,—*continued.*
    High events as these
Strike those that make them : and their story is
No less in pity, than his glory, which
Brought them to be lamented.   *A.C.* v. 2
    Nay then, farewell !
I've touch'd the highest point of all my greatness!
And, from that full meridian of my glory,
I haste now to my setting. I shall fall
Like a bright exhalation in the evening,
And no man see me more.   *H.VIII.* iii, 2.

 Where is thy husband now ? where be thy brothers ?
Where be thy two sons ? wherein dost thou joy ?
Who sues, and kneels, and says—God save the queen ?
Where be the bending peers that flatter'd thee ?
Where be the thronging troops that follow'd thee ?
Decline all this, and see what now thou art. *R. III.* iv. 4.

 A falcon, tow'ring in her pride of place,
Was, by a mousing owl, hawk'd at, and kill'd. *M.* ii. 4.

An argument that he is pluck'd, when hither
He sends so poor a pinion of his wing,
Which had superfluous kings for messengers,
Not many moons gone by.   *A.C.* iii. 10.

O wither'd is the garland of the war,
The soldier's pole is fallen ; young boys, and girls
Are level now with men ; the odds is gone,
And there is nothing left remarkable
Beneath the visiting moon.   *A.C.* iv. 13.

O mighty Cæsar! Dost thou lie so low ?
Are all thy conquests, glories, triumphs, spoils,
Shrunk to this little measure ?   *J.C.* iii. 1.

'Tis certain, greatness, once fallen out with fortune,
Must fall out with men too : What the declin'd is,
He shall as soon read in the eyes of others,
As feel in his own fall :—for men, like butterflies,
Show not their mealy wings but to the summer.
          T.C. iii. 3

 Never so truly happy, my good Cromwell.
I know myself now ; and I feel within me
A peace above all earthly dignities,
A still and quiet conscience. The king has cur'd me,
I humbly thank his grace ; and from these shoulders,
These ruin'd pillars, out of pity, taken
A load would sink a navy, too much honour:
O, 'tis a burden, Cromwell, 'tis a burden,
Too heavy for a man that hopes for heaven. *H.VIII.* iii. 2

FALLEN GREATNESS,—*continued.*
My lord of Winchester, you are a little,
By your good favour, too sharp ; men so noble,
However faulty, yet should find respect,
For what they have been : 'tis a cruelty,
To load a falling man.   *H. VIII.* v. 2.

His overthrow heap'd happiness upon him ;
For then, and not till then, he felt himself,
And found the blessedness of being little.   *H. VIII.* iv. 2

        What, amazed
At my misfortunes ? can thy spirit wonder,
A great man should decline ? Nay, an you weep,
I am fallen indeed.   *H. VIII.* iii. 2

There was the weight that pull'd me down. O Cromwell,
The king has gone beyond me, all my glories
In that one woman I have lost for ever :
No sun shall ever usher forth mine honours,
Or gild again the noble troops that waited
Upon my smiles. Go, get thee from me, Cromwell ;
I am a poor fallen man, unworthy now
To be thy lord and master.   *H. VIII.* iii. 2.

     Brave Percy : Fare thee well, great heart !
Ill-weav'd ambition, how much art thou shrunk !
When that this body did contain a spirit,
A kingdom for it was too small a bound ;
But now, two paces of the vilest earth
Is room enough.   *H. IV.* PT. I. v. 4.

Let's talk of graves, of worms, and epitaphs,
Make dust our paper, and with rainy eyes,
Write sorrow on the bosom of the earth.
Let's choose executors, and talk of wills :
And yet not so, for what can we bequeath,
Save our deposed bodies to the ground ?
Our lands, our lives, and all are Bolingbroke's,
And nothing can we call our own, but death ;
And that small model of the barren earth,
Which serves as paste and cover to our bones.
For heaven's sake let us sit upon the ground,
And tell sad stories of the death of kings :—
How some have been depos'd, some slain in war ;—
Some haunted by the ghosts they have depos'd ;
Some poison'd by their wives, some sleeping kill'd ;
All murder'd.   *R. II.* iii. 2

    O, my lord,
Press not a falling man too far ; 'tis virtue :
His faults lie open to the laws ; let them,

FAL   *Shakespearian Dictionary.*   FAM

FALLEN GREATNESS,—*continued.*
Not you, correct him. My heart weeps to see him
So little of his great self.   *H. VIII.* iii. 2.

     I must now forsake ye; the last hour
Of my long weary life is come upon me.
Farewell:
And when you would say something that is sad,
Speak how I fell.   *H. VIII.* ii. 4.

     Pry'thee go hence,
Or I shall show the cinders of my spirit
Through the ashes of my chance.   *A. C.* v. 2.

Now boast thee, death! in thy possession lies
A lass unparallel'd.—Downy windows, close;
And golden Phœbus never be beheld
Of eyes again so royal!   *A. C.* v. 2.

FALSE CHARACTERS.
     I am damned in hell, for swearing to gentlemen, my friends, you were good soldiers, and tall fellows: and when Mistress Bridget lost the handle of her fan, I took't upon mine honour, thou hadst it not.   *M. W.* ii. 2.

—— HAIR.
So are those crisped snaky golden locks,
Which make such wanton gambols with the wind,
Upon supposed fairness, often known
To be the dowry of a second head,
The scull that bred them in the sepulchre.   *M. V.* iii. 2.

FALSEHOOD.
Falser than vows made in wine.   *A. Y.* iii. 5.
As false as dicers' oaths.   *H.* iii. 4.
O what a goodly outside falsehood hath.   *M. V.* i. 3.

     That same Diomed is a false-hearted rogue, a most unjust knave; I will no more trust him when he leers, than I will a serpent when he hisses; he will spend his mouth, and promise, like Brabler the hound; but when he performs, astronomers fortel it; it is prodigious; there will come some change; the sun borrows of the moon, when Diomed keeps his word.   *T. C.* v. 1.

FALLSTAFF.
I have much to say on behalf of that Fallstaff.
                                   H. IV. PT. I. ii. 4.

FAME (See also CELEBRITY).
Let fame, that all hunt after in their lives,
Live register'd upon our brazen tombs,

FAME,—*continued.*
And then grace us in the disgrace of death;
When, spite of cormorant devouring Time,
The endeavour of this present breath may buy
That honour which shall bate his scythe's keen edge,
And make us heirs of all eternity. *L.L.* i. 1.

All-telling Fame. *L. L.* ii. 1.

It deserves with characters of brass,
A forted residence, 'gainst the tooth of time
And razure of oblivion. *M. M.* v. 1.

The evil that men do lives after them;
The good is oft interred with their bones. *J. C.* iii. 2.

Men's evil manners live in brass: their virtues
We write in water. *H. VIII.* iv. 2.

Death makes no conquest of this conqueror;
For now he lives in fame, though not in life.
R. III. iii. 1.

He lives in fame, that died in virtue's cause.
Tit. And. i. 2.

After my death, I wish no other herald,
No other speaker of my living actions,
To keep mine honour from corruption,
But such an honest chronicler as Griffith. *H. VIII.* iv. 2.

Adieu, and take thy praise with thee to heaven!
Thy ignominy sleep with thee in the grave,
But not remember'd in thy epitaph. *H. IV.* PT. I. v. 4.

Fame, at the which he aims,—
In whom already he is well grac'd,—cannot
Better be held, nor more attain'd, than by
A place below the first: for what miscarries
Shall be the general's fault, though he perform
To the utmost of a man; and giddy censure
Will then cry out of Marcius, *O, if he
Had borne the business!* *C.* i. 1.

O, Harry, thou hast robb'd me of my youth,
I better brook the loss of brittle life,
Than those proud titles thou hast won of me;
They wound my thoughts, worse than thy sword my flesh:
But thought's the slave of life, and life, time's fool;
And time, that takes survey of all the world,
Must have a stop. *H. IV.* PT. I. v. 4.

Having his ear full of his airy fame,
Grows dainty of his worth, and in his tent
Lies mocking our designs. *T. C.* I. 3.

FAME,—*continued.*
If a man do not erect, in this age, his own tomb ere he dies, he shall live no longer in monument, than the bell rings, and the widow weeps. * * * An hour in clamour, and a quarter in rheum.   *M. A.* v. 2.

I would give all my fame for a pot of ale, and safety.
H. V. iii. 2.

FANCY.
So full of shapes is fancy,
That it alone is high-fantastical.   *T. N.* i. 1.

An old hat, and the humour of forty fancies stuck in it for a feather.   *T. S.* iii. 2.

Nature wants stuff
To vie strange forms with fancy.   *A. C.* v. 2.

Tell me, where is fancy bred;
Or in the heart, or in the head?
How begot, how nourished?
It is engender'd in the eyes,
With gazing fed: and fancy dies
In the cradle where it lies.   *M. V.* iii. 2.

She knew her distance, and did angle for me,
Madding my eagerness with her restraint,
As all impediments in fancy's course
Are motives of more fancy.   *A. W.* v. 3.

We must every one be a man of his own fancy.
A. W. iv. 1.

In maiden meditation, fancy-free.   *M. N.* ii. 2.

FASHION.
See'st thou not, I say, what a deformed thief this fashion is? how giddily he turns about all the hot bloods between fourteen and five-and-thirty?   *M. A.* iii. 3.

Eat, speak, and move, under the influence of the most received star; and though the devil lead the measure, such are to be followed.   *A. W.* ii. 1.

I see that the fashion wears out more apparel than the man.   *M. A.* iii. 3.

New customs,
Though they be never so ridiculous,
Nay, let them be unmanly, yet are follow'd.   *H. VIII.* i. 3.

These remnants
Of fool and feather, that they got in France,
With all their honourable points of ignorance
Pertaining thereunto.   *H. VIII.* i. 3.

FASHION,—*continued.*
　　Death! my lord,
　　Their clothes are after such a pagan cut too.　*H. VIII.* i. 3.

　　　Still, wars and letchery; nothing else holds fashion: a burning devil take them!　*T. C.* v. 2.

FATE.
　　O heavens! that one might read the book of fate;
　　And see the revolutions of the times
　　Make mountains level, and the continent
　　(Weary of solid firmness) melt itself
　　Into the sea! and, other times, to see
　　The beachy girdle of the ocean
　　Too wide for Neptune's hips: how chances mock,
　　And changes fill, the cup of alteration,
　　With divers liquors!　*H. IV.* PT. II. iii. 1.

　　What fates impose, that men must needs abide,
　　It boots not to resist both wind and tide.
　　　　　　　　　　　　H. IV. PT. III. iv. 3.

　　　We defy augury; there is a special providence in the fall of a sparrow. If it be now, 'tis not to come; if it be not to come, it will be now; if it be not now, yet it will come: the readiness is all.　*H.* v. 2.

　　　　But, O vain boast!
　　Who can controul his fate?　*O.* v. 2.

　　Well, heaven forgive him, and forgive us all!
　　Some rise by sin, and some by virtue fall:
　　Some run from brakes of vice and answer none;
　　And some condemned for one fault alone.　*M. M.* ii. 1

　　If thou read this, O Cæsar, thou may'st live;
　　If not, the fates with traitors do contrive.　*J. C.* ii. 3.

　　Men, at some times, are masters of their fates.　*J. C.* i. 2.

　　But, orderly to end where I begun,
　　Our wills and fates do so contrary run,
　　That our devices still are overthrown;
　　Our thoughts are ours, their ends none of our own.
　　　　　　　　　　　　H. iii. 2.

FATHER.
　　　Fathers, that wear rags,
　　　　Do make their children blind;
　　　But fathers that bear bags,
　　　　Shall see their children kind.　*K. L.* ii. 4.

　　Who would be a father?　*O.* i. 1.

FAVOUR.

For taking one's part that's out of favour: Nay, an thou canst not smile as the wind sits, thoul't catch cold shortly. *K. L.* i. 4.

    O, who shall believe,
But you misuse the reverence of your place;
Employ the countenance and grace of heaven,
As a false favourite does his prince's name
In deeds dishonourable. *H. IV.* PT. II. iv. 2.

Sickness is catching: O, were favour so! *M. N.* i. 1.

I'll set thee in a shower of gold, and hail
Rich pearls upon thee. *A. C.* ii. 5.

FAVOURITES, PRESUMPTION OF.

Where honeysuckles, ripen'd by the sun,
Forbid the sun to enter;—like favourites,
Made proud by princes, that advance their pride
Against that power that bred it. *M. A.* iii. 1.

FAULT.

I need not be barren of accusations; he hath faults, with surplus, to tire in repetition. *C.* i. 1.

Time shall unfold what plaited cunning hides;
Who cover faults, at last shame them derides. *K. L.* i. 1.

    You shall find there
A man, who is the abstract of all faults
That all men follow. *A. C.* i. 4.

Condemn the fault, and not the actor of it!
Why every fault's condemn'd ere it be done:
Mine were the very cipher of a function,
To find the faults whose fine stands in record,
And let go by the actor. *M. M.* ii. 2.

There's something in me that reproves my fault;
But such a headstrong potent fault it is,
That it but mocks reproof. *T. N.* iii. 4.

 There were none principal; they were all like one another, as halfpence are; every one fault seeming monstrous, till his fellow fault came to match it. *A. Y.* iii. 2.

 His worst fault is, he's given to prayer; he is something peevish that way; but nobody but has his fault:—but let that pass. *M. W.* i. 4.

I will not open my mouth so wide as a bristle may enter, in way of thy excuse. *T. N.* i. 5.

FAWNING.

Tut, tut!
Grace me no grace, nor uncle me no uncle;

FAWNING,—*continued.*
 I am no traitor's uncle ;—and that word grace,
 In an ungracious mouth, is but profane.   *R. II.* ii. 3.

FEAR.
 Fears makes devils of cherubims.   *T.C.* iii. 2.
 Of all base passions, fear is most accurs'd.
        H.VI. PT. I. v. 2.
 His flight was madness : When our actions do not,
 Our fears do, make us traitors.   *M.* iv. 2.
    Those linen cheeks of thine
 Are counsellors to fear.   *M.* v. 3.
    Nothing routs us
 But the villainy of our fears.   *Cym.* v. 2.
    O, a sin in war,
 Damn'd in the first beginners!   *Cym.* v. 3.
 If Cæsar hide himself, shall they not whisper,
 Lo, Cæsar is afraid ?   *J.C.* ii. 2
 In time we hate that which we often fear.   *A.C.* i. 3.
    O, these flaws and starts,
 (Impostors to true fear) would well become
 A woman's story at a winter's fire.   *M.* iii. 4.
 This is the very painting of your fear.   *M.* iii. 4.
    You make me strange,
 Even to the disposition that I owe,
 When now I think you can behold such sights,
 And keep the natural ruby of your cheeks,
 While mine are blanch'd with fear.   *M.* iii. 4.
  Blind fear, that seeing reason leads, finds safer footing
 than blind reason stumbling, without fear.   *T.C.* iii. 2.
 The devil damn thee black, thou cream-fac'd loon !
 Where got'st thou that goose look ?   *M.* v. 3.
  O, let my lady apprehend no fear: in all Cupid's pageant
 there is presented no monster.   *T.C.* iii. 2.
    There is not such a word
 Spoke of in Scotland, as this term of fear.
        H.IV. PT. I. iv. 1.
 The love of wicked friends converts to fear;
 That fear, to hate; and hate turns one, or both,
 To worthy danger, and deserved death.   *R. II.* v. 1.
    Why, what should be the fear?
 I do not set my life at a pin's fee ;
 And, for my soul, what can it do to that,
 Being a thing immortal?   *H.* i. 4.

FEAR,—*continued.*
Let not the world see fear and sad distrust
Govern the motion of a kingly eye.   *K. J.* v. 1.
I am sick and capable of fears;
Oppress'd with wrongs, and therefore full of fears;
A widow, husbandless, subject to fears;
A woman, naturally born to fears.   *K. J.* iii. 1.
I have almost forgot the very taste of fears:
The time has been my senses would have cool'd
To hear a night-shriek; and my fell of hair
Would, at a dismal treatise, rouse, and stir,
As life were in't: I have supp'd full of horrors;
Direness, familiar to my slaughterous thoughts,
Cannot once start me.   *M.* v. 5.

FEINT.
'Tis a pageant
To keep us in false gaze.   *O.* i. 3.

FICKLENESS.
Novelty is only in request; and it is dangerous to be aged in any kind of course, as it is virtuous to be constant in any undertaking. There is scarce truth enough alive to make societies secure; but security enough, to make fellowships accursed: much upon this riddle runs the wisdom of the world.   *M.M.* iii. 2.

FICTIONS.
More strange than true. I never may believe
These antique fables, nor these fairy toys.   *M. N.* v. 1.

——— TRAGIC.
What's Hecuba to him, or he to Hecuba,
That he should weep for her?   *H.* ii. 2.

FIDELITY (See also CONSTANCY, LOVE).
I'll yet follow
The wounded chance of Antony, though my reason
Sits in the wind against me.   *A.C.* iii. 8.

Though all the world should crack their duty to you,
And throw it from their soul; though perils did
Abound, as thick as thought could make them, and
Appear in forms more horrid; yet my duty,
As doth a rock against the chiding flood,
Should the approach of this wild river break,
And stand unshaken yours.   *H.VIII.* iii. 2.

Why look you so upon me?
I am but sorry, not afear'd; delay'd,

FIDELITY,—*continued.*

But nothing alter'd: What I was, I am:
More straining on for plucking back. *W.T* iv. 3.

The loyalty well held to fools, does make
Our faith mere folly:—yet, he, that can endure
To follow with allegiance a fallen lord,
Does conquer him that did his master conquer,
And earns a place i' the story. *A.C.* iii. 11.

His words are bonds, his oaths are oracles;
His love sincere, his thoughts immaculate;
His tears, pure messengers sent from his heart;
His heart as far from fraud, as heaven from earth.
T.G. ii. 7.

Thou'rt a good boy: this secresy of thine shall be a tailor to thee, and shall make thee a new doublet and hose.
M.W. iii. 3.

For all the sun sees, or
The close earth wombs, or the profound seas hide
In unknown fathoms, will I break my oath
To this my fair belov'd. *W.T.* iv. 3.

Countrymen!
My heart doth joy, that yet, in all my life,
I found no man but he was true to me. *J.C.* v. 5.

Thou shalt not see me blush,
Nor change my countenance for this arrest;
A heart unspotted is not easily daunted.
The purest spring is not so free from mud,
As I am clear from treason to my sovereign.
H.VI. PT. II. iii. 1.

FILCHING.
His thefts were too open; his filching was like an unskilful singer, he kept not time. *M.W.* i. 3.

FILIAL INGRATITUDE (See also CHILDREN).
How sharper than a serpent's tooth it is
To have a thankless child. *K.L.* i. 4.

—— RESENTMENT OF PARENTAL WRONGS.
That drop of blood that's calm proclaims me bastard.
H. iv. 5.

FISHING.
There's nothing to be got now-a-days, unless thou canst fish for't. *P.P.* ii. 1.

FIT FOR A THIEF.
Every true man's apparel fits your thief: If it be too little for your thief, your true man thinks it big enough; if

FIT FOR A THIEF,—*continued.*
it be too big for your thief, your thief thinks it little enough:
so every true man's apparel fits your thief. *M. M.* iv. 2.

FLATTERY (See also ADULATION, PARAS*I*TES).
        O, that men's ears should be
To counsel deaf, but not to flattery! *T. A.* i. 2.
            The learned pate
• Ducks to the golden fool: All is oblique;
There's nothing level in our cursed natures,
But direct villainy. *T. A.* iv. 3.
Why this
Is the world's soul; and just of the same piece
Is every flatterer's spirit. *T. A.* iii. 2.
Every one that flatters thee,
Is no friend in misery. *Poems.*
He does me double wrong,
That wounds me with the flatteries of his tongue.
       R. II. iii. 2.
O villains, vipers, damn'd without redemption!
Dogs, easily won to fawn on any man! *R. II.* iii. 2.

Ah! when the means are gone that buy this praise,
The breath is gone whereof this praise is made. *T. A.* ii. 2.

He that loves to be flatter'd is worthy the flatterer.
Heavens, that I were a lord! *T. A.* i. 1.

Why, what a candy deal of courtesy
This fawning greyhound then did proffer me!
       H. IV. PT. I. i. 3.

But when I tell him, he hates flatterers,
He says, he does; being then most flatter'd. *J. C.* ii. 1.

Flattery's the bellows blows up sin. *P. P.* i. 2.

Because I cannot flatter, and speak fair,
Smile in men's faces, smooth, deceive, and cog,
Duck with French nods and apish courtesy,
I must be held a rancorous enemy. *R. III.* i. 3.
        Why these looks of care?
Thy flatterers yet wear silk, drink wine, lie soft;
Hug their diseas'd perfumes, and have forgot
That ever Timon was. Shame not these woods,
By putting on the cunning of a carper.
Be thou a flatterer now, and seek to thrive
By that which has undone thee: hinge thy knee,
And let his very breath whom thou'lt observe,
Blow off thy cap; praise his most vicious strain,
And call it excellent. *T. A.* iv. 3.

FLATTERY,—*continued.*

              I must prevent thee, Cimber.
These couchings, and these lowly courtesies,
Might fire the blood of ordinary men,
And turn pre-ordinance, and first decree,
Into the law of children. Be not fond,
To think that Cæsar bears such rebel blood,
That will be thaw'd from the true quality,
With that which melteth fools; I mean, sweet words,
Low-crooked curt'sies, and base spaniel fawning. *J. C.* iii. 1.

              For the love of grace,
Lay not that flattering unction to your soul.   *H.* iii. 4.

Nay, do not think I flatter:
For what advancement may I hope from thee,
That no revenue hast, but thy good spirits,
To feed and clothe thee? Why should the poor be flatter'd?
No, let the candied tongue lick absurd pomp,
And crook the pregnant hinges of the knee
Where thrift may follow fawning.   *H.* iii. 2.

'Tis holy sport to be a little vain
When the sweet breath of flattery conquers strife.
                                     C. E. iii. 2.

Sweet poison for the age's tooth.   *K. J.* i. 1.

They clap the lubber Ajax on the shoulder;
As if his foot were on brave Hector's breast. *T. C.* iii. 3.

FOLLOWERS.

I follow him to serve my turn upon him:
We cannot all be masters, nor all masters
Cannot be truly followed.   *O.* i. 1.

FOOL.

Why, thou silly gentleman!   *O.* i. 3.

    Let the doors be shut upon him; that he may play the fool nowhere but in his own house. *H.* iii. 1.

Fools on both sides!   *T. C.* i. 1.

Alas, poor fool! how have they baffled thee! *T. N.* v. 1.

I dare not call them fools; but this I think,
When they are thirsty, fools would fain have drink.
                                     L. L. v. 2.

This fellow's wise enough to play the fool;
And, to do that well, craves a kind of wit:
He must observe their mood on whom he jests,
The quality of persons, and the time;
And, like the haggard, check at every feather
That comes before his eye. This is a practice,

FOOL,—*continued.*
As full of labour as a wise man's art:
For folly, that he wisely shows, is fit;
But wise men, folly-fallen, quite taint their wit. *T. N.* iii 1.
A fool, a fool!—I met a fool i' the forest,
A motley fool;—a miserable world!
As I do live by food, I met a fool;
Who laid him down, and bask'd him in the sun,
And rail'd on lady Fortune in good terms,
In good set terms,—and yet a motley fool. *A. Y.* ii. 7.
I am sprighted with a fool. *Cym.* ii. 3.

FOOLERY.
Foolery, Sir, does walk about the orb, like the sun; it shines every where. *T. N.* iii. 1.
Observe him for the love of mockery. *T. N.* ii. 5.
What folly I commit, I dedicate to you. *T. C.* iii. 2.

FOOLING.
I do not like this fooling. *T. C.* v. 2.
They fool me to the top of my bent. *H.* iii. 2.
Beshrew me, the knight's in admirable fooling. *T. N.* ii. 3.

FOP.
The soul of this man is in his clothes. *A. W.* ii. 5.

——— FOREIGN.
Whose manners still our tardy apish nation,
Limps after, in base imitation. *R. II.* ii. 1.

FORBEARANCE (See STRENGTH).

FOREBODING.
Yet, again, methinks,
Some unborn sorrow, ripe in fortune's womb,
Is coming toward me. *R. II.* ii. 2.
A heavy summons lies like lead upon me. *M.* ii. 1.
I have an ill-divining soul:
Methinks I see thee now thou art below,
As one dead in the bottom of a tomb:
Either my eye-sight fails, or thou look'st pale. *R. J* iii. 5.
The skies look grimly,
And threaten present blusters. In my conscience,
The heavens with that we have in hand are angry,
And frown upon us. *W. T.* iii. 3.
For my mind misgives,
Some consequence, yet hanging in the stars,
Shall bitterly begin his fearful date

FOREBODING,—*continued.*
With this night's revels; and expire the term
Of a despised life, clos'd in my breast,
By some vile forfeit of untimely death. *R. J.* i. 4.
In what particular thought to work, I know not;
But, in the gross and scope of mine opinion,
This bodes some strange eruption to our state. *H.* i. 1.

FORE-DOOM.
　　　　Come, seeling night,
Scarf up the tender eye of pitiful day;
And, with thy bloody and invisible hand,
Cancel and tear to pieces that great bond
Which keeps me pale. *M.* iii. 2.
I will drain him dry as hay;
Sleep shall, neither night nor day,
Hang upon his pent-house lid;
He shall live a man forbid. *M.* i. 3.
　　　Ere the bat hath flown
His cloister'd flight; ere, to black Hecate's summons,
The shard-borne beetle, with his drowsy hums,
Hath rung night's yawning peal, there shall be done
A deed of dreadful note. *M.* iii. 2.

FORE-STALLER.
Hang'd himself on the expectation of plenty. *M.* ii. 3

FORGETFULNESS.
　　　'Tis far off;
And rather like a dream than an assurance
That my remembrance warrants. *T.* i. 2
　　　Like a dull actor now,
I have forgot my part, and I am out,
Even to a full disgrace. *C.* v. 3

FORGIVENESS.
　　　The rarer action is
In virtue than in vengeance: they being penitent,
The sole drift of my purpose doth extend
Not a frown further. *T.* v. 1.
Kneel not to me;
The power that I have on you, is to spare you;
The malice toward you, to forgive you: Live,
And deal with others better. *Cym.* v. 5.
　　　Then I'll look up;
My fault is past. But, O, what form of prayer
Can serve my turn? Forgive me my foul murder!—
That cannot be; since I am still possess'd

FOR   *Shakespearian Dictionary.*   FOR

FORGIVENESS,—*continued.*
    Of those effects for which I did the murder,—
My crown, mine own ambition, and my queen.
May one be pardon'd, and retain the offence?   *H.* iii. 3.
             His great offence is dead,
And deeper than oblivion do we bury
The incensing relicks of it.   *A.W.* v. 3.

FORLORN.
    Even as men wrecked upon a sand, that look to be washed
off the next tide.   *H.V.* iv. 1.

FORTITUDE.
    Nay, good my fellows, do not please sharp fate
To grace it with your sorrows; bid that welcome
Which comes to punish us, and we punish it,
Seeming to bear it lightly.   *A C.* iv. 12.
             In the reproof of chance
Lies the true proof of men: The sea being smooth,
How many shallow bauble boats dare sail
Upon her patient breast, making their way
With those of nobler bulk!
But let the ruffian Boreas once enrage
The gentle Thetis, and, anon, behold
The strong-ribb'd bark through liquid mountains cut,
Bounding between the two moist elements,
Like Perseus' horse: Where's then the saucy boat,
Whose weak untimber'd sides but even now
Co-rivall'd greatness? either to harbour fled,
Or made a toast for Neptune. Even so,
Doth valour's show, and valour's worth, divide
In storms of fortune: for, in her ray and brightness,
The herd hath more annoyance by the brize,
Than by the tiger; but when the splitting wind
Makes flexible the knees of knotted oaks,
And flies fled under shade,—why, then, the thing of courage,
As rous'd with rage, with rage doth sympathize,
And, with an accent tun'd in self-same key,
Returns to chiding fortune.   *T.C.* i. 3.
    Mine honour keeps the weather of my fate.   *T.C.* v. 3.

FORTUNE.
             I have upon a high and pleasant hill,
Feign'd Fortune to be thron'd: The base o' the mount
Is rank'd with all deserts, all kind of natures,
That labour on the bosom of this sphere,
To propagate their states: amongst them all,
Whose eyes are on this sovereign lady fix'd,
One do I personate of Timon's frame,

FORTUNE,—*continued.*
Whom Fortune, with her ivory hand, wafts to her,
Whose present grace to present slaves and servants
Translates his rivals.   *   *   *
All those which were his fellows but of late
(Some better than his value,) on the moment
Follow his strides, his lobbies fill with tendance,
Rain sacrificial whisperings in his ear,
Make sacred even his stirrup, and through him
Drink the free air.   *   *   *,
When Fortune, in her shift and change of mood,
Spurns down her late belov'd, all his dependants,
Which labour'd after him to the mountain's top,
Even on their knees and hands, let him slip down,
Not one accompanying his declining foot.   *T. A.* i. 1.
O Fortune, Fortune! all men call thee fickle.   *R. J.* iii. 5.
Will Fortune never come with both hands full,
But write her fair words still in foulest letters?
She either gives a stomach and no food,—
Such are the poor, in health;—or else a feast,
And takes away the stomach,—such are the rich,
That have abundance, and enjoy it not.   *H.IV.* PT. II. iv 4.
            Twinn'd brothers of one womb,—
Whose procreation, residence, and birth,
Scarce is dividant,—touch them with several fortunes,
The greater scorns the lesser: Not nature,
To whom all sores lay siege, can bear great fortune,
But by contempt of nature.
Raise me this beggar, and denude that lord;
The senator shall bear contempt hereditary,
The beggar, native honour.
It is the pasture lards the brother's sides,
The want that makes him lean.   *T. A.* iv. 3.
            Here's the scroll,
The continent, and summary, of my fortunes.   *M. V.* iii. 2.
            Why, then, you princes,
Do you with cheeks abash'd behold our works;
And think them shames, which are, indeed, nought else
But the protractive trials of great Jove,
To find persistive constancy in men?
The fineness of which metal is not found
In Fortune's love; for then, the bold and coward,
The wise and fool, the artist and unread,
The hard and soft, seem all affin'd and kin:
But in the wind and tempest of her frown,
Distinction, with a broad and powerful fan,
Puffing at all, winnows the light away;

FORTUNE,—*continued*.
And what hath mass, or matter, by itself
Lies, rich in virtue, and unmingled.   *T.C.* i. 3.
How some men creep in skittish Fortune's hall,
While others play the idiots in her eyes!
How one man eats into another's pride,
While pride is fasting in his wantonness!   *T.C.* iii. 3.
Many dream not to find, neither deserve,
And yet are steep'd in favours.   *Cym.* v. 4.
A thousand moral paintings I can show,
That shall demonstrate these quick blows of Fortune,
More pregnantly than words. Yet you do well,
To show lord Timon, that mean eyes have seen
The foot above the head.   *T.A.* i. 1.
        I see men's judgments are
A parcel of their fortunes; and things outward
To draw the inward quality after them,
To suffer all alike.   *A.C.* iii. 11.
        When Fortune means to men most good,
She looks upon them with a threatening eye.   *K.J.* iii. 4.
        Be cheerful; wipe thine eyes:
Some falls are means the happier to arise.   *Cym.* iv. 2.
A good man's fortune may grow out at heels.   *K.L.* ii. 2.
That strumpet, Fortune.   *K.J.* iii. 1.
Fortune brings in some boats that are not steer'd.
   Cym. iv. 3.
Since you will buckle Fortune on my back,
To bear her burden, whe'r I will or no,
I must have patience to endure the load.   *R.III.* iii. 7.
Though Fortune's malice overthrow my state,
My mind exceeds the compass of her wheel.
   H.VI. PT. III. iv. 3.
        Fortune is merry,
And in this mood will give us any thing.   *J.C.* iii. 2.
A man whom Fortune hath cruelly scratch'd.
   A.W. v. 2.

FORTUNE TELLING (See also CONJUROR).
    We do not know what is brought to pass under the profession of fortune-telling.   *M.W.* iv. 2.

FRACTURED LIMB, HEALED, STRONGER FOR THE ACCIDENT.
And therefore be assur'd, my good lord marshal,
If we do now make our atonement well,
Our peace will, like a broken limb united,
Grow stronger for the breaking   *H.IV.* PT. II. iv 1

FRAILTY.
Frailty, thy name is woman! *H.* 1. 2
   Sometimes we are devils to ourselves,
When we will tempt the frailty of our powers,
Presuming on their changeful potency. *T. C.* iv. 4
Nay, women are frail too:
Ay, as the glasses where they view themselves,
Which are as easy broke as they make forms. *M. M.* ii. 4.

Look, here comes one; a gentlewoman of mine,
Who, falling in the flames of her own youth,
Hath blistered her report. *M. M.* ii. 3.

FRIBBLES (See also COXCOMBS).
   Ah, how the poor world is pestered with such water-flies;
diminutives of nature! *T. C.* v. 1.

   I remember, when the fight was done,
When I was dry with rage and extreme toil,
Breathless and faint, leaning upon my sword,
Came there a certain lord, neat, trimly dress'd,
Fresh as a bridegroom; and his chin, new reap'd,
Show'd like a stubble land at harvest home.
He was perfumed like a milliner;
And 'twixt his finger and his thumb he held
A pouncet-box, which ever and anon
He gave his nose, and took't away again;—
Who, therewith angry, when it next came there,
Took it in snuff;—and still he smil'd, and talk'd;
And, as the soldiers bore dead bodies by,
He call'd them untaught knaves, unmannerly,
To bring a slovenly unhandsome corse
Betwixt the wind and his nobility.
With many holiday and lady terms
He question'd me: among the rest, demanded
My prisoners, in your Majesty's behalf.
I then, all smarting, with my wounds being cold,
To be so pester'd with a popinjay,
Out of my grief and my impatience,
Answer'd neglectingly, I know not what;
He should, or should not; for he made me mad,
To see him shine so brisk, and smell so sweet,
And talk so like a waiting gentlewoman,
Of guns, and drums, and wounds, (God save the mark!)
And telling me, the sovereign'st thing on earth
Was parmaceti, for an inward bruise;
And that it was great pity, so it was,
That villainous saltpetre should be digg'd
Out of the bowels of the harmless earth,

FRIBBLES,—*continued.*
Which many a good tall fellow had destroy'd
So cowardly; and, but for these vile guns,
He would himself have been a soldier.
This bald unjointed chat of his, my lord,
I answer'd indirectly, as I said;
And, I beseech you, let not this report
Come current for an accusation,
Betwixt my love and your high Majesty. *H. IV.* PT. I. i. 3.

FRIEND.
Since my dear soul was mistress of her choice,
And could of men distinguish her election,
She had seal'd thee for herself: for thou hast been
As one, in suffering all, that suffers nothing;
A man, that fortune's buffets and rewards
Hast ta'en with equal thanks; and bless'd are those
Whose blood and judgment are so well commingled,
That they are not a pipe for Fortune's finger
To sound what stop she please: Give me that man
That is not passion's slave, and I will wear him
In my heart's core, ay, in my heart of heart,
As I do thee. *H.* iii. 2.

Who, in want, a hollow friend doth try,
Directly seasons him an enemy. *H.* iii. 2.

O, you gods! think I, what need we have any friends? they were the most needless creatures living, if we should never have need of them? They would most resemble sweet instruments hung up in cases, that keep their sounds to themselves.. We are born to do benefits. O what a precious comfort 'tis to have so many like brothers, commanding one another's fortunes! *T. A.* i. 2.

Commend me to him; I will send his ransom;
And, being enfranchis'd, bid him come to me;—
'Tis not enough to help the feeble up,
But to support him after. *T. A.* i. 1.

The dearest friend to me, the kindest man,
The best-condition'd and unweary'd spirit
In doing courtesies; and one in whom
The antient Roman honour more appears,
Than any that draws breath in Italy. *M. V.* iii. 2.

I count myself in nothing else so happy,
As in a soul remembering my good friends;
And as my fortune ripens with my love,
It shall be still my true love's recompense. *R. II.* ii. 3.

We still have slept together,
Rose at an instant, learn'd, play'd, eat together;

FRIEND,—*continued.*

And wheresoe'er we went, like Juno's swans
Still we went coupled and inseparable. *A. Y.* i. 3.
      So we grew together,
Like to a double cherry, seeming parted,
But yet a union in partition,
Two lovely berries moulded on one stem. *M. N.* iii. 2.

Pay him six thousand, and deface the bond,
Double six thousand, and then treble that,
Before a friend of this description
Shall lose a hair through my Bassanio's fault. *M. V.* iii. 2.

The amity that wisdom knits not, folly may easily untie.
                                          T. C. ii. 3.

I should fear those, who dance before me now,
Would one day stamp upon me: It has been done;
Men shut their doors against a setting sun. *T. A.* i. 2.

Every man will be thy friend
While thou hast wherewithal to spend;
But if store of crowns be scant,
No man will supply thy want. *Poems.*

There are no tricks in plain and simple faith;
But hollow men, like horses hot at hand,
Make gallant show and promise of their mettle;
But when they should endure the bloody spur,
They fall their crests, and, like deceitful jades,
Sink in the trial. *J. C.* iv. 2.

Is all the counsel that we two have shar'd,
The sisters' vows, the hours that we have spent,
When we have chid the hasty-footed time
For parting us,—O, is all now forgot?
All school-days' friendship, childhood innocence?
                                            M. N. iii. 2.

The great man down, you mark his favourite flies,
The poor advanc'd makes friends of enemies.
And hitherto doth love on fortune tend;
For who not needs, shall never lack a friend;
And who in want a hollow friend doth try,
Directly seasons him an enemy. *H.* iii. 2.

Friendship's full of dregs. *T. A.* i. 2.

      Canst thou the conscience lack,
To think I shall lack friends? Secure thy heart;
If I could broach the vessels of my love,
And try the argument of hearts by borrowing,
Men, and men's fortunes, could I frankly use,
As I can bid thee speak. *T. A.* ii. 2.

FRIEND,—*continued*.
Thou dost conspire against thy friend, Iago,
If thou but think'st him wrong'd, and mak'st his ear
A stranger to thy thoughts.   *O.* iii. 3

        O let me twine
Mine arms about that body, where against
My grained ash an hundred times hath broke,
And scar'd the moon with splinters! Here I clip
The anvil of my sword; and do contest
As hotly and as nobly with thy love,
As ever in ambitious strength I did
Contend against thy valour.   *C.* iv. 5.

Friendship is constant in all other things,
Save in the office and affairs of love.   *M. A.* ii. 1.

By heaven, I cannot flatter! I defy
The tongues of soothers; but a braver place
In my heart's·love, hath no man than yourself;
Nay, task me to my word; approve me, lord.
    H. IV. PT. I. iv. 1.

      Brutus hath riv'd my heart:
A friend should bear his friend's infirmities,
But Brutus makes mine greater than they are.   *J. C.* iv. 3.

Give him all kindness: I had rather have
Such men my friends, than enemies.   *J. C.* v. 4.

    That we have been familiar,
Ingrate forgetfulness shall poison, rather
Than pity note how much.   *C.* v. 2.

        Now do I play the touch,
To try if thou be current gold indeed.   *R. III.* iv. 2.

——————— COOLING.
I have not from your eyes that gentleness,
And show of love, as I was wont to have:
You bear too stubborn, and too strange a hand,
Over your friend that loves you.   *J. C.* i. 2.

      Thou hast describ'd
A hot friend cooling: Ever note, Lucilius,
When love begins to sicken and decay,
It useth an enforced ceremony.   *J. C.* iv. 2.

      Mere fetches:
The images of revolt and flying off.   *K. L.* ii. 4.

FRIENDSHIP ASSIMILATES FRIENDS.
        For in companions
That do converse and waste the time together,
Whose souls do bear an equal yoke of love,

Shakespearian Dictionary.

FRIENDSHIP ASSIMILATES FRIENDS,—*continued.*
There must be needs a like proportion
Of lineaments, of manners, and of spirit. *M. V.* iii. 4.

FRIGIDITY (See also COLDNESS).
What a frosty-spirited rogue is this! *H. IV.* PT. I. ii. 3.

FROWN.
He parted frowning from me, as if ruin
Leap'd from his eyes. *H. VIII.* ii. 2

FUNERAL RITES.
Her obsequies have been as far enlarg'd
As we have warranty: Her death was doubtful;
And, but that great command o'er-sways the order,
She should in ground unsanctified have lodg'd
Till the last trumpet; for charitable prayers,
Shards, flints, and pebbles, should be thrown on her;
Yet here she is allow'd her virgin rites,
Her maiden strewments, and the bringing home
Of bell, and burial. *H* v. 1.

Let it be so, and let Andronicus
Make this his latest farewell to their souls.
In peace and honour rest you here, my sons;
Rome's readiest champions, repose you here,
Secure from worldly chances and mishaps. *Tit. And.* i. 2

——— TEARS.
Though fond nature bids us all lament,
Yet nature's tears are reason's merriment. *R. J.* iv. 5

But yet
It is our trick; nature her custom holds,
Let shame say what it will. *H.* iv. 7

Comfort, dear mother; God is much displeas'd,
That you take with unthankfulness his doing;
In common worldly things, 'tis call'd—ungrateful,
With dull unwillingness to repay a debt,
Which with a bounteous hand was kindly lent. *R. III.* ii. 2

FURY.
O, I warrant, how he mammock'd it! *C.* i. 3

Let me speak; and let me rail so high,
That the false housewife, Fortune, break her wheel,
Provok'd by my offence. *A. C.* iv. 13

I understand a fury in your words,
But not the words. *O.* iv. 2.

FUTURITY.
O that a man might know
The end of this day's business, ere it come! *J. C.* v. 1.

G.

GAIETY.
See, where she comes, apparell'd like the spring. *P. P.* i. 1.
Flora, peering in April's front. *W. T.* iv. 3.

GALLANTS.
Trim gallants, full of courtship and of state. *L. L.* v. 2.
Travell'd gallants
That fill the court with quarrels, talk, and tailors.
H. VIII. i. 3.

GENTLEMAN.
I'll be sworn thou art;
Thy tongue, thy face, thy limbs, actions, and spirit,
Do give thee five-fold blazon. *T. N.* i. 4.
A gentleman born, master parson, who writes himself armigero; on any bill, warrant, quittance, or obligation, armigero. *M. W.* i. 1.

GENTLEMEN.
We are gentlemen,
That neither in our hearts, nor outward eyes,
Envy the great, nor do the low despise. *P. P.* ii. 3.

GEOGRAPHY.
Peering in maps for ports, and piers, and roads. *M. V.* i. 1.

GHOST (See also APPARITIONS, SPIRITS, TERROR, GUILT).
For it is, as the air, invulnerable,
And our vain blows malicious mockery. *H.* i. 1.
Angels, and ministers of grace, defend us!
Be thou a spirit of health, or goblin damn'd,
Bring with thee airs from heaven, or blasts from hell,
Be thy intents wicked or charitable,
Thou com'st in such a questionable shape,
That I will speak to thee. *H.* i. 4.

But, soft: behold! lo where it comes again!
I'll cross it, though it blast me.—Stay, illusion!
If thou hast any sound, or use a voice,
Speak to me. *H.* i. 1.
What may this mean,
That thou, dead corse, again, in complete steel,
Revisit'st thus the glimpses of the moon,
Making night hideous; and we, fools of nature,
So horridly to shake our disposition,

GHOST.—*continued.*

With thoughts beyond the reaches of our souls?
Say, why is this? *H.* i. 4.
    My hour is almost come,
When I to sulphurous and tormenting flames
Must render up myself. *H.* i. 5.
     O, answer me:
Let me not burst in ignorance! but tell,
Why thy canoniz'd bones, hears'd in death,
Have burst their cerements! why the sepulchre,
Wherein we saw thee quietly inurn'd
Hath op'd his ponderous and marble jaws,
To cast thee up again. *H.* i. 4.
  Why, what care I? If thou canst nod, speak too,—
If charnel-houses, and our graves, must send
Those that we bury, back, our monuments
Shall be the maws of kites. *M.* iii. 4.
The ghost of Cæsar hath appear'd to me
Two several times by night: at Sardis, once;
And, this last night, here in Philippi fields.
I know, my hour is come. *J.C.* v. 5.

GIFTS (See also LOVE TOKENS).
 Well, God give them wisdom that have it: and those that
are fools, let them use their talents. *T. N.* i. 5.
 A giving hand, though foul, shall have fair praise.
L. L. iv. 1.
     Gifts then seem
Most precious, when the giver we esteem. *Poems.*
Win her with gifts, if she respect not words;
Dumb jewels often, in their silent kind,
More quick than words, do move a woman's mind.
T. G. iii. 1.
She prizes not such trifles as these are:
The gifts, she looks from me, are pack'd and lock'd
Up in my heart; which I have given already,
But not deliver'd. *W. T.* iv. 3.
Seven hundred pounds, and possibilities, is good gifts.
M. W. i. 1.
I am not in the giving vein to day. *R. III.* iv. 2.

GLORY.
 Glory is like a circle in the water,
Which never ceaseth to enlarge itself,
'Till, by broad spreading, it disperse to nought.
H. VI. PT. I. i. 2.

GOLD (See also MONEY).

Saint-seducing gold.   *R. J.* i. 1.

O thou sweet king-killer, and dear divorce
'Twixt natural son and sire! thou bright defiler
Of Hymen's purest bed! thou valiant Mars!
Thou ever young, fresh, lov'd, and delicate wooer,
Whose blush doth thaw the consecrated snow
That lies on Dian's lap! thou visible god,
That solder'st close impossibilities,
And mak'st them kiss! that speak'st with every tongue,
To every purpose!   *T. A.* iv. 3.

For this the foolish over-careful fathers
Have broke their sleep with thoughts, their brains with care,
Their bones with industry;
For this they have engrossed and pil'd up
The canker'd heaps of strange-achieved gold;
For this they have been thoughtful to invest
Their sons with arts, and martial exercises:
When, like the bee, tolling from every flower,
The virtuous sweets;
Our thighs are pack'd with wax, our mouths with honey,
We bring it to the hive; and, like the bees,
Are murder'd for our pains.   *H. IV.* PT. II. iv. 4.

           And 'tis gold
Which makes the true man kill'd, and saves the thief;
Nay, sometimes hangs both thief and true man: what
Can it not do, and undo?   *Cym.* ii. 3.

Thus much of this, will make black white; foul, fair;
Wrong, right; base, noble; old, young; coward, valiant.
Ha, ye gods! Why this? What, this, you gods? Why this
Will lug your priests and servants from your sides;
Pluck stout men's pillows from below their heads:
This yellow slave
Will knit and break religions; bless the accurs'd;
Make the hoar leprosy ador'd; place thieves,
And give them title, knee, and approbation,
With senators on the bench: this is it,
That makes the wappen'd widow wed again;
She, whom the spital house, and ulcerous sores,
Would cast the gorge at; this embalms and spices
To the April day again.   *T. A.* iv. 3.

There is thy gold; worse poison to men's souls,
Doing more murders in this loathsome world,
Than these poor compounds that thou mayest not sell.
                                       R. J. v. 1.

GOLD,—*continued.*
        See, sons,—what things you are!
How quickly nature falls into revolt,
When gold becomes her object.   *H. IV.* PT. II. iv. 4
Know'st thou not any whom corrupting gold
Would tempt into a close exploit of death?   *R. III.* iv. 2.
I know a discontented gentleman,
Whose humble means match not his haughty mind:
Gold were as good as twenty orators,
And will, no doubt, tempt him to any thing.   *R. III.* iv. 2.
O thou touch of hearts!   *T. A.* iv. 3.

GOOD MAN, COMMERCIAL DEFINITION OF A.
    My meaning in saying he is a good man, is to have you understand me, he is sufficient.   *M. V.* i. 3.

GOOD MANNERS.
    When good manners shall lie all in one or two men's hands, and they unwash'd too, 'tis a foul thing. *R. J.* i. 5.

GOODNESS TO BE ALWAYS PREFERRED.
    Angels are bright still, though the brightest fell. *M.* iv. 3.

GOOD THINGS.
    Well, I cannot last for ever: But it was always yet the trick of our English nation, if they have a good thing, to make it too common. If you will needs say I am an old man, you should give me rest. I would to God my name were not so terrible to the enemy as it is. I were better to be eaten to death with rust, than to be scoured to nothing with perpetual motion.   *H. IV.* PT. II. i. 2.

GOOD WOMEN.
    One in ten, quoth a'! an we might have a good woman born but every blazing star, or at an earthquake, 'twould mend the lottery well: a man may draw his heart out ere he pluck one.   *A. W.* i. 3.

GOOD WORKS
    How far that little candle throws his beams!
So shines a good deed in a naughty world. *M. V.* v. i.

GORMANDIZING.
    Fat paunches have lean pates; and dainty bits
Make rich the ribs, but bank'rout quite the wits. *L. L.* i. 1.
Make less thy body, hence, and more thy grace:
Leave gormandizing.   *H. IV.* PT. II. v. 5.
        Thou shalt not gormandize,
As thou has done with me:
And sleep, and snore, and rend apparel out. *M. V.* ii. 5.

GRANDAM.
A grandam's name is little less in love,
Than is the doating title of a mother;
They are as children, but one step below;
Even of your mettle, of your very blood. *R. III.* iv. 4.

GRATITUDE.
    I have five hundred crowns,
The thrifty hire I sav'd under your father,
Which I did store to be my foster nurse,
When service should in my old limbs lie lame,
And unregarded age in corners thrown;
Take that: and He that doth the ravens feed,
Yea, providently caters for the sparrow,
Be comfort to mine age.   *A.Y.* ii. 3.
Thou canst not in the course of gratitude, but be a diligent
 follower of mine.   *Cym.* iii. 5.
    Kind gentleman, your pains
Are register'd, where every day I turn
The leaf to read them.   *M.* i. 3.
Let never day nor night unhallow'd pass,
But still remember what the Lord hath done.
         H.VI. PT. II. ii. 1.
   Would thou had'st less deserv'd;
That the proportion both of thanks and payment
Might have been mine!   *M.* i. 4.

GRAVE.
Secure from worldly chances and mishaps!
Here lurks no treason, here no envy swells,
Here grow no damned grudges; here are no storms,
No noise, but silence and eternal sleep. *Tit. And.* i. 2.
The grave doth gape, and doting death is near. *H.V.* ii. 1.
     Let us
Find out the prettiest daisied spot we can,
And make him, with our pikes and partizans,
A grave.   *Cym.* iv. 2.

GRAVE-STONE.
And let my grave-stone be your oracle. *T. A.* v. 3.

GRAVITATION.
  —— And you may know by my size, that I have a kind
of alacrity in sinking; if the bottom were as deep as hell,
I should down.   *M.W.* iii. 5

GRAVITY, AFFECTED.
There are a sort of men, whose visages
Do cream and mantle, like a standing pond;

GRAVITY, Affected,—*continued.*
And do a wilful stillness entertain,
With purpose to be dress'd in an opinion
Of wisdom, gravity, profound conceit;
As who should say, I am Sir Oracle,
And when I ope my lips, let no dog bark! *M. V.* i. 1.

GREATNESS (See also Kings, Authority).
Some are born great:—some achieve greatness;—some have greatness thrust upon them. *T. N.* iii. 4.

Rightly to be great,
Is, not to stir without great argument;
But greatly to find quarrel in a straw,
When honour's at the stake. *H.* iv. 4.

Would you praise Cæsar, say,—Cæsar; go no further.
A. C. iii. 2.

Why, man, he doth bestride the narrow world,
Like a Colossus; and we petty men
Walk under his huge legs, and peep about,
To find ourselves dishonourable graves. *J. C.* i. 2.

This man
Is now become a god; and Cassius is
A wretched creature, and must bend his body,
If Cæsar carelessly but nod at him. *J. C.* i. 2.

The abuse of greatness is, when it disjoins
Remorse from power. *J. C.* ii. 1.

Great men may jest with saints: 'tis wit in them:
But, in the less, foul profanation.
That, in the captain's but a choleric word,
Which in the soldier is flat blasphemy. *M. M.* ii. 2.

GREETING (See also Salutation).
A hundred thousand welcomes: I could weep,
And I could laugh; I am light, and heavy: Welcome:
A curse begin at very root of his heart,
That is not glad to see thee! *C.* ii. 1.

The Lord in heaven bless thee, noble Harry! *H. V.* iv. 1.

God-a-mercy, old heart! thou speakest cheerfully.
H. V. iv. 1.

Why have you stolen upon us thus! You come not
Like Cæsar's sister; the wife of Antony
Should have an army for an usher, and
The neighs of horse to tell of her approach,
Long ere she did appear; the trees by the way,
Should have borne men; and expectation fainted.
Longing for what it had not: nay, the dust

GREETING,—*continued.*
Should have ascended to the roof of heaven,
Rais'd by your populous troops : But you are come
A market-maid to Rome; and have prevented
The ostentation of our love, which, left unshown,
Is often left unlov'd : we should have met you
By sea, and land ; supplying every stage
With an augmented greeting. *A. C* iii. 6.

———— SIMPLE.
             Trust me, sweet,
Out of this silence yet I pick'd a welcome;
And in the modesty of fearful duty
I read as much, as from the rattling tongue
Of saucy and audacious eloquence.
Love, therefore, and tongue-tied simplicity
In least, speak most, to my capacity. *M. N.* v. 1.

GRIEF (See also LAMENTATION, SORROW, TEARS).
          Men
Can counsel, and speak comfort to that grief
Which they themselves not feel ; but, tasting it,
Their counsel turns to passion, which before
Would give preceptial medicine to rage,
Fetter strong madness with a silken thread,
Charm ache with air, and agony with words.
No, no ; 'tis all men's office to speak patience
To those that wring under a load of sorrow;
But no man's virtue, nor sufficiency,
To be so moral, when he shall endure
The like himself: therefore give me no counsel;
My griefs cry louder than advertisement. *M. A.* v. 1.

When remedies are past, the griefs are ended,
By seeing the worst, which late on hopes depended.
To mourn a mischief that is past and gone,
Is the next way to draw new mischief on.
What cannot be preserv'd when fortune takes,
Patience her injury a mockery makes.
The robb'd, that smiles, steals something from the thief:
He robs himself, that spends a bootless grief. *O.* i. 3.

I cannot but remember such things were
That were most precious to me. *M.* iv. 3.

Why tell you me of moderation?
The grief is fine, full, perfect, which I taste,
And no less in a sense as strong
As that which causeth it: How can I moderate it ?
If I could temporize with my affection,
Or brew it to a weak and colder palate,

GRI   **Shakespearian Dictionary.**   GRI

GRIEF,—*continued.*
The like allayment could I give my grief;
My love admits no qualifying cross:
No more my grief, in such a precious loss.   *T.C.* iv. 4.

        The heart hath treble wrong,
When it is barr'd the aidance of the tongue.   *Poems.*

        Some grief shows much of love;
But much of grief shows still some want of wit.
                                           R.J. iii. 5.

        My grief lies all within,
And these external manners and laments
Are merely shadows to the unseen grief,
That swells with silence in the tortur'd soul.   *R.II.* iv. 1.

A plague of sighing and grief! it blows a man up like a bladder.   *H.IV.* PT. I. ii. 4.

The gods rebuke me, but it is a tidings
To wash the eyes of kings.   *A.C.* v. 1.

I pray thee, cease thy counsel,
Which falls into mine ears as profitless
As water in a sieve: give not me counsel,
Nor let no comforter delight mine ear,
But such a one whose wrongs do suit with mine.
                                           M.A. v. 1.

Give sorrow words: the grief that does not speak,
Whispers the o'er-fraught heart, and makes it break.
                                           M. iv. 3.

              Like the lily,
That once was mistress of the field, and flourish'd,
I'll hang my head, and perish.   *H.VIII.* iii. 1.

          Your cause of sorrow
Must not be measur'd by its worth, for then
It hath no end.   *M.* v. 7.

Is there no pity sitting in the clouds,
That sees into the bottom of my grief?   *R.J.* iii. 5

Had he the motive and the cue for passion,
That I have, he would drown the stage with tears,
And cleave the general ear with horrid speech;
Make mad the guilty, and appal the free,
Confound the ignorant, and amaze, indeed,
The very faculties of eyes and ears.   *H.* ii. 2.

Thou canst not speak of what thou dost not feel:
Wert thou as young as I, Juliet thy love,
An hour but married, Tybalt murdered,
Doating like me, and like me banished,
Then might'st thou speak, then might'st thou tear thy hair,

GRIEF,—*continued.*
And fall upon the ground, as I do now,
Taking the measure of an unmade grave.   *R. J.* iii. 3.
    Grief softens the mind, and makes it fearful and degenerate.   *H. VI.* PT. II. iv. 4

         There she shook
The holy water from her heavenly eyes,
And clamour-moisten'd: then away she started,
To deal with grief alone.   *K. L.* iv. 3

    O, insupportable! O, heavy hour!
Methinks it should be now a huge eclipse
Of sun and moon, and that the affrighted globe
Should yawn at alteration.   *O.* v. 2.

      Good, my lords,
I am not prone to weeping, as our sex
Commonly are; the want of which vain dew,
Perchance, shall dry your pities; but I have
That honourable grief lodg'd here, which burns
Worse than tears drown.   *W. T.* ii. 1.

     Woe doth the heavier sit,
Where it perceives it is but faintly borne.   *R. II.* i. 3.

My lord;—I found the prince in the next room,
Washing with kindly tears his gentle cheeks;
With such a deep demeanour in great sorrow,
That tyranny, which never quaff'd but blood,
Would, by beholding him, have wash'd his knife
With gentle eye-drops.   *H. IV.* PT. II. iv. 4.

    One of the prettiest touches of all, and that which angled for mine eyes (caught the water, though not the fish) was, when at the relation of the queen's death, with the manner how she came to it, (bravely confessed and lamented by the king), how attentiveness wounded his daughter: till, from one sign of dolour to another, she did, with an *alas!* I would fain say, bleed tears; for, I am sure, my heart wept blood. Who was most marble there, changed colour; some swooned, all sorrowed: if all the world could have seen it, the woe had been universal.   *W. T.* v. 2.

Care is no cure, but rather corrosive,
For things that are not to be remedied.   *H. VI.* PT. I. iii. 3.

    Why do you keep alone,
Of sorries' fancies your companions making?
Using those thoughts, which should indeed have died
With them they think on? Things without all remedy
Should be without regard.   *M.* iii. 2.

GRIEF.—*continued.*

These tidings nip me: and I hang the head,
As flowers with frost, or grass beat down with storms.
Tit. And. iv. 4.

    Nor doth the general care
Take hold on me; for my particular grief
Is of so flood-gate and o'erbearing nature,
That it engluts and swallows other sorrows,
And it is still itself.   *O.* i. 3.

Many a morning hath he there been seen,
With tears augmenting the fresh morning's dew,
Adding to clouds more clouds with his deep sighs.
R. J. i. 1.

O, I could play the woman with mine eyes,
And braggart with my tongue!   *M.* iv. 3.

Now my soul's palace is become a prison:
Ah, would she break from hence! that this my body
Might in the ground be closed up in rest;
For never henceforth shall I joy again. *H. VI.* PT. III. ii. 1.

How now! has sorrow made thee dote already?
Tit. And. iii. 2.

His grief grew puissant, and the strings of life
Began to crack.   *K. L.* v. 3.

But let not therefore my good friends be griev'd,
Nor construe any further my neglect,
Than that poor Brutus, with himself at war,
Forgets the shows of love to other men.   *J. C.* i. 2.

All things that we ordained festival,
Turn from their office to black funeral:
Our instruments, to melancholy bells:
Our wedding cheer, to a sad burial feast;
Our solemn hymns to sullen dirges change;
Our bridal flowers serve for a buried corse,
And all things change them to the contrary.   *R. J.* iv. 5.

    Once a day I'll visit
The chapel where they lie: and tears, shed there,
Shall be my recreation: so long as Nature
Will bear up with this exercise, so long
I daily vow to use it.   *W. T.* iii. 2.

O break, my heart!—poor bankrupt, break at once!
To prison, eyes! ne'er look on liberty!
Vile earth, to earth resign; end, motion, here;
And thou, and Romeo, press one heavy bier. *R. J.* iii. 2.

    Sorrow, and grief of heart,
Made him speak fondly, like a frantic man.   *R. II.* iii. 3

GRIEF,—*continued*.
Most subject is the fattest soil to weeds;
And he, the noble image of my youth,
Is overspread with them: therefore my grief
Stretches itself beyond the hour of death.
H. IV. PT. II. iv. 4.

We must be patient: but I cannot choose but weep, to think they should lay him i' the cold ground. *H.* iv. 5.

Bind up those tresses: O, what love I note
In the fair multitude of those her hairs!
Where but by chance a silver drop hath fallen,
Even to that drop ten thousand wiry friends
Do glew themselves in sociable grief;
Like true, inseparable, faithful loves,
Sticking together in calamity. *K. J.* iii 4.

There's nothing in this world can make me joy:
Life is as tedious as a twice-told tale,
Vexing the dull ear of a drowsy man. *K. J.* iii. 4.

Every one can master a grief, but he that has it.
M. A. iii. 2.

What fates impose, that men must needs abide;
It boots not to resist both wind and tide.
H. VI. PT. III. iv. 3.

Wise men ne'er sit and wail their loss,
But cheerly seek how to redress their harms.
H. VI. PT. III. v. 4.

What is he whose grief
Bears such an emphasis? whose phrase of sorrow
Conjures the wand'ring stars, and makes them stand
Like wonder-wounded hearers? *H.* v. i.

Friend, I owe more tears
To this dead man, than thou shalt see me pay. *J. C.* v. 3.

Strange it is,
That nature must compel us to lament
Our most persisted deeds. *A. C.* v. 1.

Great griefs, I see, medicine the less. *Cym.* iv. 2.

What's gone, and what's past help,
Should be past grief. *W. T.* iii. 2.

Spirits of peace, where are ye? Are ye all gone?
And leave me here in wretchedness behind ye?
H. VIII. iv. 2.

O, that I were as great
As is my grief! *R. II.* iii 3.

GRIEF,—continued.
     And but he's something stain'd
With grief, that's beauty's canker, thou might'st call him
A goodly person.   *T.* i. 2.

I have in equal balance justly weigh'd,
What wrongs our arms may do, what wrongs we suffer,
And find our griefs heavier than our offences.
              H. IV. PT. II. iv. 1.

     All of us have cause
To wail the dimming of our shining star;
But none can cure their harms by wailing them.
              R. III. ii. 2.

Why, courage, then! what cannot be avoided,
'Twere childish weakness to lament, or fear.
              H. VI. PT. III. v. 4.

———— MATERNAL.
And, father cardinal, I have heard you say,
That we shall see and know our friends in heaven
If that be true, I shall see my boy again;
For, since the birth of Cain, the first male child,
To him that did but yesterday suspire,
There was not such a gracious creature born.
But now will canker sorrow eat my bud,
And chase the native beauty from his cheek;
And he will look as hollow as a ghost,
As dim and meagre as an ague's fit;
And so he'll die; and, rising so again,
When I shall meet him in the court of heaven
I shall not know him: therefore, never, never,
Must I behold my pretty Arthur more. *K. J.* iii. 4.

He talks to me that never had a son.   *K. J.* iii. 4

Grief fills the room up of my absent child,
Lies in his bed, walks up and down with me;
Puts on his pretty looks, repeats his words,
Remembers me of all his gracious parts,
Stuffs out his vacant garments with his form;
Then have I reason to be fond of grief.
Fare you well: had you such a loss as I,
I could give better comfort than you do.—
I will not keep this form upon my head,
When there is such disorder in my wit.
O lord, my boy, my Arthur, my fair son!
My life, my joy, my food, my all the world!
My widow-comfort, and my sorrow's cure! *K. J.* iii. 4.

GRIEF AND JOY.
The violence of either grief or joy,
Their own enactures with themselves destroy:
Where joy most revels, grief doth most lament;
Grief joys, joy grieves, on slender accident. *H.* iii. 2.

GROUP.
O thus, quoth Dighton, lay the gentle babes,—
Thus, thus, quoth Forrest, girdling one another,
Within their alabaster innocent arms. *R. III.* iv. 3

GUILT.
So full of artless jealousy is guilt,
It spills itself in fearing to be spilt. *H.* iv. 5.
        Guiltiness will speak
Though tongues were out of use. *O.* v. 1.
Have you heard the argument? Is there no offence in it?
H. iii. 2.
And then it started like a guilty thing
Upon a fearful summons. *H.* i. 1
The guilt being great, the fear doth still exceed. *Poems.*
I'll haunt thee like a wicked conscience still,
That mouldeth goblins swift as frenzy thoughts. *T.C.* v. ii.
        Infected minds
To their deaf pillows will discharge their secrets. *M.* v. 1.
My words fly up, my thoughts remain below;
Words without thoughts never to heaven go. *H.* iii. 3.

GUILTY CAREER, THE CLOSE OF A.
I have liv'd long enough; my way of life
Is fallen into the sear, the yellow leaf;
And that which should accompany old age,
As honour, love, obedience, troops of friends,
I must not look to have; but, in their stead,
Curses not loud, but deep, mouth-honour, breath,
Which the poor heart would fain deny, but dare not.
M. v. 3.

―――――― PURSUITS.
What win the guilty, gaining what they seek?
A dream, a breath, a froth of fleeting joy!
For one sweet grape, who will the vine destroy?
Who buys a minute's mirth to wail a week?
Or sells eternity to get a toy? *Poems.*

H.

HABIT (See also CUSTOM).
For use almost can change the stamp of nature
And either curb the devil, or throw him out
With wondrous potency. *H.* iii. 4.

The tyrant custom, most grave senators,
Hath made the flinty and steel couch of war
My thrice driven bed of down. *O.* i. 3.

HABITATION.
Fore God, you have here a goodly dwelling, and a rich.
H. IV. PT. II. v. 3.

——— HUMBLE.
Stoop, boys: this gate
Instructs you how to adore the heavens; and bows you
To morning's holy office: The gates of monarchs
Are arch'd so high, that giants jet through
And keep their impious turbans on, without
Good morrow to the sun. Hail, thou fair heaven!
We house i' the rock, yet use thee not so hardly
As prouder livers do. *Cym.* iii. 3.

HALTER.
A halter, gratis; nothing else, for God's sake. *M. V.* iv. 7

HAND.
O, that her hand,
In whose comparison all whites are ink,
Writing their own reproach; To whose soft seizure
The cygnet's down is harsh, and spirit of sense
Hard as the palm of ploughmen. *T. C.* i. 1.

HANGER-ON.
O Lord! he will hang upon him like a disease: he is
sooner caught than the pestilence, and the taker runs presently mad. *M. A.* i. 1.

HANGING.
O the charity of a penny cord! it sums up thousands in
a trice: you have no true debitor and creditor but it: of
what's past, is, and to come, the discharge: Your neck, Sir,
is pen, book, and counters, so the acquittance follows.
Cym. v. 4.

A heavy reckoning for you, Sir; but the comfort is, you
shall be called to no more payments, fear no more tavern
bills: which are often the sadness of parting, as the procuring of mirth: you come in faint for want of meat, depart

HAN **Shakespearian Dictionary.** HAT

HANGING,—*continued.*
reeling with too much drink;— * * * purse and brain both
empty. *Cym.* v. 4.
 Hanging is the word, Sir; if you be ready for that, you
are well cook'd. *Cym.* v. 4.
 I have great comfort from this fellow: methinks he hath
no drowning mark upon him; his complexion is perfect
gallows. Stand fast, good fate, to his hanging! make the
rope of his destiny our cable, for our own doth little advantage! If he be not born to be hang'd, our case is miserable.
T. i. 1.

HANGMEN.
 Some of the best of them were hereditary hangmen.
C. ii. 1.

HAPPINESS.
         Hitting
Each object with a joy; the counterchange
Is severally in all. *Cym.* v. 5.
 But, O, how bitter a thing it is to look into happiness
through another man's eyes! *A.Y.* v. 2.

———— CONNUBIAL.
      If it were now to die,
'Twere now to be most happy; for, I fear,
My soul hath her content so absolute,
That not another comfort like to this
Succeeds in unknown fate. *O.* ii. 1.

HARMONY OF THE SPHERES.
There's not the smallest orb which thou behold'st,
But in his motion like an angel sings,
Still quiring to the young-eyed cherubim:
Such harmony is in immortal souls;—
But, whilst this muddy vesture of decay
Doth grossly close it in, we cannot hear it. *M.V.* v. 1.

HATRED.
Were half to half the world by th' ears, and he
Upon my party, I'd revolt, to make
Only my wars with him: he is a lion
That I am proud to hunt. *C.* i. 1.
     Nor sleep, nor sanctuary,
Being naked, sick: nor fane, nor capitol,
The prayers of priests, nor times of sacrifice,
Embarquements all of fury, shall lift up
Their rotten privilege and custom 'gainst
My hate to Marcius: where I find him, were it
At home, upon my brother's guard, even there.

HATRED,—*continued.*
Against the hospitable canon, would I
Wash my fierce hand in 's heart. *C.* i. 10.
Cancel his bond of life, dear God, I pray,
That I may live to say,—the dog is dead! *R. III.* iv. 4.
How like a fawning publican he looks!
I hate him, for he is a christian:
But more, for that, in low simplicity,
He lends out money gratis, and brings down
The rate of usance here with us in Venice. *M.V.* i. 2.
　　Alas, poor York! but that I hate thee deadly,
I should lament thy miserable state.
I pr'ythee, grieve, to make me merry, York;
Stamp, rave, and fret, that I may sing and dance.
　　　　　　　　　　　　H.VI. PT. III. i. 4.
I'll not be made a soft and dull-ey'd fool,
To shake the head, relent, and sigh, and yield
To christian intercessors. *M.V.* iii. 3.
If I can catch him once upon the hip,
I will feed fat the antient grudge I bear him. *M.V.* i. 3.

HEART.
　　A good leg will fall; a strait back will stoop; a black beard will turn white; a curled pate will grow bald; a fair face will wither; a full eye will wax hollow: but a good heart, Kate, is the sun and moon; or, rather, the sun, and not the moon; for it shines bright, and never changes, but keeps his course truly. *H.V.* v. 2.
　　A light heart lives long. *L.L.* v. 2.

──── BREAKING.
　　　　　　But his flaw'd heart,
(Alack, too weak the conflict to support!)
'Twixt two extremes of passion, joy and grief,
Burst smilingly. *K.L.* v. 3

HEIR-LOOM.
Of six preceding ancestors, that gem
Conferr'd by testament to the sequent issue,
Hath it been own'd and worn. *A.W.* v . 3
It is an honour 'longing to our house,
Bequeathed down from many ancestors,
Which were the greatest obloquy i' the world,
In me to lose. *A.W.* iv. 2.

HERNE'S OAK.
There is an old tale goes, that Herne, the hunter,
Some time a keeper here in Windsor forest,
Doth all the winter time, at still midnight,

HERNE'S OAK,—*continued.*
Walk round about an oak, with great ragg'd horns;
And there he blasts the tree, and takes the cattle;
And makes milch kine yield blood, and shakes a chain
In a most hideous and dreadful manner.   *M. W.* iv. 4.

HERO, MILITARY, PRETENDED.
Such fellows are perfect in great commanders' names:
and they will learn you by rote where services are done.
H. V. iii. 6.
What a beard of the general's cut, and a horrid suit of the camp, will do among foaming bottles, and ale-washed wits, is wonderful to be thought on!   *H. V.* iii. 6.

HEROISM.
Either our history shall, with full mouth,
Speak freely of our acts; or else our grave,
Like Turkish mute, shall have a tongueless mouth,
Nor worship'd with a waxen epitaph.   *H. V.* i. 2.

By his light,
Did all the chivalry of England move
To do brave acts: he was, indeed, the glass
Wherein the noble youth did dress themselves.
H. IV. PT. II. ii. 3.

A true knight;
Not yet mature, yet matchless; firm of word,
Speaking in deeds, and deedless in his tongue;
Not soon provok'd, nor, being provok'd, soon calm'd:
His heart and hand both open, and both free;
For what he has, he gives; what thinks, he shows;
Yet gives he not till judgment guide his bounty,
Nor dignifies an impair thought with breath:
Manly as Hector, but more dangerous;
For Hector, in his blaze of wrath, subscribes
To tender objects, but he, in heat of action,
Is more vindicative than jealous love.   *T. C.* iv. 5.

HESITATION (See also IRRESOLUTION).
Now, whether it be
Bestial oblivion, or some craven scruple
Of thinking too precisely on the event,—
A thought, which, quarter'd, hath but one part wisdom,
And, ever, three parts coward,—I do not know
While yet I live to say,—*This thing's to do.*   *H.* iv. 4.

HIGHWAYMEN,
Gentlemen of the shade, minions of the moon.
H. IV. PT. I. i. 2.

HISTORIAN.
Instructed by the antiquary times,
He must, he is, he cannot but be wise.   *T. C.* ii. 3.

HIT.
A hit, a very palpable hit.   *H.* v. 5.

HOLIDAY.
To solemnize this day, the glorious sun
Stays in his course, and plays the alchemist;
Turning, with splendour of his precious eye,
The meagre cloddy earth to glittering gold:
The yearly course, that brings this day about,
Shall never see it but a holyday.   *K. J.* iii. 1.

HOMAGE OF SIMPLICITY.
For never any thing can be amiss,
When simpleness and duty tender it.   *M. N.* v. 1.

HOME-BREEDING (See also TRAVELLING).
Out of your proof we speak: we, poor unfledg'd,
Have never wing'd from view o' the nest; nor know not
What air's from home.   *Cym.* iii. 3.

HONESTY.
Ay, Sir; to be honest, as this world goes, is to be one man picked out of ten thousand.   *H.* ii. 2.

We need no grave to bury honesty;
There's not a grain of it the face to sweeten
Of the whole dungy earth.   *W. T.* ii. 1.

    Take note, take note, O world,
To be direct and honest is not safe.   *O.* iii. 3.

I am myself indifferent honest: but yet I could accuse me of such things, that it were better my mother had not borne me: I am very proud, revengeful, ambitious; with more offences at my beck, than I have thoughts to put them in, imagination to give them shape, or time to act them in: What should such fellows as I do crawling between earth and heaven? We are arrant knaves all; believe none of us.   *H.* iii. 1.

    Let me behold
Thy face.—Surely this man was born of woman.—
Forgive my general and exceptless rashness,
Perpetual sober-gods! I do proclaim
One honest man,—mistake me not,—but one;
No more, I pray,—and he's a steward.   *T. A.* iv. 3.

There is no terror, Cassius, in your threats
For I am armed so strong in honesty,
That they pass by me, as the idle wind,
Which I respect not.   *J. C.* iv. 3.

HONESTY,—*continued.*
This tyrant, whose sole name blisters our tongues,
Was once thought honest. *M.* iv. 3.

Ha, ha, what a fool Honesty is! and Trust, his sworn
brother, a very simple gentleman! *W.T.* iv. 3.

Though I am not naturally honest, I am so sometimes by
chance. *W.T.* iv. 3.

Every man has his fault, and honesty is his; I have told
him on't, but I could never get him from it. *T. A.* iii. 1.

Though honesty be no puritan, yet it will do no hurt.
A. W. i. 3.

Mine honesty and I begin to square. *A. C.* iii. 11.

HONOUR (See also TITLES, REPUTATION).
The purest treasure mortal times afford,
Is spotless reputation; that away,
Men are but gilded loam or painted clay.
A jewel in a ten-times barr'd up chest,
Is a bold spirit in a loyal breast.
Mine honour is my life; both grow in one;
Take honour from me, and my life is done. *R. II.* i. 1.

For 'tis the mind that makes the body rich;
And as the sun breaks through the darkest clouds,
So honour peereth in the meanest habit.
What, is the jay more precious than the lark,
Because his feathers are more beautiful?
Or is the adder better than the eel,
Because his painted skin contents the eye? *T. S.* iv. 3.

By heaven, methinks it were an easy leap,
To pluck bright honour from the pale-fac'd moon;
Or dive into the bottom of the deep,
Where fathom-line could never touch the ground,
And pluck up drowned honour by the locks;
So he, that doth redeem her thence, might wear,
Without corrival, all her dignities:
But out upon this half-fac'd fellowship! *H. IV.* PT. I. i. 3.

By Jove, I am not covetous of gold,
Nor care I, who doth feed upon my cost;
It yearns me not if men my garments wear;
Such outward things dwell not in my desires;
But, if it be a sin to covet honour,
I am the most offending soul alive. *H. V.* iv. 3.

Life every man holds dear; but the dear man
Holds honour far more precious-dear than life. *T. C.* v. 3.

For life, I prize it,
As I weigh grief, which I would spare: for honour,

HONOUR,—*continued.*

'Tis a derivative from me to mine,
And only that I stand for. *W. T.* iii. 2

   The king has cur'd me,
I humbly thank his grace: and from these shoulders,
These ruin'd pillars, out of pity, taken
A load would sink a navy,—too much honour.
            H. VIII. iii. 2

He sits 'mongst men, like a descended god
He hath a kind of honour sets him off,
More than a mortal seeming. *Cym.* i. 7.

Your presence glads our days; honour we love,
For who hates honour, hates the gods above. *P. P.* ii. 3.

    For men, like butterflies,
Show not their mealy wings but to the summer;
And not a man, for being simply man,
Hath any honour; but honour for those honours
That are without him; as place, riches, favour,
Prizes of accident as oft as merit:
Which, when they fall, as being slippery standers,
The love that lean'd on them as slippery too,
Do one pluck down another, and together
Die in the fall. *T. C.* iii. 3.

Thou art a fellow of a good respect;
Thy life hath had some smatch of honour in it. *J. C.* v. 5.

A scar nobly got,
Or a noble scar, is a good livery of honour. *A. W.* iv. 5.

From lowest place when virtuous things proceed,
The place is dignified by the doer's deed:
Where great additions swell, and virtue none,
It is a dropsied honour: good alone
Is good, without a name: vileness is so;
The property by what it is should go,
Not by the title. *A. W.* ii. 3.

For nought I did in hate, but all in honour. *O.* v. 2.

     Let none presume
To wear an undeserved dignity.
O, that estates, degrees, and offices,
Were not deriv'd corruptly! and that clear honour
Were purchas'd by the merit of the wearer!
How many then should cover that stand bare!
How many be commanded that command!
How much low peasantry would then be glean'd
From the true seed of honour! and how much honour
Pick'd from the chaff and ruin of the times,
To be new varnish'd! *M. V.* ii. 9.

HON   *Shakespearian Dictionary.*   HON

HONOUR,—*continued.*
By deed-achieving honour newly nam'd.   *C.* ii. 1.
If it be honour, in your wars, to seem
The same you are not, (which for your best ends,
You adopt your policy,) how is it less, or worse,
That it shall hold companionship in peace
With honour, as in war; since that to both
It stands in like request?   *C.* iii. 2.
Who does i' the wars more than his captain can,
Becomes his captain's captain: and ambition,
The soldier's virtue, rather makes choice of loss,
Than gain, which darkens him.   *A.C.* iii. 1.
Meddle you must, that's certain; or forswear to wear iron about you.   *T.N.* iii. 4.

    New honours come upon him
Like our strange garments; cleave not to their mould,
But with the aid of time.   *M.* i. 3.

You stand upon your honour!—Why, thou unconfinable baseness, it is as much as I can do to keep the terms of mine honour precise. I, I, I myself sometimes, leaving the fear of heaven on the left hand, and hiding mine honour in my necessity, am fain to shuffle, to hedge, and to lurch; and yet you, rogue, will ensconce your rags, your cat-a-mountain looks, your red-lattice phrases, and your bold-beating oaths under the shelter of your honour? *M.W.* ii. 2.

    I have heard you say,
Honour and policy, like unsever'd friends,
I' the war do grow together: Grant that, and tell me,
In peace, what each of them by'the other lose,
That they combine not there.   *C.* iii. 2.

              You come
Not to woo honour, but to wed it.   *A.W.* ii. 1.

Signs of nobleness, like stars, shall shine
On all deservers.   *M.* i. 4.

    Give me life; which, if I can save, so; if not, honour comes unlook'd for, and there's an end. *H.IV.* PT. I. v. 3.

    Well, 'tis no matter; Honour pricks me on. Yea, but how if honour prick me off when I come on; how then? Can honour set to a leg?—No. Or an arm?—No. Or take away the grief of a wound?—No. Honour hath no skill in surgery then?—No. What is honour?—A word. What is that word?—Honour. What is that honour?—Air. A trim reckoning! Who hath it?—He that died o' Wednesday. Doth he feel it?—No. Doth he hear it?—No. Is it insensible then?—Yea, to the dead. But will it not live

HON   **Shakespearian Dictionary.**   HOP

HONOUR,—*continued.*
    with the living?—No. Why?—Detraction will not suffer
    it:—therefore I'll none of it. Honour is a mere scutcheon,
    and so ends my catechism.   *H. IV.* PT. I. v. 1.

HONOURS, WORLDLY, UNCERTAINTY OF.
    The painefull warrior famosed for worth,
      After a thousand victories once foil'd,
    Is from the booke of honour razed quite,
      And all the rest forgot for which he toil'd.   *Poems.*

HOPE.
    The ample proposition that hope makes
    In all designs begun on earth below,
    Fails in the promis'd largeness: checks and disasters
    Grow in the veins of actions, highest rear'd;
    As knots by the conflūx of meeting sap,
    Infect the sound pine and divert his grain,
    Tortive and errant from his course of growth.   *T. C.* i. 3.

               A cause on foot
    Lives so in hope, as in an early spring
    We see the appearing buds; which, to prove fruit,
    Hope gives not so much warrant, as despair,
    That frosts will bite them.   *H. IV.* PT. II. i. 3.

    Like one that stands upon a promontory,
    And spies a far-off shore where he would tread,
    Wishing his foot were equal with his eye;
    And chides the sea that sunders him from thence,
    Saying,—he'll lade it dry to have his way.
                           H. VI. PT. III. iii. 2.

    True hope is swift, and flies with swallows' wings,
    Kings it makes gods, and meaner creatures kings.
                           R. III. v. 2.

    The miserable have no other medicine,
    But only hope.   *M. M.* iii. 1.

    Hope is a lover's staff; walk hence with that,
    And manage it against despairing thoughts.   *T. G.* iii. 1.

    There is a credence in thy heart,
    An esperance so obstinately strong,
    That doth invert the attest of eyes and ears;
    As if those organs had deceptious functions,
    Created only to calumniate.   *T. C.* v. 2.

               It never yet did hurt,
    To lay down likelihoods, and forms of hope.
                           H. IV. PT. II. i. 3.

    In that hope, I throw mine eyes to heaven,
    Scorning whate'er you can afflict me with.   *H. VI.* III. i. 4.

HOPE,—*continued.*
I spy life peering; but I dare not say
How near the tidings of our comfort is.   *R. II.* ii. 1.
    O, out of that no hope,
What great hope have you! no hope, that way, is
Another way so high an hope, that even
Ambition cannot pierce a wink beyond.   *T.* ii. 1.
Do not satisfy your resolution with hopes that are fallible
                                    M. M. iii. 1.
I have lost my hopes,
Perhaps even there, where I did find my doubts.   *M.* iv. 3.
And he that will not fight for such a hope,
Go home to bed, and, like the owl by day,
If he arise, be mock'd and wonder'd at.   *H. VI.* PT. III. v. 4.
What! we have many goodly days to see;
The liquid drops of tears that you have shed,
Shall come again, transform'd to orient pearl;
Advantaging their loan, with interest
Of ten-times-double gain of happiness.   *R. III.* iv. 4.
Hope is a curtail dog in some affairs.   *M. W.* ii. 1.
I will despair, and be at enmity
With cozening hope; he is a flatterer,
A parasite, a keeper-back of death,
Who gently would dissolve the bands of life,
Which false hope lingers in extremity.   *R. II.* ii. 2.

HOPELESSNESS (See also DESPONDENCY).
Had I but died an hour before this chance,
I had liv'd a blessed time; for, from this instant,
There's nothing serious in mortality:
All is but toys: renown, and grace, are dead;
The wine of life is drawn, and the mere lees
Is left this vault to brag of.   *M.* ii. 3.

HORNS.
    Why, horns; which such as you are fain to be beholden
to your wives for.   *A. Y.* iv. 1.
    Horns! even so:—Poor men alone?—No, no; the noblest
deer hath them as huge as the rascal.   *A. Y.* iii. 3.

HORROR.
    But that I am forbid
To tell the secrets of my prison-house,
I could a tale unfold, whose lightest word
Would harrow up thy soul; freeze thy young blood;
Make thy two eyes, like stars, start from their spheres;
Thy knotted and combined locks to part,

HOR   *Shakesperian Dictionary.*   HUN

HORROR,—*continued.*
And each particular hair to stand on end,
Like quills upon the fretful porcupine.   *H.* i. 5

HUMILITY.
    Often to our comfort shall we find
The sharded beetle in a safer hold
Than is the full-wing'd eagle.   *Cym.* iii. 3.
I have sounded the very base string of humility.
                           H. IV. PT. I. ii. 4.
    I heard him swear,
Were he to stand for consul, never would he
Appear i' the market-place, nor on him put
The napless vesture of humility.   *C.* ii. 1.
    Wilt thou, pupil-like,
Take thy correction mildly, kiss the rod,
And fawn on rage with base humility?   *R. II.* v. 1.
O happy 'vantage of a kneeling knee.   *R. II.* v. 3.

HUMOUR.
    "The humour of it," quoth 'a! here's a fellow frights humour out of its wits.   *M. W.* ii. 1.
    I'll tell thee what, prince; a college of wit-crackers cannot flout me out of my humour.   *M. A.* v. 4.
    I am now of all humours, that have showed themselves humours, since the old days of goodman Adam, to the pupil age of this present twelve o'clock at midnight.
                           H. IV. PT. I. ii. 4.

HUNTING.
    Say, thou wilt course; thy greyhounds are as swift
As breathed stags, ay, fleeter than the roe.   *T. S.* IND. 2.

Come, shall we go and kill us venison?
And yet it irks me, the poor dappled fools,
Being native burghers of this desert city,
Should, in their own confines, with forked heads
Have their round haunches gor'd.   *A. Y.* ii. 1

My hounds are bred out of the Spartan kind,
So flew'd, so sanded; and their heads are hung
With ears that sweep away the morning dew;
Crook-knee'd, and dew-lapp'd like Thessalian bulls;
Slow in pursuit, but match'd in mouth like bells,
Each under each. A cry more tuneable
Was never holla'd to, nor cheer'd with horn.   *M. N.* iv. 1

Uncouple in the western valley; go:
Despatch, I say, and find the forester.—

168

HUNTING,—*continued.*
•We will, fair queen, up to the mountain's top,
And mark the musical confusion
Of hounds and echo in conjunction.   *M. N.* iv. 1.
I was with Hercules, and Cadmus, once,
When in a wood of Crete they bay'd the bear
With hounds of Sparta: never did I hear
Such gallant chiding; for, besides the groves,
The skies, the fountains, every region near
Seem'd all one mutual cry: I never heard
So musical a discord, such sweet thunder.   *M. N.* iv. 1.

HUSBANDMEN.
Sun-burnt sicklemen.   *T.* iv. 1.

HYPOCRISY (See also DISSIMULATION, QUOTING SCRIPTURE).
Now step I forth to whip hypocrisy.   *L. L.* iv. 3.
A huge translation of hypocrisy.   *L. L.* v. 2.
Ah, that deceit should steal such gentle shapes,
And with a virtuous visor hide deep vice!   *R. III.* ii. 2.

    A knave very voluble; no further conscionable, than in putting on the mere form of civil and humane seeming.
    O. ii. 1.
Knavery cannot, sure, hide itself in such reverence.
    M. A. ii. 3.

O Buckingham, beware of yonder dog; ·
Look, when he fawns, he bites; and, when he bites,
His venom tooth will rankle to the death;
Have not to do with him, beware of him;
Sin, death, and hell have set their marks on him;
And all their ministers attend on him.   *R. III.* i. 3.

           Show men dutiful?
Why, so didst thou: or seem they grave and learned?
Why, so didst thou: come they of noble family?
Why, so didst thou: seem they religious?
Why, so didst thou: or are they spare in diet,
Free from gross passion, or of mirth, or anger;
Constant in spirit, not swerving with the blood;
Garnish'd and deck'd in modest compliment;
Not working with the eye, without the ear,
And, but in purged judgment, trusting neither?
Such, and so finely bolted, didst thou seem.   *H. V.* ii. 2.

Seems he a dove? his feathers are but borrow'd,
For he's disposed as the hateful raven.
Is he a lamb? his skin is surely lent him,
For he's inclin'd as are the ravenous wolves.
Who cannot steal a shape, that means deceit?

HYPOCRISY,—*continued.*

Take heed my lord; the welfare of us all
Hangs on the cutting short that fraudful man.
H. VI. PT. II. iii. 1.

Tut, I can counterfeit the deep tragedian;
Speak, and look back, and pry on every side,
Tremble and start at wagging of a straw,
Intending deep suspicion: ghastly looks
Are at my service, like enforced smiles;
And both are ready in their offices,
At any time, to grace my stratagems. *R. III.* iii. 5.

Be not you spoke with, but by mighty suit:
And look you get a prayer-book in your hand,
And stand between two churchmen, good my lord;
For on that ground I'll make a holy descant:
And be not easily won to our requests;
Play the maid's part, still answer nay, and take it.
R. III. iii. 7.

There is no vice so simple, but assumes
Some mark of virtue on his outward parts. *M. V.* iii. 2.

This outward-sainted deputy,—
Whose settled visage and deliberate word
Nips youth i' the head, and follies doth enmew,
As falcon doth the fowl,—is yet a devil. *M. M.* iii. 1.

Gloster's show
Beguiles him, as the mournful crocodile
With sorrow snares relenting passengers;
Or as the snake, roll'd in a flowering bank,
With shining checker'd slough, doth sting a child,
That, for the beauty, thinks it excellent.
H. VI. PT. II. iii. 1.

Smooth runs the water, where the brook is deep;
And in his simple show he harbours treason.
The fox barks not, when he would steal the lamb.
No, no, my sovereign; Gloster is a man
Unsounded yet, and full of deep deceit.
H. VI. PT. II. iii. 1.

So smooth he daub'd his vice with show of virtue,
That,—his apparent open guilt omitted—
He liv'd from all attainder of suspect. *R. III.* iii. 5.

Ah, that deceit should steal such gentle shapes,
And with a virtuous visor hide deep vice! *R. III.* ii. 2.

O, what authority and show of truth
Can cunning sin cover itself withal! *M. A.* iv. 1.

HYP   *Shakespearian Dictionary.*   JEA

HYPOCRISY,—*continued.*
And thus I clothe my naked villainy
With old odd ends, stol'n forth of holy writ;
And seem a saint when most I play the devil.   *R. III.* i. 3.
The secret mischief that I set abroach,
I lay unto the grievous charge of others.   *R. III.* i. 3.
I do the wrong, and first begin to brawl.   *R. III.* i. 3.
     Your great goodness, out of holy pity,
Absolv'd him with an axe.   *H. VIII.* iii. 2.

J & J.

JACKS IN OFFICE.
     The little dogs and all,
Tray, Blanch, and Sweetheart, see, they bark at me.
   K. L. iii. 6.

JARGON.
     They have been at a great feast of languages, and stolen
the scraps.   *L. L.* v. 1.

IDOLATRY.
     'Tis mad idolatry,
That makes the service greater than the god.   *T. C.* ii. 2.
This is the liver vein, which makes flesh a deity;
A green goose, a goddess: pure, pure idolatry.   *L. L.* iv. 3.

JEALOUSY.
     How many fond fools serve mad jealousy!   *C. E.* ii. 1.
     Trifles, light as air,
Are, to the jealous, confirmations strong
As proofs of holy writ.   *O.* iii. 3.
     Good, my lord, be cur'd
Of this diseas'd opinion, and betimes;
For 'tis most dangerous.   *W. T.* i. 2.
Look where he comes! Not poppy, nor mandragora,
Nor all the drowsy syrups of the world,
Shall ever medicine thee to that sweet sleep
Which thou ow'd'st yesterday.   *O.* iii. 3.
     How blest am I
In my just censure, in my true opinion!
Alack, for lesser knowledge! How accurs'd,
In being so bless'd!—There may be in the cup
A spider steep'd, and one may drink; depart,
And yet partake no venom; for his knowledge
Is not infected: but if one present

JEALOUSY,—*continued.*

The abhorr'd ingredient to his eye, make known
How he hath drunk, he cracks his gorge, his sides,
With violent hefts :—I have drunk, and seen the spider.
W.T. ii. 1.

Of one, that lov'd not wisely, but too well;
Of one, not easily jealous, but being wrought,
Perplex'd in the extreme. *O.* v. 2.

That same knave, Ford, her husband, hath the finest mad devil of jealousy in him, master Brook, that ever govern'd frenzy. *M.W.* v. 1.

Poor, and content, is rich, and rich enough;
But riches, fineless, is as poor as winter,
To him that ever fears he shall be poor. *O.* iii. 3.

O beware, my lord, of jealousy;
It is the green-eyed monster, which doth mock
The meat it feeds on: That cuckold lives in bliss,
Who, certain of his fate, loves not his wronger;
But, O, what damned minutes tells he o'er,
Who dotes, yet doubts ; suspects, yet strongly loves!
O. iii. 3.

These are the forgeries of jealousy:
And never, since the middle summer's spring,
Met we on hill, in dale, forest, or mead,
By paved fountain, or by rushy brook,
Or on the beached margent of the sea,
To dance our ringlets to the whistling wind,
But with thy brawls thou hast disturb'd our sport.
M.N. ii. 2.

Self-harming jealousy. *C.E.* ii. 1.

The venom clamours of a jealous woman
Poison more deadly than a mad dog's tooth. *C.E.* v. 1

The shrug, the hum, or ha; these pretty brands,
That calumny doth use:—O, I am out,
That mercy does; for calumny will seer
Virtue itself;—these shrugs, these hums, and has,
When you have said, she's goodly, come between,
Ere you can say she's honest. *W.T.* ii. 1.

The forgeries of jealousy. *M.N.* ii. 2.

How novelty may move, and parts with person,
Alas, a kind of godly jealousy
(Which, I beseech you, call a virtuous sin)
Makes me afeard. *T.C.* iv. 4.

I will possess him with yellowness. *M.W.* i. 3.

JEALOUSY,—*continued.*
Think'st thou I'd make a life of jealousy,
To follow still the changes of the moon
With fresh suspicions? No: to be once in doubt,
Is—once to be resolved.   *O.* iii. 3.

    Is whispering nothing?
Is leaning cheek to cheek? is meeting noses?
Kissing with inside lip? stopping the career
Of laughter with a sigh? (a note infallible
Of breaking honesty?) horsing foot on foot?
Skulking in corners? wishing clocks more swift?
Hours, minutes? noon, midnight? and all eyes blind
With the pin and web, but theirs, theirs only,
That would unseen be wicked?—is this nothing
Why, then, the world, and all that's in't, is nothing;
The covering sky is nothing; Bohemia nothing;
My wife is nothing; nor nothing have these nothings,
If this be nothing.   *W.T.* i. 2.

But to be paddling palms, and pinching fingers,
As now they are; and making practis'd smiles,
As in a looking-glass;—and then to sigh, as 'twere
The mort o' the deer; O, that is entertainment
My bosom likes not, nor my brows.   *W.T.* i. 2.

What sense had I of her stolen hours of lust?
I saw it not, thought it not, it harm'd not me;
I slept the next night well, was free and merry;
I found not Cassio's kisses on her lips:
He that is robb'd, not wanting what is stol'n,
Let him not know it, and he's not robb'd at all.   *O.* iii. 3

Avaunt! begone! thou hast set me on the rack:—
I swear 'tis better to be much abus'd,
Than but to know't a little.   *O.* iii. 3.

I'll see, before I doubt; when I doubt, prove;
And, on the proof, there is no more but this,—
Away at once with love and jealousy.   *O.* iii. 3.

All my fond love thus do I blow to heaven:
Arise, black vengeance, from thy hollow cell!
Yield up, O love, thy crown, and hearted throne,
To tyrannous hate! swell, bosom, with thy fraught,
For 'tis of aspicks' tongues.   *O.* iii. 3.

Make me to see it; or (at the least) so prove it,
That the probation bear no hinge, nor loop,
To hang a doubt on; or, woe upon thy life.   *O.* iii. 3.

If thou dost slander her and torture me,
Never pray more; abandon all remorse:
On horror's head, horrors accumulate:

JEALOUSY,—*continued.*
Do deeds to make heaven weep, all earth amaz'd,
For nothing canst thou to damnation add,
Greater than that. *O.* iii. 3.
Villain, be sure thou prove my wife a whore;
Be sure of it; give me the ocular proof;
Or, by the worth of mine eternal soul,
Thou hadst been better have been born a dog,
Than answer my wak'd wrath. *O.* iii. 3.
Have you not seen, Camillo,
(But that's past doubt: you have; or your eye-glass
Is thicker than a cuckold's horn); or heard,
(For, to a vision so apparent, rumour
Cannot be mute); or thought, (for cogitation
Resides not in that man, that does not think it)
My wife is slippery? If thou wilt confess,
(Or else be impudently negative,
To have nor eyes, nor ears, nor thought), then say,
My wife's a hobby-horse; deserves a name
As rank as any flax-wench, that puts to
Before her troth-plight: say it, and justify it. *W.T.* i. 2.
My wife hath sent to him, the hour is fixed, the match is made. Would any man have thought this?—See the hell of having a false woman! *M.W.* ii. 2.
Page is an ass, a secure ass: he will trust his wife. He will not be jealous; I will rather trust a Fleming with my butter, parson Hugh the Welshman with my cheese, an Irishman with my aqua-vitæ bottle, or a thief to walk my ambling gelding, than my wife with herself.—Heaven be praised for my jealousy! *M.W.* ii. 2.
By gar, 'tis no de fashion of France; it is not jealous in France. *M.W.* iii. 3.

JEST.
O, it is much, that a lie, with a slight oath, and a jest, with a sad brow, will do with a fellow that never had the ache in his shoulders. *H. IV.* PT. II. v. 1.
A jest's prosperity lies in the ear
Of him that hears it, never in the tongue
Of him that makes it. *L. L.* v. 2.
I will bite thee by the ear for that jest. *R. J.* ii. 4.
That very oft,
When I am dull with care and melancholy,
Lightens my humour with his merry jests. *C. E.* i. 2.
Reply not to me with a fool-born jest. *H. IV.* PT. II. v. 5.
To see now, how a jest shall come about! *R. J.* i. 3.

JEST,—*continued.*
Jesters do oft prove prophets.   *K. L.* v. 3.
Jest a twelvemonth in an hospital.   *L. L.* v. 2.
—— MISAPPLIED.
His jest will savour but of shallow wit,
When thousands weep more than did laugh at it. *H.V.* i. 2.
He jests at scars that never had a wound.   *R. J.* ii. 2.

JEWEL.
Can the world buy such a jewel?   *M. A.* i. 1.

IF.
Talk'st thou to me of *ifs*.   *R. III.* iii. 4.
—— THE VIRTUES OF AN.
All these you may avoid but the lie direct; and you may avoid that too, with an *if*. I knew when seven justices could not make up a quarrel; but when the parties were met themselves, one of them thought but of an *if*; as, *if* you said so, then I said so; and they shook hands, and swore brothers. Your *if* is the only peace-maker; much virtue in *if*.   *A.Y.* v. 4.

IGNORANCE.
O thou monster, ignorance, how deform'd dost thou look
    L. L. iv. 2.
Ignorance is the curse of God.   *H.VI.* PT. II. iv. 7.
Dull, unfeeling, barren ignorance.   *R. II.* i. 3.
Short-arm'd ignorance.   *T. C.* ii. 3.

ILL-FAVOURED.
He is deformed, crooked, old, and sere,
Ill-faced, worse-bodied, shapeless every where;
Vicious, ungentle, foolish, blunt, unkind,
Stigmatical in making, worse in mind.   *C. E.* iv. 2.

ILLITERATE.
Sir, he hath never fed of the dainties that are bred in a book; he hath not eat paper, as it were; he hath not drunk ink: his intellect is not replenished; he is only an animal; only sensible in the duller parts.   *L. L.* iv. 2.

ILLUSION (See DELUSION).
Our revels now are ended: these our actors,
As I foretold you, were all spirits, and -
Are melted into air, into thin air:
And like the baseless fabric of their vision,
The cloud-capp'd towers, the gorgeous palaces,
The solemn temples, the great globe itself,
Yea, all which it inherit, shall dissolve;

ILLUSION,—continued.

And like this insubstantial pageant faded,
Leave not a rack behind. We are such stuff
As dreams are made of, and our little life
Is rounded with a sleep. *T.* iv. 1.

IMAGINATION.

Such tricks hath strong imagination;
That if it would but apprehend some joy,
It comprehends some bringer of that joy;
Or, in the night imagining some fear,
How easy is a bush suppos'd a bear! *M. N.* v. 1.

Conceit, more rich in matter than in words,
Brags of his substance, not of ornament:
They are but beggars that can count their worth.
R. J. ii. 6.

Lovers and madmen have such seething brains,
Such shaping fantasies, that apprehend
More than cool reason ever comprehends.
The lunatic, the lover, and the poet,
Are of imagination all compact:
One sees more devils than vast hell can hold;
That is, the madman: the lover, all as frantic,
Sees Helen's beauty in a brow of Egypt:
The poet's eye, in a fine frenzy rolling,
Doth glance from heaven to earth, from earth to heaven;
And, as imagination bodies forth
The forms of things unknown, the poet's pen
Turns them to shapes, and gives to airy nothing
A local habitation and a name. *M. N.* v. 1.

O, who can hold a fire in his hand,
By thinking on the frosty Caucasus?
Or cloy the hungry edge of appetite,
By bare imagination of a feast?
Or wallow naked in December's snow,
By thinking on fantastic summer's heat
O, no! the apprehension of the good,
Gives but the greater feeling to the worse:
Fell sorrow's tooth doth never rankle more,
Than when it bites, but lanceth not the sore. *R. II.* i. 3

Dangerous conceits, are, in their natures, poisons,
Which, at the first, are scarce found to distaste;
But, with a little act upon the blood,
Burn like the mines of sulphur. *O.* iii. 3.

He waxes desperate with imagination. *H.* i. 4.

IMA   **Shakesperian Dictionary.**   IMP

IMAGINARY EVILS CAUSE REAL CARES.
The passions of the mind,
That have their first conception by mis-dread,
Have after-nourishment and life by care;
And what was first but fear what might be done,
Grows elder now, and cares it be not done.   *P. P.* i. 2.

IMMACULATE.
Chaste and immaculate in very thought.   *H. VI.* PT. I. v. 4.

IMMOLATION.
O cruel, irreligious piety!   *Tit. And.* i. 2.

IMMORAL READING.
Lascivious metres, to whose venom sound
The open ear of youth doth always listen.   *R. II.* ii. 1.

IMPATIENCE SUPPRESSED.
Bondage is hoarse, and may not speak aloud;
Else would I tear the cave where Echo lies,
And make her airy tongue more hoarse than mine
With repetition of my Romeo's name.   *R. J.* ii. 2.

IMPETUOSITY.
The ocean, overpeering of his list,
Eats not the flats with more impetuous haste.   *H.* iv. 5.

Let me go, Sir,
Or I'll knock you o'er the mazzard.   *O.* ii. 3.

IMPLACABILITY (See INFLEXIBILITY).

IMPOLICY.
Neglecting an attempt of ease and gain,
To wake, and wage, a danger profitless.   *O.* i. 3.

IMPOSSIBILITIES.
Then let the pebbles on the hungry beach
Fillip the stars; then let the mutinous winds
Strike the proud cedars 'gainst the fiery sun;
Murd'ring impossibility, to make
What cannot be, slight work.   *C.* v. 3.

IMPRISONMENT.
By my christendom,
So I were out of prison, and kept sheep,
I should be merry as the day is long.   *K. J.* iv. 1.

IMPROVIDENCE.
'Tis not unknown to you, Antonio,
How much I have disabled mine estate,
By something showing a more swelling port
Than my faint means would grant continuance.   *M. V.* i. 1.

IMPUDENCE.
What! canst thou say all this, and never blush?
Tit. And. v. 1.

IMPUTATION.
To vouch this, is no proof;
Without more certain and more overt test,
Than these thin habits and poor likelihoods
Of modern seeming do prefer against him. *O.* i. 3.

INCLINATION.
To business that we love, we rise betimes,
And go to it with delight. *A. C.* iv. 4.

INCONSTANCY.
    O heaven! were man
But constant, he were perfect; that one error
Fills him with faults. *T. G.* v. 4.

INCONTINENCE.
     Such an act,
That blurs the grace and blush of modesty:
Calls virtue hypocrite: takes off the rose
From the fair forehead of an innocent love,
And sets a blister there: makes marriage vows
As false as dicers' oaths; O, such a deed,
As from the body of contraction plucks
The very soul; and sweet religion makes
A rhapsody of words. *H.* iii. 4.

    O, she is fallen
Into a pit of ink? that the wide sea
Hath drops too few to wash her clean again;
And salt too little, which may season give
To her foul tainted flesh. *M. A.* iv. 1.

     Had it pleas'd heaven
To try me with affliction; had he rain'd
All kinds of sores, and shames, on my bare head;
Steep'd me in poverty to the very lips;
Given to captivity me and my utmost hopes;
I should have found in some part of my soul
A drop of patience: but.(alas!) to make me
A fixed figure, for the type of scorn
To point his low unmoving finger at,
O! O! *O.* iv. 2.

I should make very forges of my cheeks,
That would to cinders burn up modesty,
Did I but speak thy deeds. *O.* iv. 2.

Look to her, Moor; have a quick eye to see;
She has deceiv'd her father, and may thee. *O.* i. 3.

INCONTINENCE,—*continued.*
          O thou weed,
Who art so lovely fair, and smell'st so sweet,
That the sense aches at thee,—would, thou hadst ne'er been
born.   *O.* iv. 2.
O shame! where is thy blush? Rebellious hell,
If thou canst mutine in a matron's bones
To flaming youth let virtue be as wax,
And melt in her own fire: proclaim no shame,
When the compulsive ardour gives the charge;
Since frost itself as actively doth burn,
And reason panders will.   *H.* iii. 4.
              If I do prove her haggard,
Though that her jesses were my dear heart strings,
I'd whistle her off, and let her down the wind,
To prey at fortune.   *O.* iii. 3

INCORRIGIBLE.
    Double and treble admonition, and still forfeit in the same kind. This would make mercy swear and play the tyrant.   *M. M.* iii. 2.

INDEPENDENCE.
    I cannot tell, what you and other men
Think of this life.; but, for my single self,
I had as lief not be, as live to be
In awe of such a thing as I myself.   *J. C.* i. 2

INDIGNATION.
    His indignation derives itself out of a very competent injury.   *T. N* iii. 4.

INFAMY.
    Wine lov'd I deeply; dice dearly; and in woman, out-paramour'd the Turk. False of heart, light of ear, bloody of hand; hog in sloth, fox in stealth, wolf in greediness, dog in madness, lion in prey.   *K. L.* iii. 4.

INFANT RULER.
    Woe to that land that's govern'd by a child! *R. III.* ii. 3.

INFATUATION.
        When we in our viciousness grow hard,
(O, misery on't!) the wise gods seel our eyes;
In our own filth drop our clear judgments; make us
Adore our errors; laugh at us, while we strut
To our confusion.   *A. C.* iii. 11.
Thus hath the candle sing'd the moth.   *M. V.* ii. 9.
It was young Hotspur's case at Shrewsbury.
* * * * Who lin'd himself with hope,

INFATUATION,—*continued.*
Eating the air on promise of supply,
Flattering himself with project of a power
Much smaller than the smallest of his thoughts
And so, with great imagination,
Proper to madmen, led his powers to death,
And, winking, leap'd into destruction.   *H. IV.* PT. II. i. 3.

INFECTION.
     And one infect another
Against the wind a mile.   *C.* i. 4.

INFIRMITY.
Infirmity doth still neglect all office,
Whereto our health is bound; we are not ourselves,
When nature, being oppress'd, commands the mind
To suffer with the body.   *K. L.* ii. 4.

——————— GREATNESS NOT EXEMPT FROM.
He had a fever when he was in Spain,
And, when the fit was on him, I did mark
How he did shake: 'tis true, this god did shake:
His coward lips did from their colours fly;
And that same eye, whose bend doth awe the world,
Did lose its lustre.   *J.C.* i. 2.

INFLEXIBILITY. (See also BOND).
You may as well go stand upon the beech,
And bid the main flood bate his usual height;
You may as well use question with the wolf,
Why he hath made the ewe bleat for the lamb;
You may as well forbid the mountain pines
To wag their high tops and to make no noise,
When they are fretted with the gusts of heaven
You may as well do any thing most hard,
As seek to soften that—(than which what's harder?)
His Jewish heart!   *M. V.* iv. 1.

    Swear his thought over
By each particular star in heaven, and
By all their influences, you may as well
Forbid the sea for to obey the moon,
As or, by oath, remove, or counsel, shake,
The fabric of his folly; whose foundation
Is pil'd upon his faith, and will continue
The standing of his body.   *W.T.* i. 2.

I'll have my bond; I will not hear thee speak:
I'll have my bond: and therefore speak no more.   *M. V.* iii. 3.

 There's no more mercy in him than there is milk in a male tiger.   *C.* v. 4.

INFLUENCE.
   So our leader's led,
And we are women's men.   *A.C.* iii. 7.

INGRATITUDE.
Monster ingratitude!   *K.L.* i. 5
The ingratitude of this Seleucus does
Even make me wild.   *A.C.* v. 2.
    Must I be unfolded
With one that I have bred? The gods!—It smites me
Beneath the fall I have.   *A.C.* v. 2.
   Blow, blow, thou winter wind,
   Thou art not so unkind
    As man's ingratitude;
   Thy tooth is not so keen,
   Because thou art not seen
    Although thy breath be rude.
   Freeze, freeze, thou bitter sky,
   That dost not bite so nigh,
    As benefits forgot;
   Though thou the waters warp,
   Thy sting is not so sharp
    As friend remember'd not. *A.Y.* ii. 7.
I hate ingratitude more in a man,
Than lying, vainness, babbling, drunkenness,
Or any taint of vice, whose strong corruption
Inhabits our frail blood.   *T.N.* iii. 4.
    I have kept back their foes
While they have told their money; and let out
Their coin upon large interest; I myself,
Rich only in large hurts,—All those for this?
Is this the balsam, that the usuring senate
Pours into captains' wounds?   *T.A.* iii. 5.
   Pr'ythee lead me in:
There take an inventory of all I have,
To the last penny; 'tis the king's: my robe,
And my integrity to heaven, is all
I dare now call my own. O Cromwell, Cromwell,
Had I but serv'd my God with half the zeal
I serv'd my king, he would not in mine age
Have left me naked to mine enemies. *H.VIII.* iii. 2.
   I had my trial;
And, must needs say, a noble one; which makes me
A little happier than my wretched father:
Yet thus far we are one in fortunes,—Both
Fell by our servants, by those men we lov'd most;
A most unnatural and faithless service!

INGRATITUDE,—*continued.*
Heaven has an end in all; yet, you that hear me,
This from a dying man receive as certain:
Where you are liberal of your loves, and counsels,
Be sure you be not loose; for those you make friends
And give your hearts to, when they once perceive
The least rub in your fortunes, fall away
Like water from ye, never found again
But where they mean to sink ye. *H. VIII.* ii. 1.

For Brutus, as you know, was Cæsar's angel;
Judge, O you gods, how dearly Cæsar lov'd him!
This was the most unkindest cut of all:
For when the noble Cæsar saw him stab,
Ingratitude, more strong than traitors' arms,
Quite vanquish'd him: then burst his mighty heart;
And, in his mantle muffling up his face,
Even at the base of Pompey's statue,
Which all the while ran blood, great Cæsar fell. *J.C.* iii. 2.

Time hath, my lord, a wallet at his back,
Wherein he puts alms for oblivion,
A great-siz'd monster of ingratitudes:
Those scraps are good deeds past; which are devour'd
As fast as they are made, forgot as soon
As done. *T.C.* iii. 3.

Ingratitude is monstrous: and for the multitude to be ingrateful, were to make a monster of the multitude.
C. ii. 3.

I am rapt, and cannot cover
The monstrous bulk of this ingratitude
With any size of words. *T.A.* v. 1.

Being fed by us, you us'd us so,
As that ungentle gull, the cuckoo's bird,
Useth the sparrow: did oppress our nest;
Grew by our feeding to so great a bulk,
That even our love durst not come near your sight,
For fear of swallowing. *H.IV.* PT. I. v. 1.

——————— FILIAL (See also CHILDREN).
Is it not as this mouth should tear this hand,
For lifting food to't? *K.L.* iii. 4.

Ingratitude! thou marble-hearted fiend;
More hideous when thou show'st thee in a child,
Than the sea monster. *K.L.* i. 4.

Beloved Regan,
Thy sister's naught: O Regan, she hath tied
Sharp-tooth'd unkindness, like a vulture here;
I can scarce speak to thee. *K.L.* ii. 4.

INHUMANITY.
I am sorry for thee; thou art come to answer
A stony adversary, an inhuman wretch
Uncapable of pity, void and empty
From any dram of mercy. *M.V.* iv. 1.
O, be thou damn'd, inexorable dog!
And for thy life let justice be accurs'd.
Thou almost mak'st me waver in my faith
To hold opinion with Pythagoras,
That souls of animals infuse themselves
Into the trunks of men. *M.V.* iv. 1.

INJURED MAN.
He hath wronged me; indeed, he hath;—at a word, he hath;—believe me;—Robert Shallow, esquire, saith he is wrong'd. *M.W.* i. 1.
I leave my duty a little unthought of, and speak out of my injury. *T.N.* v. 1.

INN.
What, will you make a younker of me? shall I not take mine ease in mine inn, but I shall have my pocket picked.
H.IV. PT. I. iii. 3.

INNOCENCE.
The trust I have is in mine innocence. *H.IV.* PT. II. iv. 4.
Unstained thoughts do seldom dream of evil. *Poems.*
Pure innocence hath never practis'd how
To cloak offences. *Poems.*
  I humbly thank your highness:
And am right glad to catch this good occasion
Most thoroughly to be winnow'd, where my chaff
And corn shall fly asunder; for, I know,
There's none stands under more calumnious tongues
Than I myself. *H.VIII.* v. 1.
  We do not know
How he may soften at the sight o' the child;
The silence often of pure innocence
Persuades, when speaking fails. *W.T.* ii. 2.
Did I not tell you she was innocent? *M.A.* v. 4.
  I have mark'd
A thousand blushing apparitions start
Into her face; a thousand innocent shames
In angel whiteness bear away those blushes;
And in her eye there hath appear'd a fire,
To burn the errors that these princes hold
Against her maiden truth. *M.A.* iv. 1.

INNOCENCE,—*continued.*
　　　　　If powers divine
　Behold our human actions, (as they do)
　I doubt not then, but innocence shall make
　False accusation blush, and tyranny
　Tremble at patience.　　　　　　　　*W.T.* iii. 2.

——————— ITSELF, NOT EXEMPT FROM MISFORTUNE.
　Some innocents 'scape not the thunderbolt.　*A.C.* ii. 5.

INNOVATION.
　　　　　Thus we debase
　The nature of our seats, and make the rabble
　Call our cares, fears; which will in time break ope
　The locks o' th' senate, and bring in the crows
　To peck the eagles.　　　　　　　　*C.* iii. 1.

INSANITY.
　We are not ourselves, when nature, being oppress'd,
　Commands the mind to suffer with the body.　*K. L.* ii. 4

INSECURITY.
　We have scotch'd the snake, not kill'd it;
　She'll close, and be herself; whilst our poor malice
　Remains in danger of her former tooth.　.　*M.* iii. 2.

　　I am cabin'd, cribb'd, confin'd, bound in
　To saucy doubts and fears.　　　　　*M.* iii. 4.

INSINUATION.
　　　　　Thou cried'st, *Indeed?*
　And didst contract and purse thy brow together,
　As if thou had'st then shut up in thy brain
　Some horrible conceit.　　　　　　*O.* iii. 3.

INSOLENCE.
　Ill deeds are doubled with an evil word.　*C. E.* iii. 2.

INSTRUMENT (See also PIPING, TOOL).
　　　　　How poor an instrument
　May do a noble deed!　　　　　　*A.C.* v. 2.

INTEGRITY.
　　　　　Delay'd,
　But nothing alter'd: What I was, I am.　*W.T.* iv. 3.

　There is a kind of character in thy life,
　That, to the observer, doth thy history
　Fully unfold: Thyself and thy belongings
　Are not thine own so proper, as to waste
　Thyself upon thy virtues, them on thee.　*M. M.* i. 1.

INTEMPERANCE.
Boundless intemperance
In nature is a tyranny; it hath been
The untimely emptying of the happy throne,
And fall of many kings.   *M.* iv. 3.

INTENTIONS, GOOD, DEFEATED.
We are not the first,
Who, with best meaning, have incurr'd the worst
   K. L. v. 3.

INTENTS AND ACTS.
His act did not o'ertake his bad intent;
And must be buried but as an intent,
That perish'd by the way: thoughts are no subjects;
Intents but merely thoughts.   *M. M.* v. 1.
Between the acting of a dreadful thing
And the first motion, all the interim is
Like a phantasma, or a hideous dream:
The genius, and the mortal instruments,
Are then in council; and the state of man,
Like to a little kingdom, suffers then
The nature of an insurrection.   *J.C.* ii. 1.

INTERRUPTION, VIOLENT.
And, like the tyrannous breathing of the north,
Shakes all our buds from growing.   *Cym.* i. 4.

INTRUDER.
What! dares the slave
Come hither, cover'd with an antic face,
To fleer and scorn at our solemnity?   *R. J.* i. 5.

INVASION.
There comes a power
Into this scatter'd kingdom; who already,
Wise in our negligence, have secret feet
In some of our best ports, and are at point
To show their open banner.   *K.L.* iii. 1.
Shall we, upon the footing of our land,
Send fair-play orders, and make compromise,
Insinuation, parley, and base truce,
To arms invasive? shall a beardless boy,
A cocker'd silken wanton brave our fields,
And flesh his spirit in a warlike soil,
. Mocking the air with colours idly spread,
And find no check?   *K. J.* v. 1.

INVITATION.
If your love do not persuade you to come, let not my letter.
   M. V. iii. 2.

INVOCATION.
My father's wit, and my mother's tongue, assist me!
L. L. i. 2.

————— LOYAL.
God, and his angels, guard your sacred throne,
And make you long become it! *H. V.* i. 2.

————— POET'S.
O, for a muse of fire, that would ascend
The brightest heaven of invention! *H. V.* i. *chorus.*

————— SOLDIER'S.
St. George,—that swing'd the dragon, and e'er since,
Sits on his horseback at mine hostess' door,
Teach us some fence! *K. J.* ii. 1.

JOY.
Take my cap, Jupiter, and I thank thee :—Hoo! Marcius
is coming home! *C.* ii. 1

Why, hark you;
The trumpets, sackbuts, psalteries, and fifes,
Tabors, and cymbals, and the shouting Romans,
Make the sun dance. *C.* v. 4

But that I see thee here,
Thou noble thing! more dances my rapt heart
Than when I first my wedded mistress saw
Bestride my threshold. *C.* iv. 5.

There appears much joy in him; even so much that joy
could not show itself modest enough, without a badge of
bitterness. * * * A kind overflow of kindness: There are
no faces truer than those that are so washed. How much
better is it to weep at joy, than to joy at weeping!
M. A. i. 1.

IRRESOLUTION (See also HESITATION).
Our doubts are traitors,
And make us lose the good we oft might win,
By fearing to attempt. *M. M.* i. 5.

That we would do,
We should do when we would; for this *would* changes,
And hath abatements and delays as many,
As there are tongues, are hands, are accidents;
And then this *should* is like a spendthrift's sigh,
That hurts by easing. *H.* iv. 7.

IRREVERENCE.
Quaff'd off the muscadel, and threw the sops all in the
sexton's face. *T. S.* iii. 2.

IRRITABILITY (See also QUARREL).
Come, come, thou art as hot a Jack in thy mood as any in Italy. *R. J.* iii. 1.
     Being incens'd, he's flint;
As humorous as winter, and as sudden
As flaws congealed in the spring of day.
His temper therefore must be well observ'd:
Chide him for faults, and do it reverently,
When you perceive his blood inclin'd to mirth;
But, being moody, give him line and scope,
Till that his passions, like a whale on ground,
Confound themselves with working.   *H. IV.* PT. II. iv. 4.
 A very little thief of occasion will rob you of a great deal of patience.   *C.* ii. 1.

JUDGES, DILATORY.
 You dismiss the controversy bleeding, the more entangled by your hearing.   *C.* ii. 1.

JUDGMENT, JUSTICE.
I stand for judgment: answer; shall I have it? *M. V.* iv. 1.
Forbear to judge, for we are sinners all. *H. VI.* PT. II. iii. 3.
A Daniel come to judgment! yea, a Daniel! *M. V.* iv. 1
To offend and judge, are distinct offices,
And of opposed natures.   *M. V.* ii. 9.
O judgment, thou art fled to brutish beasts,
And men have lost their reason.   *J. C.* iii. 2.
 The urging of that word judgment hath bred a kind of remorse in me.   *R. III.* i. 4.
      I charge you by the law,
Whereof you are a well-deserving pillar,
Proceed to judgment.   *M. V.* iv. 4
Under your good correction, I have seen,
When, after execution, judgment hath
Repented o'er his doom.   *M. M.* ii. 2.
       This shows you are above,
You justicers, that these poor nether crimes
So speedily can venge!   *K. L.* iv. 2.
O, I were damn'd beyond all depth in hell,
But that I did proceed upon just grounds
To this extremity.   *O.* v. 2.
       All friends shall taste
The wages of their virtue, and all foes
The cup of their deservings.   *K. L.* v. 3.
The gods are just, and of our pleasant vices
Make instruments to scourge us.   *K. L.* v. 3.

JUDGMENT, JUSTICE,—*continued.*

      Thyself shalt see the act:
For, as thou urgest justice, be assur'd,
Thou shalt have justice, more than thou desir'st.
                M. V. iv. 1.
And where the offence is, let the great axe fall. *H.* iv. 5.
Robes and furr'd gowns hide all. Plate sin with gold,
And the strong lance of justice hurtless breaks:
Arm it in rags, a pigmy's straw doth pierce it. *K. L.* iv. 6.

  In the corrupted currents of this world,
Offence's gilded hand may shove by justice;
And oft 'tis seen, the wicked prize itself
Buys out the law: But 'tis not so above:
There is no shuffling, there the action lies
In his true nature; and we ourselves compell'd,
Even to the teeth and forehead of our faults,
To give in evidence.   *H.* iii. 3.

     I do believe,
Induc'd by potent circumstances, that
You are mine enemy; and make my challenge,
You shall not be my judge.   *H. VIII.* ii. 4.

     If I shall be condemn'd
Upon surmises; all proofs sleeping else,
But what your jealousies await; I tell you,
'Tis rigour, and not law.   *W. T.* iii. 2.

    Impartial are our eyes, and ears:
Were he my brother, nay, my kingdom's heir,
Now by my sceptre's awe I make a vow,
Such neighbour nearness to our sacred blood
Should nothing privilege him, nor partialize
The unstooping firmness of my upright soul. *R. II.* i. 1.

He shall have merely justice, and his bond. *M. V.* iv. 1.

JUSTICE OF PEACE.

  He's a justice of peace in his county, simple though I stand here.   *M. W.* i. 1.

K.

KENT.
  Kent, in the commentaries Cæsar writ,
Is term'd the civil'st place of all this isle:
Sweet in the country, because full of riches;
The people liberal, valiant, active, wealthy.
              H. VI. PT. II. iv. 7

KIL   *Shakesperian Dictionary.*   KIN

KILLING.
- To kill, I grant, is sin's extremest gust;
But, in defence, by mercy, it is just.   *T. A.* iii. 5.

KINDNESS.
              When your head did but ache,
I knit my handkerchief about your brows,
(The best I had, a princess wrought it me,)
And I did never ask it you again:
And with my hand at midnight held your head;
And, like the watchful minutes to the hour,
Still and anon cheer'd up the heavy time;
Saying,—What lack you?—and,—Where lies your grief?
                                     K. J. iv. 1.
What would you have? your gentleness shall force,
More than your force move us to gentleness.   *A. Y.* ii. 7.
                Blunt not his love;
Nor lose the good advantage of his grace,
By seeming cold, or careless of his will,
For he is gracious if he be observ'd.   *H. IV.* PT. II. iv. 1.
              You may ride us,
With one soft kiss, a thousand furlongs, ere
With spur we heat an acre.   *W. T.* i. 2.

KINGS (See also AUTHORITY, CROWN, FALLEN GREATNESS).
He may not, as unvalu'd persons do,
Carve for himself; for on his choice depends
The safety and the health of the whole state;
And therefore must his choice be circumscrib'd
Unto the voice and yielding of that body,
Whereof he is the head.   *H.* i. 3.
O hard condition, twin-born with greatness,
Subject to the breath of every fool,
Whose sense no more can feel but his own wringing!
What infinite heart's ease must kings neglect,
That private men enjoy!
And what have kings, that privates have not too,
Save ceremony, save general ceremony?
And what art thou, thou idol ceremony?
What kind of god art thou, that suffer'st more
Of mortal griefs than do thy worshippers?
What are thy rents? what are thy comings in?
O, ceremony, show me but thy worth
What, is thy soul of adoration?
Art thou aught else but place, degree, and form,
Creating awe and fear in other men?
Wherein thou art less happy, being fear'd,
Than they in fearing

KINGS,—*continued.*
What drink'st thou oft instead of homage sweet,
But poison'd flattery? O, be sick, great greatness,
And bid thy ceremony give thee cure!
Think'st thou, the fiery fever will go out
With titles blown from adulation?
Will it give place to flexure and low bending?
Canst thou, when thou command'st the beggar's knee,
Command the health of it? No, thou proud dream;
That play'st so subtly with a king's repose;
I am a king, that find thee; and I know,
'Tis not the balm, the sceptre, and the ball,
The sword, the mace, and crown imperial,
The inter-tissued robe of gold and pearl,
The farced title running 'fore the king,
The throne he sits on, nor the tide of pomp,
That beats upon the high shore of this world:
No, not all these, thrice gorgeous ceremony,
Not all these, laid in bed majestical,
Can sleep so soundly as the wretched slave;
Who, with a body fill'd, and vacant mind,
Gets him to rest, cramm'd with distressful bread;
Never sees horrid night, the child of hell;
But like a lackey, from the rise to set,
Sweats in the eye of Phœbus, and all night
Sleeps in Elysium; next day, after dawn,
Doth rise, and help Hyperion to his horse;
And follows so the ever-running year
With profitable labour, to his grave:
And, but for ceremony, such a wretch,
Winding up his days with toil, and nights with sleep,
Had the fore-hand and vantage of a king. *H. V.* iv. 1.

Draw not thy sword to guard iniquity,
For it was lent thee all that brood to kill. *Poems.*

Ay, every inch a king. *K. L.* iv. 6.

Kings are earth's gods: in vice their law's their will;
And if Jove stray, who dares say, Jove doth ill? *P. P.* i. 1.

   Princes are
A model which heaven makes like to itself:
As jewels lose their glory, if neglected,
So princes their renown if not respected. *P. P.* ii. 2.

Ha, majesty! how high thy glory towers,
When the rich blood of kings is set on fire!
O, now doth death line his dead chaps with steel;
The swords of soldiers are his teeth, his fangs;
And now he feasts, mouthing the flesh of men,
In undetermin'd differences of kings. *K. J.* ii. 2.

KIN   *Shakespearian Dictionary.*   **KIN**

KINGS,—*continued.*
                Do but think,
How sweet a thing it is to wear a crown;
Within whose circuit is Elysium,
And all that poets feign of bliss and joy!
                                        H. VI. PT. III. i. 2.
                O majesty!
When thou dost pinch thy bearer, thou dost sit
Like a rich armour worn in heat of day,
That scalds with safety.   *H. IV.* PT. II. iv. 4.
Yet looks he like a king; behold, his eye,
As bright as is the eagle's, lightens forth
Controlling majesty : Alack, alack, for woe,
That any harm should stain so fair a show.   *R. II.* iii. 3.
Not all the water in the rough, rude sea
Can wash the balm from an anointed king!   *R. II.* iii. 2.
Is not the king's name forty thousand names? *R. II.* iii. 2.
There's such divinity doth hedge a king,
That treason can but peep to what it would,
Acts little of his will.   *H.* iv. 5

How long a time lies in one little word,
Four lagging winters, and four wanton springs,
End in a word; such is the breath of kings.   *R. II.* i. 3
               High heaven forbid,
That kings should let their ears hear their faults hid.
                                             P. P. i. 2.
When we are wrong'd, and would unfold our griefs,
We are denied access unto his person,
Even by those men that most have done us wrong.
                                           H. IV. PT. II. iv. 1.

   The king is a good king; but it must be as it may; he passes some humours and careers.   *H. V.* ii. 1.

He is a happy king, since from his subjects
He gains the name of good, by his government. *P. P.* ii. 1.

The hearts of princes kiss obedience,
So much they love it; but, to stubborn spirits,
They swell, and grow as terrible as storms.   *H. VIII.* iii. 1.

Gives not the hawthorn bush a sweeter shade
To shepherds, looking on their silly sheep
Than doth a rich embroider'd canopy,
To kings that fear their subjects' treachery?
O, yes, it doth; a thousand fold it doth.
And, to conclude,—The shepherd's homely curds,
His cold thin drink out of his leather bottle,

KIN **Shakesperian Dictionary.** KIN

KINGS,—*continued.*
His wonted sleep under a fresh tree's shade,
All which secure and sweetly he enjoys,
Is far beyond a prince's delicates;
His viands sparkling in a golden cup,
His body couched in a curious bed,
When care, mistrust, and treason, wait on him.
H. VI. PT. III. ii. 5

    Mulmutius,
Who was the first of Britain, that did put
His brows within a golden crown, and called
Himself a king.   *Cym.* iii. 1

Who has a book of all that monarchs do,
He's more secure to keep it shut than shown. *P. P.* i. 1

Peace, peace, my lords, and give experience tongue.
They do abuse the king that flatter him:
For flattery is the bellows blows up sin;
The thing the which is flatter'd, but a spark,
To which that breath gives heat and stronger glowing;
Whereas reproof, obedient, and in order,
Fits kings, as they are men, for they may err. *P. P.* i. 2

The mightier man, the mightier is the thing
That makes him honour'd, or begets him hate. *Poems*

A thousand flatteries sit within thy crown,
Whose compass is no bigger than thy head;
And yet, incaged in so small a verge,
The waste is no whit lesser than thy land. *R. II.* ii. 1

    What?
I will be jovial; come, come; I am a king,
My masters, know you that?   *K. L.* iv. 6

Landlord of England art thou now, not king:
Thy state of law is bond-slave to the law. *R. II.* ii. 1

The king is not himself, but basely led by flatterers.
    R. II. ii 1

The skipping king he ambled up and down,
With shallow jesters and rash bavin wits.
    H. IV. PT. I. iii 2.

Princes have but their titles for their glories,
An outward honour for an inward toil;
And, for unfelt imaginations,
They often feel a world of restless cares:
So that, between their titles, and low name,
There's nothing differs but the outward fame. *R. III.* i. 4.

  For within the hollow crown,
That rounds the mortal temples of a king,

KINGS,—*continued.*
Keeps death his court: and there the antic sits,
Scoffing his state, and grinning at his pomp;
Allowing him a breath, a little scene
To monarchise, be fear'd, and kill with looks;
Infusing him with self and vain conceit,—
As if this flesh, that walls about our life,
Were brass impregnable; and humour'd thus,
Comes at the last, and with a little pin
Bores through his castle wall, and—farewell, king.
R.II. iii. 2.

Cover your heads, and mock not flesh and blood
With solemn reverence; throw away respect,
Tradition, form, and ceremonious duty,
For you have but mistook me all this while:
I live on bread like you, feel want like you,
Taste grief, need friends, like you: subjected thus,
How can you say to me—I am a king! *R. II.* iii. 2.

O Cromwell, Cromwell,
Had I but serv'd my God, with half the zeal
I serv'd the king, he would not in mine age
Have left me naked to mine enemies. *H.VIII.* iii. 2.

I think the king is but a man, as I am: the violet smells to him as it doth to me; the element shows to him as it doth to me; all his senses have but human conditions; his ceremonies laid by, in his nakedness he appears but a man; and though his affections are higher mounted than ours, yet, when they stoop, they stoop with the like wing; therefore, when he sees reason of fears, as we do, his fears, out of doubt, be of the same relish as ours are. *H.V.* iv. 1.

Well, I perceive he was a wise fellow, and had good discretion, that being bid to ask what he would of the king, desired he might know none of his secrets. Now do I see he had some reason for it: for if a king bid a man be a villain, he is bound by the indenture of his oath to be one.
P.P. i. 3

But not a minute, king, that thou can'st give:
Shorten my days, thou can'st, with sullen sorrow,
And pluck nights from me, but not lend a morrow:
Thou canst help time to furrow me with age,
But stop no wrinkle in his pilgrimage;
Thy word is current with him for my death;
But, dead, thy kingdom cannot buy my breath. *R. II.* i. 3.

——— HENRY V.
I saw young Harry with his beaver on,
His cuisses on his thighs, gallantly arm'd,—

KING Henry V.,—*continued.*
    Rise from the ground, like feather'd Mercury,
And vaulted with such ease into his seat,
As if an angel dropp'd down from the clouds,
To turn and wind a fiery Pegasus,
And witch the world with noble horsemanship.
                            H. IV. PT. I. iv. 1.
England ne'er had a king until his time.
Virtue he had, deserving to command;
His brandish'd sword did blind men with his beams;
His arms spread wider than a dragon's wings;
His sparkling eyes, replete with wrathful fire,
More dazzled and drove back his enemies,
Than mid-day sun, fierce bent against their faces.
What should I say? his deeds exceed all speech:
He ne'er lift up his hand, but conquered. *H. VI.* PT. I. i. 1.
Hear him but reason in divinity,
And, all-admiring, with an inward wish
You would desire the king were made a prelate:
Hear him debate of commonwealth affairs,
You would say—it hath been all-in-all his study;
List his discourse of war, and you shall hear
A fearful battle render'd you in music:
Turn him to any cause of policy,
The Gordian knot of it he will unloose,
Familiar as his garter; that, when he speaks,
The air, a charter'd libertine, is still,
And the mute wonder lurketh in men's ears,
To steal his sweet and honey'd sentences.   *H. V.* i. 1.
―――― Henry VI.
But all his mind is bent to holiness,
To number *Ave-Maries* on his beads;
His champions are—the prophets and apostles;
His weapons, holy saws of sacred writ;
His study is his tilt-yard, and his loves
Are brazen images of canoniz'd saints.   *H. VI.* PT. II. i. 3.
―――― Richard III.
Tetchy and wayward was thy infancy;
Thy school-days frightful, desperate, wild, and furious;
Thy prime of manhood daring, bold, and venturous;
Thy age confirm'd, proud, subtle, sly, and bloody.
                                R. III. iv. 4.
·――――'s Absence and Return, Typified.
                        Know'st thou not,
That when the searching eye of heaven is hid
Behind the globe, and lights the lower world,
Then thieves and robbers range abroad unseen,

KIN   **Shakesperian Dictionary.**   KIS

KING'S ABSENCE AND RETURN, TYPIFIED,—*continued.*
In murders and in outrage, bloody here ;
But when, from under this terrestrial ball,
He fires the proud tops of the eastern pines,
And darts his light through every guilty hole,
Then murders, treasons, and detested sins,
The cloak of night being pluck'd from off their backs,
Stand bare and naked, trembling at themselves? *R.II.* iii. 2

———'s ADVISER.
That man, that sits within a monarch's heart,
And ripens in the sunshine of his favour,
Would he abuse the countenance of the king,
Alack, what mischiefs might he set abroach,
In shadow of such greatness!   *H.IV.* PT. II. iv. 2.

——— DEATH OF A.
The cease of majesty
Dies not alone ; but, like a gulf, doth draw
What's near it with it: it is a massy wheel,
Fix'd on the summit of the highest mount,
To whose huge spokes ten thousand lesser things
Are mortis'd and adjoin'd ; which, when it falls,
Each small annexment, petty consequence,
Attends the boisterous ruin.   *H.* iii. 3.

———'s EVIL.
'Tis call'd the evil:
A most miraculous work in this good king :
Which often, since my here-remain in England,
I have seen him do. How he solicits heaven,
Himself best knows: but strangely visited people,
All swoln and ulcerous, pitiful to the eye,
The mere despair of surgery, he cures;
Hanging a golden stamp about their necks,
Put on with holy prayers ; and 'tis spoken,
To the succeeding royalty he leaves
The healing benediction.   *M.* iv. 3.

Ay, Sir ; there are a crew of wretched souls,
That stay his cure ; their malady convinces
The great assay of art ; but, at his touch,
Such sanctity hath heaven given his hand,
They presently amend.   *M.* iv. 3.

KISS.
O, a kiss
Long as my exile, sweet as my revenge !
Now, by the jealous queen of heaven, that kiss
I carried from thee, dear ; and my true lip
Hath virgin'd it o'er since.   *C.* v. 3.

KISS,—*continued.*
Very good; well kissed ! an excellent courtesy. *P.* ii. 1.
This done, he took the bride about the neck;
And kiss'd her lips with such a clamorous smack,
That, at the parting, all the church did echo. *T. S.* iii. 2.
Teach not thy lip such scorn; for it was made
For kissing, lady, not for such contempt. *R. III.* i. 2.

KISSES, COLD.
He hath bought a pair of cast lips of Diana; a nun of winter's sisterhood kisses not more religiously; the very ice of chastity is in them. *A.Y.* iii. 4.
And his kissing is as full of sanctity as the touch of holy bread. *A.Y.* iii. 4.

——— EXPRESSIVE.
I understand thy kisses, and thou mine,
And that's a feeling disputation. *H. IV.* PT. I. iii. 1.

KNAVES.
A knave; a rascal, an eater of broken meats; a base, proud, shallow, beggarly, three-suited, hundred-pound, filthy worsted-stocking knave; a lily-liver'd, action-taking knave; a whoreson, glass-gazing, superserviceable, finical rogue; a one-trunk-inheriting slave: one whom I will beat into clamorous whining, if thou denyest the least syllable of thy additions. *K. L.* ii. 2.
A shrewd knave, and an unhappy. *A.W.* iv. 5.

A slippery and subtle knave; a finder out of occasions; that has an eye can stamp and counterfeit advantages, though true advantage never present itself: a devilish knave! *O.* ii. 1.
What a pestilent knave is this same ! *R. J.* iv. 5.

I grant your worship, that he is a knave, Sir; but yet, God forbid, Sir, but a knave should have some countenance at his friend's request. An honest man, Sir, is able to speak for himself, when a knave is not. I have served your worship truly, Sir, for this eight years; and if I cannot once or twice in a quarter bear out a knave against an honest man, I have but very little credit with your worship. The knave is mine honest friend, Sir; therefore, I beseech your worship, let him be countenanced. *H. IV.* PT. II. v. 1.

A beetle-headed, flat-ear'd knave. *T.S.* iv. 1
Use his men well, for they are arrant knaves, and will backbite. *H.IV.* PT. II. v. 1
That such a slave as this should wear a sword,

KNAVES,—*continued.*
Who wears no honesty. Such smiling rogues as these
Like rats, oft bite the holy cords atwain,
Which are too intrinse. t' unloose.   *K. L.* ii. 2.
By holy Mary, Butts, there's knavery.   *H. VIII.* v. 2.

KNIGHTHOOD.
Sweet knight, thou art now one of the greatest men in the realm.   *H. IV:* PT. II. v. 3.

Well, now can I make any Joan a lady :
Good-den, Sir Richard,—God-a-mercy, fellow ;—
And if his name be George, I'll call him Peter ;
For new-made honour doth forget men's names;
'Tis too respective, and too sociable,
For your conversion.   *K. J.* i. 1.

He is a knight, dubbed with unhacked rapier, and on carpet consideration.   *T. N.* iii. 4.

There lay he stretch'd along, like a wounded knight.
    A. Y. iii. 2.

KNIGHTS OF THE GARTER.
When first this order was ordain'd, my lords,
Knights of the garter were of noble birth ;
Valiant, and virtuous, full of haughty courage,
Such as were grown to credit by the wars :
Not fearing death, nor shrinking for distress,
But always resolute in most extremes.
He then that is not furnish'd in this sort,
Doth but usurp the sacred name of knight.
Profaning this most honourable order.   *H. VI.* PT. I. iv. 1.

KNOCKING.
Here's a knocking, indeed ! If a man were porter of hell-gate, he should have old turning the key. Who's there, i' the name of Belzebub ?   *M.* ii. 3.

KNOTS IN TIMBER.
As knots, by the conflux of meeting sap,
Infect the sound pine, and divert his grain,
Tortive and errant from his course of growth.   *T. C.* i. 3.

KNOWING MAN.
This fellow's of exceeding honesty,
And knows all qualities with a learned spirit
Of human dealings.   *O.* iii. 3.
Is this the man ? Is't you, Sir, that know things ?
    A. C i. 2.

KNOWLEDGE.
Too much to know, is to know nought but fame. *L. L.* i. 1.

L.

LABOUR IN VAIN.
 Numbering sands and drinking oceans dry.   *R. II.* ii. 2.
 You may as well go about to turn the sun to ice, by fanning in his face with a peacock's feather.   *H. V.* iv. 1.
 I have seen a swan
With bootless labour swim against the tide,
And spend her strength with over-matching waves.
            H. VI. PT. III. i. 4.

LABYRINTH.
  Here's a maze trod, indeed,
Through forth-rights, and meanders!   *T.* iii. 3.

LAMENTATIONS (See also SORROW, TEARS).
 Why should calamity be full of words?   *R. III.* iv. 4.
Windy attorneys to their client woes,
Airy succeeders to intestate joys,
Poor breathing orators of miseries!
Let them have scope: though what they do impart,
Help nothing else, yet do they ease the heart. *R.III.* iv. 4.
 Alas, poor Yorick!   *H.* v. 1.
  Wise men ne'er sit and wail their loss,
But cheerly seek how to redress their harms.
          H. VI. PT. III. v. 4.
Cry, Trojans, cry! lend me ten thousand eyes,
And I will fill them with prophetic tears.
Virgins and boys, mid-age and wrinkled elders,
Soft infancy, that nothing canst but cry,
Add to my clamours! let us pay betimes
A moiety of that mass of moan to come.   *T. C.* ii. 2.

LAND OWNER.
 He hath much land, and fertile:—'Tis a chough; but, as I say, spacious in the possession of dirt.   *H.* v. 2.

LANGUAGE, ENGAGING.
 He speaks holiday.   *M. W.* iii. 2.

LARK.
    The lark, whose notes do beat
The vaulty heaven so high above our heads.   *R. J.* iii. 5.

LATE HOURS.
 Have you no wit, manners, nor honesty, but to gabble like tinkers at this time of night?   *T. N.* ii. 3.
 What doth gravity out of his bed at midnight!
            H. IV. PT. I. ii. 4.

LAT **Shakespearian Dictionary.** LAW

LATIN.

Away with him, away with him! He speaks Latin.
H. VI. PT. II..v. 2.
O, good my lord, no Latin;
I am not such a truant since my coming,
As not to know the language I have liv'd in. *H. VIII.* iii. 1.
You do ill to teach the child such words: he teaches him to hick, and to hack, which they'll do fast enough of themselves; and to call horum;—fye upon you! *M. W.* iv. 1.
O, I smell false Latin. *L. L.* v. 1.

LAUGHTER.

With his eyes in flood with laughter. *Cym.* i. 7.
O, you shall see him laugh, till his face be like a wet cloak, ill laid up. *H. IV.* PT. II. v. 1.
With such a zealous laughter, so profound. *L. L.* v. 2.
Stopping the career of laughter with a sigh. *W.T.* i. 2.
Making that idiot, laughter, keep men's eyes,
And strain their cheeks to idle merriment,
A passion hateful to my purposes. *K. J.* iii. 3.
O, I am stabb'd with laughter. *L. L.* v. 2
More merry tears
The passion of loud laughter never shed. *M. N.* v. 1

LAW (See also LITIGATION).

We have strict statutes and most biting laws. *M. M.* i. 4.
When law can do no right,
Let it be lawful, that law bar no wrong. *K. J.* iii. 1.
In law, what plea so tainted and corrupt,
But, being season'd with a gracious voice,
Obscures the show of evil? *M. V.* iii. 2.
Help, master, help; here's a fish hangs in the net, like a poor man's right in the law; 'twill hardly come out.
P. P. ii. 1.
The brain may devise laws for the blood; but a hot temper leaps over a cold decree: such a hare is madness the youth, to skip o'er the meshes of good counsel the cripple.
M. V. i. 2.
We must not make a scarecrow of the law,
Setting it up to fear the birds of prey,
And let it keep one shape till custom make it
Their perch, and not their terror. *M. M.* ii. 1.
There is no power in Venice
Can alter a decree established:
'Twill be recorded for a precedent;

LAW *Shakespearian Dictionary.* LEA

LAW,—*continued.*
And many an error, by the same example,
Will rush into the state: it cannot be. *M. V.* iv. 1.
We are for law, he dies. *T. A.* iii. 5.
It pleases time and fortune to lie heavy
Upon a friend of mine, who, in hot blood,
Hath stepp'd into the law, which is past depth
To those that, without heed, plunge into it. *T. A.* iii. 5.
    Now, as fond fathers,
Having bound up the threatening twigs of birch,
Only to stick it in their children's sight,
For terror, not to use; in time the rod
Becomes more mock'd than fear'd: so our decrees,
Dead to infliction, to themselves are dead;
And liberty plucks justice by the nose. *M. M.* i. 4.
   What's open made to justice,
That justice seizes. What know the laws,
That thieves do pass on thieves? 'Tis very pregnant,
The jewel that we find we stoop and take it,
Because we see it; but what we do not see,
We tread upon, and never think of it. *M. M.* ii. 1.
    The bloody book of law
You shall yourself read in the bitter letter,
After your own sense. *O.* i. 3.
If by this crime he owes the law his life,
Why, let the war receiv't in valiant gore;
For law is strict, and war is nothing more. *T. A.* iii. 5.
Faith, I have been a truant in the law;
And never yet could frame my will to it;
And, therefore, frame the law unto my will.
          H. VI. PT. I. ii. 4.
 But, I pr'ythee, sweet wag, shall there be gallows standing in England when thou art king?—and resolution thus fobb'd as it is, with the rusty curb of old father antic, the law? *H. IV.* PT. I. i. 2.
―――― ABUSE OF.
The usurer hangs the cozener.. *K. L.* iv. 6.
LAWYERS.
The first thing we do, let's kill all the lawyers.
          H. VI. PT. II. iv. 2.
Do as adversaries in law, strive mightily,
But eat and drink as friends. *T. S.* i. 2.
LEADER.
Another of his fashion they have not;
To lead their business. *O.* i. 1.

LEAN VISAGE.
Would he were fatter:—But I fear him not:—
Yet if my name were liable to fear,
I do not know the man I should avoid
So soon as that spare Cassius. He reads much;
He is a great observer, and he looks
Quite through the deeds of men ; he loves no plays,
As thou dost, Antony ; he hears no music :
Seldom he smiles ; and smiles in such a sort,
As if he mock'd himself, and scorn'd his spirit
That could be mov'd to smile at any thing.
Such men as he be never at heart's ease,
Whiles they behold a greater than themselves ;
And therefore are they very dangerous.   *J.C.* i. 2.

LEARNING (See also LIGHT, KING HENRY V., STUDY).
O this learning! what a thing it is!   *T. S.* i. 2.

Learning is but an adjunct to ourself.   *L. L.* iv. 3.

A mere hoard of gold, kept by a devil; till sack commences it, and sets it in use.   *H. IV.* PT. II. iv. 3

LEEK, THE
Will you mock at an antient tradition, begun upon an honourable respect, and worn as a memorable trophy of predeceased valour,—and dare not avouch in your deeds any of your words?   *H. V.* v. 1.

LEERING.
I spy entertainment in her; she discourses, she carves, she gives the leer of invitation.   *M. W.* i. 3.

LEGITIMACY.
Sirrah, your brother is legitimate :
Your father's wife did after wedlock bear him :
And if she did play false, the fault was her's ;
Which fault lies on the hazards of all husbands
That marry wives.   *K. J.* i. 1.

LENITY.
For what doth cherish weeds but gentle air?
And what makes robbers bold, but too much lenity?
H. VI. PT. III. ii. 6.

My gracious liege, this too much lenity
And harmful pity, must be laid aside.   *H.VI.* PT. III. ii. 2.

LETTER.
An' it shall please you to break up this, it shall seem to signify.   *M. V.* ii. 4.

LETTER,—continued.
     Why, what read you there,
That hath so cowarded and chas'd your blood,
Out of appearance?   *H.V.* ii. 2.
       Let us see :—
Leave, gentle wax; and manners, blame us not. *K.L.* iv. 6.
   Read o'er this;
And after, this; and then to breakfast, with
What appetite you have.   *H.VIII.* iii. 2.
Here are a few of the unpleasant'st words
That ever blotted paper.   *M.V.* iii. 2.
  Why, thou picture of what thou seemest, and idol of idiot-worshippers, here's a letter for thee. *T.C.* v 1.

LIAR. LIES. LYING.
  One that lies three-thirds, and uses a known truth to pass a thousand nothings with, should be once heard, and thrice beaten.   *A W.* ii. 5.
You told a lie; an odious, damned lie;
Upon my soul, a lie; a wicked lie.   *O.* v. 2
  He will lie, Sir, with such volubility, that you would think truth were a fool.   *A.W.* iv. 3.
     Two beggars told me,
I could not miss my way: Will poor folks lie,
That have afflictions on them; knowing 'tis
A punishment, or trial? Yes; no wonder,
When rich ones scarce tell true: To lapse in fulness
Is sorer than to lie for need; and falsehood
Is worse in kings than beggars.   *Cym.* iii. 6.
  Let me have no lying; it becomes none but tradesmen.
             W. T. iv. 3.
Detested kite! thou liest.   *K. L.* i. 4.
  These lies are like the father that begets them; gross as a mountain, open, palpable.   *H. IV.* PT. I. ii. 4.
  This same starved justice hath done nothing but prate to me of the wildness of his youth, and the feats he hath done about Turnbull-street; and every third word a lie, duer paid to the hearer than the Turk's tribute.
           H. IV. PT. II. iii. 2.
Thou liest, thou jesting monkey, thou.   *T.* iii. 2.
     Whose tongue soe'er speaks false,
Not truly speaks; who speaks not truly, lies. *K. J.* iv. 3.
  A very honest woman, but something given to lie; as a woman should not do, but in the way of honesty.
              A.C. v. 2.

LIA   Shakespearian Dictionary.   LIF

LIAR,—*continued.*
Lord, Lord, how subject we old men are to this vice of lying!   *H. IV.* PT. II. iii. 4.

—— HIS OWN DUPE.
Like one,
Who having, unto truth, by telling of it,
Made such a sinner of his memory,
To credit his own lie.   *T.* i. 2.

LIBERTY.
Blessed be those,
How mean soe'er, that have their honest wills,
Which seasons comfort.   *Cym.* i. 7.

LICENTIOUSNESS.
As surfeit is the father of much fast,
So every scope, by the immoderate use,
Turns to restraint.   *M. M.* i. 3.

LIFE (See also ILLUSION, MAN, DEATH).
Thy life's a miracle.   *K. L.* iv. 6.
Life's but a walking shadow, a poor player,
That struts and frets his hour upon the stage,
And then is heard no more; it is a tale
Told by an idiot, full of sound and fury,
Signifying nothing.   *M.* v. 5.
O gentlemen, the time of life is short;
To spend that shortness basely, were too long,
If life did ride upon a dial's point,
Still ending at th' arrival of an hour.   *H. IV.* PT. I. v. 2.
I see, a man's life is a tedious one.   *Cym.* iii. 6.
Like madness is the glory of this life.   *T. A.* i. 2.
Reason thus with life:—
If I do lose thee, I do lose a thing,
That none but fools would keep.   *M. M.* iii. 1.

The web of our life is of a mingled yarn, good and ill together: our virtues would be proud, if our faults whipp'd them not; and our crimes would despair, if they were not cherished by our virtues.   *A. W.* iv. 3.

The sands are number'd that make up my life.
   H. VI. PT. III. i. 4.
Life is a shuttle.   *M. W.* v. 1.
Thus play I, in one person, many people,
And none contented.   *R. II.* 5.
O excellent! I love long life better than figs!   *A. C.* i. 2.

LIFE,—*continued.*
                Think, ye see
The very persons of our noble story,
As they were living; think, you see them great,
And follow'd with the general throng, and sweat,
Of thousand friends, then, in a moment, see
How soon this mightiness meets misery! *H. VIII. prologue.*

It is silliness to live, when to live is a torment: and then we have a prescription to die, when death is our physician.
O. 1. 3.

That life is better life, past fearing death,
Than that which lives to fear. *M. M.* v. 1.

Thus, sometimes, hath the brightest day a cloud;
And, after summer, evermore succeeds
Barren winter, with his wrathful nipping cold:
So cares and joys abound, as seasons fleet.
H. VI. PT. II. ii. 4.

——— EPITOMIZED (See WORLD).

——— DESIRE OF.
        Camillo.—I very well agree with you in the hopes of him: it is a gallant child; one that, indeed, physics the subject, makes old hearts fresh: they, that went on crutches ere he was born, desire yet their life, to see him a man.
        Archidamus.—Would they else be content to die?
        Camillo.—Yes; if there were no other excuse why they should desire to live.
        Archidamus.—If the king had no son, they would desire to live on crutches till he had one. *W. T.* i. 1.

LIGHT (See also STUDY).
Light, seeking light, doth light of light beguile:
So, ere you find where light in darkness lies,
Your light grows dark by losing of your eyes. *L. L.* i. 1.

LIGHT INFANTRY.
        And this same half-fac'd fellow, Shadow,—give me this man; he presents no mark to the enemy; the foeman may with as great aim level at the edge of a pen-knife: And, for a retreat,—how swiftly will this Feeble, the woman's tailor, run off! O, give me the spare men, and spare me the great ones. *H. IV.* PT. II. iii. 2.

LIGHTNING (See also QUICKNESS).
        Like the lightning, which doth cease to be,
Ere one can say,—It lightens! *R. J.* ii. 2.

Brief as the lightning in the collied night,
That, in a spleen, unfolds both heaven and earth;

LIGHTNING,—*continued.*
And ere a man can say,—Behold!
The jaws of darkness do devour it up.   *M. N.* i. 1.

To stand against the deep dread-bolted thunder,
In the most terrible and nimble stroke
Of quick, cross lightning.   *K. L.* iv. 7.

LINEAGE (See also ANCESTRY).
A plague of both your houses!   *R. J.* iii. 1.

    There's neither honesty, manhood, nor good fellowship in thee, nor thou camest not of the blood-royal, if thou dar'st not stand for ten shillings.   *H. IV.* PT. I. i. 2.

LION.
                'Tis
The royal disposition of that beast,
To prey on nothing that doth seem as dead.   *A. Y.* iv. 3.

So looks the pent-up lion o'er the wretch,
That trembles under his devouring paws:
And so he walks, insulting o'er his prey;
And so he comes to rend his limbs asunder.
    H. VI. PT. III. i. 3.

LITIGATION (See also LAW).
    I'll have an action of battery against him, if there be any law in Illyria.   *T. N.* iv. 1.

    Persuade me not, I will make a star chamber matter of it.
    M. W. i. 1

    I'll answer him by law: I'll not budge an inch.
    T. S. IND. 1.

LIVELIHOOD.
                You take my life,
When you do take the means whereby I live.   *M. V.* iv. 1.

LONELINESS.
Alack, the night comes on, and the bleak winds
Do sorely ruffle; for many miles about
There's scarce a bush.   *K. L.* ii. 4.

———————— INSUPPORTABLE.
                 But whate'er I am,
Nor I, nor any man, that but man is,
With nothing shall be pleas'd, till he be eas'd
With being nothing.   *R. II.* v. 5.

LONGEVITY.
    A light heart lives long.

LONG (Stories).
Men, pleas'd themselves, think others will delight
In such like circumstance, with such like sport,
Their copious stories, oftentimes begun,
End without audience, and are never done. *Poems.*

LORD.
Thou art a lord, and nothing but a lord. *T. S.* Ind. 2
Upon my life I am a lord, indeed;
And not a tinker, nor Christophero Sly. *T. S.* Ind. 2.

LORD'S Anointed.
A flourish, trumpets!—strike alarum, drums!
Let not the heavens hear these tell-tale women
Rail on the Lord's anointed. *R. III.* iv. 4.

LOVE (See also Courtship, Fidelity).
Let me not to the marriage of true minds
 Admit impediments. Love is not love,
Which alters when it alteration finds,
 Or bends with the remover to remove.
O no, it is an ever-fixed mark,
 That looks on tempests, and is never shaken;
It is the star to every wand'ring bark,
 Whose worth's unknown, although his height be taken.
Love's not Time's fool, though rosy lips and cheeks
 Within his bending sickle's compass come;
Love alters not with his brief hours and weeks,
 But bears it out even to the edge of doom. *Poems.*

To be wise, and love, exceeds man's might. *T. C.* iii. 2.

Good shepherd, tell this youth what 'tis to love.
It is to be all made of sighs and tears,
It is to be all made of faith and service,
It is to be all made of fantasy.
All made of passion, and all made of wishes;
All adoration, duty, and observance,
All humbleness, all patience, and impatience,
All purity, all trial, all observance. *A. Y.* v. 2.

As love is full of unbefitting strains;
All wanton as a child, skipping, and vain;
Form'd by the eye, and, therefore, like the eye,
Full of strange shapes, of habits, and of forms,
Varying in subjects as the eye doth roll
To every varied object in his glance. *L. L.* v. 2.

But love, first learned in a lady's eyes,
Lives not alone immured in the brain:
But with the motion of all elements,
Courses as swift as thought in every power;

LOVE,—*continued.*
And gives to every power a double power,
Above their functions and their offices.
It adds a precious seeing to the eye;
A lover's eyes will gaze an eagle blind;
A lover's ear will hear the lowest sound,
When the suspicious head of theft is stopp'd;
Love's feeling is more soft, and sensible,
Than are the tender horns of cockled snails;
Love's tongue proves dainty Bacchus gross in taste:
For valour, is not love a Hercules,
Still climbing trees in the Hesperides?
Subtle as Sphynx, as sweet and musical
As bright Apollo's lute, strung with his hair;
And, when love speaks, the voice of all the gods
Makes heaven drowsy with the harmony.
Never durst poet touch a pen to write,
Until his ink were temper'd with love's sighs;
O then his lines would ravish savage ears,
And plant in tyrants mild humility. *L. L.* iv. 3.

Love is a smoke rais'd with the fume of sighs;
Being purg'd, a fire sparkling in a lover's eyes;
Being vex'd, a sea nourish'd with lovers' tears:
What is it else? a madness most discreet,
A choking gall, and a preserving sweet. *R. J.* i. 1.

Love like a shadow flies, when substance love pursues;
Pursuing that that flies, and flying what pursues.
M. W. ii. 2.

Didst thou but know the inly touch of love,
Thou would'st as soon go kindle fire with snow,
As seek to quench the fire of love with words. *T. G.* ii. 7.

Things base and vile, holding no quantity,
Love can transpose to form and dignity.
Love looks not with the eyes, but with the mind;
And therefore is wing'd Cupid painted blind;
Nor hath love's mind of any judgment taste;
Wings, and no eyes, figure unheedy haste;
And therefore is love said to be a child,
Because in choice he is so oft beguil'd. *M. N.* i. 1.

Love is a familiar: love is a devil: there is no evil angel but love. Yet Sampson was so tempted; and he had an excellent strength: yet was Solomon so seduced; and he had a very good wit. *L. L.* i. 2.

Adieu, valour! rust, rapier! be still, drum! for your manager is in love; yea, he loveth. *L. L.* i. 2.

LOVE,—continued.

O king, believe not this hard-hearted man;
Love, loving not itself, none other can. *R. II.* v. 3.

O spirit of love, how quick and fresh art thou! *T. N.* i. 1

Come hither, boy: If ever thou shalt love,
In the sweet pangs of it, remember me;
For, such as I am, all true lovers are;
Unstaid and skittish in all motions else,
Save in the constant image of the creature
That is belov'd. *T. N.* ii. 4.

It is as easy to count atomies, as to resolve the propositions of a lover. *A. Y.* iii. 2.

The strongest, love will instantly make weak:
Strike the wise dumb; and teach the fool to speak. *Poems.*

Excellent wretch! Perdition catch my soul,
But I do love thee! and when I love thee not,
Chaos is come again. *O.* iii. 3.

I know I love in vain, strive against hope;
Yet in this captious and intenible sieve,
I still pour in the waters of my love,
And lack not to lose still: thus, Indian-like,
Religious in mine error, I adore
The sun, that looks upon his worshipper,
But knows of him no more. *A. W.* i. 3.

We, that are true lovers, run into strange capers; but as all is mortal in nature, so is all nature in love mortal in folly. *A. Y.* ii. 4.

Love is merely a madness; and, I tell you, deserves as well a dark house and a whip, as madmen do: and the reason why they are not so punished and cured, is, that the lunacy is so ordinary, that the whippers are in love too. *A. Y.* iii. 2.

O coz, coz, coz, my pretty little coz, that thou didst know how many fathom deep I am in love! But it cannot be sounded; my affection hath an unknown bottom, like the bay of Portugal. *A. Y.* iv. 1.

Break an hour's promise in love! *A. Y.* iv. 1.

By heaven, I do love; and it hath taught me to rhyme, and to be melancholy. *L. L.* iv. 3.

If he be not in love with some woman, there is no believing old signs: he brushes his hat o' mornings;—what should that bode? *M. A.* iii. 3.

The greatest note of it is his melancholy. *M. A.* iii. 2.

LOVE,—*continued.*
I found him under a tree, like a dropped acorn.
A. Y. iii. 2.
But love is blind, and lovers cannot see
The pretty follies that themselves commit;
For, if they could, Cupid himself would blush. *M. V.* ii. 6.
This is the very ecstacy of love:
Whose violent property foredoes itself,
And leads the will to desperate undertakings,
As oft as any passion under heaven,
That does afflict our natures. *H.* ii. 1.
Cressid, I love thee in so strain'd a purity,
That the bless'd gods—as angry with my fancy,
More bright in zeal than the devotion which
Cold lips blow to their deities. *T. C.* iv. 4.

   I do much wonder that one man, seeing how much another man is a fool when he dedicates his behaviour to love, will, after he hath laughed at such shallow follies in others, become the argument of his own scorn, by falling in love. *M. A.* ii. 3.

The more thou damm'st it up, the more it burns;
The current, that with gentle murmur glides,
Thou know'st, being stopp'd, impatiently doth rage:
But when his fair course is not hindered,
He makes sweet music with th' enamel'd stones,
Giving a gentle kiss to every sedge
He overtaketh in his pilgrimage;
And so, by many winding nooks, he strays,
With willing sport, to the wild ocean. *T. G.* ii. 7.

O, pardon me, my lord; it oft falls out,
To have what we'd have, we speak not what we mean:
I something do excuse the thing I hate,
For his advantage that I dearly love. *M. M.* ii. 4.

   If I do not take pity of her, I'm a villain'; if I do not love her, I am a Jew: I will go get her picture.
M. A. ii. 3.

   Not only, Mistress Ford, in the simple office of love, but in all accoutrement, complement, and ceremony of it.
M. W. iv. 2.

Tell her, my love, more noble than the world,
Prizes not quantity of dirty lands;
The parts that fortune hath bestow'd upon her,
Tell her, I hold as giddily as fortune;
But 'tis that miracle, and queen of gems,
That nature pranks her in, attracts my soul. *T. N.* ii. 4.

LOV   Shakespearian Dictionary.   LOV

LOVE,—*continued.*

     As the most forward bud
Is eaten by the canker ere it blow,
Ev'n so by love the young and tender wit
Is turn'd to folly; blasting in the bud,
Losing his verdure even in the prime,
And all the fair effects of future hopes.   *T.G.* i. 1
O, how this spring of love resembleth
 The uncertain glory of an April day;
Which now shows all the beauty of the sun,
 And by-and-by a cloud takes all away.   *T.G.* i. 2
    As in the sweetest bud
The eating canker dwells, so eating love
Inhabits in the finest wits of all.   *T.G.* i. 1.

 Your brother and my sister no sooner met, but they looked; no sooner looked, but they loved; no sooner loved, but they sighed; no sooner sighed, but they asked one another the reason; no sooner knew the reason, but they sought the remedy: and in these degrees they have made a pair of stairs to marriage.   *A.Y.* v. 2.

 Indeed, he was mad for her, and talk'd of Satan, and of limbo, and of furies.   *A.W.* v. 3.

But if thy love were ever like to mine,
How many actions most ridiculous
Hast thou been drawn to by thy fantasy!   *A.Y.* ii. 4.

 He was wont to speak plain, and to the purpose, like an honest man, and a soldier; and now he has turn'd orthographer; his words are a very fantastical banquet, just so many strange dishes.   *M.A.* ii. 3.

If thou remember'st not the slightest folly
That ever love did make thee run into,
Thou hast not lov'd.   *A.Y.* ii. 4.

O!—And I, forsooth, in love!
I, that have been love's whip;
A very beadle to a humorous sigh;
A critic; nay, a night-watch constable;
A domineering pedant o'er the boy,
Than whom no mortal so magnificent!
This wimpled, whining, purblind, wayward boy;
This senior-junior, giant-dwarf, Dan Cupid;
Regent of love-rhymes, lord of folded arms,
The anointed sovereign of sighs and groans,
Liege of all loiterers and malcontents:
 *   *   *   *

What? I! I love! I sue! I seek a wife!
A woman, that is like a German clock,

LOVE,—*continued.*
Still a repairing; ever out of frame;
And never going aright, being a watch,
But being watch'd that it may still go right!   *L. L.* iii. 1.

   For aught that ever I could read,
Could ever hear by tale or history,
The course of true love never did run smooth;
But, either it was different in blood;
O cross! too high to be enthrall'd to low!
Or else misgraffed, in respect of years;
O spite! too old to be engag'd to young!
Or else it stood upon the choice of friends:
O hell! to choose love by another's eye!
Or, if there were a sympathy in choice,
War, death, or sickness did lay siege to it;
Making it momentary as a sound,
Swift as a shadow, short as any dream;
Brief as the lightning in the collied night,
That, in a spleen, unfold both heaven and earth,
And ere a man hath power to say,—Behold!
The jaws of darkness do devour it up:
So quick bright things come to confusion.   *M. N.* i. 1.

   For know, Iago,
But that I love the gentle Desdemona,
I would not my unhoused free condition
Put into circumspection and confine,
For the sea's worth.   *O.* i. 2.

Love's reason's without reason.   *Cym.* iv. 2.

   The gods themselves,
Humbling their deities to love, have taken
The shapes of beasts upon them: Jupiter
Became a bull and bellow'd; the green Neptune
A ram, and bleated; and the fire-rob'd god,
Golden Apollo, a poor humble swain,
As I seem now: Their transformations
Were never for a piece of beauty, rarer;
Nor in a way so chaste: since my desires
Run not before mine honour.   *W. T.* iv. 3.

   He says, he loves my daughter;
I think so too; for never gaz'd the moon
Upon the water, as he'll stand and read,
As 'twere, my daughter's eyes: and, to be plain,
I think, there is not half a kiss to choose,
Who loves another best.   *W. T.* iv. 3.

LOVE,—*continued.*

Still harping on my daughter :—yet he knew me not at first; he said, I was a fishmonger: He is far gone, far gone.
H. ii. 2.

Ever till now,
When men were fond, I smil'd, and wonder'd how.
M. M. ii. 2.

All fancy-sick she is, and pale of cheer,
With sighs of love. *M. N.* iii. 2.

They are but beggars that can count their worth;
But my true love is grown to such excess,
I cannot sum up half my sum of wealth. *R. J.* ii. 6.

Mine eyes
Were not in fault, for she was beautiful;
Mine ears, that heard her flattery; nor mine heart,
That thought her like her seeming; it had been vicious
To have mistrusted her. *Cym.* v. 5.

Soft, let us see ;—
Write, " Lord have mercy upon us" on these three ;
They are infected, in the heart it lies ;
They have the plague, and caught it of your eyes.
L. L. v. 2.

A lean check,—a blue eye, and sunken,—an unquestionable spirit,—a beard neglected :—Then your hose should be ungartered, your bonnet unbanded, your sleeve unbuttoned, your shoe untied, and every thing about you demonstrating a careless desolation. *A. Y.* iii. 2.

If he love her not,
And be not from his reason fall'n thereon,
Let me be no assistant for a state,
But keep a farm and carters. *H.* ii. 2.

O then, give pity
To her, whose state is such, that cannot choose
But lend and give, where she is sure to lose ;
That seeks not to find what her search implies,
But, riddle-like, live sweetly where she dies. *A. W.* i. 3.

He is far gone, far gone: and truly in my youth I suffered much extremity for love; very near this. *H.* ii. 2.

Here comes the lady.—O, so light a foot
Will ne'er wear out the everlasting flint.
A lover may bestride the gossamers
That idle in the wanton summer air,
And yet not fall. *R. J.* ii. 6.

She never told her love,
But let concealment, like a worm i' the bud,

LOVE,—*continued.*
Feed on her damask'd cheek: she pin'd in thought;
And, with a green and yellow melancholy,
She sat, like Patience on a monument,
Smiling at grief. *T. N.* ii. 4.

However we do praise ourselves.
Our fancies are more giddy and unfirm,
More longing, wavering, sooner lost and won,
Than women's are. *T. N.* ii. 4.

We men may say more, swear more: but indeed,
Our shows are more than will; for still we prove
Much in our vows, but little in our love. *T. N.* ii. 4.

O, she that hath a heart of that fine frame,
To pay this debt of love but to a brother,
How will she love, when the rich golden shaft
Hath kill'd the flock of all affections else
That live in her! when liver, brain, and heart,
These sovereign thrones, are all supplied and fill'd
(Her sweet perfections,) with one self king!—
Away before me to sweet beds of flowers;·
Love-thoughts lie rich, when canopied with bowers.
T. N. i. 1.

In love, the heavens themselves do guide the state,
Money buys lands, and wives are sold by fate. *M. W.* v. 5.

I have done penance for contemning love;
Whose high imperious thoughts have punish'd me
With bitter fasts, with penitential groans,
With nightly tears, and daily heart-sore sighs,
For in revenge of my contempt of love,
Love hath chas'd sleep from my enthralled eyes,
And made them watchers of mine own heart's sorrow.
T. G. ii. 4.

I know no ways to mince it in love, but directly to say, I love you; then, if you urge me further than to say, Do you in faith? I wear out my suit. Give me your answer; i' faith do, and so clap hands, and a bargain. *H. V.* v. 2.

She, sweet lady, dotes,
Devoutly dotes, dotes in idolatry,
Upon this spotted and inconstant man. *M. N.* i. 1

So loving to my mother,
That he might not beteem the winds of heaven,
Visit her face too roughly. *H.* i. 2.

Hang him, truant; there's no true drop of blood in him, to be truly touch'd with love: if he be sad, he wants money. *M.A.* iii. 9

LOVE,—*continued.*

Sweet love, I see, changing his property,
Turns to the sourest and most deadly hate.   *R. II.* iii. 2.

It is the show and seal of nature's truth,
Where love's strong passion is impressed in youth.
  A. W. i. 3.

To hear with eyes belongs to love's fine wit.   *Poems.*

I lov'd Ophelia; forty thousand brothers
Could not, with all their quantity of love,
Make up my sum.   *H.* v. 1.

My love till death, my humble thanks, my prayers;
That love, which virtue begs, and virtue grants.
  H. VI. PT. III. iii. 2.

    Why, man, she is mine own;
And I as rich in having such a jewel,
As twenty seas, if all their sands were pearl,
The water, nectar, and the rocks pure gold.   *T. G.* ii. 4.

What dangerous action, stood it next to death,
Would I not undergo for one calm look?
O, 'tis the curse in love, and still approv'd,
When women cannot love where they're beloved.   *T. G.* v. 4.

    Go to; it is a plague
That Cupid will impose for my neglect
Of his almighty dreadful little might.
Well; I will love, write, sigh, pray, sue, and groan;
Some men must love my lady, and some Joan.   *L. L.* iii. 1.

Good Mistress Page, for that I love your daughter
In such a righteous fashion as I do,
Perforce, against all checks, rebukes, and manners,
I must advance the colours of my love,
And not retire.   *M. W.* iii. 4.

With adorations, and with fertile tears,
With groans that thunder love, with sighs of fire.   *T. N.* i. 5.

    How now?
Even so quickly may one catch the plague?
Methinks, I feel this youth's perfections,
With an invisible and subtle stealth,
To creep in at mine eyes.   *T. N.* i. 5.

A murd'rous guilt shows not itself more noon
Than love that would seem hid; love's night is soon.
  T. N. iii. 1.

Fie, Fie! how wayward is this foolish love,
That, like a testy babe, will scratch the nurse,
And presently, all humbled, kiss the rod!   *T. G.* i. 2.

LOVE,—*continued.*

What? do I love her,
That I desire to hear her speak again,
And feast upon her eyes?   *M.M.* ii. 2.

There's beggary in the love that can be reckon'd.
     A.C i. 1.

Drawn in the flattering table of her eye!
Hang'd in the frowning wrinkle of her brow!
And quarter'd in her heart!   *K.J.* ii. 2.

    They are in the very wrath of love, and they will together; clubs cannot part them.   *A.Y.* v. 2.

Alas, that love, so gentle in his view,
Should be so tyrannous and rough in proof!   *R.J.* i. 1.

Love will suspect where is no cause of fear;
And there not fear where it should most distrust.   *Poems.*

Alas, that love, whose view is muffled still,
Should, without eyes, see path-ways to his will!   *R.J.* i. 1.

    Were I crown'd the most imperial monarch,
Thereof most worthy; were I the fairest youth
That ever made eye swerve; had force,and knowledge,
More than was ever man's,—I would not prize them,
Without her love: for her, employ them all;
Commend them, and condemn them, to her service,
Or to their own perdition.   *W.T.* iv. 3.

    If thou be'st valiant, as (they say) base men, being in love, have then a nobility in their natures, more than is native to them,—listen to me.   *O.* ii. 1.

I saw Othello's visage in his mind;
And to his honours and his valiant parts,
Did I my soul and fortunes consecrate.   *O.* i. 3.

Madam, you have bereft me of all words,
Only my blood speaks to you in my veins.   *M.V.* iii. 2.

    Thou art most rich, being poor;
Most choice, forsaken; and most lov'd, despis'd.
Thee and thy virtues here I seize upon.   *K.L.* i. 1.

In truth, fair Montague, I am too fond;
And therefore thou may'st think of my 'haviour light:
But trust me, gentlemen, I'll prove more true
Than those that have more cunning to be strange.
     R.J. ii. 2.

Ah me! how sweet is love itself possess'd,
When but love's shadows are so rich in joy?   *R.J.* v. 1.
Love's invisible soul.   *T.C.* iii. 1.

LOVE,—continued.
Her virtues, graced with external gifts,
Do breed love's settled passions in my heart.
H. VI. pt. i. v. 5.

His love was an eternal plant;
Whereof the root was fix'd in virtue's ground,
The leaves and fruit maintain'd with beauty's sun.
H. VI. pt. iii. iii. 3

First you have learn'd like Sir Proteus, to wreath your arms, like a malecontent; to relish a love-song, like a robin-red-breast; to walk alone, like one that had the pestilence; to sigh, like a school-boy that had lost his A B C; to weep, like a young wench that had buried her grandam; to fast, like one that takes diet; to watch, like one that fears robbing; to speak puling, like a beggar at Hallowmas.
T. G. ii. 1.

Holy St. Francis, what a change is here!
Is Rosaline, whom thou didst love so dear,
So soon forsaken? Young men's love then lies
Not truly in their hearts, but in their eyes.
Jesu Maria! what a deal of brine
Hath wash'd thy sallow cheeks for Rosaline!
How much salt water thrown away in waste,
To season love, that of it doth not taste!
The sun not yet thy sighs from heaven clears,
Thy old groans ring yet in my antient ears;
Lo, here upon thy cheek the stain doth sit
Of an old tear that is not wash'd off yet:
If e'er thou wast thyself, and these woes thine,
Thou and these woes were all for Rosaline;—
And art thou chang'd? *R. J.* ii. 3.

There lives within the very flame of love
A kind of wick, or snuff, that will abate it:
And nothing is at a like goodness still;
For goodness, growing to a pleurisy,
Dies in its own too-much. *H.* iv. 7.

O, gentle Romeo,
If thou dost love, pronounce it faithfully
Or if thou think'st I am too quickly won,
I'll frown, and be perverse, and say thee nay,
So thou wilt woo: but, else, not for the world. *R. J.* iii. 2.

See, how she leans her cheek upon her hand!
O, that I were a glove upon that hand,
That I might touch that cheek! *R. J.* ii. 2.

She lov'd me for the dangers I had pass'd;
And I lov'd her that she did pity them. *O.* i. 3.

LOVE,—*continued.*

Men have died from time to time, and worms have eaten
them, but not for love. *A. Y.* iv. 1.

Ay, but hearken, Sir; though the cameleon love can feed
on the air, I am one that am nourished by my victuals, and
would fain have meat. *T. G.* ii. 1.

Love is your master, for he masters you:
And he that is so yoked by a fool
Should'st not, methinks, be chronicled for wise. *T. G* i. 1.

If it prove so, then loving goes by haps;
Some Cupids kill with arrows, some with traps.
M. A. iii. 1.

For now my love is thaw'd;
Which, like a waxen image 'gainst a fire,
Bears no impression of the thing it was. *T. G.* ii. 4.

With love's light wings did I o'er-perch these walls;
For stony limits cannot hold love out. *R. J.* ii. 2.

Tut, man! one fire burns out another's burning,
One pain is lessen'd by another's anguish;
Turn giddy, and be holp by backward turning;
One desperate grief cures with another's languish:
Take thou some new infection to thy eye,
And the rank poison of the old will die. *R. J.* i. 3.

How silver-sweet sound lovers' tongues by night,
Like softest music to attending ears! *R. J.* ii. 2.

O, ten times faster Venus' pigeons fly
To seal love's bonds new made, than they are wont
To keep obliged faith unforfeited. *M. V.* ii. 6.

Time goes on crutches till love have all his rites.
M. A. ii. 1.

The wound's invisible
That love's keen arrows make. *A. Y.* iii. 5.

Love is not love when it is mingled with regards that
stand aloof from the entire point. *K. L.* i. 1.

Dove-drawn Venus. *T.* iv. 1.

One woman is fair; yet I am well: another is wise; yet
I am well: another is virtuous; yet I am well: but till all
graces be in one woman, one woman shall not come into
my grace. Rich she shall be, that's certain; wise, or I'll
none; virtuous, or I'll never cheapen her; fair, or I'll
never look on her; mild, or come not near me; noble, or
not I for an angel; of good discourse, an excellent musician, and her hair shall be of what colour it please God.
M. A. ii. 3.

LOVE, ETERNITY OF.
So that eternal love in love's fresh case,
Weighs not the dust and injuries of age,
Nor gives to necessary wrinkles place,
But makes antiquities for aye his page:
  Finding the first conceit of love there bred,
  Where time and outward forms would show it dead.
                                            Poems.

———— LETTER.
               As much love in rhyme,
As would be cramm'd up in a sheet of paper,
Writ on both sides the leaf, margent and all;
That he was fain to seal in Cupid's name.   *L. L.* v. 2.
She makes it strange; but she would be best pleas'd
To be so anger'd with another letter.   *T. G.* i. 2.

————'s MESSENGERS.
            Love's heralds should be thoughts,
Which ten times faster glide than the sun's beams,
Driving back shadows over low'ring hills.   *R. J.* ii. 5

LOVERS' POETRY.
Speak but one rhyme and I am satisfied;
Cry but,—Ah me! couple but—*love* and *dove.*   *R. J.* ii. 1.
Woo in rhyme, like a blind harper's song.   *L. L.* v. 2.
But are you so much in love as your rhymes speak?
                                              A. Y. iii. 2.

———— TOKENS.
Wear this from me; one out of suits with fortune,
That could give more, but that her hand lacks means.
                                              A. Y. i. 2.
            But she so loves the token,
(For he conjur'd her she would ever keep it,)
That she reserves it evermore about her,
To kiss and talk to.   *O.* iii. 3.
         Sooth, when I was young,
And handed love, as you do, I was wont
To load my she with knacks; I would have ransack'd
The pedlar's silken treasury, and have pour'd it
To her acceptance.   *W. T.* iv. 3.

Take these again; for, to the noble mind,
Rich gifts wax poor, when givers prove unkind.   *H.* iii. 1

————'s Vows (See also OATHS).
Ay, springes to catch wood-cocks. I do know,
When the blood burns, how prodigal the soul
Lends the tongue vows: these blazes, daughter,

LOVER'S Vows,—*continued.*
Giving more light than heat,—extinct in both,
Even in their promise, as it is a making,—
You must not take for fire.   *H.* i. 3.

  I swear to thee by Cupid's strongest bow;
By his best arrow with the golden head;
By the simplicity of Venus' doves;
By that which knitteth souls and prospers loves;
And by that fire which burn'd the Carthage queen,
When the false Trojan under sail was seen;
By all the vows that ever men have broke,
In number more than ever woman spoke;—
In that same place thou hast appointed me,
To-morrow truly will I meet with thee.   *M. N.* i. 1.

           Yet, if thou swear'st,
Thou may'st prove false; at lovers' vows,
They say, Jove laughs.   *R. J.* ii. 2.

Lady, by yonder blessed moon I swear,
That tips with silver all these fruit-tree tops.   *R. J.* ii. 2.

     Swearing, till my very roof was dry
With oaths of love.   *M. V.* iii. 2.

    Doubt thou the stars are fire;
      Doubt that the sun doth move:
    Doubt truth to be a liar;
      But never doubt I love.   *H.* ii. 2.

Do not swear at all;
Or, if thou wilt, swear by thy gracious self,
Which is the god of my idolatry,
And I'll believe thee.   *R. J.* ii. 2.

  Was is not *is;* besides, the oath of a lover is no stronger than the word of a tapster; they are both the confirmers of false reckonings.   *A. Y.* iii. 4.

Stealing her soul with many vows of faith,
And ne'er a true one.   *M. V.* v. 1.

That suck'd the honey of his music vows.   *H.* iii. 1.

O, men's vows are women's traitors.   *Cym.* iii. 4.

LOVELINESS.
She is full of most blessed conditions.   *O.* ii. 1.

      Diana's lip
Is not more smooth and rubious.   *T. N.* i. 4.

Of Nature's gifts thou may'st with lilies boast,
And with the half-blown rose.   *K. J.* iii. 1.

LOVE-WOUND.
Shot, by heaven! Proceed, sweet Cupid; thou hast thump'd him with thy bird-bolt under the left pap.
L. L. iv. 3.

Alas, poor Romeo, he is already dead; stabbed with a white wench's black eye; shot through the ear with a love-song; the very pin of his heart cleft with the blind bow-boy's butt-shaft. *R. J.* ii. 4.

LUCK.
You're a made old man; if the sins of your youth are forgiven you, you're well to live. Gold! all gold!
W. T. iii. 3.

M.

MACBETH.
Yet I do fear thy nature;
It is too full o' the milk of human kindness,
To catch the nearest way: Thou would'st be great;
Art not without ambition; but without
The illness should attend it. What thou would'st highly,
That would'st thou holily; would'st not play false,
And yet would'st wrongly win; thou'dst have, great Glamis,
That which cries, "Thus thou must do, if thou have it;
And that which rather thou dost fear to do
Than wishest should be undone." *M.* i. 5.

MAD-CAP.
Why, what a mad-cap hath heaven lent us here! *K. J.* i. 1.
Well, then, once in my days I'll be a mad-cap.
H. IV. PT. I. i. 2.

MADNESS (See also DESPONDENCY, DERANGEMENT).
Your noble son is mad:
Mad, call I it: for, to define true madness,
What is't, but to be nothing else but mad? *H.* ii. 2.

A sight most pitiful in the meanest wretch;
Past speaking of in a king. *K. L.* iv. 6.

And he repulsed, (a short tale to make,)
Fell into a sadness, then into a fast;
Thence to a watch; thence into a weakness;
Thence to a lightness: and, by this declension,
Into the madness wherein now he raves. *H.* ii. 2.

Alack, 'tis he; why, he was met even now
As mad as the vex'd sea; singing aloud;
Crown'd with rank fumitor, and furrow weeds,

MAD   *Shakespearian Dictionary.*   MAD

MADNESS,—*continued.*
With hardocks, hemlock, nettles, cuckoo-flowers,
Darnel, and all the idle weeds that grow
In our sustaining corn.   *K. L.* iv. 4.

          Oh, he is more mad
Than Telamon for his shield; the boar of Thessaly
Was never so imbost.   *A. C.* iv. 11.

O, what a noble mind is here o'erthrown!
The courtier's, soldier's, scholar's eye, tongue, sword:
The expectancy and rose of the fair state,
The glass of fashion, and the mould of form,
The observ'd of all observers; quite, quite down.
And I, of ladies most deject and wretched,
That suck'd the honey of his music vows,
Now see that sovereign and most noble reason,
Like sweet bells jangled, out of tune and harsh;
That unmatch'd form and feature of blown youth,
Blasted with ecstacy: O, woe is me!
To have seen what I have seen, see what I see!   *H.* iii. 1

         This is mere madness:
And thus awhile the fit will work on him;
Anon, as patient as the female dove,
When that her golden couplets are disclos'd,
His silence will sit drooping.   *H.* v. i.

Essentially mad, without seeming so.   *H. IV.* PT. I. ii. 4.

She speaks much of her father; says, she hears,
There's tricks i' the world; and hems, and beats her heart;
Spurns enviously at straws; speaks things in doubt,
That carry but half sense: her speech is nothing,
Yet the unshaped use of it, doth move
The hearers to collection.   *H.* iv. 5.

O let me not be mad, not mad, sweet heaven!
Keep me in temper; I would not be mad!   *K. L.* i. 5.

   How pregnant sometimes his replies are! a happiness
that often madness hits on, which reason and sanity could
not so prosperously be delivered of!   *H.* ii. 2.

It is the very error of the moon;
She comes more near the earth than she was wont;
And makes men mad.   *O.* v. 2.

O, matter and impertinency mix'd!
Reason in madness!   *K. L.* iv. 6

That he is mad, 'tis true; 'tis true, 'tis pity;
And pity 'tis, 'tis true.   *H.* ii. 2.

Mad world, mad kings, mad composition.   *K. J.* ii. 2.

MADNESS,—*continued.*

     I am as mad as he,
If sad and merry madness equal be.   *T. N.* iii. 4.
    O prince, I conjure thee, as thou believ'st
There is another comfort than this world,
That thou neglect me not, with that opinion
That I am touch'd with madness.   *M. M.* v. 1.
      It is not madness,
That I have utter'd: bring me to the test,
And I the matter will re-word; which madness
Would gambol from.   *H.* iii. 4.
Madness in great ones must not unwatch'd go. *H.* iii. 1.

———, METHODICAL.
      By mine honesty,
If she be mad, (as I believe no other,)
Her madness hath the oddest frame of sense,
Such a dependency of thing on thing,
As e'er I heard in madness.   *M. M.* v. 1.

MAGNANIMITY.
     Our spoils he kick'd at;
And look'd upon things precious, as they were
The common muck o' the world: he covets less
Than misery itself would give; rewards
His deeds with doing them; and is content
To spend the time to end it.   *C.* ii. 2.
     Had I great Juno's power,
The strong-wing'd Mercury should fetch thee up,
And set thee by Jove's side.   *A. C.* iv. 13.
     Your honours' pardon;
I had rather have my wounds to heal again,
Than hear say how I got them.   *C.* ii. 2.
I had rather have one to scratch my head i' the sun,
When the alarum was struck, than idly sit
To hear my nothings monster'd.   *C.* ii. 2.
He had rather venture all his limbs for honour,
Than one of his ears to hear it.   *C.* ii. 2.
Bettering thy loss makes the bad causer worse;
Revolving this will teach thee how to curse. *R. III.* iv. 4.
And those that leave their valiant bones in France,
Dying like men, though buried in your dunghills,
They shall be fam'd; for there the sun shall greet them,
And draw their honours reeking up to heaven. *H. V.* iv. 3.
If we are mark'd to die, we are enough
To do our country loss; and if to live,
The fewer men, the greater share of honour. *H. V.* iv. 3.

MAGNANIMITY,—*continued.*
O! the blood more stirs,
To rouse a lion than to start a hare.   *H. IV.* PT. I. i. 3.
My noble girls!—Ah, women, women! look,
Our lamp is spent, its out: Good Sirs, take heart:
We'll bury him: and then, what's brave, what's noble,
Let's do it after the high Roman fashion,
And make death proud to take us.   *A. C.* iv. 13.
His valour, shown upon our crests to-day,
Hath taught us how to cherish such high deeds,
Even in the bosom of our adversaries.   *H. IV.* PT. I. v. 5.

MAL-ADMINISTRATION.
I have misused the king's press damnably.
H. IV. PT. I. iv. 2

MALEDICTION.
     All the charms
Of Sycorax, toads, beetles, bats, light on you.   *T.* i. 2

The common curse of mankind, folly and ignorance, be thine in great revenue! heaven bless thee from a tutor, and discipline come not near thee! Let thy blood be thy direction till thy death! then if she, that lays thee out, says, thou art a fair corse, I'll be sworn, and sworn upon't, she never shrouded any but lazars. Amen.   *T. C.* ii. 3.

You nimble lightnings, dart your blinding flames
Into her scornful eyes! Infect her beauty,
You fen-suck'd fogs, drawn by the powerful sun,
To fall and blast her pride!   *K. L.* ii. 4.

Feed not thy sovereign's foe, my gentle earth,
Nor, with thy sweets, comfort his ravenous sense:
But let thy spiders, that suck up thy venom,
And heavy gaited toads, lie in their way;
Doing annoyance to the treacherous feet,
Which with usurping steps do trample thee.
Yield stinging nettles to mine enemies;
And when they from thy bosom pluck a flower,
Guard it I pray thee, with a lurking adder.   *R. II.* iii. 2.

As wicked dew, as e'er my mother brush'd,
With raven's feather, from unwholesome fen,
Drop on you both: a south-west blow on ye,
And blister you all o'er.   *T.* i. 2.

Richard yet lives, hell's black intelligencer;
Only reserv'd their factor to buy souls,
And send them thither: But at hand, at hand,
Ensues his piteous and unpitied end;
Earth gapes, hell burns, fiends roar, saints pray,

MALEDICTION,—*continued.*
To have him suddenly convey'd from hence;
Cancel his bond of life, dear God, I pray,
That I may live to say—The dog is dead!   *R. III.* iv. 4.

The plague of Greece upon thee, thou mongrel beef-witted
lord!   *T.C.* ii. 1.

Hear, Nature, hear; dear goddess, hear!
*   *   *   Suspend thy purpose, if
Thou didst intend to make this creature fruitful!
*   *   *   If she must teem,
Create her child of spleen; that it may live
And be a thwart disnatur'd torment to her!
Let it stamp wrinkles on her brow of youth!
With cadent tears fret channels in her cheeks;
Turn all her mother's pains and benefits
To laughter and contempt; that she may feel
How sharper than a serpent's tooth it is
To have a thankless child!   *K. L.* i. 4.

The worm of conscience still be-gnaw thy soul!
Thy friends suspect for traitors whilst thou liv'st,
And take deep traitors for thy dearest friends!
No sleep close up that deadly eye of thine,
Unless it be while some tormenting dream
Affrights thee with a hell of ugly devils!   *R. III.* i. 3.

You taught me language; and my profit on't
Is, I know how to curse: the red plague rid you
For learning me your language.   *T.* i. 2.

Now the red pestilence strike all trades in Rome,
And occupations perish!   *C.* iv. 1.

All the stor'd vengeance of heaven fall
On her ingrateful top! Strike her young bones,
You taking airs with lameness!   *K. L.* ii. 4.

If heaven have any grievous plague in store,
Exceeding those that I can wish upon thee,
O, let them keep it till thy sins be ripe,
And then hurl down their indignation
On thee, the troubler of the poor world's peace.   *R.* iii. 3.

Now, all the plagues that in the pendulous air
Hang fated o'er men's faults, light on thy daughters.
   K. L. iii. 4

A plague upon your epileptic visage.   *K. L.* ii. 2

Let this pernicious hour
Stand aye accursed in the calendar!   *M.* iv. 1.

All the infections that the sun sucks up,

MALEDICTION,—*continued.*
From bogs, fens, flats, on Prosper fall, and make him
By inch-meal a disease! *T.* ii. 2.
If ever he have child, abortive be it,
Prodigious, and untimely brought to light,
Whose ugly and unnatural aspéct
May fright the hopeful mother at the view;
And that be heir to his unhappiness. *R. III.* i. 2.
Dower'd with our curse, and stranger'd with an oath. *K.L.* i. 1.
Why, thou damnable box of envy, thou, what meanest
thou, to curse thus. *T.C.* v. 1.

MALEVOLENCE.
Had I power, I should ·
Pour the sweet milk of concord into hell,
Uproar the universal peace, confound
All unity on earth. *M.* iv. 3.
I will fight
Against my canker'd country, with the spleen
Of all the under fiends. *C.* iv. 5.

MALICE.
Men, that make
Envy, and crooked malice nourishment,
Dare bite the best. *H.VIII.* v. 2.

MALIGNITY.
A dagger of the mind; a false creation,
Proceeding from the heat-oppressed brain. *M.* ii. 1.

MAN (See also ILLUSION, LIFE, DEATH).
What a piece of work is man! How noble in reason!
how infinite in faculties! in form, and moving, how express
and admirable! in action, how like an angel! in apprehen-,
sion, how like a god! the beauty of the world! the para-
gon of animals! *H.* ii. 2.
They say, best men are moulded out of faults,
And, for the most, become much more the better,
For being a little bad. *M. M.* v. 1
Ay, in the catalogue ye go for men;
As hounds, and greyhounds, mongrels, spaniels, curs,
Shoughs, water-rugs, and demi-wolves are clep'd,
All by the name of dogs: the valued file
Distinguishes the swift, the slow, the subtle,
The house-keeper, the hunter, every one
According to the gift which bounteous Nature
Hath in him clos'd; whereby he doth receive
Particular addition, from the bill
That writes them all alike: and so of men. *M.* iii. 1.

MAN,—*continued.*
　　We came crying hither.　　　　　　　　　*K. L.* iv. 6.
　　Lord, we know what we are, but know not what we may
be. .　　　　　　　　　　　　　　　　　　　*H.* iv. 5.
　　　　　　Know thou this:—that men
Are as the time is.　　　　　　　　　　　　*K. L.* v. 3.
O momentary grace of mortal men,
Which we more hunt for than the grace of God!
Who builds his hope in air of your fair looks
Lives like a drunken sailor on a mast;
Ready, with every nod, to tumble down
Into the fatal bowels of the deep.　　　　*R. III.* iii. 4.

This was the noblest Roman of them all:
All the conspirators, save only he,
Did that they did in envy of great Cæsar;
He, only, in a general honest thought,
And common good to all, made one of them.
His life was gentle; and the elements
So mix'd in him, that nature might stand up,
And say to all the world, *This was a man!*　*J.C.* v. 5.
Is man no more than this?　　　　　　　　· *K. L.* iii. 4.
　　　　　　A breath thou art,
(Servile to all the skiey influences),
That dost this habitation, where thou keep'st,
Hourly afflict; merely, thou' art death's fool;
For him thou labour'st by thy flight to shun,
And yet runn'st toward him still: Thou art not noble:
For all the accommodations that thou bear'st,
Are nurs'd by baseness: Thou art by no means valiant;
For thou dost fear the soft and tender fork
Of a poor worm: Thy best of rest is sleep,
And that thou oft provok'st; yet grossly fear'st
Thy death, which is no more. Thou art not thyself;
For thou exist'st on many a thousand grains
That issue out of dust: Happy thou art not;
For what thou hast not, still thou striv'st to get:
And what thou hast, forget'st: Thou art not certain;
For thy complexion shifts to strange effects,
After the moon: If thou art rich, thou art poor;
For, like an ass, whose back with ingots bows,
Thou bear'st thy heavy riches but a journey,
Till death unloads thee: Friend hast thou none;
For thine own bowels, which do call thee sire,
The mere effusion of thy proper loins,
Do curse the gout, serpigo, and the rheum,
For ending thee no sooner: Thou hast nor youth, nor age ·

MAN   Shakesperian Dictionary.   MAN

MAN,—*continued.*
But, as it were, an after-dinner's sleep,
Dreaming on both; for all thy blessed youth
Becomes as aged, and does beg the alms
Of palsied eld; and when thou art old, and rich,
Thou hast neither heat, affection, limb, nor beauty,
To make thy riches pleasant. What's yet in this,
That bears the name of life? Yet in this life
Lie hid more thousand deaths: yet death we fear,
That makes these odds all even.   *M. M.* iii. 1.
     Foolish wench!
To the most of men this is a Caliban,
And they to him are angels.   *T.* i. 2.
O the difference of man and man!   *K. L.* iv. 2.
God made him, therefore let him pass for a man. *M. V.* i. 2.
    There is no trust,
No faith, no honesty in men; all perjur'd,
All forsworn, all naught, all dissemblers.   *R. J.* iii. 2.
   A rarer spirit never
Did steer humanity; but you, gods, will give us
Some faults to make us men.   *A. C.* v. 1.
When we are born, we cry, that we are come
To this great stage of fools.   *K. L.* iv. 6.
   He was not born to shame:
Upon his brow shame is asham'd to sit;
For 'tis a throne where honor may be crown'd
Sole monarch of the universal earth.   *R. J.* iii. 2.
 He was a man, take him for all in all,
I shall not look upon his like again.   *H.* i. 2.

 You rogue, here's lime in this sack too: There is nothing but roguery to be found in villainous man.
        H. IV. pt. i. ii. 4.
Every man is odd.   *T. C.* iv. 5.
   Who lives, that's not
Depraved, or depraves? who dies, that bears
Not one spurn to their graves of their friends' gift?
        T. A. i 2.
Man is a giddy thing, and this is my conclusion.
        M. A. v. 4.

MANHOOD Deteriorated.
 But manhood is melted into courtesies, valour into compliment, and men are turned into tongue, and trim ones too: he is now as valiant as Hercules that only tells a lie, and swears to it.   *M. A.* iv. 1.

MANHOOD DETERIORATED,—*continued.*
Go thy ways, old Jack; die when thou wilt, if manhood, good manhood, be not forgot upon the face of the earth, then am I a shotten herring. *II. IV.* PT. I. ii. 4.

MANUSCRIPT.
I once did hold it, as our statists do,
A baseness to write fair, and labour'd much
How to forget that learning; but, sir, now
It did me yeoman's service. *II.* v. 2.

MARRIAGE (SEE also ESPOUSAL).
A contract of eternal bond of love,
Confirmed by mutual joinder of your hands,
Attested by the holy close of lips,
Strengthened by interchangement of your rings;
And all the ceremony of this compáct
Seal'd in my function by my testimony. *T. N.* v. 1.

Marriage is a matter of more worth
Than to be dealt in by attorneyship.
For what is wedlock forced, but a hell,
An age of discord and continual strife?
Whereas the contrary bringeth forth bliss,
And is a pattern of celestial peace. *H. VI.* PT. I. v. 5.

Earthlier happy is the rose distill'd,
Than that, which, withering on the virgin thorn,
Grows, lives, and dies, in single blessedness. *M. N.* i. 1.

She's not well married, that lives married long;
But she's best married, that dies married young.
R. J. iv. 5.

Pale primroses,
That die unmarried, ere they can behold
Bright Phœbus in his strength, a malady
Most incident to maids. *W. T.* iv. 3

But, mistress, know yourself; down on your knees,
And thank heaven, fasting, for a good man's love:
For I must tell you friendly in your ear,—
Sell when you can; you are not for all markets.
A. Y. iii. 5

MARRIAGES, MERCENARY.
The hearts of old, gave hands;
But our new heraldry is—hands, not hearts. *O.* iii. 4

MARTLET.
This guest of summer,
The temple-hunting martlet, does approve,
By his lov'd mansionry, that the heaven's breath,
Smells wooingly here: no jutty, frieze, buttress,

MAR   **Shakespearian Dictionary.**   MEE

MARTLET,—*continued*.
Nor coigne of 'vantage, but this bird hath made
His pendent bed, and procreant cradle: Where they
Most breed and haunt, I have observ'd the air
Is delicate.   *M.* i. C.
     The martlet
Builds in the weather on the outward wall,
Even in the force and road of casualty.   *M. V.* ii. 9.

MASKED LADIES.
Fair ladies, mask'd, are roses in their bud:
Dismask'd, their damask sweet commixture shown,
Are angels veiling clouds, or roses blown.   *L. L.* v. 2.

MATURITY.
Mellow'd by the stealing hours of time.   *R. III.* iii. 7.

MEALS.
Unquiet meals make ill digestions.   *C. E.* v. 1.

MEANING.
Take our good meaning; for our judgment sits
Five times in that, ere once in our five wits.   *R. J.* i. 4.

MEDDLER.
'Tis dangerous, when the baser nature comes
Between the pass and fell incensed points
Of mighty opposites.   *H.* v. 2.

Thou wretched, rash, intruding fool; farewell!
I took thee for thy better; take thy fortune:
Thou find'st, to be too busy, is some danger.   *H.* iii. 4.

    Why, the devil, came you between us? I was hurt under
your arm.   *R. J.* iii. 1.

MEDIATOR.
    I was hardly moved to come to thee; but being assured
none but myself could move thee, I have been blown out
of your gates with sighs; and conjure thee to pardon Rome,
and thy petitionary countrymen.   *C.* v. 2.

MEDITATION.
Measuring his affections by my own,
That most are busied when they're most alone.   *R. J.* i. 1.

MEEKNESS.
                      'Beseech your majesty,
Forbear sharp speeches to her: she's a lady
So tender of rebukes, that words are strokes,
And strokes death to her.   *Cym.* iii. 5

MEETING.
Here is like to be a great presence of worthies.   *L. L.* v. 2.

MELANCHOLY (See also DESPONDENCY, MADNESS).
Melancholy is the nurse of frenzy. *T. S.* IND. 2.
Thick-ey'd musing, and curs'd melancholy. *H.IV.* PT. I. ii. 3.
Besieged with sable-coloured melancholy. *L. L.* i. 1
The sad companion, dull-ey'd melancholy. *P. P.* i. 2.
I am wrapp'd in dismal thinkings. *A. W.* v. 3.
Chanting faint hymns to the cold fruitless moon. *M. N.* i. 1.

My cue is villanous melancholy, with a sigh like Tom o' Bedlam. *K. L.* i. 2.

I have of late (but wherefore I know not) lost all my mirth, foregone all custom of exercises: and, indeed, it goes so heavily with my disposition, that this goodly frame, the earth, seems to me a sterile promontory; this most excellent canopy, the air, look you, this brave o'erhanging firmament, this majestical roof fretted with golden fire, why, it appears no other thing to me, than a foul and pestilent congregation of vapours. *H.* ii. 2.
Melancholy as a lover's lute. *H. IV.* PT. I. i. 2.

Boy, what sign is it, when a man of great spirit grows melancholy? *L. L.* i. 2.

We have been up and down to seek for thee; for we are high proof melancholy, and would fain have it beaten away: Wilt thou use thy wit? *M. A.* v. 1.

I have neither the scholar's melancholy, which is emulation; nor the musician's, which is fantastical; nor the courtier's, which is proud; nor the soldier's, which is ambitious; nor the lawyer's, which is politic; nor the lady's, which is nice; nor the lover's, which is all these; but it is a melancholy of mine own, compounded of many simples, extracted from many objects: and, indeed, the sundry contemplation of my travels, in which my often rumination wraps me, is a most humorous sadness. *A. Y.* iv. 1.

Why, he will look upon his boot, and sing; mend the ruff, and sing; ask questions, and sing; pick his teeth, and sing: I knew a man that had this trick of melancholy, sold a goodly manor for a song. *A. W.* iii. 2.

Would the fountain of your mind were clear again, that I might water an ass at it. *T. C.* iii. 3.

There's something in his soul,
O'er which his melancholy sits on brood;
And, I do doubt, the hatch, and the disclose,
Will be some danger. *H.* iii. 1.

O, melancholy!
Who ever yet could sound thy bottom? find

MELANCHOLY,—*continued.*
The ooze, to show what coast thy sluggish crare
Might easiest harbour in? *Cym.* iv. 2.

MEMORY, THE STORES OF THE (See also REMEMBRANCE).
This is a gift that I have, simple, simple; a foolish extravagant spirit, full of forms, figures, shapes, objects, ideas, apprehensions, motions, revolutions: these are begot in the ventricle of memory, nourished in the womb of *pia mater*, and delivered upon the mellowing of occasion.
L. L. iv. 2.

MEN, DESTROYER OF.
Cannibally given. *C.* iv. 5.

MERCENARY.
Sir, for a *quart d'écu* he will sell the fee-simple of his salvation, the inheritance of it; and cut the entail from all remainders. *A. W.* iv. 3.

O, dishonest wretch!
Wilt thou be made a man out of my vice! *M. M.* iii. 1.

O fie, fie, fie!
Thy sin's not accidental, but a trade. *M. M.* iii. 1.

Think'st thou, I'll endanger my soul *gratis?* *M. W.* ii. 2.

MERCHANTMEN.
Your mind is tossing on the ocean;
There, where your argosies with portly sail,
Like signiors and rich burghers of the flood,
Or, as it were, the pageants of the sea,—
Do overpeer the petty traffickers,
That curt'sy to them, do them reverence,
As they fly by them with their woven wings. *M. V.* i. 1.

MERCY.
Wilt thou draw near the nature of the gods?
Draw near them then in being merciful:
Sweet mercy is nobility's true badge. *Tit. And.* i. 2.

The quality of mercy is not strain'd;
It droppeth, as the gentle rain from heaven,
Upon the place beneath: it is twice bless'd;
It blesseth him that gives, and him that takes ·
'Tis mightiest in the mightiest; it becomes
The throned monarch better than his crown:
His sceptre shows the force of temporal power,
The attribute to awe and majesty,
Wherein doth sit the dread and fear of kings;
But mercy is above this sceptred sway,
It is enthroned in the heart of kings,
It is an attribute to God himself:

Shakespearian Dictionary.

MERCY,—*continued.*

And earthly pow'r doth then show likest God's,
When mercy seasons justice. *M. V.* iv. 1.
    Alas! alas!
Why, all the souls that are, were forfeit once;
And He that might th' advantage best have took,
Found out the remedy: How would you be,
If He, who is the top of judgment, should
But judge you as you are? O, think on that;
And mercy then will breathe within your lips,
Like man new made. *M M.* ii. 2.

I am an humble suitor to your virtues;
For pity is the virtue of the law,
And none but tyrants use it cruelly. *T. A.* iii. 5.

If little faults, proceeding on distemper,
Shall not be wink'd at, how shall we stretch our eye,
When capital crimes, chew'd, swallow'd, and digested,
Appear before us? *H. V.* ii. 2.

Press not a falling man too far; 'tis virtue:
His faults lie open to the laws; let them,
Not you, correct him. *H. VIII.* iii. 2.
    Well, believe this;
No ceremony that to great ones 'longs,
Not the king's crown, nor the deputed sword,
The marshal's truncheon, nor the judge's robe,
Become them with one half so good a grace,
As mercy does. *M. M.* ii. 2.
    Lawful mercy is
Nothing akin to foul redemption. *M. M.* ii. 4.

Though justice be thy plea, consider this:—
That in the course of justice, none of us
Should see salvation: we do pray for mercy;
And that same prayer doth teach us all to render
The deeds of mercy. *M. V.* iv. 1.

Mercy is not itself that oft looks so;
Pardon is still the nurse of second woe. *M. M.* ii. 1.

You must not dare, for shame, to talk of mercy;
For your own reasons turn into your bosoms,
As dogs upon their masters, worrying them. *H. V.* ii. 2.

MERIT.

 There is more owing her than is paid; and more shall be paid her than she'll demand. *A. W.* i. 3.

 You see, my good wenches, how men of merit are sought after. *H. IV.* PT. II. ii. 4.

MERIT,—*continued.*
    Thou art so far before,
That swiftest wing of recompense is slow
To overtake thee..   *M.* i. 4.

—— DEPENDENT.
Better it is to die, better to starve,
Than crave the hire which first we do deserve. *C.* ii. 3.

MERRY WIVES.
Wives may be merry, and yet honest too.   *M. W.* iv. 2.

MESSENGER (See also NEWS).
    The first bringer of unwelcome news
Hath but a losing office; and his tongue
Sounds ever after as a sullen bell,
Remember'd knolling a departed friend. *H. IV.* PT. II. i. 1.

Though it be honest, it is never good
To bring bad news: Give to a gracious message
A host of tongues; but let ill tidings tell
Themselves, when they be felt.   *A. C.* ii. 5.

Here is a dear and true industrious friend,
Sir Walter Blount, new lighted from his horse, .
Stain'd with the variation of each soil
Betwixt that Holmedon, and this seat of ours;
And he hath brought us smooth and welcome news.
            H. IV. PT. I. i. 1.

    I have not seen
So likely an ambassador of love;
A day in April never came so sweet,
To show how costly summer was at hand,
As this fore-spurrer comes before his lord. *M. V.* ii. 9.

Be thou as lightning in the eyes of France;
For ere thou canst report, I will be there;
The thunder of my cannon shall be heard. *K. J.* i. 1.

    Why, he is dead.
See what a ready tongue suspicion hath!
He, that but fears the thing he would not know,
Hath, by instinct, knowledge from others' eyes.
That which he fear'd is chanc'd. Yet speak, Morton,
Tell thou thy earl, his divination lies;
And I will take it as a sweet disgrace;
And make thee rich for doing me much wrong.
            H. IV. PT. II. i. 1.

    How doth my son, and brother?
Thou tremblest, and the whiteness in thy cheek
Is apter than thy tongue to tell thy errand.
Even such a man, so faint, so spiritless,

MESSENGER,—*continued.*
So dull, so dead in look, so woe-begone,
Drew Priam's curtain in the dead of night,
And would have told him, half his Troy was burn'd;
But Priam found the fire, ere he his tongue,
And I my Percy's death, ere thou report'st it.
This thou would'st say,—Your son did thus, and thus;
Your brother thus; so fought the noble Douglas;
Stopping my greedy ear with their bold deeds;
But in the end, to stop mine ear indeed,
Thou hast a sigh to blow away this praise,
Ending with—brother, son, and all are dead.
H. IV. PT. II. i. 1.

Yea, this man's brow, like to a title leaf,
Foretells the nature of a tragic volume;
So looks the strong, whereon the imperial flood
Hath left a witness'd usurpation.
Say, Morton, didst thou come from Shrewsbury?
H. IV. PT. II. i. 1.

Pr'ythee, say on;
The setting of thine eye, and cheek, proclaim
A matter from thee; and a birth, indeed,
Which throes thee much to yield. *T.* ii. 1.

If thou speak'st false,
Upon the next tree shalt thou hang alive,
Till famine cling thee; if thy speech be sooth,
I care not if thou dost for me as much. *M.* v. 5

MIGHTY DEAD (See also LIFE, DEATH, MAN, FALLEN GREATNESS).
Here none but soldiers, and Rome's servitors,
Repose in fame. *Tit. And.* i. 2.

———— ANTONY.
His legs bestrid the ocean: his rear'd arm
Crested the world; his voice was propertied
As all the tuned spheres, and that to friends;
But when he meant to quail and shake the orb,
He was as rattling thunder. For his bounty,
There was no winter in't. *A. C.* v. 2.

In his livery
Walk'd crowns and crownets; realms and islands were
As plates dropp'd from his pockets. *A. C.* v. 2.

The death of Antony
Is not a single doom; in the name lay
A moiety of the world. *A. C.* v. 1.

———— DUKE OF BEDFORD.
But yet, before we go, let's not forget

MIGHTY DEAD,—*continued*.
The noble Duke of Bedford, late deceas'd,
But see his exequies fulfill'd in Roüen;
A braver soldier never couched lance,
A gentler heart did never sway in court:
But kings and mightiest potentates must die:
For that's the end of human misery. *H. VI.* PT. I. iii. 2.

——————— BRUTUS.
Free from the bondage you are in, Messala;
The conquerors can but make a fire of him;
For Brutus only overcame himself,
And no man else hath honour by his death. *J. C.* v. 5.
According to his virtue let us use him,
With all respect and rites of burial.
Within my tent his bones to-night shall lie,
Most like a soldier, order'd honourably. *J. C.* v. 4.

——————— CORIOLANUS.
Bear from hence his body,
And mourn you for him; let him be regarded
As the noblest corse, that ever herald
Did follow to his urn. *C.* v. 5.

——————— JULIUS CÆSAR.
O, pardon me, thou bleeding piece of earth,
That I am meek and gentle with these butchers!
Thou art the ruins of the noblest man,
That ever lived in the tide of times.
Woe to the hand that shed this costly blood!
Over thy wounds now do I prophecy,—
Which, like dumb mouths, do ope their ruby lips,
To beg the voice and utterance of my tongue!
A curse shall light upon the limbs of men;
Domestic fury, and fierce civil strife,
Shall cumber all the parts of Italy;
Blood and destruction shall be so in use,
And dreadful objects so familiar,
That mothers shall but smile, when they behold
Their infants quarter'd by the hands of war:
All pity chok'd with custom of fell deeds:
And Cæsar's spirit, raging for revenge,
With Até by his side, come hot from hell,
Shall in these confines, with a monarch's voice,
Cry *Havoc*, and let slip the dogs of war. *J C.* iii. 1.

——————— SALISBURY.
And, that hereafter ages may behold
What ruin happen'd in revenge of him,

MIGHTY DEAD,—*continued.*
Within their chiefest temple I'll erect
A tomb, wherein his corpse shall be interr'd.
H. VI. PT. I. ii. 2.

MIND.
When the mind's free the body's delicate. *K. L.* iii. 4.

MIRACLES.
It must be so: for miracles are ceas'd;
And therefore we must needs admit the means
How things are perfected. *H. V.* i. 1.
   Great floods have flown
From simple sources; and great seas have dried,
While miracles have by the greatest been denied.
A. W. ii. 1.

MIRTH.
Awake the pert and nimble spirit of mirth;
Turn melancholy forth to funerals,
The pale companion is not for our pomp. *M. N.* i. 1.
 Hostess, clap to the doors; watch to-night, pray to-morrow.—Gallants, lads, boys, hearts of gold, all the titles of good fellowship come to you! What, shall we be merry? Shall we have a play extempore? *H. IV.* PT. I. ii. 4.
  See, your guests approach:
Address yourself to entertain them sprightly,
And let's be red with mirth. *W. T.* iv. 3
  Frame your mind to mirth and merriment,
Which bars a thousand harms, and lengthens life.
T. S. IND. 2.

    A merrier man,
Within the limit of becoming mirth,
I never spent an hour's talk withal. *L. L.* ii. 1.
And then the old quire hold their lips, and loffe;
And waxen in their mirth, and neeze, and swear
A merrier hour was never wasted there. *M. N.* ii. 1.
Jog on, jog on, the foot-path way
 And merrily hent the stile-a,
A merry heart goes all the day,
 Your sad tires in a mile-a. *W. T.* iv. 3
He makes a July's day short as December;
And, with his varying childness, cures in me
Thoughts that would thick my blood. *W. T.* i. 2.
 From the crown of his head to the sole of his foot, he is all mirth; he hath twice or thrice cut Cupid's bow-string, and the little hangman dare not shoot at him: he hath a

MIRTH,—*continued.*
heart as sound as a bell, and his tongue is the clapper; for
what his heart thinks, his tongue speaks. *M. A.* iii. 2.
Let me play the fool:
With mirth and laughter let old wrinkles come;
And let my liver rather heat with wine,
Than my heart cool with mortifying groans. *M. V.* i. 1.
I would entreat you rather to put on
Your boldest suit of mirth, for we have friends
That purpose merriment. *M. V.* ii. 2.
Had she been light like you,
Of such a merry, nimble, stirring spirit,
She might have been a grandam ere she died;
And so may you: for a light heart lives long. *L. L.* v. 2.
Be large in mirth; anon, we'll drink a measure
The table round. *M.* iii. 4.

MISANTHROPY.
I am misanthropos, and hate mankind,
For thy part, I do wish thou wert a dog,
That I might love thee something. *T. A.* iv. 3.
Tell Athens, in the sequence of degree,
From high to low throughout, that whoso please
To stop affliction, let him take his haste,
Come hither, ere my tree hath felt the axe,
And hang himself. *T. A.* v. 2.

MISCHIEF.
O mischief strangely thwarting! *M. A.* iii. 2
As prone to mischief, as able to perform it. *H. VIII.* i. 1
O mischief! thou art swift
To enter in the thoughts of desperate men! *R. J.* v. 1.
Ha! what, so rank? Ah, ha!
There's mischief in this man. *H. VIII.* i. 2.
O, this is full of pity!—Sir, it calls,
I fear, too many curses on their heads,
That were the authors. *H. VIII.* ii. 1.

MISER, Sick.
Having no other pleasure of his gain
But torment, that it cannot ease his pain. *Poems.*

I can compare our rich misers to nothing so fitly as to a
Whale; that plays and tumbles, driving the poor fry before
him, and at last devours them all at a mouthful. Such
whales I have heard of on land, who never leave gaping,
till they have swallowed up a whole parish, church, steeple,
bells, and all. *P. P.* ii. 1.

MISERY.
    Misery acquaints a man with strange bed-fellows. *T.* ii. 2.
    Misery makes sport to mock itself.   *R. II.* ii. 1.

MISERY, Appeal of.
    O, let those cities, that of Plenty's cup
    And her prosperities so largely taste,
    With their superfluous riots, hear these tears ! *P. P.* i. 4.

MISFORTUNE.
    My stars shine darkly over me.   *T. N.* ii. 1.
    I am now, Sir, muddied in fortune's moat, and smell
somewhat strong of her strong displeasure. *A. W.* v. 2.
    A most poor man, made tame by fortune's blows ;
    Who, by the art of known and feeling sorrows,
    Am pregnant to good pity.   *K. L.* iv. 6.
    When we were happy, we had other names. *K. J.* v. 4.

—————————— Sometimes brings Contentment.
    My long sickness
Of health and living, now begins to mend,
And nothing brings me all things.   *T. A.* v. 2.

MISNOMER.
    Benefactors ? Well ; what benefactors are they ? are they
not malefactors ?   *M. M.* ii. 1.

MISRULE.
        Beaten for loyalty,
Excited me to treason.   *Cym.* v. 5

MISTAKE.
    Then my dial goes not true ; I took this lark for a bunting.
        A. W. ii. 5.
        What a thrice double ass
Was I, to take this drunkard for a god,
And worship this dull fool !   *T.* v. 1.

MISTRUST.
        I hold it cowardice,
To rest mistrustful, where a noble heart
Hath pawn'd an open hand in sign of love.
    H. VI. pt. iii. iv. 2.

MOB (See also Commotion, Popularity.)
    Here come the clusters.   *C.* iv. 6.
    The mutable, rank-scented many.   *C.* iii. 1
    There's a trim rabble let in ; Are all these
Your faithful friends o' the suburbs ?   *H. VIII.* v. 3.

MOB,—*continued*.
    They threw their caps
As they would hang them on the horns o' the moon,
Shouting their emulation.   *C*. i. 1.
He that will give good words to thee, will flatter
Beneath abhorring. What would you have, you curs,
That like nor peace, nor war? The one affrights you,
The other makes you proud. He that trusts you,
Where he should find you lions, finds you hares;
Where foxes, geese: You are no surer, no,
Than is the coal of fire upon the ice,
Or hailstone in the sun. Your virtue is,
To make him worthy, whose offence subdues him,
And curse that justice did it. Who deserves greatness,
Deserves your hate; and your affections are
A sick man's appetite, who desires most that
Which would increase his evil. He that depends
Upon your favours, swims with fins of lead,
And hews down oaks with rushes. Hang ye! Trust ye?
With every minute you do change a mind;
And call him noble, that was now your hate;
Him vile, that was your garland. *C*. i. 1.

    You are they
That made the air unwholesome, when you cast
Your stinking, greasy caps, in hooting at
Coriolanus' exile.   *C*. iv. 6.

What work's, my countrymen, in hand? Where go you
With bats and clubs? The matter? Speak, I pray you.
    C. i. 1.

You common cry of curs! whose breath I hate
As reek o' the rotten fens; whose love I prize
As the dead carcasses of unburied men
That do corrupt my air.   *C*. iii. 3.

    Mechanic slaves,
With greasy aprons, rules, and hammers, shall
Uplift us to the view; in their thick breaths,
Rank of gross diet, shall we be enclouded,
And forc'd to drink their vapour. *A.C.* v. 2.

  The fool multitude, that choose by show,
Not learning more than the fond eye doth teach;
Which prize not to the interior, but, like the martlet,
Builds in the weather on the outward wall,
Even in the force and road of casualty. *M.V.* ii. 9

The rabble should have first unroof'd the city,
Ere so prevail'd with me: it will in time

MOB,—*continued.*
 Win upon power, and throw forth greater themes
 For insurrection's arguing.   *C.* i. 1
   The beast
 With many heads butts me away.   *C.* iv. 1
   You have made good work,
 You, and your apron-men.   *C.* iv. 6
 Hence; home, you idle creatures, get you home:
 Is this a holiday? What! know you not,
 Being mechanical, you ought not walk,
 Upon a labouring day, without the sign
 Of your profession? Speak, what trade art thou?
 I will not choose what many men desire,
 Because I will not jump with common spirits,
 And rank me with the barbarous multitudes. *M. V.* ii. 9
 Cats, that can judge as fitly of his worth,
 As I can of those mysteries which heaven
 Will not have earth to know.   *C.* iv. 2

 They said they were an hungry, sigh'd forth proverbs;
 That, hunger broke stone walls; that, dogs must eat;
 That, meat was made for mouths; that, the gods sent not
 Corn for the rich men only:—With these shreds
 They vented their complainings.   *C.* i. 1
   Whose rage doth rend
 Like interrupted waters, and o'erbear
 What they are us'd to bear.   *C.* iii. 1.
 The shouting varletry.   *A.C.* v. 2.
 This inundation of mistemper'd humour. *K. J.* v. 1.

—— LEADER.
 The horn and noise o' the monsters.   *C.* iii. 1.
 The tongues o' the common mouth.   *C.* iii. 1.
 The herdsman of the beastly plebeians. *C.* ii. 1.

MOCKERY.
 By heaven, all dry-beaten with pure scoff. *L. L.* v. 2.
 But who dare tell her so? If I should speak,
 She'd mock me into air; O, she would laugh me
 Out of myself, press me to death with wit.
 Therefore let Benedick, like cover'd fire,
 Consume away in sighs, waste inwardly:
 It were a better death than die with mocks;
 Which is as bad as die with tickling.   *M. A.* iii. 1
 Never did mockers waste more idle breath. *M. N.* iii. 2
 How my achievements mock me.   *T.C.* iv. 2

MOCKERY,—*continued.*
A pestilence on him!—now will he be mocking. *T. C.* iv. 2.
To mock the expectation of the world. *H. IV.* PT. II. v. 2.
They do it but in mocking merriment;
And mock for mock is only my intent. *L. L.* v. 2.

————— SOLEMN.
    O, such a deed
As from the body of contraction plucks
The very soul; and sweet religion makes
A rhapsody of words. *H.* iii. 4.

MODERATION.
Let's teach ourselves that honourable stop,
Not to out-sport discretion. *O.* ii. 3.

 For aught I see, they are as sick, that surfeit with too much, as they that starve with nothing; it is no mean happiness, therefore, to be seated in the mean; superfluity comes sooner by white hairs, but competency lives longer.
M. V. i. 2.
    What's amiss,
May it be gently heard: When we debate
Our trivial difference loud, we do commit
Murder in healing wounds: Thou, noble partner,
(The rather, for I earnestly beseech,)
Touch you the sourest points with sweetest terms,
Nor curstness grow to the matter. *A. C.* ii. 2.

MODESTY.
It is the witness still of excellency,
To put a strange face on his own perfection. *M. A.* ii. 3.

Bashful sincerity and comely love. *M. A.* iv. 1.

    Can it be,
That modesty may more betray our sense
Than woman's lightness? Having waste ground enough,
Shall we desire to raze the sanctuary,
And pitch our evils there? *M. M.* ii. 2.

    Too modest are you;
More cruel to your good report, than grateful
To us that give you truly. *C.* i. 9.

————— ITS INFLUENCE.
 I perceive in you so excellent a touch of modesty, that you will not extort from me what I am willing to keep in; therefore it charges me in manners the rather to express myself. *T. N.* ii. 1

MONEY.

For they say, if money go before, all ways do lie open.
M. W. ii. 2.
Money is a good soldier, Sir, and will on.   *M W.* ii. 2.
O what a world of vile, ill-favour'd faults,
Looks handsome in three hundred pounds a year!
M. W. iii. 4.
But, by the Lord, lads, I am glad you have the money.
H. IV. PT. I. ii. 4.
Bell, book, and candle, shall not drive me back,
When gold and silver becks me to come on.   *K. J.* iii. 1.
All gold and silver rather turn to dirt!
As 'tis no better reckon'd but of those
Who worship dirty gods.   *Cym.* iii. 6.

MONSTER.

By this good light this is a very shallow monster: I afeard of him?—a very weak monster: The man in the moon?—a most poor credulous monster:—well drawn monster, in good sooth.   *T.* ii. 2.

I shall laugh myself to death at this puppy-headed monster! A most scurvy monster.   *T.* ii. 2.

—————— ATTRACTIVENESS OF, IN ENGLAND.

Were I in England now, (as once I was,) and had but this fish painted, not a holiday fool there but would give a piece of silver: there would this monster make a man; any strange beast there makes a man: when they will not give a doit to relieve a lame beggar, they will lay out ten to see a dead Indian.   *T.* ii. 2.

MOODY.

I cannot hide what I am: I must be sad when I have cause, and smile at no man's jests; eat when I have stomach, and wait for no man's leisure; sleep when I am drowsy, and tend to no man's business; laugh when I am merry, and claw no man in his humour.   *M. A.* i. 3.

I love to cope him in these sullen fits,
For then he's full of matter.   *A. Y.* ii. 1.

MOON.

O sovereign mistress of true melancholy.   *A. C.* iv. 9
        The moon, the governess of floods,
Pale in her anger, washes all the air,
That rheumatic diseases do abound:
And, through this distemperature, we see
The seasons alter.   *M. N.* ii. 2.
The pale-fac'd moon.   *R. II.* ii. 4.

MOON,—*continued.*
How sweet the moonlight sleeps upon this bank!
Here will we sit, and let the sounds of music
Creep in our ears.   *M. V.* v. 1.
——— LINGERING.
                    Methinks, how slow
This old moon wanes! she lingers my desires,
Like to a step-dame, or a dowager,
Long withering out a young man's revenue.   *M. N.* i. 1

MORNING.
See, how the morning opes her golden gates,
And takes her farewell of the glorious sun!
How well resembles it the prince of youth,
Trimm'd like a younker prancing to his love!
                                H. VI. PT. III. ii. 1.
             The busy day,
Wak'd by the lark, hath rous'd the ribald crows.
                                T. C. iv. 2.
The sun is on the heaven; and the proud day,
Attended with the pleasures of the world,
Is all too wanton.   *K. J.* iii. 3.

MORTALITY.
Even so must I run on, and even so stop.   *K. J.* v .
This muddy vesture of decay.   *M.V.* v ..

MOTION.
        Things in motion sooner catch the eye,
Than what not stirs.   *T. C.* iii. 3

MOURNING.
'Tis sweet and commendable in your nature, Hamlet,
To give these mourning duties to your father:
But, you must know, your father lost a father;
That father lost his; and the survivor bound
In filial obligation, for some term
To do obsequious sorrow: But to persévere
In obstinate condolement, is a course
Of impious stubbornness: 'tis unmanly grief:
It shows a will most incorrect to heaven:
A heart unfortified, a mind impatient;
An understanding simple and unschool'd:
For what we know, must be, and is as common
As any the most vulgar thing to sense,
Why should we, in our peevish opposition,
Take it to heart? Fie! 'tis a fault to heaven,
A fault against the dead, a fault to nature,
To reason most absurd; whose common theme

MOURNING,—*continued.*
　　Is death of fathers, and who still hath cried.
　　From the first corse, till he that died to-day,
　　"This must be so."　　　　　　　　　　　*H.* i. 2.
　　'Tis not alone my inky cloak, good mother
　　Nor customary suits of solemn black,
　　Nor windy suspiration of forc'd breath,
　　No, nor the fruitful river in the eye,
　　Nor the dejected 'haviour of the visage,
　　Together with all forms, modes, shows of grief,
　　That can denote me truly: These, indeed, seem.
　　For they are actions that a man might play:
　　But I have that within, which passeth show;
　　These, but the trappings and the suit of woe.　　*H.* i. 2.

MUCH ADO ABOUT NOTHING.
　　To tear with thunder the wide cheeks o' the air,
　　And yet to charge thy sulphur with a bolt
　　That should but rive an oak.　　　　　*C.* v. 3.

MUNIFICENCE.
　　The best ward of mine honour, is, rewarding my dependents.
　　　　　　　　　　　　　　　　　　L. L. iii. 1.

MURDER.
　　　　　　The great King of kings
　　Hath in the table of his law commanded,
　　That thou shalt do no murder: Wilt thou then
　　Spurn at his edict, and fulfil a man's?
　　Take heed; for he holds vengeance in his hand,
　　To hurl upon their heads that break his law.　*R. III.* i. 4
　　There is no sure foundation set on blood;
　　No certain life achiev'd by others' death.　　*K. J.* iv. 2.
　　　Not afraid to kill him, having a warrant for it; but to be damned for killing him, from the which no warrant can defend me.　　　　　　　　　　　　　　　　　　*R. III.* i. 4.
　　　　　　This is the bloodiest shame,
　　The wildest savag'ry, the vilest stroke,
　　That ever wall-eyed wrath, or staring rage,
　　Presented to the tears of soft remorse.　　*K. J.* iv. 3.
　　　　　　　Thou sure and firm-set earth,
　　Hear not my steps, which way they walk, for fear
　　The very stones prate of my whereabout,
　　And take the present horror from the time,
　　Which now suits with it.　　　　　　*M.* ii. 1
　　The tyrannous and bloody act is done;
　　The most arch deed of piteous massacre,
　　That ever yet this land was guilty of.

MUR   **Shakespearian Dictionary.**   MUR

MURDER,—*continued.*
Dighton, and Forrest, whom I did suborn
To do this piece of ruthless butchery,
Albeit they were flesh'd villains, blood dogs.
Melting with tenderness, and mild compassion,
Wept like two children, in their death's sad story.
R. III. iv. 3.
Mercy but murders, pardoning those that kill.   *R. J.* iii. 1.
No place, indeed, should murder sanctuarize.   *H.* iv. 7.
Blood hath been shed ere now, i' the olden time,
Ere human statute purg'd the general weal;
Ay, and since, too, murders have been perform'd
Too terrible for the ear; the times have been,
That when the brains were out, the man would die,
And there an end: but now, they rise again,
With twenty mortal murders on their crowns,
And push us from our stools: This is more strange
Than such a murder is.   *M.* iii. 4.
It will have blood; they say, blood will have blood;
Stones have been known to move, and trees to speak;
Augures, and understood relations, have
By magot-pies, and choughs, and rooks, brought forth
The secret'st man of blood.   *M.* iii. 4.
For murder, though it have no tongue, will speak
With most miraculous organ.   *H.* ii. 2
Who finds the heifer dead and bleeding fresh,
And sees fast by a butcher with an axe,
But will suspect 'twas he that made the slaughter?
Who finds the partridge in the puttock's nest,
But may imagine how the bird was dead,
Although the kite soar with unbloodied beak,
Even so suspicious is this tragedy.   *H. VI.* PT. II. iii. 2.
             Wither'd murder,
Alarum'd by his sentinel, the wolf,
Whose howl's his watch, thus, with his stealthy pace,
With Tarquin's ravishing strides, towards his design
Moves like a ghost.   *M.* ii. 1
With all great Neptune's ocean wash this blood
Clean from my hand? No; this my hand will rather
The multitudinous seas incarnadine,
Making the green one, red.   *M.* ii. 2.
Butchers and villains, bloody cannibals!
How sweet a plant have you untimely cropp'd!
You have no children, butchers! if you had,
The thought of them would have stirr'd up remorse.
H. VI. PT. III. v. 5.

MURDER,—*continued.*
Murder most foul, as in the best it is;
But this most foul, strange, and unnatural. *H.* i. 5.
    The bell invites me.
Hear it not, Duncan; for it is a knell
That summons thee to heaven, or to hell. *M.* ii. 1.
    Safe in a ditch he bides,
With twenty trenched gashes on his head;
The least a death to nature. *M.* iii. 4.

——— THE DUKE OF CLARENCE.
Hast thou that holy feeling in thy soul,
To counsel me to make my peace with God,
And art thou yet to thy own soul so blind,
That thou wilt war with God, by murd'ring me?
Ah, sirs, consider, he, that set you on
To do this deed, will hate you for the deed.
Not to relent, is beastly savage, devilish.
Which, of you, if you were a prince's son,
Being pent from liberty, as I am now,
If two such murderers as yourselves came to you,
Would not entreat for life?
My friend, I spy some pity in thy looks;
O, if thine eye be not a flatterer,
Come thou on my side, and entreat for me,
As you would beg, were you in my distress.
A begging prince what beggar pities not?
  2nd Murderer.—Look behind you, my lord.
  1st Murderer.—Take that, and that. (*Stabbing him.*)
            R. III. i. 4.

——— YOUNG PRINCES (WALES and YORK).
O thus, quoth Dighton, lay the gentle babes,—
Thus, thus, quoth Forrest, girdling one another
Within their alabaster innocent arms;
Their lips were four red roses on a stalk,
Which, in their summer beauty, kiss'd each other.
A book of prayers on their pillow lay;
Which, once, quoth Forrest, almost chang'd my mind;
But, O, the devil—there the villain stopp'd
When Dighton thus told on,—we smothered
The most replenished sweet work of nature,
That, from the prime creation, e'er she fram'd.
            R. III. iv. 3.

——— RICHARD THE SECOND.
  Exton.—From your own mouth, my lord, did I this deed.
  Bolingbroke.—They love not poison that do poison need,
Nor do I thee; though I did wish him dead,

MUR   **Shakespearian Dictionary.**   MUR

MURDER, RICHARD THE SECOND,—*continued.*
I hate the murderer, love him murdered.
The guilt of conscience take thou for thy labour,
But neither my good word, nor princely favour;
With Cain go wander through the shade of night,
And never shew thy head by day, nor light.   *R.II.* v. 6.

———— PRINCE ARTHUR.
Hubert.—Here is your hand and seal for what I did.
King John.—O, when the last account 'twixt heaven and
  earth
Is to be made, then shall this hand and seal
Witness against us to damnation!
How oft the sight of means to do ill deeds,
Makes deeds ill done! Hadst not thou been by,
A fellow by the hand of nature mark'd,
Quoted, and sign'd, to do a deed of shame,
This murder had not come into my mind:
But, taking note of thy abhor'd aspect,
Finding thee fit for bloody villany,
Apt, liable, to be employ'd in danger,
I faintly broke with thee of Arthur's death;
And thou, to be endeared to a king,
Made it no conscience to destroy a prince.
Hadst thou but shook thy head, or made a pause,
When I spake darkly what I purposed;
Or turn'd an eye of doubt upon my face,
As bid me tell my tale in express words;
Deep shame had struck me dumb, made me break off,
And those thy fears might have wrought fears in me;
But thou didst understand me by my signs,
And didst in signs again parley with sin;
Yea, without stop, didst let thy heart consent,
And, consequently, thy rude hand to act
The deed, which both our tongues held vile to name.—
Out of my sight, and never see me more!   *K.J.* iv. 2.

. ———— SUSPICION OF.
         If thou didst but consent
To this most cruel act, do but despair,
And, if thou want'st a cord, the smallest thread
That ever spider twisted from her womb
Will serve to strangle thee; a rush will be.
A beam to hang thee on; or would'st thou drown thyself,
Put but a little water in a spoon,
And it shall be as all the ocean,
Enough to stifle such a villain up.—
I do suspect thee very grievously.   *K J.* iv 3.

MUSIC.
Come, ho, and wake Diana with a hymn;
With sweetest touches pierce your mistress' ear,
And draw her home with music. *M.V.* v. 1.
Let music sound while he doth make his choice;
Then, if he lose, he makes a swan-like end,
Fading in music. That the comparison
May stand more proper, my eye shall be the stream,
And wat'ry death-bed for him : He may win ;
And what is music then? Then music is
Even as the flourish when true subjects bow
To a new-crowned monarch; such it is,
As are those dulcet sounds in break of day,
That creep into the dreaming bridegroom's ear,
And summon him to marriage. *M.V.* iii. 2.

    Come on; tune: If you can penetrate her with your fingering, so ; we'll try with tongue too: if none will do, let her remain; but I'll never give o'er. First, a very excellent good-conceited thing, after a wonderful sweet air, with admirable rich words to it,—and then let her consider. *Cym.* ii. 3.

How sweet the moonlight sleeps upon this bank!
Here will we sit, and let the sounds of music
Creep in our ears ; soft stillness, and the night,
Become the touches of sweet harmony. *M.V.* v. 1.
              Sitting on a bank,
Weeping against the king my father's wreck,
This music crept by me upon the waters ;
Allaying both their fury and my passion,
With its sweet air. *T.* i. 2.
'Tis good tho' music oft hath such a charm,
To make bad good ; and good provoke to harm. *M.M.* iv. 1.
And it will discourse most eloquent music. *H.* iii. 2.
Preposterous ass! that never read so far,
To know the cause why music was ordain'd!
Was it not to refresh the mind of man,
After his studies, or his usual pain?.
Then give me leave to read philosophy,
And, while I pause, serve in your harmony. *T.S.* iii. 1.
I'm never merry, when I hear sweet music.—
The reason is, your spirits are attentive:
For do but note a wild and wanton herd,
Or race of youthful and unhandled colts,
Fetching mad bounds, bellowing and neighing loud,
Which is the hot condition of their blood:
If they perchance but hear a trumpet sound,

MUSIC,—*continued.*
Or any air of music touch their ears,
You shall perceive them make a mutual stand,
Their savage eyes turn'd to a modest gaze,
By the sweet power of music: Therefore, the poet
Did fein that Orpheus drew trees, stones, and floods;
Since nought so stockish, hard, and full of rage,
But music for the time doth change his nature. *M.V.* v. 1.

The man that hath not music in himself,
Nor is not moved with concord of sweet sounds,
Is fit for treasons, stratagems, and spoils;
The motions of his spirit are dull as night,
And his affections dark as Erebus :
Let no such man be trusted. *M.V.* v. 1.

For Orpheus' lute was stung with poets' sinews,
Whose golden touch could soften steel and stones;
Make tigers tame, and huge leviathans
Forsake unsounded deeps to dance on sands. *T.G.* iii. 2.

If music be the food of love, play on,
Give me excess of it; that, surfeiting,
The appetite may sicken, and so die.—
That strain again;—it had a dying fall:
O, it came o'er mine ear like the sweet south,
That breathes upon a bank of violets,
Stealing and giving odour. *T.N.* i. 1.

  Once I sat upon a promontory,
And heard a mermaid, on a dolphin's back,
Uttering such dulcet and harmonious breath,
That the rude sea grew civil at her song;
And certain stars shot madly from their spheres,
To hear the sea-maid's music. *M.N.* ii. 2.

Let there be no noise made, my gentle friends;
Unless some dull and favourable hand
Will whisper music to my weary spirit. *H.IV.* PT. II. iv. 4.

Then music, with her silver sound,
With speedy help doth lend redress. *R.J.* iv. 5.

  Tax not so bad a voice
To slander music any more than once. *M.A.* ii. 3.

  But, masters, here's money for you: and the general so likes your music, that he desires you, of all loves, to make no more noise with it. *O.* iii. 1.

Wilt thou have music? hark! Apollo plays,
And twenty caged nightingales do sing. *T.S.* IND. 2.

Give me some music; music, moody food
Of us that trade in love. The music, ho! *A.C.* ii. 5.

MUSIC,—*continued.*
I am advised to give her music o'mornings: they say it will penetrate. *Cym.* ii. 3
　　　　　The choir,
With all the choicest music of the kingdom,
Together sung *Te Deum.* *H. VIII.* iv. 1.

MUSICIAN.
He plays o' th' viol-de-gambo. *T. N.* i. 3.

MUSTERING.
Call forth your actors by the scroll. Masters, spread yourselves. *M. N.* i. 2.

MUTABILITY.
　　　　　How chances mock,
And changes fill the cup of alteration
With divers liquors! *H. IV.* PT. II. iii. 1.
　　To what base uses we may return, Horatio! Why may not imagination trace the noble dust of Alexander till he find it stopping a bung-hole? *H.* v. 1.
Imperious Cæsar, dead, and turn'd to clay,
Might stop a hole, to keep the wind away:
O, that the earth, which kept the world in awe,
Should patch a wall to expel the winter's flaw! *H.* v. 1.
All things that we ordained festival,
Turn from their office to black funeral:
Our instruments, to melancholy bells;
Our wedding cheer, to a sad burial feast;
Our solemn hymns, to sullen dirges change;
Our bridal flowers serve for a buried corse,
And all things change them to the contrary. *R. J.* iv. 5.
This world is not for aye; nor 'tis not strange,
That even our love should with our fortunes change;
For 'tis a question left us yet to prove,
Whether love lead fortune, or else fortune love. *H.* iii. 2.
　　Lord, we know what we are, but know not what we may be! *H.* iv. 5.

MYSTERIES.
There are more things in heaven and earth, Horatio,
Than are dreamt of in your philosophy *H.* i. 5.
Canst tell how an oyster makes his shell? *K. L.* i. 5.

MYSTERIOUS.
　　It was not brought me, my lord, there's the cunning of it: I found it thrown in at the casement of my closet.
　　　　　　　　　　　　　　　　　K. L. i 2.

N.

NAIADS.
You nymphs, call'd Naiads, of the wand'ring brooks,
With your sedg'd crowns and ever harmless looks,
Leave your crisp'd channels, and on this green land
Answer your summons. *T* iv. 1.

NAME.
Brutus and Cæsar: what should be in that Cæsar?
Why should that name be sounded more than yours?
Write them together, yours is as fair a name;
Sound them, it doth become the mouth as well;
Weigh them, it is as heavy; conjure with them,
Brutus will start a spirit as soon as Cæsar.
Now in the names of all the gods at once,
Upon what meat doth this our Cæsar feed,
That he is grown so great. *J. C.* i. 2.

'Tis but thy name that is my enemy,—
Thou art thyself, though not a Montague.
What's Montague? it is nor hand, nor foot,
Nor arm, nor face, nor any other part
Belonging to a man. O, be some other name!
What's in a name? that which we call a rose,
By any other name would smell as sweet. *R. J.* ii. 2.

   I do beseech you,
(Chiefly, that I might set it in my prayers,)
What is your name? *T.* iii. 1.

   Romeo, doff thy name;
And for that name, which is no part of thee,
Take all myself. *R. J.* ii. 2.

   Go back; the virtue of your name
Is not here passable. *C.* v. 2.

NARRATION, Long.
   No more yet of this;
For 'tis a chronicle of day by day,
Not a relation for a breakfast, nor
Befitting this first meeting *T.* v. 1.

NATURE.
Nature hath meal, and bran; contempt, and grace.
Cym. iv. 2.
One touch of nature makes the whole world kin.
T. C. iii. 3.
How hard it is to hide the sparks of nature! *Cym.* iii. 3.

NATURE,—continued.
Nature, what things there are,
Most abject in regard, and dear in use;
What things again most dear in the esteem,
And poor in worth!   .   *T. C.* iii. 3.

Labouring art can never ransom Nature
From her inaidable estate.   ·   *A. W.* ii. 1.

NATURAL PRODUCTIONS.
Many for many virtues excellent,
None but for some, and yet all different.
O, mickle is the powerful grace, that lies
In herbs, plants, stones, and their true qualities:
For nought so vile that on the earth doth live,
But to the earth some special good doth give;
Nor aught so good, but, strain'd from that fair use,
Revolts from true birth, stumbling on abuse:
Virtue itself turns vice, being misapplied:
And vice sometime's by action dignified.
Within the infant rind of this small flower
Poison hath residence, and med'cine power:
For this, being smelt, with that part cheers each part;
Being tasted, stays all senses with the heart.
Two such opposed foes encamp them still
In man as well as herbs, grace, and rude will;
And, where the worser is predominant,
Full soon the canker death eats up that plant. *R. J.* ii. 3.

NECESSITY. NEED.
Necessity's sharp pinch.   *K. L.* ii. 4.

Teach thy necessity to reason thus;
There is no virtue like necessity.   *R. II.* i. 3.

Where is this straw, my fellow?
The art of our necessities is strange,
That can make vile things precious.   *K. L.* iii. 2.

Necessity will make us all forsworn.   *L. L.* i. 1.

O, reason not the need: our basest beggars
Are in the poorest thing superfluous:
Allow not nature more than nature needs,
Man's life is cheap as beast's.   *K. L.* ii. 4

But, for true need,—
You heavens, give me that patience: patience I need.
K. L. ii. 4.

I am sworn brother, sweet,
To grim Necessity; and he and I
Will keep a league till death.   *R. II.* v. 1

NEG   **Shakespearian Dictionary.**   NEW

NEGLECT (See also DELAY, OPPORTUNITY).
    O, then, beware;
Those wounds heal ill that men do give themselves:
Omission to do what is necessary
Seals a commission to a blank of danger;
And danger, like an ague, subtly taints
Even then when we sit idly in the sun.   *T. C.* iii. 3.
    O negligence,
Fit for a fool to fall by!   *H. VIII.* iii. 2.
    And you are now sailed into the north of my lady's opinion, where you will hang like an icicle in a Dutchman's beard, unless you do redeem it by some laudable attempt, either of valour, or policy.   *T. N.* iii. 2.
    They pass'd by me
As misers do by beggars.   *T. C.* iii. 3.
Omittance is no quittance.   *A. Y.* iii. 5.

NEWS (See also MESSENGER).
    Let me speak, to the yet unknowing world,
How these things came about; so shall you hear
Of carnal, bloody, and unnatural acts;
Of accidental judgments, casual slaughters;
Of deaths put on by cunning, and forc'd cause;
And, in this upshot, purposes mistook
Fall'n on the inventor's heads; all this can I
Truly deliver.   *H.* v. 2.
    But I have words,
That should be howl'd out in the desert air
Where hearing should not latch them.   *M.* iv. 3.

And there are twenty weak and wearied posts,
Come from the north; and, as I came along,
I met, and overtook, a dozen captains,
Bareheaded, sweating, knocking at the taverns.
    H. IV. PT. II. ii. 4.

Is thy news good, or bad? answer to that:
Say either, and I'll stay the circumstance;
Let me be satisfied,—Is't good or bad?   *R. J.* ii. 5.

Old men, and beldams, in the streets
Do prophesy upon it dangerously;
Young Arthur's death is common in their mouths:
And when they talk of him, they shake their heads,
And whisper one another in the ear:
And he that speaks, doth gripe the hearer's wrist;
Whilst he that hears, makes fearful action,
With wrinkled brows, with nods, with rolling eyes.
I saw a smith stand with his hammer, thus,

NEWS,—*continued.*
The whilst the iron did on the anvil cool,
With open mouth swallowing a tailor's news;
Who, with his shears and measure in his hand,
Standing on slippers, (which his nimble haste
Had falsely thrust upon contrary feet,)
Told of a many thousand warlike French,
That were embattalled and rank'd in Kent;
Another lean unwash'd artificer
Cuts off his tale, and talks of Arthur's death. *K. J.* iv. 2.

Tell him, there's a post come from my master, with his horn full of news. *M. V.* v. 1.

Ere I was risen from the place that show'd
My duty kneeling, came there a reeking post,
Stew'd in his haste, half breathless, panting forth
From Goneril, his mistress, salutations;
Deliver'd letters, spite of intermission,
Which presently they read. *K. L.* ii. 4.

After him, came spurring hard,
A gentleman almost forspent with speed;
That stopp'd by me to breathe his bloodied horse;
He ask'd the way to Chester, and of him
I did demand what news from Shrewsbury.
He told me, that rebellion had bad luck,
And that young Harry Percy's spur was cold;
With that, he gave his able horse the head,
And, bending forward, struck his armed heels
Against the panting sides of his poor jade,
Up to the rowel head; and, starting so,
He seem'd in running to devour the way,
Staying no further question. *H. IV.* PT. II. i. 1.

Seek him, Titinius; whilst I go to meet
The noble Brutus, thrusting this report
Into his ears: I may say, thrusting it;
For piercing steel, and darts envenomed,
Shall be as welcome to the ears of Brutus,
As tidings of this sight. *J. C.* v. 3.

Tedious it were to tell, and harsh to hear. *T. S.* iii. 2.

My ears are stopp'd, and cannot hear good news,
So much of bad already hath possess'd them. *T. G.* iii. 1.

I drown'd these news in tears. *H. VI.* PT. III. ii. 1.

News, fitted to the night:
Black, fearful, comfortless, and horrible. *K. J.* v. 6

Master, master! news, old news, and such news as you never heard of. *T. S.* iii. 2.

Shakespearian Dictionary.

NEWS,—*continued*.

Ram thou thy fruitful tidings in mine ears,
That long time have been barren.   *A.C.* ii. 5

    Such a deal of wonder is broken out within this hour, that the ballad-makers cannot be able to express it.
                                          W.T. v. 2.

Let not your ears despise my tongue for ever,
Which shall possess them with the heaviest sound,
That ever yet they heard.   *M.* iv. 3.

My heart hath one poor string to stay it by,
Which holds but till thy news be uttered.   *K.J.* v. 7.

There's villainous news abroad.   *H.IV.* PT. I. ii. 4.

O, slaves, I can tell you news; news, you rascals.   *C.* iv. 5.

    There might you have beheld one joy crown another; so, and in such manner, that, it seemed, sorrow wept to take leave of them; for their joy waded in tears. There was casting up of eyes, holding up of hands; with countenance of such distraction, that they were to be known by garment, not by favour.   *W.T.* v. 2.

    Thy father's beard is turned white with the news; you may buy land now as cheap as stinking mackarel.
                                          H.IV. PT. I. ii. 4.

                     Pr'ythee, friend,
Pour out the pack of matter to mine ear,
The good and bad together.   *A.C.* ii. 5.

Where have you lurk'd, that you make doubt of it?   *C.* v. 4.

What news, Lord Bardolph? every minute now
Should be the father of some stratagem;
The times are wild.   *H.IV.* PT. II. i. 1.

    Like an old tale still; which will have matter to rehearse, though credit be asleep, and not an ear open.   *W.T.* v. 2.

    How goes it now, Sir; this news, which is called true, is so like an old tale, that the verity of it is in strong suspicion.   *W.T.* v. 2.

The nature of bad news infects the teller.   *A.C.* i. 2

With news the time's with labour; and throes forth
Each minute, some.   *A.C.* iii. 7.

Thy letters have transported me beyond
This ignorant present, and I feel now
The future in the instant.   *M.* i. 5.

What a haste looks through his eyes!
So should he look,
That seems to speak things strange.   *M.* i. 2

NEW   **Shakesperian Dictionary.**   NIG

NEWS, Stale.
    There needs no ghost, my lord, come from the grave,
    To tell us this.   *H.* i, 5.

NEW Governor.
    Whether it be the fault and glimpse of newness;
    Or whether that the body public be
    A horse whereon the governor doth ride,
    Who, newly in the seat, that it may know
    He can command, let's it straight feel the spur:
    Whether the tyranny be in his place,
    Or in his eminence that fills it up,
    I stagger in:—But this new governor
    Awakes me all the enrolled penalties,
    Which have, like unscour'd armour, hung by the wall
    So long, that nineteen zodiacs have gone round,
    And none of them been worn; and, for a name,
    Now puts the drowsy and neglected act
    Freshly on me.   *M. M.* i. 3.

NICETY.
    Here's goodly gear!   *R. J.* ii. 4.

NIGHT.
    When creeping murmur, and the poring dark,
    Fill the wide vessel of the universe.   *H. V.* iv. *chorus.*

    The dragon wing of night o'er-spreads the earth.   *T. C.* v. 9.

    The gaudy, blabbing, and remorseful day
    Is crept into the bosom of the sea;
    And now loud howling wolves arouse the jades
    Who, with their drowsy, slow, and flagging wings
    Clip dead men's graves, and from their misty jaws
    Breathe foul contagious darkness in the air.
                                 H. VI. pt. ii. iv. 1.

            Now o'er the one half world
    Nature seems dead, and wicked dreams abuse
    The curtain'd sleep; now witchcraft celebrates
    Pale Hecate's offerings: and wither'd murder,
    Alarum'd by his sentinel, the wolf,
    Whose howl's his watch, thus, with his stealthy pace,
    With Tarquin's ravishing strides, towards his design
    Moves like a ghost.   *M.* ii. 1.

    Stumbling night.   *K. J.* v. 5.

            Look how the floor of heaven
    Is thick inlaid with patines of bright gold;
    There's not the smallest orb which thou behold'st,
    But in his motion like an angel sings,
    Still quiring to the young ey'd cherubim.   *M. V.* v. 1.

Shakesperian Dictionary.

NIGHT,—*continued.*
Vaporous night approaches. *M. M.* iv. 1.
Now the hungry lion roars,
   And the wolf behowls the moon;
Whilst the heavy ploughman snores,
   All with weary task fore-done.
Now the wasted brands do glow,
   Whilst the screech-owl, screeching loud,
Puts the wretch that lies in woe,
   In remembrance of a shroud.
Now it is the time of night,
   That the graves all gaping wide,
Every one lets forth his sprite,
   In the church-way paths to glide:
And we fairies, that do run,
   By the triple Hecate's team,
From the presence of the sun,
   Following darkness like a dream,
Now are frolic; not a mouse
Shall disturb this hallow'd house:
I am sent, with broom, before,
To sweep the dust behind the door. *M. N.* v. 2.

Come, gentle night; come, loving, black-brow'd night,
Give me my Romeo; and, when he shall die,
Take him, and cut him out in little stars,
And he shall make the face of heaven so fine,
That all the world will be in love with night,
And pay no worship to the garish sun. *R. J.* iii. 2.

The iron tongue of midnight hath told twelve:—
Lovers to bed; 'tis almost fairy time. *M. N.* v. 1.

To bed, to bed: Sleep kill those pretty eyes,
And give as soft attachment to thy senses,
As infants empty of all thought. *T. C.* iv. 2.

Beshrew the witch: with venomous wights she stays,
As tediously as hell; but flies the grasps of love,
With wings more momentary-swift than thought. *T. C.* iv. 2
Pitchy night. *A. W.* iv. 4.

'Tis now the very witching time of night,
When churchyards yawn, and hell itself breathes out
Contagion to the world. *H.* iii. 1.

The time when screech-owls cry, and ban-dogs howl.
H. VI. PT. II. i. 4.

    Hark! peace!
It was the owl that shriek'd, the fatal bell-man,
Which gives the stern'st good night. *M.* ii. 2.

Shakespearian Dictionary.

NIGHT,—*continued.*
Come, civil night,
Thou sober-suited matron, all in black. *R. J.* iii. 2

NIGHTINGALE.
And to the nightingale's complaining notes,
Tune my distresses, and record my woes. *T. G.* v. 4.

NOBILITY.
He seems to be the more noble in being fantastical: a great man, I'll warrant. *W. T.* iv. 3.
O, that your young nobility could judge,
What 'twere to lose it, and be miserable!
They that stand high, have many blasts to shake them;
And if they fall, they dash themselves to pieces.
R. III. i. 3.

NOSE.
A good nose is requisite, to smell out work for the other senses. *W. T.* iv. 3.
All that follow their noses are led by their eyes, but blind men; and there's not a nose among twenty but can smell him that's stinking. *K. L.* ii. 4.
Fool.—Can'st tell, why one's nose stands i' the middle of his face?
Lear.—No.
Fool.—Why, to keep his eyes on either side his nose; that what a man cannot smell out, he may spy into. *K. L.* i. 5.
There is a fellow somewhat near the door, he should be a brazier by his face, for o' my conscience, twenty of the dog-days now reign in's nose; all that stand about him are under the line, they need no other penance.
H. VIII. v. 3.

NOTES.
I will make a prief of it in my note book. *M. W.* i. 1

NOVELTIES.
That all, with one consent, praise new born gawds,
Though they are made and moulded of things past;
And give to dust, that is a little gilt,
More laud than gilt o'er-dusted.
The present eye praises the present object. *T. C.* iii. 3.
New customs,
Though they be never so ridiculous,
Nay, let them be unmanly, yet are follow'd. *H. VIII.* i. 3

NUN.
Question your desires;
Know of your youth, examine well your blood,

NUN,—*continued*.
    Whether, if you yield not to your father's choice,
    You can endure the livery of a nun;
    For aye to be in shady cloister mew'd,
    To live a barren sister all your life,
    Chaunting faint hymns to the cold fruitless moon.
    Thrice blessed they, that master so their blood,
    To undergo such maiden pilgrimage ;
    But earthlier happy is the rose distill'd,
    Than that, which, withering on the virgin thorn,
    Grows, lives, and dies, in single blessedness.   *M. N.* i. 1.
    I hold you as a thing ensky'd and sainted;
    By your renouncement, an immortal spirit;
    And to be talk'd with in sincerity,
    As with a saint.   *M. M.* i. 5.

O

OAK.
    The unwedgeable and gnarled oak.   *M.M.* ii. 2.
    I have seen tempests, when the scolding winds
    Have riv'd the knotty oaks. .   *J.C.* i. 3.
———— AGED.
    Under an oak whose boughs were moss'd with age,
    And high top bald with dry antiquity.   *A.Y.* iv. 3.
OATHS (See also LOVERS' VOWS).
    No, not an oath : If not the face of men,
    The sufferance of our souls, the time's abuse,—
    If these be motives weak, break off betimes,
    And every man hence to his idle bed ;
    So let high-sighted tyranny range on,
    Till each man drop by lottery : But if these,
    As I am sure they do, bear fire enough
    To kindle cowards, and to steel with valour
    The melting spirits of women ; then, countrymen,
    What need we any spur, but our own cause,
    To prick us to redress? what other bond,
    Than secret Romans, that have spoke the word,
    And will not palter? and what other oath
    Than honesty to honesty engag'd,
    That this shall be, or we will fall for it?
    Swear priests, and cowards, and men cautelous,
    Old feeble carrions, and such suffering souls
    That welcome wrongs; unto bad causes swear
    Such creatures as men doubt; but do not stain
    The even virtue of our enterprise.

OATHS,—*continued.*
Nor the unsuppressive metal of our spirits,
To think, that, or our cause, or our performance,
Did need an oath; when every drop of blood,
That every Roman bears, and nobly bears,
Is guilty of a several bastardy,
If he do break the smallest particle
Of any promise that hath pass'd from him.   *J. C.* ii. 1.

'Tis not the many oaths that make the truth;
But the plain single vow, that is vow'd true.   *A. W.* iv. 2.

    Not yours, in good sooth! 'Heart, you swear like a comfit-maker's wife! Not you, in good sooth; and, As true as I live; and, As God shall mend me; and, As sure as day; And giv'st such sarcenet surety for thy oaths, as if thou never walk'dst further than Finsbury. Swear me, Kate, like a lady as thou art, a good mouth-filling oath; and leave *in sooth*, and such protest of pepper gingerbread, to velvet-guards, and Sunday citizens.   *H. IV.* PT. I. iii. 1.

Trust none;
For oaths are straws, men's faiths are wafer-cakes,
And hold-fast is the only dog, my duck;
Therefore, *caveto* be thy counsellor.   *H. V.* ii. 3.

           Myself, myself confound!
Heaven, and fortune, bar me happy hours!
Day, yield me not thy light; nor night, thy rest!
Be opposite, all planets of good luck,
To my proceeding, if, with pure heart's love,
Immaculate devotion, holy thoughts,
I tender not thy beauteous princely daughter.   *R. III.* iv. 4

An oath, an oath; I have an oath in heaven:
Shall I lay perjury upon my soul?
No, not for Venice.   *M. V.* iv. 1.

I'll take thy word for faith, not ask thine oath;
Who shuns not to break one, will sure crack both.
                                          P. P. i. 2.

Do not believe his vows; for they are brokers,
Not of that die which their investments show,
But mere implorators of unholy suits,
Breathing like sanctified and pious bonds,
The better to beguile.   *H.* i. 3

Your oaths are past, and now subscribe your name,
That his own hand may strike his honour down,
That violates the smallest branch herein.   *L. L.* i. 1

                  Come, swear it, damn thyself,
Lest, being like one of heaven, the devils themselves

OATHS,—*continued.*
Should fear to seize thee: therefore be double-damn'd,
Swear—thou art honest. *O.* iv. 2.
O, swear not by the moon, the inconstant moon,
That monthly changes in her circled orb,
Lest that thy love prove likewise variable. *R. J.* ii. 2.
Look thou be true; do not give dalliance
Too much the rein; the strongest oaths are straw
To the fire i' the blood; be more abstemious,
Or else good night your vow. *T.* iv. 1.
Thou see'st that all the grace that she hath left,
Is that she will not add to her damnation
A sin of perjury. She not denies it. *M. A.* iv. 1.
    I have no cunning in protestation; only downright oaths, which I never use till urged, nor never break for urging.
H. V. v. 2.
    He professes not keeping of oaths; in breaking them, he is stronger than Hercules. *A. W.* iv. 3.
It is a great sin, to swear unto a sin;
But greater sin, to keep a sinful oath.
Who can be bound by any solemn vow
To do a murderous deed, to rob a man,
To force a spotless virgin's chastity,
To 'reave the orphan of his patrimony,
To wrong the widow from her custom'd right;
And have no other reason for this wrong,
But that he was bound by a solemn oath?
H. VI. PT. II. v. 1.
    By mine honour, I will; and when I break that oath, let me turn monster. *A. Y.* i. 2.
    But if you swear by that that is not, you are not forsworn; no more was the knight, swearing by his honour, for he never had any. *A. Y.* i. 2.
By all pretty oaths that are not dangerous. *A. Y.* iv. 1.
OBJECT.
A mote it is, to trouble the mind's eye. *H.* i. 1.
——————— OLD AND FAMILIAR.
    Now he thanks the old shepherd, which stands by, like a weather-bitten conduit of many kings' reigns.
W. T. v. 2.
OBLIVION.
    In the swallowing gulf
Of dark forgetfulness and deep oblivion. *R. III.* iii. 7.
And all the clouds that lowr'd upon our house
In the deep bosom of the ocean buried. *R. III.* i. 1.

OBLIVION,—*continued.*
    When time is old and hath forgot itself,
    When water-drops have worn the stones of Troy,
    And blind oblivion swallow'd cities up,
    And mighty states characterless are grated
    To dusty nothing.   *T. C.* iii. 2.
    The dark backward and abysm of Time.   *T.* i. 2.
      He no more remembers his mother now, than an eight year old horse.   *C.* v. 4.

OBSEQUIOUSNESS.
    So play the foolish throngs with one that swoons,
    Come all to help him, and so stop the air
    By which he should revive: and even so,
    The general, subject to a well-wish'd king,
    Quit their own part, and in obsequious fondness
    Crowd to his presence, where their untaught love
    Must needs appear offence.   *M. M.* ii. 4.

OBSERVATION.
    For he is but a bastard to the time,
    That doth not smack of observation.   *K. J.* i. 1.
    There is a history in all men's lives
    Figuring the nature of the times deceas'd:
    The which observ'd, a man may prophecy,
    With a near aim, of the main chance of things
    As yet to come to life; which in their seeds,
    And weak beginnings, lie intreasured.   *H. IV.* PT. II. iii. 1.
    Squandering glances.   *A. Y.* ii. 7.

ODDITY.
    What a Herod of Jewry is this!   *M. W.* ii. 1.
      I have lived four score years and upward; I never heard of a man of his place, gravity, and learning, so wide of his own respect.   *M. W.* iii. 1.
      How oddly he is suited! I think he bought his doublet in Italy, his round hose in France, his bonnet in Germany, and his behaviour every where.   *M. V.* i. 2.

ODIUM.
              You are smelt
    Above the moon.   *C.* v. 1.

OFFENCE.
    The very head and front of my offending
    Hath this extent, no more.   *O.* i. 3.
              How have I offended?
    All's not offence that indiscretion finds,
    And dotage terms so.   *K. L.* ii. 4.

OFFENCE,—*continued.*
What is my offence?
Where is the evidence that doth accuse me?
What lawful quest have given their verdict up
Unto the frowning judge. *R. III.* i. 4.
In such a time as this, it is not meet
That every nice offence should bear its comment. *J.C.* iv. 3.

OFFICE.
Having both the key of officer and office. *T.* i. 2.
He was a fool;
For he would needs be virtuous: That good fellow,
If I command him, follows my appointment;
I will have none so near else. Learn this, brother,
We' live not to be grip'd by meaner persons. *H. VIII.* ii. 2.
Fear not your advancement; I will be the man yet that
shall make you great. *H. IV.* PT. II. v. 5.

OFFICE, ITS EVILS.
If I am traduc'd by tongues, which neither know
My faculties, nor person, yet will be
The chronicles of my doing,—let me say,
'Tis but the fate of place, and the rough brake
That virtue must go through. We must not stint
Our necessary actions, in the fear
To cope malicious censurers; which ever,
As ravenous fishes, do a vessel follow
That is new trimm'd; but benefit no further
Than vainly longing. What we oft do best,
By sick interpreters, (once weak ones) is
Not ours, or not allow'd; what worst, as oft,
Hitting a grosser quality, is cried up
For our best act. If we shall stand still,
In fear our motion will be mock'd or carp'd at,
We should take root here where we sit, or sit
State statues only. *H. VIII.* i. 2

- ——— INSOLENCE OF.
I'd have beaten him like a dog, but for disturbing the
lords within. *C.* iv. 5.

OMENS, (See also PORTENTS).
The bay trees in our country are all wither'd,
And meteors fright the fixed stars of heaven;
The pale-faced moon looks bloody on the earth,
And lean-look'd prophets whisper fearful change;
Rich men look sad, and ruffians dance and leap. *R. II.* ii. 4.
There is some ill a-brewing towards my rest,
For I did dream of money-bags to-night. *M. V* ii. 5.

OMNIPOTENCE, INSCRUTABLE.
He that of greatest works is finisher,
Oft does them by the weakest minister:
So holy writ in babes hath judgment shown
When judges have been babes.   *A. W.* ii. 1.

OPENNESS.
    I must be found;
My parts, my title, and my perfect soul,
Shall manifest me rightly.   *O.* i. 2.

OPHELIA DROWNING.
There is a willow grows aslant a brook,
That shows his hoar leaves in the glassy stream;
There, with fantastic garlands did she come,
Of crow-flowers, nettles, daisies, and long purples,
That liberal shepherds give a grosser name,
But our cold maids do dead men's fingers call them.
There on the pendant boughs her coronet weeds
Clamb'ring to hang, an envious sliver broke;
When down her weedy trophies, and herself,
Fell in the weeping brook. Her clothes spread wide;
And mermaid-like, awhile they bore her up:
Which time she chanted snatches of old tunes;
As one incapable of her own distress,
Or like a creature native and endu'd
Unto that element: but long it could not be,
Till that her garments, heavy with their drink,
Pull'd the poor wretch from her melodious lay,
To muddy death.   *H. IV.* 7.

OPINION (See also CENSURE.)
I am that I am, and they that level
At my abuses, reckon up their owne,
I may be straight, though they themselves be bevell,
By their rank thoughts, my deeds must not be showne:
    Unless this general evil they maintaine,
    All men are bad, and in their badness raigne. *Poems.*

Because you want the grace that others have,
You judge it straight a thing impossible
To compass wonders, but by help of devils.
    H. VI. PT. I. v. 4.

There's nothing good or bad, but thinking makes it so.
    H. ii. 2.

    Our virtues
Lie in the interpretation of the time.   *C.* iv. 7.

Opinion, a sovereign mistress of effects.   *O.* i. 3

OPINION,—*continued.*
But fish not with this melancholy bait,
For this fool's gudgeon, this opinion. *M. V.* i. 1.
Opinion's but a fool, that makes us scan
The outward habit for the inward man. *P. P.* ii. 2.
A plague of opinion! a man may wear it on both sides,
like a leather jerkin. *T. C.* iii. 3.

OPPORTUNITY (See also DELAY, IRRESOLUTION, NEGLECT).
There is a tide in the affairs of men,
Which, taken at the flood, leads on to fortune;
Omitted, all the voyage of their life
Is bound in shallows, and in miseries.
On such a full sea are we now afloat;
And we must take the current when it serves,
Or lose out ventures. *J. C.* iv. 3.
Who seeks, and will not take, when once 'tis offer'd,
Shall never find it more. *A. C.* ii. 7.
When the sun shines, let foolish gnats make sport,
But creep in crannies, when he hides his beams.
C. E. ii. 2.

A little fire is quickly trodden out;
Which, being suffer'd, rivers cannot quench.
H. VI. PT. III. iv. 8.
The means that heaven yields must be embrac'd,
And not neglected; else, if heaven would,
And we will not, heaven's offer we refuse. *R. II.* iii. 2.
I find my zenith doth depend upon
A most auspicious star; whose influence
If now I court not, but omit, my fortunes
Will ever after droop. *T.* i. 2

OPPOSITION.
Back, I say, go; lest I let forth your half pint of blood;—
back,—that's the utmost of your having:—back. *C.* v. 2.

OPPRESSION.
I love not to see wretchedness o'ercharg'd,
And duty in his service perishing. *M. N.* v. 1.

I am an ass, indeed; you may prove it by my long ears.
I have served him from the hour of my nativity to this instant, and have nothing at his hands for my service, but
blows; when I am cold, he heats me with beating: when
I am warm, he cools me with beating; I am awak'd with
it, when I sleep; rais'd with it, when I sit; driven out of
doors with it, when I go from home; welcomed home with
it, when I return: nay, I bear it on my shoulders, as a

OPPRESSION,—*continued.*
beggar her brat; and, I think, when he hath lam'd me, I
shall beg with it from door to door. *C. E.* iv. 4.
     Each new morn,
New widows howl, new orphans cry, new sorrows
Strike heaven on the face. *M.* iv. 2

—————— THE NATURAL DUTY OF RESISTANCE TO.
To whom do lions cast their gentle looks?
Not to the beast that would usurp their den.
Whose hand is that the forest bear doth lick?
Not his, that spoils her young before her face.
Who 'scapes the lurking serpent's mortal sting?
Not he that sets his foot upon her back.
The smallest worm will turn, being trodden on,
And doves will peck, in safeguard of their brood.
           II. VI. PT. III. ii. 2.

     The poor wren,
The most diminutive of birds, will fight,
Her young ones in the nest, against the owl. *M.* iv. 2.

OPTICS (See EYE).

ORATION, PEDANTIC.
Taffeta phrases, silken terms precise,
 Three pil'd hyperboles, spruce affectation,
Figures pedantical; these summer flies
 Have blown me full of maggot ostentation. *L. L.* v. 2

ORATOR.
Doubt not, my lord; I'll play the orator,
As if the golden fee, for which I plead,
Were for myself. *R. III.* iii. 5.

ORATORY, POPULAR.
     For in such business,
Action is eloquence, and the eyes of the ignorant
More learned than their ears. *C.* iii. 2.

     Pray, be content;
Mother, I am going to the market-place;
Chide me no more. I'll mountebank their loves,
Cog their hearts from them, and come home belov'd
Of all the trades in Rome. *C.* iii. 2

ORDER.
    Degree being vizarded,
The unworthiest shows as fairly in the mask.
The heavens themselves, the planets, and this centre,
Observe degree, priority, and place,
Insisture, course, proportion, season, form,

Shakespearian Dictionary.

ORDER,—*continued*.
    Office, and custom, in all line of order:
    And therefore is the glorious planet, Sol,
    In noble eminence enthron'd and spher'd
    Amidst the other; whose med'cinable eye
    Corrects the ill aspécts of planets evil,
    And posts, like the commandment of a king,
    Sans check, to good and bad: But when the planets,
    In evil mixture, to disorder wander,
    What plagues, and what portents! what mutiny!
    What raging of the sea! shaking of earth!
    Commotion in the winds! frights, changes, horrors,
    Divert and crack, rend and deracinate
    The unity and married calm of states
    Quite from their fixture! O, when degree is shak'd,
    Which is the ladder of all high designs,
    The enterprise is sick! How could communities,
    Degrees in schools, and brotherhoods in cities,
    Peaceful commerce from divided shores,
    The primogeniture and due of birth,
    Prerogative of age, crowns, sceptres, laurels,
    But by degree, stand in authentic place?
    Take but degree away, untune that string,
    And, hark, what discord follows! each thing meets
    In mere oppugnancy: The bounded waters
    Should lift their bosoms higher than the shores,
    And make a sop of all this solid globe:
    Strength should be lord of imbecility,
    And the rude son should strike his father dead:
    Force should be right; or, rather, right and wrong
    (Between whose endless jar justice resides)
    Should lose their names, and so should justice too.
    Then every thing includes itself in power,
    Power into will, will into appetite:
    And appetite, a universal wolf,
    So doubly seconded with will and power,
    Must make perforce a universal prey,
    And, last, eat up himself. Great Agamemnon;
    This chaos, when degree is suffocate,
    Follows the choking:
    And this neglection of degree it is,
    That by a pace goes backward, with a purpose
    It hath to climb. The general's disdain'd
    By him one step below; he, by the next;
    That next, by him beneath: so every step,
    Exampled by the first pace that is sick
    Of his superior, grows to an envious fever
    Of pale and bloodless emulation.   *T.C.* i. 3.

ORDER,—*continued.*
The world is still deceiv'd with ornament.
In law, what plea so tainted and corrupt,
But, being season'd with a gracious voice,
Obscures the show of evil? In religion,
What damned error, but some sober brow
Will bless it, and approve it with a text,
Hiding the grossness with fair ornament? *M. V.* iii. 2.

ORNAMENT.
Thus ornament is but the guiled shore
To a most dangerous sea; the beauteous scarf
Veiling an Indian beauty; in a word,
The seeming truth which cunning times put on
To entrap the wisest. *M. V.* iii. 2.

OTHELLO'S Apology.
                Rude am I in speech,
And little bless'd with the soft phrase of peace;
For since these arms of mine had seven years' pith,
Till now some nine moons wasted, they have us'd
Their dearest action in the tented field;
And little of this great world can I speak,
More than pertains to feats of broil and battle;
And therefore little shall I grace my cause,
In speaking for myself: Yet, by your gracious patience,
I will a round unvarnish'd tale deliver
Of my whole course of love; what drugs, what charms,
What conjuration, and what mighty magic,
(For such proceeding I am charg'd withal)
I won his daughter with.
    Her father lov'd me; oft invited me;
Still question'd me the story of my life,
From year to year; the battles, sieges, fortunes,
That I have pass'd.
I ran it through, even from my boyish days,
To the very moment that he bade me tell it.
Wherein I spoke of most disastrous chances,
Of moving accidents by flood and field;
Of hair-breadth 'scapes i' the imminent deadly breach;
Of being taken by the insolent foe,
And sold to slavery; of my redemption thence,
And portance in my travel's history:
Wherein of antres vast, and desarts wild,
Rough quarries, rocks, and hills whose heads touch heaven,
It was my hint to speak. Such was my process;
And of the cannibals that each other eat,
The Anthropophagi, and men whose heads
Do grow beneath their shoulders. These things to hear,

Shakespearian Dictionary.

OTHELLO'S APOLOGY,—*continued.*
Would Desdemona seriously incline:
But still the house affairs would draw her thence;
Which ever as she could with haste despatch,
She'd come again, and with a greedy ear
Devour up my discourse: Which I observing,
Took once a pliant hour; and found good means
To draw from her a prayer of earnest heart,
That I would all my pilgrimage dilate,
Whereof by parcels she had something heard,
But not distinctively. I did consent;
And often did beguile her of her tears,
When I did speak of some distressful stroke,
That my youth suffer'd. My story being done,
She gave me for my pains a world of sighs;
She swore,—In faith, 'twas strange, 'twas passing strange;
'Twas pitiful, 'twas wondrous pitiful:
She wish'd' she had not heard it; yet she wish'd
That heaven had made her such a man. She thank'd me;
And bade me, if I had a friend that lov'd her,
I should but teach him how to tell my story,
And that would woo her. Upon this hint I spake;
She lov'd me for the dangers I had pass'd;
And I lov'd her, that she did pity them:
This only is the witchcraft I have us'd;
Here comes the lady, let her witness it.   *O.* i. 3.

―――――― FAREWELL.
            O now, for ever,
Farewell the tranquil mind! Farewell content!
Farewell the plumed troop, and the big wars,
That make ambition virtue! O, farewell!
Farewell the neighing steed, and the shrill trump,
The spirit-stirring drum, the ear-piercing fife,
The royal banner; and all quality,
Pride, pomp, and circumstance of glorious war!
And, O, you mortal engines, whose rude throats
The immortal Jove's dread clamours counterfeit,
Farewell!—Othello's occupation's gone!   *O.* iii. 3.

――――――― HANDKERCHIEF.
     There's magic in the web of it:
A sybil, that had number'd in the world
The sun to make two hundred compasses,
In her prophetic fury sew'd the work:
The worms were hallow'd that did breed the silk;
And it was dy'd in mummy, which the skilful
Conserv'd of maidens' hearts.   *O.* iii. 4.

OVERMATCHED.
  If there were not two or three and fifty upon poor old
  Jack, I am no two-legged creature.   *H.IV.* PT. I. ii. 4.

OUTCAST
            I am one my liege,
  Whom the vile blows and buffets of the world
  Have so incens'd, that I am reckless what
  I do to spite the world.   *M.* iii. 1.
  So weary with disasters, tugg'd with fortune,
  That I would set my life on any chance
  To mend it, or be rid on't.   *M.* iii. 1.
  Sick in the world's regard, wretched, and low,
  A poor unminded outlaw.   *H. IV.* PT. I. iv. 3.

OUTRAGEOUSNESS.
  Why, this passes, Mister Ford: you are not to go loose
  any longer, you must be pinioned.   *M. W.* iv. 2.
  Why, this is lunatics.   ·   *M. W.* iv. 2.

OUTWITTED.
            Thou art not vanquish'd,
  But cozen'd and beguil'd.   *K. L.* v. 3.

· **P.**

PACIFICATION.
  Each word thou hast spoke hath weeded from my heart
  A root of antient envy.   *C.* iv. 5.
            O, let me twine
  Mine arms about that body, where against
  My grained ash an hundred times hath broke,
  And scarr'd the moon with splinters!   *C.* iv 5.

PAINTING (See also PORTRAIT).
  Dost thou love pictures? We will fetch thee straight
  Adonis, painted by a running brook :
  And Cytherea, all in sedges hid ;
  Which seem to move and wanton with her breath,
  Even as the waving sedges play with wind.
  We'll show thee Io, as she was a maid ;
  And how she was beguiled and surpris'd,
  As lively painted as the deed was done.
  Or Daphne, roaming through a thorny wood ;
  Scratching her legs that one shall swear she bleeds ;
  And at that sight shall sad Apollo weep,
  So workmanly the blood and tears are drawn. *T. S.* IND. 2.

PAINTING,—continued.

Painting is welcome,
The painting is almost the natural man;
For since dishonour trafficks with man's nature,
He is but outside: These pencil'd figures are
Ev'n such as they give out. *T. A.* i. 1.
It is a pretty mocking of the life. *T. A.* i. 1.
    I'll say of it
It tutors nature: artificial strife
Lives in these touches, livelier than life. *T. A.* i. 1.
    How this grace
Speaks his own standing! what a mental power
This eye shoots forth! How big imagination
Moves in this lip! to the dumbness of the gesture
One might interpret. *T. A.* i. 1

    Timon.—Wrought he not well that painted this?
Apemantus.—He wrought better that made the painter;
and yet he's but a filthy piece of work. *T. A.* i. 1

PALLIATION.
Some sins do bear their privilege on earth,
And so doth your's. *K. J.* i. 1.

PALPABILITY.
Day-light and champian discovers not more. *T.N.* ii. 5.

PANIC.
    Norweyan banners flout the sky,—
And fan our people cold. *M.* i. 2.

PARADOX.
You undergo too strict a paradox,
Striving to make an ugly deed look fair. *T.A.* iii. 5.

PARADOXES.
These are old fond paradoxes, to make fool's laugh i' the alehouse. *O.* ii. 1.

PARASITES (See also FLATTERY).
That, Sir, which serves and seeks for gain,
    And follows but for form;
Will pack, when it begins to rain,
    And leave thee in the storm. *K. L.* ii. 4.

    O, you gods! what a number
Of men eat Timon, and he sees them not!
It grieves me, to see so many dip their meat
In one man's blood; and all the madness is,
He cheers them up too. *T.A.* i. 2.

PARASITES,—*continued.*
     'Tis such as you,
That creep like shadows by him, and do sigh
At each his needless heavings,—such as you
Nourish the cause of his awakings: I
Do come with words as med'cinal as true,
Honest, as either; to purge him of that humour
That presses him from sleep. *W.T.* ii. 3.
It is the curse of kings, to be attended
By slaves, that take their humour for a warrant
To break within the bloody house of life;
And, on the winking of authority,
To understand a law: to know the meaning
Of dangerous majesty, when, perchance, it frowns
More upon honour than advis'd respect. *K.J.* iv. 2.
Feast-won, fast-lost; one cloud of winter showers;
These flies are couch'd. *T.A.* ii. 2.
To me you cannot reach, you play the spaniel,
And think with wagging of your tongue to win me
But whatso'er thou tak'st me for, I am sure
Thou hast a cruel nature, and a bloody. *H.VIII.* v. 2.
O villains, vipers, damn'd without redemption!
Dogs, easily won to fawn on any man!
Snakes, in my heart-blood warm'd, that sting my heart!
          R.II. iii. 2.

  When the rain came to wet me once, and the wind to make me chatter; when the thunder would not peace at my bidding; there I found them, there I smelt them out. Go to, they are not men o' their words: they told me I was every thing;—'tis a lie; I'm not ague-proof. *K.L.* iv. 6.

May you a better feast never behold,
You knot of mouth-friends! Smoke and luke-warm water
Is your perfection. This is Timon's last;
Who stuck and spangled you with flatteries,
Washes it off, and sprinkles in your faces
Your reeking villainy. Live loath'd, and long,
Most smiling, smooth, detested parasites,
Courteous destroyers, affable wolves, meak bears,
You fools of fortune, trencher friends, time's flies,
Cap and knee slaves, vapours, and minute-jacks!
Of man, and beast, the infinite malady
Crust you quite o'er' *T.A.* ii. 6

PARDON
Yes, I do think that you might pardon him,
And neither heaven nor man grieve at the mercy.
          M.M. ii. 2.

PARENTAL AFFECTION (See also AFFLICTION).
How sometimes nature will betray its folly,
Its tenderness, and make itself a pastime
To harder bosoms! Looking on the lines
Of my boy's face, methought I did recoil
Twenty-three years, and saw myself unbreech'd,
In my green velvet coat; my dagger muzzled,
Lest it should bite its master, and so prove
As ornaments oft do, too dangerous. *W.T.* i. 2.

You have no children, butchers! if you had,
The thought of them would have stirr'd up remorse.
H. VI. PT. III. v. 5.

    And my young boy
Hath an aspéct of intercession, which
Great nature cries, *deny not*. *C.* v. 3.

Unreasonable creatures feed their young:
And though man's face be fearful to their eyes,
Yet in protection of their tender ones,
Who hath not seen them (even with those wings
Which sometimes they have us'd with fearful flight)
Make war with him that climb'd unto their nest,
Offering their own lives in their young's defence?
H. VI. PT. III. ii. 2.

PARLIAMENT.
 God speed the parliament! *H. VI.* PT. I. iii. 2.

PARRYING.
 Truly, madam, he holds Belzebub at the stave's end, as well as a man in his case may do. *T. N.* v. 1.

 Thou knowest my old ward;—here I lay, and thus I bore my point. *H. IV.* PT. I. ii. 4.

PARTING.
    Parting is such sweet sorrow,
That I shall say—good night, till it be morrow. *R. J.* ii. 2.

    For so long
As he could make me with this eye or ear
Distinguish him from others, he did keep
The deck, with glove, or hat, or handkerchief,
Still waving, as the fits or stirs of his mind
Could best express how slow his soul sail'd on,
How swift his ship. *Cym.* i 4

Farewell! the leisure and the fearful time
Cuts off the ceremonious vows of love,
And ample interchange of sweet discourse,
Which so long sunder'd friends should dwell upon;

PARTING,—*continued.*
God give us leisure for these rites of love!
Once more, adieu! *R. III.* v. 3.
    O, my lord,
Must I then leave you? Must I needs forego
So good, so noble, and so true a master?
Bear witness, all that have not hearts of iron,
With what a sorrow Cromwell leaves his lord.
The king shall have my service; but my prayers,
For ever, and for ever, shall be yours. *H. VIII.* iii. 2.

Farewell! God knows when we shall meet again.
I have a faint cold fear thrills through my veins,
That almost freezes up the heat of life. *R. J.* ii. 2.

And even there, his eyes being big with tears,
Turning his face, he put his hand behind him,
And with affection wondrous sensible,
He wrung Bassanio's hand, and so they parted. *M. V.* ii. 8.

I would have broke mine eye-strings; crack'd them, but
To look upon him; till the diminution
Of space had pointed him sharp as my needle;
Nay, follow'd him, till he had melted from
The smallness of a gnat, to air; and then
Have turn'd mine eye, and wept. *Cym.* i. 4.

    What! gone without a word?
Ay, so true love should do: it cannot speak;
For truth had better deeds than words, to grace it.
    T. G. ii. 2.

We make woe wanton with this foul delay;
Once more, adieu! the rest let sorrow say. *R. II.* v. 1

And whether we shall meet again, I know not.
Therefore, our everlasting farewell take:—
For ever, and for ever, farewell, Cassius!
If ever we do meet again, why we shall smile:
If not, why then this parting was well made. *J. C.* v. 1.

   Should we be taking leave
As long a term as yet we have to live,
The loathness to depart would grow. *Cym.* i. 2.

We two, that with so many thousand sighs
Did buy each other, must poorly sell ourselves
With the rude brevity and discharge of one.
Injurious time, now with a robber's haste,
Crams his rich thievery up, he knows not how;
As many farewells as be stars in heaven,
With distinct breath and consign'd kisses to them,
He fumbles up into a loose adieu;

PARTING,—*continued.*
And scants us with a single famish'd kiss,
Distasted with the salt of broken tears.   *T.C.* iv. 4.
Portia, adieu! I have too griev'd a heart
To take a tedious leave.   *M.V.* ii. 7.
    At once, good night:—
Stand not upon the order of your going,
But go at once.   *M.* iii. 4
    Come;
Our separation so abides, and flies,
That thou, residing here, go'st yet with me,
And I, hence fleeting, here remain with thee.   *A.C.* i. 3.
And so, without more circumstance at all,
I hold it fit, that we shake hands and part;
You, as your business, and desire, shall point you:—
For every man hath business, and desire,
Such as it is,—and for mine own poor part,
Look you, I will go pray.   *H.* i. 5.
'Tis almost morning, I would have thee gone:
And yet no further than a wanton's bird;
Who lets it hop a little from her hand,
Like a poor prisoner in his twisted gyves,
And with a silk thread plucks it back again,
So loving jealous of his liberty.   *R.J.* ii. 2.
Here is my hand for my true constancy;
And when that hour o'er-slips me in the day,
Wherein I sigh not, Julia, for thy sake,
The next ensuing hour some foul mischance
Torment me for my love's forgetfulness.   *T.G.* ii. 2.
Wilt thou begone? it is not yet near day:
It was the nightingale, and not the lark,
That pierc'd the fearful hollow of thine ear;
Nightly she sings on yon pomegranate tree;
Believe me, love, it was the nightingale.   *R.J.* iii. 5.
I did not take my leave of him, but had
Most pretty things to say: ere I could tell him,
How I would think on him, at certain hours,
Such thoughts, and such; * * *
* * * or have charg'd him,
At the sixth hour of morn, at noon, at midnight,
T' encounter me with orisons; for then,
I am in heaven for him; or ere I could
Give him that parting kiss, which I had set
Betwixt two charming words, comes in my father,
And, like the tyrannous breathing of the north,
Shakes all our buds from growing.   *Cym.* i. 4.

PAR   Shakesperian Dictionary.   PAT

PARTING,—*continued.*
    Tend me to-night;
May be, it is the period of your duty;
Haply, you shall not see me more: or if,
A mangled shadow: perchance, to-morrow,
You'll serve another master   I look on you,
As one that takes his leave.   Mine honest friends;
I turn you not away; but, like a master,
Married to your good service, stay till death.   *A. C.* iv. 2.

PARTY Rancour.
    These days are dangerous!
Virtue is chok'd with foul ambition,
And charity chas'd hence by rancour's hand.
    H. VI. pt. ii. iii. 1.

PASSION.
All the more it seeks to hide itself,
The bigger bulk it shows.   *T.* iii. 1.

PASSIONS, Conflicting (See also Emotions).
Thou think'st 'tis much that this contentious storm
Invades us to the skin: so 'tis to thee;
But where the greater malady is fix'd,
The lesser is scarce felt.   Thou'dst shun a bear:
But if thy flight lay towards the raging sea,
Thou'dst meet a bear i' the mouth.   When the mind's free,
The body's delicate: the tempest in my mind
Doth from my senses take all feeling else,
Save what beats there.   *K. L.* iii. 4.

PASSIONS, Guilty.
Poor chastity is rifled of her store,
And lust, the thief, far poorer than before.   *Poems.*

PASTIME.
This will be pastime passing excellent
If it be husbanded with modesty.   *T. S.* Ind. 1.

Say, what abridgment have you for this evening?
What mask? what music?   How shall we beguile
The lazy time, if not with some delight?   *M. N.* v. 1.

    Courtship, pleasant jest and courtesy,
As bombast, and as lining to the time.   *L. L.* v. 2.

PATCHING.
    Any thing that's mended, is but patched: virtue, that
transgresses, is but patched with sin; and sin, that amends
is but patched with virtue.   *T. N.* i. 5.

PATIENCE.

He, that would have a cake out of the wheat, must tarry
the grinding.   *T.C.* i. 1.
Though patience be a tired mare, yet she will plod.
  II.V. ii. 1.
How poor are they that have not patience!
What wound did ever heal but by degrees?
Thou know'st we work by wit, and not by witchcraft;
And wit depends on dilatory time.   *O.* ii. 3.
Thou young and rose-lipp'd cherubim.   *O.* iv. 2
  I do note,
That grief and patience, rooted in him both,
Mingle their spurs together.   *Cym.* iv. 2.
  Grow, patience!
And let the stinking elder, grief, untwine
His perishing root, with the increasing vine.   *Cym.* iv. 2.
Cease to lament for that thou canst not help,
And study help from that which thou lament'st.
Time is the nurse and breeder of all good.   *T.G.* iii. 1.
So let the Turk of Cyprus us beguile;
We lose it not, so long as we can smile,
He bears the sentence well, that nothing bears
But the free comfort which from thence he hears:
But he bears both the sentence and the sorrow,
That, to pay grief, must of poor patience borrow.   *O.* i. 3
Nay, patience, or we break the sinews of our plot.
  T.N. ii. 5.
That which in mean men we entitle patience,
Is pale cold cowardice in noble breasts.   *R.II.* i. 2.
  O, gentle son,
Upon the heat and flame of thy distemper,
Sprinkle cool patience.   *H.* ii. 4.
Signior Antonio, many a time and oft,
On the Rialto, you have rated me
About my monies, and my usances:
Still I have borne it with a patient shrug:
For sufferance is the badge of all our tribe.   *M.V.* i. 3.
Patience, unmov'd, no marvel though she pause;
They can be meek that have no other cause.
A wretched soul, bruis'd with adversity,
We bid be quiet when we hear it cry;
But were we burthen'd with like weight of pain,
As much, or more, we should ourselves complain.
  C.E. ii. 1.

PATIENCE,—*continued.*

I have her sovereign aid,
And rest myself content. *T.* v. 1.

I do oppose
My patience to his fury; and am arm'd
To suffer with a quietness of spirit,
The very tyranny and rage of his. *M.V.* iv. 1.

Henceforth, I'll bear
Affliction, till it do cry out itself,
Enough, enough, and die. *K.L.* iv. 6

PATRIOTISM.

If it be aught toward the general good,
Set honour in one eye, and death i' the other,
And I will look on both indifferently:
For, let the gods so speed me, as I love
The name of honour, more than I fear death. *J.C.* i. 2.

I am the son of Marcus Cato, ho!
A foe to tyrants and my country's friend. *J.C.* v. 4.

There was a Brutus once, that would have brook'd
The eternal devil to keep his state in Rome,
As easily as a king. *J.C.* i. 2.

Our subjects, Sir,
Will not endure his yoke. *Cym.* iii. 5.

PATRONAGE.

O momentary grace of mortal men,
Which we more hunt for than the grace of God!
R. III. iii. 4.

PAUSING.

Look, he is winding up the watch of his wit; by and by
it will strike. *T.* ii. 1.

PAYMENT.

He is well paid, that is well satisfied. *M.V.* iv. 1.
Fair payment for foul words, is more than due. *L.L.* iv. 1.

PEACE.

Fie, lords! that you, being supreme magistrates,
Thus contumeliously should break the peace.
H. VI. PT. I. i. 3.

Nothing but peace and gentle visitation. *L.L.* v. 2.

In her days, every man shall eat in safety,
Under his own vine, what he plants; and sing
The merry songs of peace to all his neighbours.
H. VIII. v. 4.

PEACE,—_continued._
Peace be to France; if France in peace permit
Our just and lineal entrance to our own!
If not; bleed France, and peace ascend to heaven.
K. J. ii. 1.

Now are our brows bound with victorious wreaths;
Our bruised arms hung up for monuments;
Our stern alarums chang'd to merry meetings,
Our dreadful marches to delightful measures.
Grim visag'd war hath smooth'd his wrinkled front;
And now,—instead of mounting barbed steeds,
To fright the souls of fearful adversaries,—
He capers nimbly in a lady's chamber,
To the lascivious pleasing of a lute. *R. III.* i. 1.

A peace is of the nature of a conquest;
For then both parties nobly are subdued,
And neither party loser. *H. IV.* PT. II. iv. 2.

Now is the winter of our discontent
Made glorious summer by this sun of York;
And all the clouds that lower'd upon our house,
In the deep bosom of the ocean buried. *R. III.* i. 1.

    The sea being smooth,
How many shallow bauble boats dare sail
Upon her patient breast, making their way
With those of nobler bulk. *T. C.* i. 3

Keep peace, upon your lives;
He dies, that strikes again. What is the matter?
K. L. ii. 2.

If I unwittingly, or in my rage,
Have aught committed that is hardly borne
By any in this presence, I desire
To reconcile me to his friendly peace:
'Tis death to me, to be at enmity;
I hate it, and desire all good men's love. *R. III.* ii. 1.

   Who should study to preserve a peace
If holy churchmen take delight in broils?
H. VI. PT. I. iii. 1

Peace be to me, and every one that dares not fight.
L. L. i. 1.

In peace, there's nothing so becomes a man,
As modest stillness, and humility. *H. V.* iii. 1.

What, drawn, and talk of peace? *R. J.* i. 1.

  This peace is nothing, but to rust iron, increase tailors,
and breed ballad-makers. *C.* iv. 5.

PEACE,—continued.

Peace is a very apoplexy, lethargy: mulled, deaf, sleepy, insensible.   *C.* iv. 5.

Still, in thy right hand, carry gentle peace.   *H. VIII.* iii. 2.

My tongue shall hush again this storm of war,
And make fair weather in your blust'ring land.   *K. J.* v. 1.

Thy threatening colours now wind up,
And tame the savage spirit of wild war;
That, like a lion foster'd up at hand,
It may lie gently at the foot of peace,
And be no further harmful than in show.   *K. J.* v. 2.

PEDANT.
Like a pedant, that keeps a school i' the church.
T. N. iii. 2.

PEDANTRY.
Idle words, servants to shallow fools,
Unprofitable sounds, weak arbitrators!
Busy yourselves in skull-contending schools;
Debate, where leisure serves, with dull debaters.
Poems.

PEDLAR.
He hath ribands of all the colours i' the rainbow; points more than all the lawyers in Bohemia can learnedly handle, though they come to him by the gross; inkles, caddisses, cambrics, lawns: why, he sings them over, as they were gods or goddesses; you would think, a smock were a she-angel; he so chaunts to the sleeve hand, and the work about the square on't.   *W. T.* iv. 3.

PENITENCE.
By penitence the Eternal's wrath's appeas'd.   *T. G.* v. 4.

The breath of heaven hath blown his spirit out,
And strew'd repentant ashes on his head.   *K. J.* iv. 1.

PEOPLE.
The people are the city.   *C.* iii. 1.

PERCEPTION, HUMAN.
What! are men mad? Hath nature given them eyes,
To see this vaulted arch, and the rich crop
Of sea and land, which can distinguish 'twixt
The fiery orbs above, and the twinn'd stones
Upon the unnumber'd beach; and can we not
Partition make, with spectacles so precious,
'Twixt fair and foul?   *Cym.* i. 7.

Shakespearian Dictionary.

PERDITION.
I'll be damned for ne'er a king's son in Christendom.
H. IV. PT. I. i. 2.
O thou sun,
Burn the great sphere thou mov'st in! darkling stand
The varying shore o' the world! *A. C.* iv. 13.

PERFECTION.
More than report can promise, fancy blazon,
Is true perfection. *Poems.*
Is this your perfectness?—begone, you rogue. *L. L.* v. 2.
————————, FEMALE.
She that was ever fair, and never proud;
Had tongue at will, and yet was never loud;
Never lack'd gold, and yet went never gay;
Fled from her wish, and yet said, Now I may;
She that, being anger'd, her revenge being nigh,
Bade her wrong stay, and her displeasure fly:
* * * * *
She that could think, and ne'er disclose her mind,
See suitors following, and not look behind. *O.* ii. 1.

PERIL.
Now happy he, whose cloak and cincture can
Hold out this tempest. *K. J.* iv. 3.

For mine own part, I have not a case of lives; the humour of it is too hot, that is the very plain-song of it.
H. V. iii. 2.

PERJURY.
Thus pour the stars down plagues for perjury! *L. L.* v. 2.

PERPLEXITY.
Sure one of you does not serve heaven well; that you are so crossed. *M. W.* iv. 5.

PERSECUTION.
O God, defend me! how am I beset!
What kind of catechizing call you this? *M. A.* iv. 1.
Disloyal? No:
She's punish'd for her truth; and undergoes,
More goddess-like than wife-like, such assaults
As would take in some virtue. *Cym.* iii. 2.

PERSEVERANCE.
Persévérance, dear my lord,
Keeps honour bright: To have done, is to hang
Quite out of fashion, like a rusty mail
In monumental mockery. *T. C.* iii. 3

PERSEVERANCE,—*continued.*
Do not, for one repulse, forego the purpose
That you resolv'd to effect. *T.* iii. 3.

PERSPECTIVE.
These things seem small, and undistinguishable,
Like far-off mountains turned into clouds. *M. N.* iv. 1.

PERTINACITY.
 Nay, I will; that's flat:
He said, he would not ransom Mortimer;
Forbade my tongue to speak of Mortimer;
But I will find him when he lies asleep,
And in his ear I'll holla,—Mortimer! *H. IV.* PT. I. i. 3.

Let them pull all about mine ears; present me
Death on the wheel, or at wild horses' heels;
Or pile ten hills on the Tarpeian rock,
That the precipitation might down stretch
Below the beam of sight,—yet will I still
Be thus to them. *C.* iii. 2.

You'll ask me, why I rather choose to have
A weight of carrion flesh, than to receive
Three thousand ducats: I'll not answer that:
But say, it is my humour; Is it answer'd? *M. V.* iv. 1.

 Speak of Mortimer!
Zounds, I will speak of him: and let my soul
Want mercy, if I do not join with him:
Yea, on his part, I'll empty all these veins,
And shed my dear blood, drop by drop, i' the dust.
But I will lift the down-trod Mortimer
As high i' the air as this unthankful king,
As this ingrate and canker'd Bolingbroke. *H. IV.* PT. I. i. 3.

 Pent to linger
But with a grain a day, I would not buy
Their mercy at the price of one fair word;
Nor check my courage for what they can give,
To hav't with saying,—Good morrow. *C.* iii. 3.

 Nay,
I'll have a starling shall be taught to speak
Nothing but Mortimer, and give it him,
To keep his anger still in motion. *H. IV.* PT. I. i. 3.

 Thou injurious tribune!
Within thine eyes sat twenty thousand deaths,
In thy hands clutch'd as many millions, in
Thy lying tongue both numbers, I would say,
Thou liest, unto thee, with a voice as free
As I do pray the gods. *C.* iii. 3.

PERTINACITY,—*continued.*
Choler!
Were I as patient as the midnight sleep,
Bv Jove, 'twould be my mind.   *C.* iii. 1.
It nothing steads us
To cnide him from our eaves.

PHANTASY.
This is the very coinage of your brain:
This bodiless creation ecstacy
Is very cunning in.   *H.* iii. 4.

PHILOSOPHY. PHILOSOPHERS.
Adversity's sweet milk, philosophy.   *R.J.* iii. 3.
Brave conquerors,—for so you are,
That war against your own affections,
And the huge army of the world's desires.   *L. L.* i. 1.
Of your philosophy you make no use,
If you give place to accidental evils.   *J.C.* iv. 3.
Blest are those,
Whose blood and judgment are so well commingled,
That they are not a pipe for Fortune's finger,
To sound what stop she please.   *H.* iii. 2.
Hang up philosophy!
Unless philosophy can make a Juliet,
Displant a town, reverse a prince's doom;
It helps not, it prevails not, talk no more.   *R. J.* iii. 3.
For there was never yet philosopher,
That could endure the tooth-ach patiently;
However they have writ the style of gods,
And made a pish at chance and sufferance   *M. A.* v. 1
O, cry you mercy,
Noble philosopher, your company.   *K. L.* iii. 4.
First, let me talk with this philosopher:—
What is the cause of thunder?   *K. L.* iii. 4.

———, PRETENDED.
We make trifles of terrors; ensconcing ourselves into seeming knowledge, when we should submit ourselves to an unknown fear.   *A. W.* ii. 3
We have our philosophical persons, to make modern and familiar things, supernatural and causeless.   *A. W.* ii. 3.

PHRASES.
Good phrases are surely, and ever were, very commendable.
    H. IV. PT. II. iii. 4.
The tevil and his tam! what phrase is this?   *M. W.* i. 1

PHYSIC.
Throw physic to the dogs, I'll none of it. *M.* v. 3.

———, STATE.
If thou could'st, doctor, cast
The water of my land, find her disease,
And purge it to a sound and pristine health,
I would applaud thee to the very echo,
That should applaud again.—Pull't off, I say—
What rhubarb, senna, or what purgative drug,
Would scour these English hence. *M.* v. 3.

PHYSICIAN.
Whose skill was almost as great as his honesty; had it stretched so far, 'twould have made Nature immortal, and Death should have played for lack of work. *A. W.* i. 1.

PHYSIOGNOMY.
There's no art,
To find the mind's construction in the face:
He was a gentleman on whom I built
An infinite trust. *M.* i. 1.

PICTURE.
Come, draw this curtain, and let's see your picture.
T. C. iii. 2.

But we will draw the curtain, and show you the picture.
T. N. i. 5.

PILGRIMAGE.
Which holy undertaking, with most austere sanctimony, she accomplished. *A. W.* iv. 3.

PIPING (See also TOOL).
Govern these ventages with your fingers and thumb, give it breath with your mouth, and it will discourse most excellent music. *H.* iii. 2.

Why, look you now, how unworthy a thing you make of me. You would play upon me; you would seem to know my stops; you would pluck out the heart of my mystery; you would sound me from my lowest note to the top of my compass: and there is much music, excellent voice, in this little organ; yet cannot you make it speak. 'Sblood, do you think I am easier to be played upon than a pipe?
H. iii. 2.

PIRATES' PIETY.
Thou concludest like the sanctimonious pirate, that went to sea with the ten commandments, but scraped one out of the table:—Thou shalt not steal. *M. M.* i. 2.

PIT   **Shakesperian Dictionary.**   PIT

PITY.
        Those that can pity, here
May, if they think it well, let fall a tear;
The subject will deserve it.   *H. VIII. prologue*
        But if there be
Yet left in heaven as small a drop of pity,
As a wren's eye, fear'd gods, a part of it!   *Cym.* iv. 2

And pity, like a naked new-born babe,
Striding the blast, or heaven's cherubim, hors'd
Upon the sightless couriers of the air,
Shall blow the horrid deed in every eye,
That tears shall drown the wind.   *M.* i. 7.
        It is a pity
Would move a monster.   *H. VIII.* ii. 3.

If ever you have look'd on better days;
If ever been where bells have knoll'd to church
If ever sat at any good man's feast;
If ever from your eye-lids wip'd a tear,
And know what 'tis to pity and be pitied;
Let gentleness my strong enforcement be.   *A. Y.* ii. 7.

A begging prince what beggar pities not?   *R. III.* i. 4.

Had not God, for some strong purpose, steel'd
The hearts of men, they must perforce have melted,
And barbarism itself have pitied him.   *R. II.* v. 2

    If thou tell'st this heavy story right,
Upon my soul the hearers will shed tears;
Yea, even my foes will shed fast falling tears,
And say,—Alas, it was a piteous deed!   *H. VI.* PT. III. i. 4.

I show it most of all when I show justice;
For then I pity those I do not know,
Which a dismiss'd offence would after gall;
And do him right, that, answering one foul wrong
Lives not to act another.   *M. M.* ii. 2.
        Pity's sleeping:
Strange times, that weep with laughing, not with weeping!
                                T. A. iv. 3.

        But, I perceive,
Men must learn now with pity to dispense;
For policy sits above conscience.   *T. A.* iii. 2.

The dint of pity.   *J. C.* iii. 2.

Tear-falling pity.   *R. III.* iv. 2.

O dearest soul! your cause doth strike my heart
With pity, that doth make me sick.   *Cym* I. 7.

PLA   Shakespearian Dictionary.   PLA

PLACE AND GREATNESS.
O place and greatness, millions of false eyes
Are struck upon thee! volumes of report
Run with these false and most contrarious quests
Upon thy doings! thousand 'scapes of wit
Make thee the father of their idle dreams,
And rack thee in their fancies!   *M. M.* iv. 1.

PLANETARY INFLUENCE.
This is the excellent foppery of the world; that, when we are sick in fortune, (often the surfeit of our own behaviour) we make guilty of our disasters, the sun, the moon, and the stars: as if we were villains by necessity; fools, by heavenly compulsion; knaves, thieves, and treachers, by spherical predominance; drunkards, liars, and adulterers, by an enforced obedience of planetary influence; and all that we are evil in, by a divine thrusting on: An admirable evasion of man, to lay his goatish disposition to the charge of a star!   *K. L.* i. 2.

Our remedies oft in ourselves do lie,
Which we ascribe to heaven: the fated sky
Gives us free scope; only, doth backward pull
Our slow designs, when we ourselves are dull.   *A. W.* i. 1.

Men at some time are masters of their fates:
The fault, dear Brutus, is not in our stars,
But in ourselves, that we are underlings.   *J. C.* i. 2.

PLAYS. PLAYERS.
Melancholy is the nurse of frenzy,
Therefore, they thought it good you hear a play,
And frame your mind to mirth and merriment,
Which bars a thousand harms, and lengthens life.
   T. S. IND. 2.

Is there no play,
To ease the anguish of a torturing hour?   *M. N.* v. 1.

Shall's have a play of this?   *Cym.* v. 5.

What, a play toward? I'll be an auditor.   *M. N.* iii. 1.

The play's the thing,
Wherein I'll catch the conscience of the king.   *H.* ii. 2.

Good, my lord, will you see the players well bestow'd? Do you hear, let them be well used; for they are the abstract, and brief chronicles, of the time: After your death, you were better have a bad epitaph, than their ill report while you live.   *H.* ii. 2.

The players cannot keep counsel; they'll tell all.   *H.* iii. 2.

PLEA.
Since what I am to say, must be but that
Which contradicts my accusation ; and
The testimony on my part, no other
But what comes from myself, it shall scarce boot me
To say,—Not Guilty:—mine integrity
Being counted falsehood, shall, as I express it,
Be so receiv'd. But thus,—if powers divine
Behold our human actions (as they do)
I doubt not then, but innocence shall make
False accusation blush, and tyranny
Tremble at patience. *W.T.* iii. 2.

PLEASURE AND REVENGE, RECKLESSNESS OF.
Pleasure, and revenge,
Have ears more deaf than adders to the voice
Of any true decision. *T.C.* ii. 2.

PLEDGE.
My heart is thirsty for that noble pledge. *J.C.* iv. 3.

PLODDING.
Why, universal plodding prisons up
The nimble spirits in the arteries ;
As motion, and long-during action, tires
The sinewy vigour of the traveller. *L. L.* iv. 3.

PLOT.
By the Lord, our plot is a good plot as ever was laid ;
our friends true and constant: a good plot, good friends,
and full of expectation: an excellent plot, very good friends.
H. IV. PT. I. ii. 2.

Who cannot be crush'd with a plot! *A.W.* iv. 3.

So so ; these are the limbs of the plot. *H. VIII.* i. 1.

PLUNDERERS.
Hear me, you wrangling pirates, that fall out
In sharing that which you have pill'd from me. *R. III.* i. 3.

POETRY. POET (See also BALLAD-MONGER, RHYMSTER).
Our poesy is a gum, which oozes
From whence 'tis nourish'd: the fire i'the flint
Shows not, till it be struck ; our gentle flame
Provokes itself, and, like the current, flies
Each bound it chafes. *T. A.* i. 1.

Own'st thou the heavenly influence of the muse,
Spend not thy fury on some worthless song ;
Dark'ning thy power to lend base subjects light. *Poems.*

POETRY, Poet,—*continued*.
　Assist me, some extemporal god of rhyme, for, I am sure, I shall turn sonneteer. Devise, wit; write, pen; for I am for whole volumes in folio. *L. L.* i. 2.
　The elegancy, facility, and golden cadence of poesy.
L. L. iv. 2.
And wait the season, and observe the times,
And spend his prodigal wits in bootless rhymes. *L.L.* v. 2.
　The force of heaven-bred poesy. *T. G.* iii. 2.
　Audrey.—I do not know what poetical is: Is it honest indeed and word? Is it a true thing?
　Touchstone.—No, truly; for the truest poetry is the most feigning. *A. Y.* iii. 3.

POISON.
　　　　　　Let me have
A dram of poison; such soon-speeding geer
As will disperse itself through all the veins,
That the life-weary taker may fall dead;
And that the trunk may be discharg'd of breath
As violently, as hasty powder fir'd
Doth hurry from the fatal cannon's womb. *R. J.* v. 1.
　　　　　　No cataplasm so rare,
Collected from all simples that have virtue
Under the moon, can save the thing from death,
That is but scratch'd withal. *H.* iv. 7.

POLICY.
　The devil knew not what he did, when he made man politic. *T. A.* iii. 3.
　　　　　　Plague of your policy!
You sent me deputy for Ireland;
Far from his succour, from the king, from all
That might have mercy on the fault thou gav'st him;
Whilst your great goodness, out of holy pity,
Absolv'd him with an axe. *H. VIII.* iii. 2

POLITICIANS.
　　　　　　Get thee glass eyes;
And, like a scurvy politician, seem
To see the things thou dost not. *K. L.* iv. 6.
They'll sit by the fire, and presume to know
What's done i'the Capitol: who's like to rise,
Who thrives, and who declines; side factions, and give out
Conjectural marriages; making parties strong,
And feebling such as stand not in their liking,
Below their cobbled shoes. *C.* i. 1.

POLISHED MAN.
Behaviour, what wert thou
Till this man show'd thee? and what art thou now?
L. L. v. 2.

POMP.
Why, what is pomp, rule, reign, but earth and dust?
And, live we how we can, yet die we must.
H. VI. PT. III. v. 2.

—— AND POVERTY.
Take physic, pomp;
Expose thyself to feel what wretches feel;
That thou mayest shake the superflux to them,
And show the heavens more just. *K. L.* iii. 4

POPULARITY (See also APPLAUSE, MOB).
All tongues speak of him, and the bleared sights
Are spectacled to see him. *C.* ii. 1.

Stalls, bulks, windows,
Are smother'd up, leads fill'd, and ridges hors'd
With variable complexions; all agreeing
In earnestness to see him. *C.* ii. 1.

Had I so lavish of my presence been,
So common hackney'd in the eyes of men,
So stale and cheap to vulgar company;
Opinion, that did help me to the crown,
Had still kept loyal to possession,
And left me in reputeless banishment,
A fellow of no mark, nor likelihood.
By being seldom seen, I could not stir,
But, like a comet, I was wonder'd at:
That men would tell their children, *That is he;*
Others would say, *Where? which is Bolingbroke?*
And then I stole all courtesy from heaven,
And dress'd myself in such humility,
That I did pluck allegiance from men's hearts,
Loud shouts and salutations from men's mouths,
Even in the presence of the crowned king.
Thus did I keep my person fresh and new;
My presence, like a robe pontifical,
Ne'er seen, but wonder'd at: and so my state,
Seldom, but sumptuous, showed like a feast;
And won, by rareness, such solemnity.
The skipping king, he ambled up and down,
With shallow jesters, and rash bavin wits,
Soon kindled, and soon burn'd: carded his state;
Mingled his royalty with carping fools;
Had his great name profaned with his scorns;
And gave his countenance, against his name,

POPULARITY,—*continued.*
To laugh at gibing boys, and stand the push
Of every beardless vain comparative:
Grew a companion to the common streets,
Enfeoff'd himself to popularity:
That being daily swallowed by men's eyes,
They surfeited with honey; and began
To loathe the taste of sweetness, whereof a little
More than a little is by much too much.
So, when he had occasion to be seen,
He was but as the cuckoo is in June,
Heard, not regarded; seen, but with such eyes,
As, sick and blunted with community,
Afford no extraordinary gaze,
Such as is bent on sun-like majesty
When it shines seldom in admiring eyes. *H. IV.* PT. I. iii. 2.

              I have seen
The dumb men throng to see him, and the blind
To hear him speak: the matrons flung their gloves,
Ladies and maids their scarfs and handkerchiefs,
Upon him as he pass'd: the nobles bended,
As to Jove's statue; and the commons made
A shower, and thunder, with their caps and shouts.
                                 C. ii. 1.

He's lov'd of the distracted multitude,
Who like not in their judgment, but their eyes;
And, where 'tis so, the offender's scourge is weigh'd
But never the offence.   *H.* iv. 3.

              He returns,
Splitting the air with noise.   *C.* v. 5.

It hath been taught us from the primal state,
That he, which is, was wish'd until he were;
And the ebb'd man, ne'er loved, till ne'er worth love,
Comes dear'd by being lack'd. This common body,
Like a vagabond flag upon the stream,
Goes to, and back, lackeying the varying tide,
To rot itself with motion.   *A. C.* i. 4.

            Such a noise arose
As the shrouds make at sea in a stiff tempest,
As loud, and to as many tunes: hats, cloaks,
(Doublets, I think,) flew up; and had their faces
Been loose, this day they had been lost. *H. VIII.* iv. 1

Every wretch pining and pale before,
Beholding him, plucks comfort from his looks;
A largess universal, like the sun,

POP   *Shakesperian Dictionary.*   POP

POPULARITY,—*continued.*
His lib'ral eye doth give to every one,
Thawing cold fear.   *H.V.* iv. *chorus.*
     Then, as I said, the Duke, great Bolingbroke,
Mounted upon a hot and fiery steed,
Which his aspiring rider seemed to know,
With slow, but stately pace, kept on his course ;
While all tongues cry'd,—God save thee, Bolingbroke!
You would have thought the very windows spake
So many greedy looks of young and old
Through casements darted their desiring eyes
Upon his visage ;—and that all the walls,
With painted imag'ry, had said at once,—
JESU preserve thee : Welcome, Bolingbroke!
Whilst he, from one side to the other turning,
Bare-headed, lower than his proud steed's neck,
Bespake them thus :—I thank you, countrymen ;
And thus still doing, thus he passed along.   *R. II.* v. 2.

     If the tag-rag people did not clap him, and hiss him, according as he pleased, and displeased them, as they use to do the players in the theatre, I am no true man.   *J.C.* i. 2.

     Marry, before he fell down when he perceived the common herd was glad he refused the crown, he plucked me ope his doublet, and offered them his throat to cut. An I had been a man of any occupation, if I would not have taken him at his word, I would I might go to hell, among the rogues ;—and so he fell. When he came to himself again, he said, If he had done, or said, anything amiss, he desired their worships to think it was his infirmity. Three or four wenches, where I stood, cried, *Alas, good soul,*—and forgave him with all their hearts.   *J.C.* i 2.

     Since the wisdom of their choice, is rather to have my hat than my heart, I will practise the insinuating nod, and be off to them most counterfeitly ; that is, Sir, I will counterfeit the bewitchment of some popular man, and give it bountifully to the desirers.   *C.* ii. 3.

     The rabble call him lord:
And, as the world were now but to begin,
Antiquity forgot, custom not known,
The ratifiers and props of every word,
They cry,—*Choose we ; Laertes shall be king!*   *H.* iv. 5.
Now, when the lords, and barons of the realm,
Perceiv'd Northumberland did lean to him,
The more and less came in with cap and knee ;
Met him in boroughs, cities, villages ;
Attended him on bridges, stood in lanes,

POPULARITY,—*continued.*
Laid gifts before him, proffer'd him their oaths,
Gave him their heirs, as pages follow'd him,
Even at his heels, in golden multitudes.
He presently,—as greatness knows itself,—
Steps me a little higher than his vow
Made to my father, while his blood was poor,
Upon the naked shore at Ravenspurg;
And now, forsooth, takes on him to reform
Some certain edicts, and some strait decrees,
That lie too heavy on the commonwealth:
Cries out upon abuses, seems to weep
Over his country's wrongs; and, by this face
This seeming brow of justice, did he win
The hearts of all that he did angle for. *H. IV.* PT. I. iv. 3

You see, how all conditions, how all minds,
(As well of glib and slippery creatures, as
Of grave and austere quality,) tender down
Their services to Lord Timon; his large fortune
Upon his good and gracious nature hanging,
Subdues and properties to his love and tendance
All sorts of hearts. *T. A.* i. 1.

The wisdom of their choice is, rather to have my hat
than my heart. *C.* ii. 3

     Ourself
Observ'd his courtship to the common people:
How he did seem to dive into their hearts,
With humble and familiar courtesy;
What reverence he did throw away on slaves;
Wooing poor craftsmen with the craft of smiles,
And patient underbearing of his fortune,
As 'twere to banish their effects with him
Off goes his bonnet to an oyster-wench;
A brace of draymen bid—God speed him well!
And had the tribute of his supple knee,
With—Thanks, my countrymen, my loving friends.
          R. II. i. 4.

Was ever feather so lightly blown to and fro, as this
multitude? *H. VI.* PT. II. iv. 8.

Look, as I blow this feather from my face,
And as the air blows it to me again,
Obeying with my wind when I do blow,
And yielding to another when it blows,
Commanded always by the greater gust;
Such is the lightness of you common men.
         H. VI. PT. III. iii. 1

POPULARITY,—*continued.*
The common people swarm like summer flies,
And whither fly the gnats but to the sun?
H. VI. PT. III. ii. 6.
The commonwealth is sick of their own choice,
Their over-greedy love hath surfeited :—
A habitation giddy and unsure
Hath he, that buildeth on the vulgar heart.
O thou fond many! with what loud applause
Didst thou beat heaven with blessing Bolingbroke,
Before he was what thou wouldst have him be!
And being now trimm'd in thine own desires,
Thou, beastly feeder, art so full of him,
That thou provok'st thyself to cast him up.
H. IV. PT. II. i. 3.
When he had done, some followers of mine own
At lower end of the hall, hurl'd up their caps,
And some ten voices cried, God save King Richard!
And thus I took the 'vantage of those few,—
Thanks, gentle citizens, and friends, quoth I;
This general applause, and cheerful shout,
Argues your wisdom, and your love to Richard:
And even here broke off, and came away. *R. III.* iii. 7.
I had rather have one scratch my head i' the sun,
When the alarum was struck, than idly sit
To hear my nothings monster'd. *C.* ii. 2.

Faith, there have been many great men who have flattered the people, who ne'er loved them; and there be many that they have lov'd, they know not wherefore; so that, if they love they know not why, they hate upon no better ground. *C.* ii. 2.

I have not stopp'd mine ears to their demands,
Nor posted off their suits with slow delays;
My pity hath been balm to heal their wounds,
My mildness hath allay'd their swelling griefs,
My mercy dried their water-flowing tears:
I have not been desirous of their wealth,
Nor much oppress'd them with great subsidies,
Nor forward of revenge, though they much err'd
Then why should they love Edward more than me?
H. VI. PT. III. iv. 8.
I love the people,
But do not like to stage me to their eyes;
Though it do well, I do not relish well
Their loud applause, and *aves* vehement;
Nor do I think the man of safe discretion,
That does affect it. *M. M.* i. 1.

POPULARITY,—*continued.*
Like one of two contending in a prize,
That thinks he hath done well in people's eyes,
Hearing applause, and universal shout,
Giddy in spirit, still gazing in a doubt
Whether those peals of praise be his or no. *M. V.* iii. 2.

PORTENTS (See also PRODIGIES).
The owl shriek'd at thy birth, an evil sign;
The night-crow cried, aboding luckless time;
Dogs howl'd, and hideous tempests shook down trees;
The raven rooked her on the chimney top,
And chattering pies in dismal discord sung.
H. VI. PT. III. v. 6.

Before the days of change, still is it so;
By a divine instinct, men's minds mistrust
Ensuing danger; as, by proof, we see
The water swell before a boist'rous storm. *R. III.* ii. 3.

When clouds are seen, wise men put on their cloaks;
When great leaves fall, then winter is at hand;
When the sun sets, who doth not look for night?
Untimely storms make men expect a dearth? *R. III.* ii. 3.

Warnings, and portents, and evils ominous. *J. C.* ii. 2.
    The southern wind
Doth play the trumpet to his purposes;
And, by his hollow whistling in the leaves,
Foretells a tempest and a blustering day. *H. IV.* PT. I. v. 1.

How bloodily the sun begins to peer
Above yon busky hill! the day looks pale
At his distemperature. *H. IV.* PT. I. v. 1.

Truly, the hearts of men are full of fear:
You cannot reason almost with a man
That looks not heavily, and full of dread. *R. III.* ii. 3

PORTRAIT (See also PAINTING).
See, what a grace was seated on this brow:
Hyperion's curls; the front of Jove himself;
An eye like Mars to threaten and command;
A station, like the herald Mercury,
New lighted on a heaven-kissing hill
A combination, and a form, indeed,
Where every god did seem to set his seal,
To give the world assurance of a man. *H.* iii. 4
    O thou senseless form,
Thou shalt be worsnipp'd, kiss'd, lov'd, and ador'd.
T. G. iv. 4

PORTRAIT,—*continued.*
What demi-god
Hath come so near creation? Move these eyes?
Or whether, riding on the balls of mine,
Seem they in motion? Here are sever'd lips,
Parted with sugar breath; so sweet a bar
Should sunder such sweet friends: Here in her hairs
The painter plays the spider; and hath woven
A golden mesh to entrap the hearts of men,
Faster than gnats in cobwebs: But her eyes,—
How could he see to do them? *M. V.* iii. 2.
The counterfeit presentment. *H.* iii. 4.

POSSESSION.
Have is have, however men do catch. *K. J.* i. 1.

—————— AND DEPRIVATION.
For it so falls out,
That what we have, we prize not to the worth,
Whiles we enjoy it: but being lack'd and lost,
Why, then we rack the value; then we find
The virtue, that possession would not show us
Whiles it was ours. *M. A.* iv. 1

POSTSCRIPT.
Jove and my stars be prais'd, here is yet a postscript!
T. N. ii. 5.

POVERTY.
No matter what: He's poor, and that's revenge enough.
T. A. iii. 4.
Pray you, poor gentleman, take up some other station;
here's no place for you; pray you, avoid. *C.* iv. 5.
As we do turn our backs
From our companion, thrown into his grave;
So his familiars to his buried fortunes
Slink all away; leave their false vows with him,
Like empty purses pick'd; and his poor self,
A dedicated beggar to the air,
With his disease of all shunn'd poverty,
Walks, like contempt, alone. *T. A.* iv. 2.
Anon, a careless herd
Full of the pasture, jumps along by him; Ay, quoth
Jaques,
Sweep on, you fat and greasy citizens;
'Tis just the fashion: wherefore do you look
Upon that poor and broken bankrupt then? *A. Y.* ii. 1
Art thou so bare, and full of wretchedness,
And fear's to die? famine is in thy cheeks,

POVERTY,—*continued.*
Need and oppression stareth in thine eyes,
Upon thy back hangs ragged misery,
The world is not thy friend, nor the world's law. *R.J.* v. 1.
  Who can speak broader than he that has no house to put his head in?—Such may rail against great buildings.
                T.A. iii. 4.
Through tatter'd clothes small vices do appear. *K.L.* iv. 4.
A most poor man, made tame by fortune's blows;
Who, by the art of known and feeling sorrows,
Am pregnant to good pity.   *K.L.* iv. 6.
  No, Madam, 'tis not so well that I am poor; though many of the rich are damned.   *A.W.* i. 3.
A staff is quickly found to beat a dog. *H.VI.* PT. II. iii. 1.
They say, poor suitors have strong breaths.   *C.* i. 1.

POWER.
     O perilous mouths,
That bear in them one and the self-same tongue,
Either of condemnation or approof!
Bidding the law make court'sy to their will;
Hooking both right and wrong to the appetite,
To follow as it draws!   *A.M.* ii. 4.
     We had need pray,
And heartily, for our deliverance;
Or this imperious man will work us all
From princes into pages: all men's honours
Lie in one lump before him, to be fashion'd
Into what pitch he please.   *H.VIII.* ii. 2.
     In his livery
Walk'd crowns and crownets; realms and islands were
As plates dropp'd from his pocket.   *A.C.* v. 2.

The abuse of greatness is, when it disjoins
Remorse from power.   *J.C.* ii. 1.
Mortality and mercy in Vienna
Live in thy tongue and heart.   *M.M.* i. 1.

PRAISE.
The worthiness of praise distains his worth
If that the prais'd himself bring the praise forth:
But what the rip'ning enemy commend,
That breath fame follows; that praise, sole pure, transcends.
                T.C. i. 3.
Great Timon, noble, worthy, royal Timon!
Ah! when the means are gone, that buy this praise,
The breath is gone whereof this praise is made. *T.A.* ii. 2.

Shakespearian Dictionary.

PRAISE,—*continued.*
Do not smile at me, that I boast her off,
For thou shalt find she will outstrip all praise,
And make it halt behind her. *T.* iv. 1.
    You shall not be
The grave of your deserving: Rome must know
The value of her own: 'twere a concealment
Worse than a theft, no less than a traducement,
To hide your doings. *C.* i. 9.
    Cram us with praise, and make us
As fat as tame things: One good deed, dying tongueless,
Slaughters a thousand, waiting upon that:
Our praises are our wages. *W.T.* i. 9.
    Praising what is lost
Makes the remembrance dear. *A.W.* v. 3.
Cautious they praise, who purpose not to sell. *Poems.*
To things of sale a seller's praise belongs. *L.L.* iv. 3.

————— AND CENSURE.
 Marry, Sir, they praise me and make an ass of me: now my foes tell me plainly, I'm an ass; so that by my foes, Sir, I profit in the knowledge of myself. *T.N.* v. 1.

PRAYERS.
Not with fond shekels of the tested gold;
Or stones, whose rates are either rich, or poor,
As fancy values them: but with true prayers,
That shall be up at heaven and enter there,
Ere sun-rise. *M.M.* ii. 2.
    We, ignorant of ourselves,
Beg often our own harms, which the wise powers.
Deny us for our good; so find we profit
By losing of our prayers. *A.C.* ii. 1.

When I would pray and think, I think and pray
To several subjects: heaven hath my empty words;
Whilst my invention, hearing not my tongue,
Anchors on Isabel: Heaven in my mouth,
As if I did but only chew his name;
And in my heart, the strong and swelling evil
Of my conception. *M.M.* ii. 4.

When holy and devout religious men
Are at their beads, 'tis hard to draw them thence,
So sweet is zealous contemplation. *R. III.* iii. 7.

    A thousand knees,
Ten thousand years together, naked, fasting,
Upon a barren mountain, and still winter

PRAISE,—*continued.*
In storm perpetual, could not move the gods
To look that way thou wert. *W.T.* iii. 2
I pray thee leave me to myself to-night;
For I have need of many orisons
To move the heavens to smile upon my state,
Which, well thou know'st, is cross and full of sin.
R. J. iv. 3.
. Lovers,
And men in dangerous bonds, pray not alike. *Cym.* iii. 2.
Get him to say his prayers; good Sir Toby, get him to pray.
T. N. iii. 4.

PREACHING AND PRACTICE.
Fie, uncle Beaufort! I have heard you preach,
That malice was a great and grievous sin:
And will not you maintain the thing you teach,
But prove a chief offender in the same? *H. VI.* PT. I. iii. 1.

PRECIPICE.
What, if it tempt you toward the flood, my lord,
Or to the dreadful summit of the cliff,
That beetles o'er his base into the sea?
And there assume some other horrible form,
Which might deprive your sovereignty of reason,
And draw you into madness? think of it:
The very place puts toys of desperation,
Without more motive, into every brain,
That looks so many fathoms to the sea,
And hears it roar beneath. *H.* i. 4.

PRECISE MAN.
Lord Angelo is precise;
Stand at a guard with envy; scarce confesses
That his blood flows, or that his appetite
Is more to bread than stone: Hence shall we see
If power change purpose, what our seemers be. *M. M.* i. 4.
A man whose blood
Is very snow-broth; one who never feels
The wanton stings and motions of the sense;
But doth rebate and blunt his natural edge
With profits of the mind, study and fast. *M. M.* i. 5.

PRE-EMINENCE
The observ'd of all observers. *H.* iii. 1.

PREFERMENT.
'Tis the curse of service;
Preferment goes by letter, and affection,

PREFERMENT,—*continued.*
Not by the old gradation. where each second
Stood heir to the first.   *O.* i. 1.

PREJUDICE.
Oft it chances, in particular men,
That, for some vicious mole of nature in them,
As, in their birth, (wherein they are not guilty,
Since nature cannot choose its origin,)
By the o'ergrowth of some complexion,
Oft breaking down the pales and forts of reason;
Or by some habit, which too much o'er-leavens
The fõrm of plausive manners;—that these men,—
Carrying, I say, the stamp of one defect;
Being nature's livery, or fortune's star,—
Their virtues else, (be they as pure as grace,
As infinite as man can undergo,)
Shall in the general censure take corruption
From that particular fault: the dram of base
Doth all the noble. substance often dout,
To his own scandal.   *H.* i. 4

Which warp'd the line of every other favour;
Scorn'd a fair colour, or express'd it stolen;
Extended or contracted all proportions,
To a most hideous object.   *A. W.* v. 3.

———— RELIGIOUS.
I am a Jew: Hath not a Jew eyes? hath not a Jew hands,
organs, dimensions, senses, affections, passions? fed with
the same food, hurt with the same weapons, subject to the
same diseases, healed by the same means, warmed and
cooled by the same winter and summer, as a Christian is?
if you prick us, do we not bleed? if you tickle us, do we
not laugh? if you poison us, do we not die? and if you
wrong us, shall we not revenge? if we are like you in the
rest, we will resemble you in that.   *M. V.* iii. 1.

PREPARATION.
Your vessels, and your spells, provide,
Your charms, and every thing beside.   *M.* iii. 5.

PRESENTATION.
Here's a gentleman, and a friend of mine.   *M. M.* iii. 2.

PRESENT PLEASURES AND PAINS.
Each present joy or sorrow seems the chief.   *Poems.*

PRESUMPTION.
Inspired merit so by breath is barr'd:
It is not so with him that all things knows

PRESUMPTION,—*continued.*
As 'tis with us that square our guess by shows;
But most it is presumption in us, when
The help of heaven we count the act of men. *A. W.* ii. 1.

PRETEXT.
My pretext to strike at him admits
A good construction. *C.* v. 5.

PREVARICATION.
You boggle shrewdly, every feather starts you. *A. W.* v. 3.

PRIDE.
I do hate a proud man, as I hate the engendering of toads.
T. C. ii. 3.
O world, how apt the poor are to be proud! *T. N.* iii. 4.

He that is proud, eats up himself; pride is his own glass, his own trumpet, his own chronicle; and whatever praises itself but in the deed, devours the deed in the praise.
T. C. ii 3.

He is so plaguy proud, that the death tokens of it
Cry,—*No recovery.* *T. C.* ii. 3.

Harsh rage,
Defect of manners, want of government,
Pride, haughtiness, opinion, and disdain;
The least of which, haunting a nobleman,
Loseth men's hearts. *H. IV.* PT. I. iii. 1

I am too high-born to be property'd,
To be a secondary at controul,
Or useful serving-man, and instrument,
To any sovereign. *K. J.* v. 2.

An he be proud with me, I'll pheeze his pride. *T. C.* ii. 3.

I cannot tell
What heaven hath given him, let some graver eye
Pierce into that; but I can see his pride
Peep through each part of him: Whence has he that?
If not from hell, the devil is a niggard;
Or has given all before, and he begins
A new hell in himself. *H. VIII.* i. 1

Things small as nothing, for request's sake only,
He makes important: Possess'd he is with greatness;
And speaks not to himself, but with a pride
That quarrels at self-breath. *T. C.* ii. 3.

Small things make base men proud: this villain, here,
Being captain of a pinnace, threatens more
Than Burgulus, the strong Illyrian pirate.
H. IV. PT. II. iv. 1.

PRIDE,—*continued.*
    Pride hath no other glass
To show itself, but pride; for supple knees
Feed arrogance, and are the proud man's fees.   *T. C.* iii. 3.

———— OFFENDED.
    Yes, lion-sick, sick of proud heart : you may call it melancholy if you will favour the man; but, by my head, 'tis pride.   *T. C.* ii. 3.

———— EATS UP GRATITUDE.
    Very well; and could be content to give him good report for't, but that he pays himself with being proud.   *C.* i. 1.

PRINCE, DEGENERATE.
Shall the son of England prove a thief, and take purses!
                                                  H. IV. PT. I. ii. 4.

PRISONERS.
It is not for prisoners to be too silent in their words.
                                                  L. L. i. 2.

PRODIGALITY.
    What will this come to?
He commands us to provide, and give great gifts,
And all out of an empty coffer;
Nor will he know his purse; or yield me this,
To show him what a beggar his heart is,
Being of no power to make his wishes good;
His promises fly so beyond his state,
That what he speaks is all in debt, he owes
For every word; he is so kind, that he now
Pays interest for it   *T. A.* i. 2.

PRODIGIES (See also PORTENTS).
In the most high and palmy state of Rome,
A little ere the mightiest Julius fell,
The graves stood tenantless, and the sheeted dead
Did squeak and gibber in the Roman streets.   *H.* i. 1.
    Stars with trains of fire, and dews of blood,
Disasters in the sun; and the moist star,
Upon whose influence Neptune's empire stands,
Was sick almost to doomsday, with eclipse.   *H.* i. 1
No natural exhalation in the sky,
No scape of nature, no distemper'd day,
No common wind, no customed event,
But they will pluck away his natural cause,
And call them meteors, prodigies, and signs,
Abortives, presages, and tongues of heaven,
Plainly denouncing vengeance upon John.   *K. J.* iii. 4.

PRODIGIES,—*continued.*
Fierce fiery warriors fight upon the clouds,
In ranks, and squadrons, and right form of war,
Which drizzled blood upon the capitol:
The noise of battle hurtled in the air,
Horses did neigh, and dying men did groan. *J. C.* ii. 2.
When beggars die, there are no comets seen;
The heavens themselves blaze forth the death of princes.
J. C. ii. 2.

PROFLIGACY.
His rash fierce blaze of riot cannot last;
For violent fires soon burn out themselves:
Small showers last long, but sudden storms are short;
He tires betimes, that spurs too fast betimes;
With eager feeding food doth choke the feeder:
Light vanity, insatiate cormorant,
Consuming means, soon preys upon itself. *R. II.* ii. 1.

PROGNOSTICS.
Against ill chances men are ever merry,
But heaviness fore-runs the good event. *H. IV.* PT. II. iv. 2.

PROLIXITY.
The date is out of such prolixity. *R. J.* i. 4.

PROMISES.
Promising is the very air o' the time: it opens the eyes of expectation: performance is ever the duller for his act: and, but in the plainer and simpler kind of people, the deed is quite out of use. To promise, is most courtly and fashionable; performance is a kind of will and testament, which argues a great sickness in his judgment that makes it.
T. A. v. 1.

His promises were, as he then was, mighty;
But his performance, as he now is, nothing. *H. VIII.* iv. 2.

I see, Sir, you are liberal in offers:
You taught me first to beg; and now, methinks,
You teach me how a beggar should be answer'd.
M. V. iv. 1

Thy promises are like Adonis' gardens,
That one day bloom'd, and fruitful were the next.
H. VI. PT. I. i. 6

The king is kind; and, well we know, the king
Knows at what time to promise, when to pay.
H. IV. PT. I. iv. 3.

PROMOTION.
Many so arrive at second masters, upon their first lord's neck. *T. A.* iv 3

Shakespearian Dictionary.

PROMPTITUDE.
Anticipating time with starting courage. *T. C.* iv 5.
For at hand,
Not trusting to this halting legate here,
Whom he hath used rather for sport than need,
Is warlike John. *K. J.* v. 2.

PROOF.
Let the end try the man. *H. IV.* PT. II. ii. 2.
Let proof speak. *Cym.* iii. 1

PROPERTY.
What judgment shall I dread, doing no wrong?
You have among you many a purchas'd slave;
Which, like your asses, and your dogs, and mules,
You use in abject, and in slavish parts,
Because you bought them :· shall I say to you,
Let them be free, marry them to your heirs!
Why sweat they under burdens? let their beds
Be made as soft as yours, and let their palates
Be season'd with such viands. You will answer,
The slaves are ours:—so do I answer you. *M. V.* iv. 1.

PROPELLING.
As doth a sail, fill'd with a fretting gust,
Command an argosy to stem the waves. *H. VI.* PT. III. ii. 6.

PROSCRIPTION.
No port is free; no place,
That guard, and most unusual vigilance,
Does not attend my taking. *K. L.* ii. 3

PROSECUTOR, PUBLIC.
He puts transgression to't. *M. M.* iii. 2.

PROSPERITY.
Prosperity's the very bond of love;
Whose fresh complexion, and whose heart together,
Affliction alters. *W. T.* iv. 3.
When mine hours
Were nice and lucky, men did ransom lives
Of me for jests. *A. C.* iii. 11.

PROVERBS.
Come hither, Fabian; we'll whisper o'er a couplet or two
of most sage saws. *T. N.* iii. 4.

PROVIDENCE, (See also OMNIPOTENCE).
Our indiscretion sometimes serves us well,
When our deep plots do pall: and that should teach us,

PROVIDENCE,—*continued.*
There's a divinity that shapes our ends,
Rough-hew them how we will. *H.* v. 2.

PROVOCATION.
Have you not set mine honour at the stake,
And baited it with all the unmuzzled thoughts
That tyrannous heart can think? *T. N.* iii. 1.

PRUDENCE.
Take up this mangled matter at the best:
Men do their broken weapons rather use
Than their bare hands. *O.* i. 3.
      When we mean to build,
We first survey the plot, then draw the model;
And when we see the figure of the house,
Then must we rate the cost of the erection:
Which if we find outweighs ability,
What do we then but draw anew the model
In fewer offices; or, at least, desist
To build at all? Much more, in this great work
(Which is almost to pluck a kingdom down,
And set another up) should we survey
The plot of situation, and the model;
Consent upon a sure foundation;
Question surveyors, know our own estate,
How able such a work to undergo,
To weigh against his opposite; or else
We fortify in paper, and in figures,
Using the names of men, instead of men:
Like one, that draws the model of a house
Beyond his power to build it; who, half through,
Gives o'er, and leaves his part-created cost
A naked subject to the weeping clouds,
And waste for churlish winter's tyranny. *H. IV.* pt. ii. i. 3.

PRUDERY.
Dost thou think, because thou art virtuous, there shall be
no more cakes and ale? *T. N.* ii. 3.

PRUNING.
      All superfluous branches
We lop away, that bearing boughs may live. *R. II.* iii. 4.

PURGATORY.
Doom'd for a certain time to walk the night,
And, for the day, confin'd to fast in fires,
Till the foul crimes, done in my days of nature,
Are burnt and purg'd away. *H.* i. 5.

PURITY.

The very ice of chastity is in them. *A.Y.* iii. 4.

He's honourable,
And, doubling that, most holy. *Cym.* iii. 4.

Who can blot that name
With any just reproach? *M.A.* iv. 1.

PURPOSE.

In every thing, the purpose must weigh with the folly.
H. IV. PT. II. ii. 2.

PURSUIT.

Let us score their backs,
And snatch 'em up, as we take hares, behind:
'Tis sport to maul a runner. *A.C.* iv. 7.

Mount you, my lord, tow'rd Berwick post amain;
Edward and Richard, like a brace of greyhounds,
Having the fearful flying hare in sight,
With fiery eyes, sparkling for very wrath,
And bloody steel, grasp'd in their ireful hands,
Are at our backs; and therefore hence amain.
H.VI. PT. III. ii. 5.

—————— AND POSSESSION.
All things that are
Are with more spirit chased than enjoy'd.
How like a younker, or a prodigal,
The scarfed bark puts from her native bay,
Hugg'd and embraced by the strumpet wind!
How like the prodigal doth she return,
With over-weather'd ribs, and ragged sails,
Lean, rent, and beggar'd by the strumpet wind! *M.V.* ii. 6.

Women are angels, wooing:
Things won are done, joy's soul lies in the doing:
That she belov'd knows nought, that knows not this,—
Men prize the thing ungain'd more than it is. *T.C.* i. 2.

Q.

QUALITY.

The rich stream of lords and ladies. *H.VIII.* iv. 1.

She sweeps it through the court with troops of ladies
H.VI. PT. II. i. 3.

What a sweep of vanity comes this way! *T.A.* i. 2.

QUARREL.

Good lord! what madness rules in brain-sick men;
When, for so slight and frivolous a cause,
Such factious emulations shall arise! *H. VI.* PT. I. iv. 1.

I remember a mass of things, but nothing distinctly; a quarrel, but nothing wherefore. *O.* ii. 3.

I heard the clink and fall of swords
And Cassio high in oath. *O.* ii. 3.

Thou! why thou wilt quarrel with a man that hath a hair more, or a hair less, in his beard than thou hast. Thou wilt quarrel with a man for cracking nuts, having no other reason, but because thou hast hazel eyes. *R. J.* iii. 1.

He'll be as full of quarrel and offence
As my young mistress' dog. *O.* ii. 3.

―――――― INCIPIENT.

There is division,
Although as yet the face of it be cover'd
With mutual cunning. *K. L.* iii. 1.

I dare say
This quarrel will drink blood another day.
H. VI. PT. I. ii. 4.

QUEEN.

She had all the royal makings of a queen;
As holy oil, Edward Confessor's crown,
The rod, and bird of peace, and all such emblems,
Laid nobly on her. *H. VIII.* iv. 1.

A queen in jest, only to fill the scene. *R. III.* iv. 4.

―――― MAB.

O, then, I see, queen Mab hath been with you.
She is the fairies' midwife; and she comes
In shape no bigger than an agate-stone,
On the fore-finger of an alderman,
Drawn with a team of little atomies
Athwart men's noses as they lie asleep:
Her waggon-spokes made of long spinners' legs;
The cover, of the wings of grasshoppers;
The traces, of the smallest spider's web;
The collars, of the moonshine's watery beams:
Her whip, of crickets' bone; the lash, of film:
Her waggoner, a small gray-coated gnat,
Not half so big as a round little worm
Prick'd from the lazy finger of a maid:
Her chariot is an empty hazle-nut,
Made by the joiner squirrel, or old grub,
Time out of mind the fairies' coachmakers.

Shakespearian Dictionary.

QUEEN MAB,—*continued.*
And in this state she gallops, night by night,
Through lovers' brains, and then they dream of love:
On courtiers' knees, that dream on court'sies straight:
O'er lawyers' fingers, who straight dream on fees:
O'er ladies' lips, who straight on kisses dream;
Which oft the angry Mab with blisters plagues,
Because their breaths with sweetmeats tainted are.
Sometimes she gallops o'er a courtier's nose,
And then dreams he of smelling out a suit:
And sometimes comes she with a tithe-pig's tail,
Tickling a parson's nose as he lies asleep,
Then dreams he of another benefice:
Sometimes she driveth o'er a soldier's neck,
And then dreams he of cutting foreign throats,
Of breaches, ambuscadoes, Spanish blades,
Of healths five fathom deep; and then anon
Drums in his ear; at which he starts, and wakes;
And, being thus frighted, swears a prayer or two,
And sleeps again. *R. J.* i. 4.

QUIBBLING.
O, dear discretion, how his words are suited!
The fool hath planted in his memory
An army of good words: and I do know
A many fools, that stand in better place,
Garnish'd like him, that for a tricksy word
Defy the matter. *M. V.* iii. 5.

To see this age! A sentence is but a cheverill glove to a good wit; how quickly the wrong side may be turn'd outward! *T. N.* iii. 1.
This is a riddling merchant for the nonce. *H. IV.* PT. I. ii. 3.
How every fool can play upon the word! I think, the best grace of wit will shortly turn into silence; and discourse grow commendable in none only but parrots. *M. V.* iii. 5.

QUICKNESS.
Jove's lightnings, the precursors
O' the dreadful thunder-claps, more momentary
And sight-out-running were not. *T.* i. 2.

QUIPS.
How now, how now, mad wag? What, in thy quips, and thy quiddities? *H. IV.* PT. I. i. 2.

QUOTING SCRIPTURE (See also DISSIMULATION, HYPOCRISY).
But then I sigh, and, with a piece of scripture,
Tell them,—that God bids us do good for evil.

QUOTING SCRIPTURE,—*continued.*
And thus I clothe my naked villany
With old odd ends, stol'n forth of holy writ;
And seem a saint when most I play the devil. *R. III.* i. 3.

In religion,
What damned error, but some sober brow
Will bless it, and approve it with a text,
Hiding the grossness with fair ornament? *M. V.* iii. 2.

The devil can cite scripture for his purpose.
An evil soul, producing holy witness,
Is like a villain with a smiling cheek;
A goodly apple rotten at the heart:
O, what a goodly outside falsehood hath! *M. V.* i. 3.

O thou hast damnable iteration; and art, indeed, able to corrupt a saint. *H. IV.* PT. I. i. 2.

R.

RABBLE.
These are the youths that thunder at a play-house, and fight for bitten apples. *H. VIII.* v. 3.

The cankers of a calm world. *H. IV.* PT. I. iv. 2.

I'll not march through Coventry with them, that's flat. *H. IV.* PT. I. iv. 2.

RADIANCE.
Like the wreath of radiant fire
On flickering Phœbus' front. *K. L.* ii. 2.

RAGE (See also ANGER, FURY).
Eyeless rage. *K. L.* iii. 1.
Lost in the labyrinth of thy fury. *T. C.* ii. 3.

He's in his fit now, and does not talk after the wisest. *T.* ii. 2.

In rage, deaf as the sea, hasty as fire. *R. II.* i. 1.

Darkness and devils!
Saddle my horses; call my train together. *K. L.* i. 4.

When one so great begins to rage, he's hunted
Even to falling. *A. C.* iv. 1.

The fiery Tybalt, with his sword prepar'd;
Which, as he breath'd defiance to my ears,
He swung about his head, and cut the winds,
Who, nothing hurt withal, hiss'd him in scorn. *R. J.* i. 1

RAILING

Did you ever hear such railing? *A. Y.* iv. 3.

Why, what a monstrous fellow art thou, thus to rail on one, that is neither known of thee, nor knows thee.
K. L. ii. 2.

Why, what an ass am I!—This is most brave;
That I, the son of a dear father, murder'd,
Prompted to my revenge by heaven and hell,
Must, like a whore, unpack my heart with words,
And fall a cursing, like a very drab,
A scullion! *H.* ii. 2.

I shall sooner rail thee into wit and holiness; but, I think, thy horse will sooner con an oration, than thou learn a prayer without book. *T. C.* ii. 1.

Rails on our little state of war
Bold as an oracle: and sets Thersites,
(A slave, whose gall coins slander like a mint,)
To match us in comparisons with dirt. *T. C.* i. 3.

——— AND REPROOF, WHEN WORTHY, OR UNWORTHY, OF REGARD.

There is no slander in an allowed fool, though he do nothing but rail; nor no railing in a known discreet man, though he do nothing but reprove. *T. N.* i. 5.

RAILLERY.

We may carry it thus for our pleasure, and his penance, till our very pastime, tired out of breath, prompt us to have mercy on him. *T. N.* iii. 4.

RALLYING, IN BATTLE.

With their own nobleness (which could have turn'd
A distaff to a lance,) gilded pale looks,
Part, shame, part, spirit renewed; that some, turn'd coward'
But by example (O, a sin in war,
Damn'd in the first beginners!) 'gan to look
The way that they did, and to grin like lions
Upon the pikes o' the hunters. Then began
A stop i' the chaser, a retire; anon,
A rout, confusion thick: Forthwith they fly
Chickens, the way which they stoop'd eagles; slaves
The strides of victors made; and now our cowards
(Like fragments in hard voyages) became
The life o' the need; having found the back-door open
Of the unguarded hearts, Heavens, how they wound!
Some, slain before; some, dying; some, their friends
O'erborne i' the former wave: ten, chas'd by one,
Are now each one the slaughter-man of twenty. *Cym.* v. 3.

RANCOUR.
We have been down together in my sleep,
Unbuckling helms, fisting each other's throat,
And wak'd half dead with nothing. *C.* iv. 5

RANT.
Nay, an' thou'lt mouth,
I'll rant as well as thou. *H.* v. 1.

RAT.
How now? a rat! *H.* iii. 4.

READER.
How well he's read, to reason against reading! *L. L.* i. 1.

READINESS.
Here, man, I am at thy elbow. *M. A.* iii. 3.

REALITY.
'Tis in grain, Sir; 'twill endure wind and weather.
T. N. i. 4.

REASON.
What is a man,
If his chief good, and market of his time,
Be but to sleep and feed? a beast, no more.
Sure, He, that made us with such large discourse,
Looking before, and after, gave us not
That capability and god-like reason,
To rust in us unus'd. *H.* iv. 4.

If the balance of our lives had not one scale of reason to poise another of sensuality, the blood and baseness of our natures would conduct us to most preposterous conclusions.
O. i. 3.

Strong reasons make strong actions. *K. J.* iii. 4.

Good reasons must, of force, give place to better. *J. C.* iv. 3.

The reasons you allege, do more conduce
To the hot passion of distemper'd blood,
Than to make up a free determination
'Twixt right and wrong. *T. C.* ii. 2.

Nay, if we talk of reason,
Let's shut our gates, and sleep: Manhood and honour
Should have hare hearts, would they but fat their thoughts
With this cramm'd reason: reason and respect
Make livers pale, and lustihood deject. *T. C.* ii. 2.

Larded with many several sorts of reasons. *H.* v. 4.

You fur your gloves with reason: here are your reasons:
You know an enemy intends you harm:

REASON,—*continued*.
You know a sword employ'd is perilous;
And reason flies the object of all harm.   *T. C.* ii. 2.
No marvel, though you bite so sharp at reasons,
You are so empty of them.   *T. C.* ii. 2.
  Give you a reason on compulsion! if reasons were as plenty as blackberries, I would give no man a reason on compulsion.   *H. IV.* PT. 1. ii. 4.
I have no exquisite reason for't, but I have reason good enough.   *T. N.* ii. 3.

REBEL.
        An exhal'd meteor,
A prodigy of fear, and a portent
Of broached mischief to the unborn times.   *H. IV.* PT. I. v. 1

REBELLION.
        Hear me more plainly.
I have in equal balance justly weigh'd,
What wrongs our arms may do, what wrongs we suffer,
And find our griefs heavier than our offences.
We see which way the stream of time doth run,
And are enforc'd from our most quiet sphere
By the rough torrent of occasion:
And have the summary of all our griefs,
When time shall serve, to show in articles:
Which, long ere this, we offer'd to the king;
And might by no suit gain our audience:
When we are wrong'd, and would unfold our griefs,
We are denied access unto his person,
Even by those men who most have done us wrong.
The dangers of the days but newly gone,
(Whose memory is written on the earth
With yet-appearing blood,) and the examples
Of every minute's instance, (present now,)
Have put us in these ill-beseeming arms:
Not to break peace, or any branch of it;
But to establish here a peace indeed,
Concurring both in name and quality.   *H. IV.* PT. II. iv. 1.
Now let it work: Mischief, thou art afoot,
Take thou what course thou wilt.   *J. C.* iii. 2.
        If that rebellion
Came like itself, in base and abject routs,
Led on by bloody youth, guarded with rage,
And countenanc'd by boys, and beggary;
You, reverend father, and these noble lords,
Had not been here, to dress the ugly form
Of base and bloody insurrection.   *H. IV.* PT. II. iv. 1.

REBELLION,—*continued.*
O pity, God, this miserable age!—
What stratagems, how fell, how butcherly,
Erroneous, mutinous, and unnatural,
This deadly quarrel daily doth beget. *H. VI.* PT. III. ii. 5.
   But now the Bishop
Turns insurrection to religion:
Suppos'd sincere and holy in his thoughts,
He's follow'd both with body and with mind. *H. IV.* PT. II. i. 1.

What rein can hold licentious wickedness,
When down the hill he holds his fierce career?
We may as bootless spend our vain command
Upon th' enraged soldiers in their spoil,
As send precepts to the Leviathan
To come ashore.   *H. V.* iii. 3.

   You, lord Archbishop,—
Whose see is by a civil peace maintain'd;
Whose beard the silver hand of peace hath touch'd;
Whose learning and good letters peace hath tutor'd;
Whose white investments figure innocence,
The dove and very blessed spirit of peace,—
Wherefore do you so ill translate yourself,
Out of the speech of peace, that bears such grace,
Into the harsh and boist'rous tongue of war?
Turning your books to graves, your ink to blood,
Your pens to lances: and your tongue divine
To a loud trumpet, and a point of war? *H. IV.* PT. II. iv. 1.

The rebels are in Southwark; Fly, my lord!
Jack Cade proclaims himself Lord Mortimer,
Descended from the Duke of Clarence' house,
And calls your grace usurper, openly,
And vows to crown himself in Westminster.
His army is a ragged multitude
Of hinds and peasants, rude and merciless:
Sir Humphrey Stafford, and his brothers' death,
Hath given them heart and courage to proceed:
All scholars, lawyers, courtiers, gentlemen,
They call—false caterpillars, and intend their death.
          H. VI. PT. II. iv. 4.

   Noble English, you are bought and sold;
Unthread the rude eye of rebellion,
And welcome home again discarded faith. *K. J.* v. 4.
   All the regions
Do smilingly revolt; and, who resist,
Are only mock'd for valiant ignorance,
And perish constant fools.   *C.* iv 6.

REBELLION,—*continued.*
My lord, your son had only but the corps,
But shadows, and the shows of men, to fight:
For that same word, rebellion, did divide
The action of their bodies from their souls;
And they did fight with queasiness, constrain'd
As men drink potions; that their weapons only
Seem'd on our side, but for their spirits and souls,
This word, rebellion, it had froze them up,
As fish are in a pond. *H. IV.* PT. II. i. 1.

Suffer it, and live with such as cannot rule,
Nor ever will be rul'd. *C.* iii. 1.

Wherefore do I this? so the question stands.
Briefly to this end:—We are all diseas'd;
And with our surfeiting, and wanton hours,
Have brought ourselves into a burning fever,
And we must bleed for it: of which disease,
Our late king, Richard, being infected, died.
H. IV. PT. II. iv. 1.

   You may as well
Strike at the heaven with your staves, as lift them
Against the Roman state; whose course will on
The way it takes, cracking ten thousand curbs
Of more strong link asunder, than can ever
Appear in your impediment. *C.* i. 1.

   No kind of traffic
Would I admit; no name of magistrate;
Letters should not be known: riches, poverty,
And use of service, none; contract, succession,
Bourn, bound of land, tilth, vineyard, none. *T.* ii. 1.

Abate the edge of traitors, gracious Lord,
That would reduce these bloody days again,
And make poor England weep in streams of blood.
R. III. v. 4.

RECITATION (See also SPEECH).
 'Fore God, my lord, well spoken; with good accent, and good discretion. *H.* ii. 2.

 We'll have a speech straight: Come, give us a taste of your quality; come, a passionate speech. *H.* ii. 2.

RECKONING.
 I am ill at reckoning, it fitteth the spirit of a tapster.
L. L. i. 2.

 O Lord, Sir, it were a pity you should get your living by reckoning, Sir. *L. L.* v. 2.

RECOGNITION.

Most reverend signior, do you know my voice? *O.* i. 1.
Long is it since I saw him,
But time hath nothing blurr'd those lines of favour,
Which then he wore. *Cym.* iv. 2.

Can virtue hide itself? Go to, mum, you are he; graces
will appear, and there's an end. *M. A.* ii. 1.

RECOLLECTION, Painful.

O, it comes o'er my memory,
As doth the raven o'er the infected house,
Boding to all. *O.* iv. 1.

RECOMPENCE.

Praise us as we are tasted, allow us as we prove.
T. C. iii. 2.

RECOVERY.

This feather stirs; she lives! if it be so,
It is a chance that does redeem all sorrows
That ever I have felt. *K. L.* v. 3.

RECREATION.

Sweet recreation barr'd, what doth ensue,
But moody and dull melancholy.
(Kinsman to grim and comfortless despair,)
And, at her heels, a huge infectious troop
Of pale distemperatures, and foes to life?
In food, in sport, and life-preserving rest
To be disturb'd, would mad or man, or beast. *C. E.* v. 1.

RECREANT Slave.

Yet I am thankful: if my heart were great,
'Twould burst at this: Captain, I'll be no more;
But I will eat and drink, and sleep as soft
As captain shall: simply the thing I am
Shall make me live. Who knows himself a braggart,
Let him fear this; for it will come to pass,
That every braggart shall be found an ass:
Rust, sword! cool, blushes! and, Parolles, live!
Safest in shame! being fool'd, by foolery thrive!
There's place, and means, for every man alive. *A. W.* iv. 3.

RECRUIT.

In very truth, Sir, I had as lief be hanged, Sir, as go;
and yet, for mine own part, Sir, I do not care; but rather,
because I am unwilling, and, for mine own part, I have a
desire to stay with my friends; else, Sir, I did not care, for
mine own part, so much. *H. IV.* pt. ii. iii. 4.

REFINEMENT.

By the lord, Horatio, these three years I have taken notice of it; the age is grown so picked, that the toe of the peasant comes so near the heel of the courtier, that he galls his kibe. *H.* v. 1.

I will be proud, I will read politic authors, I will baffle Sir Toby, I will wash off gross acquaintance, I will be point-device, the very man. *T. N.* ii. 5.

REFORM.

God amend us, God amend! we are much out o' the way.
L. L. iv. 3.

Consideration like an angel came,
And whipp'd the offending Adam out of him
Leaving his body as a paradise,
To envelop and contain celestial spirits. *H. V.* i. 1.

   The shame itself doth speak
For instant remedy. *K. L.* i. 4.

My reformation, glittering o'er my fault,
Shall show more goodly, and attract more eyes,
Than that which hath no foil to set it off.
H. IV. PT. I. i. 2.

I tell thee, Jack Cade, the clothier, means to dress the commonwealth, and turn it, and set a new nap upon it.
H. VI. PT. II. iv. 2.

I must give over this life, and I will give it over; by the Lord, an I do not, I am a villain. *H. IV.* PT. I. i. 2.

REGAL CEREMONIES (See also CEREMONY).

This gentle and unforc'd accord of Hamlet
Sits smiling to my heart; in grace whereof,
No jocound health, that Denmark drinks to-day,
But the great cannon to the clouds shall tell;
And the king's rouse the heaven shall bruit again,
Respeaking earthly thunder. *H.* i. 2.

  As he drains his draughts of Rhenish down,
The kettle-drum and trumpet thus bray out,
The triumph of his pledge. *H.* i. 4.

There roar'd the sea, and trumpet-clangour sounds.
H. IV. PT. II. v. 5.

The king shall drink to Hamlet's better breath;
And in the cup an union shall he throw
Richer than that which four successive kings
In Denmark's crown have worn;—Give me the cups;
And let the kettle to the trumpet speak,
The trumpet to the cannoneer without,

REGAL Ceremonies,—*continued*.
The cannons to the heavens, the heavens to earth,
Now the king drinks to Hamlet.   *H.* v. 5.

      A garish flag,
To be the aim of every dangerous shot:
A sign of dignity, a breath, a bubble.   *R. III.* iv. 4.

The flattering index of a direful pageant,
One heav'd a high, to be hurl'd down below.   *R. III.* iv. 4.

——————————————— Ill-timed.
In this, the antique and well noted face
Of plain old form is much disfigured:
And, like a shifted wind unto a sail,
It makes the course of thought to fetch about:
Startles and frights consideration;
Makes sound opinion sick, and truth suspected,
For putting on so new a fashion'd robe.   *K. J.* iv. 2.

REGARD.
Those that I reverence, those I fear; the wise:
At fools I laugh, not fear them.   *Cym.* iv. 2.

      Why, he is so made on here within, as if he were son and heir to Mars: set at upper end o' the table: no questions asked him by any of the senators, but they stand bald before him.   *C.* iv. 5.

      Our general himself makes a mistress of him; sanctifies himself with 's hand, and turns up the white o' the eye to his discourse.   *C.* iv. 5.

——————— Devotional.
I hold you as a thing enskied, and sainted;
*   *   *   an immortal spirit;
And to be talk'd with in sincerity
As with a saint.   *M. M.* i. 5.

REGICIDE.
                To do this deed,
Promotion follows: If I could find example
Of thousands, that had struck anointed kings,
And flourish'd after, I'd not do't: but since
Nor brass, nor stone, nor parchment, bears not one,
Let villainy itself forswear't.   *W. T.* i. 2.

As full of valour as of royal blood:
Both have I spilt; O, would the deed were good!
For now the devil, that told me,—I did well,
Says, that this deed is chronicled in hell.   *R. II.* v. 6.

If it were done, when 'tis done, then 'twere well
It were done quickly: If the assassination

REGICIDE,—*continued.*
Could trammel up the consequence, and catch,
With his surcease, success; that but this blow
Might be the be-all and the end-all; here,
But here, upon this bank and shoal of time,—
We'd jump the life to come.—But in these cases,
We still have judgment here; that we but teach
Bloody instructions, which, being taught, return
To plague th' inventor: This even handed justice
Commends the ingredients of our poison'd chalice
To our own lips. He's here in double trust;
First, as I am his kinsman and his subject,
Strong both against the deed; then, as his host,
Who should against his murderer shut the door,
Not bear the knife myself. Besides, this Duncan
Hath borne his faculties so meek, hath been
So clear in his great office, that his virtues
Will plead like angels, trumpet-tongued, against
The deep damnation of his taking off:
And pity, like a naked new-born babe,
Striding the blast, or heaven's cherubim, hors'd
Upon the sightless couriers of the air,
Shall blow the horrid deed in every eye,
That tears shall drown the wind.—I have no spur
To prick the sides of my intent, but only
Vaulting ambition, which o'erleaps itself,
And falls on t'other side. *M.* i. 7.

REGRET.
I had rather
Have skipp'd from sixteen years of age to sixty,
To have turn'd my leaping time into a crutch,
Than have seen this. *Cym.* iv. 2.

RELATION.
A little more than kin, and less than kind. *H.* i. 2.

RELIGION (See also Dissimulation, Hypocrisy, Quoting Scripture).
It is religion that doth make vows kept. *K. J.* iii. 1.

I see you have some religion in you, that you fear.
Cym. i. 5

REMEDIES.
Things without remedy
Should be without regard. *M.* iii. 2.

Well of that remedy can no man speak,
That heals the loss, and cures not the disgrace. *Poems.*

REMEDIES MUST BE SUITED TO THE CASE.
                  Sir, these cold ways,
That seem like prudent helps, are very poisonous
Where the disease is violent   *C.* iii. 1.

REMEMBRANCE (See also MEMORY).
              Remember thee?
Yea, from the table of my memory
I'll wipe away all trivial fond records,
All saws of books, all forms, all pressures past,
That youth and observation copied there;
And thy commandment all alone shall live
Within the book and volume of my brain,
Unmix'd with baser matter: yes, by heaven.   *H.* i. 5.

By our remembrances of days foregone.   *A.W.* i. 3.

I cannot but remember such things were
That were most precious to me.   *M.* iv. 3.

                  Rivetted,
Screw'd to my memory.   *Cym.* ii. 2.

              Beshrew your heart,
Fair daughter! you do draw my spirits from me,
With new lamenting antient oversights. *H. IV.* PT. II. ii. 3.

            His good remembrance, Sir,
Lies richer in your thoughts, than on his tomb;
So in approof lives not his epitaph,
As in your royal speech.   *A.W.* i. 2.

            So came I a widow;
And never shall have length of life enough,
To rain upon remembrance with mine eyes,
That it may grow and sprout as high as heaven,
For recordation to my noble husband. *H. IV.* PT. II. ii. 3.

            Whose remembrance yet
Lives in men's eyes: and will, to ears and tongues,
Be theme and hearing ever.   *Cym.* iii. 1.

Awake remembrance of these valiant dead,
And with your puissant arm renew their feats. *H.V.* i. 2.

Briefly thyself remember.   *K. L* iv. 6.

REMONSTRANCE.
He must be told on't, and he shall: the office
Becomes a woman best; I'll tak't upon me:
If I prove honey-mouth'd, let my tongue blister;
And never to my red-look'd anger be
The trumpet any more.   *W.T.* ii. 2.

REMORSE (See also COMPUNCTION.)
When he shall hear she died upon his words,
The idea of her life shall sweetly creep
Into his study of imagination ;
And every lovely organ of her life
Shall come apparell'd in more precious habit,
More moving delicate, and full of life,
Into the eye and prospect of his soul,
Than when she liv'd indeed. *M. A.* iv. 1.
    I'll go no more :
I am afraid to think what I have done ;
Look on't again I dare not. *M.* ii. 2.
     Nothing in his life
Became him, like the leaving it ; he died
As one that had been studied in his death,
To throw away the dearest thing he ow'd,
As 'twere a careless trifle. *M.* i. 4.
How sharp the point of this remembrance is! *T.* ii. 1.
   O, would the deed were good!
For now the devil, that told me—I did well,
Says, that this deed is chronicled in hell. *R. II.* v. 6.
   Once a day I'll visit
The chapel where they lie ; and tears shed there
Shall be my recreation. *W.T.* iii. 2.

RENUMERATION.
 Renumeration ! O, that's the Latin word for three farthings.
            L. L. iii. 1.

RENOVATION.
   And newly move   *H. V.* iv. 1.
With casted slough and fresh legerity.

RENOUNCEMENT.
   Thy truth then be thy dower :
For, by the sacred radiance of the sun ;
The mysteries of Hecate, and the night ;
By all the operations of the orbs,
From whom we do exist, and cease to be :
Here I disclaim all my paternal care,
Propinquity, and property of blood.
And as a stranger to my heart and me
Hold thee, from this, for ever. *K. L.* i. 1.

RENOWN.
 In truth, there's wondrous things spoke of him. *C.* ii. 1.
 The man is noble ; and his fame folds in
This orb o' the earth. *C.* v. 5.

Shakespearian Dictionary.

RENUNCIATION.
Legitimation, name, and all is gone.   *K. J.* i. 1.

REPAYMENT.
O, I do not like that paying back, 'tis a double labour.
    H. IV. PT. I. iii. 3.

REPENTANCE.
Who by repentance is not satisfied
Is nor of heaven, nor earth ; for these are pleas'd ;
By penitence th' Eternal's wrath's appeas'd.   *T. G.* v. 4.
Be witness to me, O thou blessed moon,
When men revolted shall upon record
Bear hateful memory, poor Enobarbus did
Before thy face repent.   *A. C.* iv. 9.
And begin to patch up thine old body for heaven.
    H. IV. PT. II. ii. 4.
    Like bright metal on a sullen ground,
My reformation, glittering o'er my fault,
Shall show more goodly, and attract more eyes,
Than that which hath no foil to set it off. *H. IV.* PT. I. i. 2.
Never came reformation in a flood,
With such a heavy current, scow'ring faults :
Nor ever hydra-headed wilfulness
So soon did lose his seat, and fall at once,
As in this king.   *H. V.* i. 1.
    What is done, cannot be now amended :
Men shall deal unadvisedly sometimes,
Which after hours give leisure to repent.   *R. III.* iv. 4.
    Sadly I survive
To mock the expectation of the world ;
To frustrate prophecies ; and to raze out
Rotten opinion, which hath writ me down
After my seeming. The tide of blood in me
Hath proudly flow'd in vanity till now ;
Now doth it turn, and ebb back to the sea ;
Where it shall mingle with the state of floods,
And flow henceforth in formal majesty. *H. IV.* PT. II. v. 2.
Hold up your hands ; say nothing, I'll speak all.
They say, best men are moulded out of faults,
And, for the most, became much more the better
For being a little bad ; so may my husband.   *M. M.* v. 1.
The prince will, in the perfectness of time,
Cast off his followers ; and their memory
Shall as a pattern or a measure live,
By which his grace must mete the lives of others :
Turning past evils to advantages.   *H. IV.* PT. II. iv. 4.

Shakespearian Dictionary.

REPENTANCE,—*continued*.
I do not shame
To tell you what I was, since my conversion
So sweetly tastes, being the thing I am. *A. Y.* iv. 3.
Forgive me, Valentine; If hearty sorrow
Be a sufficient ransom for offence,
I tender it here: I do as truly suffer,
As e'er I did commit. *T. G.* v. 4.
For heaven doth know, so shall the world perceive,
That I have turn'd away my former self;
So will I those that kept me company. *H. IV.* PT. ii. v. 5.
 Well, I'll repent, and that suddenly, while I am in some liking; I shall be out of heart shortly, and then I shall have no strength to repent. An I have not forgotten what the inside of a church is, I am a peppercorn, a brewer's horse: the inside of a church! Company, villainous company, has been the spoil of me. *H. IV.* PT. I. iii. 3.
 Well, if my wind were but long enough to say my prayers, I would repent. *M. W.* iv. 5.

REPORT.
There's gold for you; sell me your good report. *Cym.* ii. 3.
Bring me no more reports. *M.* v. 3.

REPLY.
Shall I hear more, or shall I speak at this? *R. J.* ii. 2.

REPOSE.
Our foster-nurse of nature is repose. *K. L.* iv. 4.

REPRESENTATIVE.
   It is suppos'd,
He, that meets Hector, issues from our choice:
And choice, being mutual act of all our souls,
Makes merit her election; and doth boil,
As 'twere from forth us all, a man distill'd
Out of our virtues. *T. C.* i. 3.

REPROACH.
O, Lymoges! O, Austria! thou dost shame
That bloody spoil: Thou slave, thou wretch, thou coward;
Thou little valiant, great in villainy!
Thou ever strong upon the stronger side!
Thou fortune's champion, that dost never fight
But when her humorous ladyship is by
To teach thee safety! thou art perjur'd, too,
And sooth'st up greatness. What a fool art thou,
A ramping fool, to brag, and stamp, and swear,
Upon my party! Thou cold-blooded slave,

REP   Shakesperian Dictionary.   **REP**

REPROACH,—*continued.*
Hast thou not spoke like thunder on my side?
Been sworn my soldier, bidding me depend
Upon thy stars, thy fortune, and thy strength?
And dost thou now fall over to my foes?
Thou wear a lion's hide! doff it for shame,
And hang a calf-skin on those recreant limbs!   *K. J.* iii. 1.

REPROOF.
Madam, I have a touch of your condition
And cannot bear the accent of reproof.   *R. III.* iv. 4.

REPROOF ILL-TIMED.
           My lord Sebastian,
The truth you speak doth lack some gentleness,
And time to speak it in: you rob the sore,
When you should bring the plaster.   *T.* ii. 1.

REPUGNANCE.
No, rather I abjure all roofs, and choose
To wage against the enmity o' the air;
To be a comrade with the wolf and owl,
Necessity's sharp pinch!   *K. L.* ii. 4.

I'll never see't; for, I am sure, my nails
Are stronger than mine eyes.   *A. C.* v. 2.

REPULSE.
I have said too much unto a heart of stone,
And laid my honour too unchary out.   *T. N.* iii. 4.

          What! Michael Cassio,
That came a wooing with you; and many a time,
When I have spoke of you dispraisingly,
Hath ta'en your part; to have so much to do
To bring him in!   *O.* iii. 3.

REPUTATION (See also HONOUR).
Good name, in man, and woman, dear my lord,
Is the immediate jewel of their souls:
Who steals my purse, steals trash; 'tis something, nothing;
'Twas mine, 'tis his, and has been slave to thousands:
But he, that filches from me my good name,
Robs me of that which not enriches him,
And makes me poor indeed.   *O.* iii. 3.

The bubble reputation.   *A. Y.* ii. 7.

The gravity and stillness of your youth
The world hath noted, and your name is great
In mouths of wisest censure.   *O.* ii. 3.

REPUTATION,—continued.

Be not amazed: call all your senses to you: Defend your reputation, or bid farewell to your good life for ever. *M.W.* iii. 3.

I see, my reputation is at stake;
My fame is shrewdly gor'd. *T.C.* iii. 3.

These wise men that give fools money, get themselves a good report, after fourteen years' purchase. *T.N.* iv. 1.

O, I have lost my reputation. I have lost the immortal part, Sir, of myself; and what remains is bestial. *O.* ii. 3.

Reputation is an idle and most false imposition; oft got without merit, and lost without deserving. *O.* ii. 3.

I have offended reputation;
A most unnoble swerving. *A.C.* iii. 9.

I would to God, thou and I knew where a commodity of good names were to be bought. *H.IV.* PT. I. i. 2.

REQUEST, UNSEASONABLE.

Thou troublest me, I'm not i'the vein. *R. III.* iv. 2.

RESEMBLANCE.

Youth, thou bear'st thy father's face;
Frank nature, rather curious than in haste,
Hath well compos'd thee. Thy father's moral parts
May'st thou inherit too. *A.W.* i. 2.

RESERVE.

Thou art all ice, thy kindness freezes. *R. III.* iv. 2.

Marry, before your ladyship, I grant,
She puts her tongue a little in her heart,
And chides with thinking. *O.* ii. 1.

RESIGNATION.

O, you mighty gods!
This world I do renounce; and in your sights,
Shake patiently my great affliction off:
If I could bear it longer, and not fall
To quarrel with your great opposeless wills,
My snuff, and loathed parts of nature, should
Burn itself out. *K.L.* iv. 6.

Happy is your grace,
That can translate the stubborness of fortune
Into so quiet and so sweet a style. *A.Y.* ii. 1.

O father abbot,
An old man, broken with the storms of state,
Is come to lay his weary bones among ye;
Give him a little earth for charity. *H.VIII.* iv 2.

RESIGNATION,—*continued.*

Then, dreadful trumpet, sound the general doom!
R. J. iii. 2.

I'll queen it no inch further;
But milk my ewes, and weep. *W. T.* iv. 3.

Cheer your heart:
Be you not troubled with the time, which drives
O'er your content these strong necessities;
But let determin'd things to destiny
Hold unbewail'd their way. *A. C.* iii. 6.

Grieve not that I am fall'n to this for you:
For herein fortune shows herself more kind
Than is her custom: it is still her use,
To let the wretched man outlive his wealth,
And view with hollow eye, and wrinkled brow,
An age of poverty; from the ling'ring penance
Of such a misery doth she cut me off. *M. V.* iv. 1.

God be with you!—I have done. *O.* i. 3.

RESOLVE, Murderous.

Come, come, you spirits
That tend on mortal thoughts, unsex me here;
And fill me, from the crown to the toe, top-full
Of direst cruelty! make thick my blood,
Stop up the access and passage to remorse;
That no compunctious visitings of Nature
Shake my full purpose, nor keep peace between
The effect, and it! Come to my woman's breasts,
And take my milk for gall, you murd'ring ministers,
Wherever in your sightless substances
You wait on Nature's mischief! Come, thick night,
And pall thee in the dunnest smoke of hell!
That my keen knife see not the wound it makes:
Nor heaven peep through the blanket of the dark,
To cry hold! hold! *M.* i. 5.

RESOLUTION (See also **Determination**).

We will not from the helm, to sit and weep;
But keep our course, though the rough wind say, No.
H. VI. pt. iii. v. 4.

Muse not that I thus suddenly proceed,
For what I will, I will, and there an end. *T. G.* i. 3.

The harder match'd, the greater victory:
My mind presageth happy gain and conquest
H. VI. pt. iii. v. 1.

Strike now, or else the iron cools. *H. VI.* pt. iii. v. 1.

Shakespearian Dictionary.

RESOLUTION,—*continued.*

I should be sick,
But that my resolution helps me. *Cym.* iii. 6.
The cause is in my will. *J.C.* ii. 2.
We must have bloody noses, and crack'd crowns,
And pass them current too. Gods me, my horse!
H. IV. PT. I. ii. 3.

RETIREMENT.

To forswear the full stream of the world, and to live in a
nook merely monastic. *A. Y.* iii. 2.

Are not these woods
More free from peril than the envious court?
Here feel we but the penalty of Adam,
The seasons' difference; as, the icy fang,
And churlish chiding of the winter's wind;
Which when it bites and blows upon my body,
Even till I shrink with cold, I smile, and say,—
This is no flattery; these are counsellors
That feelingly persuade me what I am. *A. Y.* ii.1.

Let me not live,—
Thus his good melancholy oft began,
On the catastrophe and heel of pastime,
When it was out,—Let me not live, quoth he,
After my flame lacks oil, to be the snuff
Of younger spirits, whose apprehensive senses
All but new things disdain; whose judgments are
Mere fathers of their garments; whose constancies
Expire before their fashions: This he wish'd
I, after him, do after him wish too,
Since I nor wax nor honey can bring home,
I quickly were dissolved from my hive,
To give some labourers room. *A. W.* i. 2.

And this our life, exempt from public haunt,
Finds tongues in trees, books in the running brooks,
Sermons in stones, and good in every thing. *A. Y.* ii. 1.

For mine own part, I could be well content
To entertain the lag-end of my life
With quiet hours. *H. IV.* PT. I. v. 1

To shake all cares and business from our age;
Conferring them on younger strengths, while we,
Unburden'd, crawl toward death. *K. L.* i. 1

RETREAT.

A poor sequester'd stag,
That from the hunter's aim had ta'en a hurt,
Did come to languish. *A. Y.* ii 1.

RETRIBUTION.

That high ALL-SEER which I dallied with,
Hath turn'd my feigned prayer on my head,
And given in earnest what I begg'd in jest. *R. III.* v. 4.

Till now you have gone on, and fill'd the time
With all licentious measure, making your wills
The scope of justice; till now, myself and such
As slept within the shadow of your power,
Have wander'd with our travers'd arms, and breath'd
Our sufferance vainly: Now the time is flush,
When crouching marrow, in the bearer strong,
Cries of itself, *No more:* now breathless wrong,
Shall sit and pant in your great chairs of ease;
And pursy insolence shall break his wind,
With fear and horrid flight. *T. A.* v. 5.

Thus hath the course of justice wheel'd about,
And left thee but a very prey to time;
Having no more but thought of what thou wert,
To torture thee the more, being what thou art.
Thou didst usurp my place. And dost thou not
Usurp the just proportion of my sorrow? *R. III.* iv 4.

So just is God to right the innocent! *R. III.* i. 3.

But it is no matter:
Let Hercules himself do what he may,
The cat will mew, the dog will have his day. *H.* v. 1.

O God! I fear, thy justice will take hold
On me, and you, and mine, and yours, for this. *R. III.* ii. 1.

For this down-trodden equity, we tread,
In warlike march, these greens before your town.
K. J. ii. 1.

And thus the whirligig of time brings in his revenges.
T. N. v. 1.

RETROSPECTION.

When to the sessions of sweet silent thought,
I summon up remembrance of things past,
I sigh the lack of many a thing I sought,
And with old woes, new waile my dear time's waste;
Then can I drown an eye (unus'd to flow)
For precious friends hid in death's dateless night,
And weep afresh love's long since cancell'd woe,
And moan the expense of many a vanisht sight.

Then can I grieve at grievances foregone,
And heavily from woe to woe tell o'er
The sad account of fore-bemoaned moan,
Which I now pay, as if not paid before. *Poems.*

REVELRY.
Heavy-headed revel. *H.* i. 4.
Our vaults have wept
With drunken spilth of wine; when every room
Hath blaz'd with lights, and bray'd with minstrelsy.
T. A. ii. 2.

REVENGE.
If a Jew wrong a Christian, what is his humility?—revenge; if a Christian wrong a Jew, what should his sufferance be, by Christian example?—why, revenge.
M. V. iii. 1.

O, I could play the woman with mine eyes,
And braggart with my tongue!—But, gentle heaven,
Cut short all intermission; front to front,
Bring thou this fiend of Scotland, and myself;
Within my sword's length set him; if he 'scape,
Heaven forgive him too! *M.* iv. 3.

To weep, is to make less the depth of grief;
Tears, then, for babes; blows, and revenge for me.
H. VI. PT. III. ii. 1.

Haste me to know it; that I, with wings as swift
As meditation, or the thoughts of love,
May sweep to my revenge. *H.* i. 5.

Had I thy brethren here, their lives, and thine,
Were not revenge sufficient for me;
No, if I digg'd up thy forefathers' graves,
And hung their rotten coffins up in chains,
It could not slake mine ire, nor ease my heart.
The sight of any of the house of York
Is as a fury to torment my soul;
And till I root out their accursed line,
And leave not one alive, I live in hell. *H. VI.* PT. III. i. 3.

Up, sword; and know thou a more horrid bent,
When he is drunk, asleep, or in his rage;
Or in the incestuous pleasures of his bed;
At gaming, swearing; or about some act
That has no relish of salvation in't:
Then trip him, that his heels may kick at heaven,
And that his soul may be as damn'd, and black
As hell, whereto it goes. *H.* iii. 3.

To hell, allegiance! vows, to the blackest devil!
Conscience, and grace, to the profoundest pit!
I dare damnation: To this point I stand,—
That both the worlds I give to negligence,
Let come what comes; only, I'll be reveng'd. *H.* iv. 5.

REVENGE,—*continued.*
I am disgrac'd, impeach'd, and baffled here;
Pierc'd to the soul with slander's venom'd spear;
The which no balm can cure, but his heart's blood
Which breath'd this poison. *R. II.* i. 1.
  My bloody thoughts, with violent pace,
Shall ne'er look back, ne'er ebb to humble love,
Till that a capable and wide revenge
Swallow them up. *O.* iii. 3.
  Cæsar's spirit, ranging for revenge,
With Até by his side, come hot from hell,
Shall, in these confines, with a monarch's voice,
Cry Havock! and let slip the dogs of war. *J.C.* iii. 1.
To revenge is no valour, but to bear. *T.A.* iii. 5.
Had all his hairs been lives, my great revenge
Had stomach for them all. *O.* v. 2.

REVERENCE.
That angel of the world doth make distinction
Of place 'twixt high and low. *Cym.* iv. 2

REVERSES.
   He seems
Proud and disdainful; harping on what I am;
Not what he knew I was: He makes me angry;
And at this time most easy 'tis to do't;
When my good stars, that were my former guides,
Have left their orbs, and shot their fires,
Into the abysm of hell. *A.C.* iii. 11.
Against the blown rose may they stop their nose,
That kneel'd unto the buds. *A.C.* iii. 11

REVIEW.
 Here, here; here's an excellent place; here we may see
most bravely: I'll tell you them all by their names as they
pass by. *T.C.* i. 2.

REVOLUTION.
  Such is the infection of the time,
That for the health and physic of our right,
We cannot deal but with the very hand
Of stern injustice and confused wrong. *K.J.* v. 2.

RHETORIC.
Sweet smoke of rhetoric! *L.L.* iii. 1.

RHYMSTER (See also POET, BALLAD-MONGER).
Ha, Ha; how vilely doth this cynic rhyme! *J.C.* iv. 3.
Hang odes upon hawthorns, and elegies on brambles.
A.Y. iii. 2.

RHYMSTER,—*continued*.
What should the wars do with the jigging fools? *J.C.* iv. 3.
This is the very false gallop of verses; why do you infect yourself with them? *A.Y.* iii. 2.
I was not born under a rhyming planet, nor I cannot woo in festival terms. *M.A.* v. 2.

RHYME.
There never was a truer rhyme. Let us cast away nothing, for we may live to have need of such a verse.
T.C. iv. 3.

RICH.
As is the ooze and bottom of the sea
With sunken wreck and sumless treasuries. *H.V.* i. 2.

RICHES AND GOODNESS.
The old proverb is pretty well parted between my master Shylock and you, Sir; you have the grace of God, Sir, and he hath enough. *M.V.* ii. 2.

RIDDANCE.
Call the rest of the watch together, and thank God you are rid of a knave. *M.A.* iii. 3.

RIDICULE.
Shall quips, and sentences, and these paper bullets of the brain, awe a man from the career of his humour?
M.A. ii. 3.

And in this fashion,
All our abilities, gifts, natures, shapes,
Severals and generals of grace exact,
Achievements, plots, orders, preventions,
Excitements to the field, or speech for truce,
Success or loss, what is, or is not, serves
As stuff for these two to make paradoxes. *T.C.* i. 3.

RIGOUR.
There is no more mercy in him, than there is milk in a male tiger. *C.* v. 4.

RIOT.
There is no fear of Got in a riot. *M.W.* i. 1.

RISIBILITY.
He does smile his face into more lines, than are in the new map, with the augmentation of the Indies. *T.N.* iii. 2.

ROAR.
O 'twas a din to fright a monster's ear;
To make an earthquake! sure it was the roar
Of a whole herd of lions. *T.* ii. 1.

ROAR,—*continued.*
    You may do it extempore, for it is nothing but roaring.
                                                          M. N. i 2.

ROBBER.
    This is the most omnipotent villain that ever cried, Stand,
to a true man.   *H. IV.* PT. I. i. 2.

ROGUE (See also KNAVE, VILLAIN).
    Here's an overwheening rogue!   *T. N.* ii. 5

ROSES(OF YORK AND LANCASTER).
                This brawl to-day,
Grown to this faction, in the Temple Garden,
Shall send, between the red rose and the white,
A thousand souls to death and deadly night.
                                                    H. VI. PT. I. ii. 4.

Well, I'll find friends to wear my bleeding roses
That shall maintain what I have said is true:
Ay, thou shalt find us ready for thee still,
And know us by these colours for thy foes.   *H. VI.* PT. I. ii. 4.

And, by my soul, this pale and angry rose,
As cognizance of my blood-drinking hate,
Will I for ever, and my faction, wear;
Until it wither with me to the grave,
Or flourish to the height of my degree.   *H. VI.* PT. I. ii. 4.

ROTTENNESS.
    Something is rotten in the state of Denmark.   *H.* i. 4.

ROVERS.
    I would have men of such constancy put to sea, that their
business might be every thing, and their intent every where;
for that's it, that always makes a good voyage of nothing.
                                                          T. N. ii. 4.

ROYALTY IN SUBJECTION.
    To be a queen in bondage, is more vile
Than is a slave in base servility;
For princes should be free.   *H. VI.* PT. I. v. 3.

RUDENESS.
    None of noble sort would so offend a virgin.   *M. N.* iii. 2.

RUINS.
    The ruin speaks, that sometime it was a worthy building.
                                                                Cym. iv. 2.

RULERS.
    He, who the sword of heaven will bear,
Should be as holy as severe;
Pattern in himself to know,

RULERS,—*continued.*
Grace to stand, and virtue go ;
More nor less to others paying,
Than by self-offences weighing.
Shame to him, whose cruel striking
Kills for faults of his own liking. *M. M.* iii. ⁊.

There be, that can rule Naples
As well as he that sleeps ; lords, that can prate
As amply and unnecessarily,
As this Gonzalo. *T.* ii. 1

RUMOUR.
Rumour doth double, like the voice and echo,
The numbers of the fear'd. *H.IV.* PT. II. iii. 1.

There's toys abroad ; anon I'll tell thee more. *K. J.* i. 1

For so I have strew'd it in the common ear,
And so it is receiv'd. *M. M.* i. 4.

By holy Paul, they love his grace but lightly,
That fill his ears with such dissentious rumours.
R. III. i. 3.

Old men, and beldams, in the streets
Do prophecy upon it dangerously. *K. J.* iv. 2.

Open your ears: for which of you will stop
The vent of hearing, when loud Rumour speaks ?
I, from the orient, to the drooping west,
Making the wind my post-horse, still unfold
The acts commenced on this ball of earth :
Upon my tongues continual slanders ride ;
The which in every language I pronounce,
Stuffing the ears of men with false reports.
I speak of peace, while covert enmity,
Under the smile of safety, wounds the world :
And who but Rumour, who but only I,
Make fearful musters, and prepar'd defence ;
Whilst the big year, swoln with some other grief,
Is thought with child by the stern tyrant war,
And no such matter ? Rumour is a pipe
Blown by surmises, jealousies, conjectures ;
And of so easy and so plain a stop,
That the blunt monster with uncounted heads,
The still discordant wavering multitude,
Can play upon it. *H. IV.* PT. II. i. *Ind.*

RUSHING OF A MULTITUDE.
Ne'er through an arch so hurried the blown tide,
As the recomforted through the gates. *C.* v. 4.

S.

SACK.
A good sherris-sack has a two-fold operation in it. It ascends me into the brain: dries me there all the foolish, and dull, and crudy vapours which environ it: makes it apprehensive, quick, and forgetive, full of nimble, fiery, and delectable shapes; which delivered o'er to the voice, (the tongue) which is the birth, becomes excellent wit. The second property of your excellent sherris is,—the warming of the blood; which, before cold, and settled, left the liver white and pale, which is the badge of pusillanimity and cowardice; but the sherris warms it, and makes it course from the inwards to the parts extreme. It illuminateth the face; which, as a beacon, gives warning to all the rest of this little kingdom, man, to arm: and then the vital commoners, and inland petty spirits muster me all to their captain, the heart; who, great, and puffed up with this retinue, doth any deed of courage; and this valour comes of sherris: So that skill in the weapon is nothing, without sack; for that sets it a-work: and learning, a mere hoard of gold, kept by a devil; till sack commences it, and sets it in act and use. Hereof comes it, that prince Harry is valiant: for the cold blood he did naturally inherit of his father, he hath, like lean, steril, and bare land, manured, husbanded, and tilled, with excellent endeavour of drinking good, and good store of fertile sherris; that he is become very hot, and valiant. If I had a thousand sons, the first human principle I would teach them, should be,—to forswear thin potations, and addict themselves to sack.
H.IV. PT. II. iv. 3.

SADNESS.
In sooth, I know not why I am so sad;
It wearies me; you say, it wearies you:
But how I caught it, found it, or came by't,
What stuff 'tis made of, whereof it is born,
I am to learn. *M.V.* i. 1

    Howe'er it be,
I cannot but be sad; so heavy sad,
As, though in thinking, on no thought I think,—
Makes me with heavy nothing faint and shrink.
R.II. ii. 2.

Such a want-wit sadness makes of me,
That I have much ado to know myself. *M.V.* i. 1.

SAD **Shakespearian Dictionary.** SAT

SADNESS,—*continued.*
      I do note,
That grief and patience, rooted in him both,
· Mingle their spurs together. *Cym.* iv. 2.
 There is no measure in the occasion that breeds it, therefore the sadness is without limit. *M.A.* i. 3.

SAGACITY.
 This learned constable is too cunning to be understood.
               M.A. v. 1.

SALUTATION (See also BENEDICTION).
Rest you fair, good Signior. *M.V.* i. 3.
The heavens rain odours on you. *T.N.* iii. 1.
Hail to thee, lady! and the grace of heaven,
Before, behind thee, and on every hand,
Enwheel thee round. *O.* ii. 1.

——————— CLERICAL.
Jove bless thee, master parson. *T.N.* iv. 2.

——————— MILITARY.
· Most military Sir, salutation. *L.L.* v. 1.

SARCASMS.
 She speaks poignards, and every word stabs; if her breath were as terrible as her terminations, there were no living near her, she would infect the north star.
               M.A. ii. 1.

SATIETY.
They surfeited with honey, and began
To loathe the taste of sweetness, whereof little
More than a little is by much too much. *H. IV.* PT. I. iii. 2.
     Who rises from a feast
With that keen appetite that he sits down?
Where is the horse that doth untread again
His tedious measures with th' unabated fire
That he did pace them first? All things that are,
Are with more spirit chased than enjoyed. *M.V.* ii. 6.
O, ten times faster Venus' pigeons fly,
To seal love's bonds new made, than they are wont,
To keep obliged faith unforfeited. *M.V.* ii. 6.
 The food that to him now is as luscious as locusts, shall be to him shortly as bitter as coloquintida. *O.* i. 3.

SATIRE.
Satire, keen and critical. *M.N.* v. 1.
Wit larded with malice. *T.C.* v. 1

SATIRE,—*continued.*
I must have liberty
Withal, as large a charter as the wind,
To blow on whom I please ; for so fools have ;
And they that are most galled with my folly,
They most must laugh : And why, sir, must they so ?
The *why* is plain as way to parish church ;
He, that a fool doth very wisely hit,
Doth very foolishly, although he smart,
Not to seem senseless of the bob ; if not,
The wise man's folly is anatomis'd
Ev'n by the squand'ring glances of the fool. *A. Y.* ii. 7.

SATIRIST.
The world's large tongue,
Proclaims you for a man replete with mocks ;
Full of comparison and wounding flouts ;
Which you on all estates will execute,
That lie within the mercy of your wit. *L. L.* v. 2.

A very dull fool ; his only gift is in devising impossible slanders ; none but libertines delight in him ; and the commendation is not in his wit, but in his villainy ; for he both pleases men, and angers them, and then they laugh at him, and beat him. *M. A.* ii. 1.

SAVAGE.
Fit for the mountains, and the barbarous caves,
Where manners ne'er were preached. *T. N.* iv. 1.

SCHEMER.
What impossible matter will he make easy next ? *T.* ii. 1.
I am not so nice
To change true rules for odd inventions. *T. S.* iii. 1.

SCHOLAR.
Thou art a scholar, speak to it, Horatio. *H.* i. 1.

SCHOOLBOY SIMPLICITY.
The flat transgression of a schoolboy ; who, being overjoyed with finding a bird's nest, shows it to his companion, and he steals it. *M. A.* ii. 1.

SCHOOLMASTER.
Sir, I praise the Lord for you ; and so may my parishioners ; for their sons are well tutored by you, and their daughters profit very greatly under you ; you are a good member of the commonwealth. *L. L.* iv. 2.

SCOLD.
Think you, a little din can daunt mine ears ?
Have I not in my time heard lions roar ?

Shakespearian Dictionary.

SCOLD,—*continued.*
Have I not heard the sea, puff'd up with winds,
Rage like an hungry boar, chafed with sweat?
Have I not heard great ordnance in the field,
And Heaven's artillery thunder in the skies?
Have I not in pitched battles heard
Loud 'larums, neighing steeds, and trumpets' clang?
And do you tell me of a woman's tongue,
That gives not half so great a blow to the ear
As will a chesnut in a farmer's fire? *T. S.* i. 2

SCORN.
You speak of the people, as if you were a god,
To punish; not a man of their infirmity. *C.* iii. 1.
You are not worth another word, else I'd call you knave.
A. W. ii. 3.
O that I were a god, to shoot forth thunder
Upon these paltry, servile, abject drudges!
H. VI. PT. II. iv. 1.
Scorn at first, makes after love the more. *T. G.* iii. 1.
I will not do't:
Lest I surcease to honour mine own truth,
And, by my body's action, teach my mind
A most inherent baseness. *C.* iii. 2.

SCULPTURE.
He so near to Hermione hath done Hermione, that, they
say, one would speak to her and stand in hope of answer.
W. T. v. 2.
Still, methinks,
There is an air comes from her: what fine chizzel
Could ever yet cut breath. *W. T.* v. 3.

SEA.
The watery kingdom, whose ambitious head
Spits in the face of heaven. *M. V.* ii. 6.

——— BED OF THE.
Methought, I saw a thousand fearful wrecks;
A thousand men, that fishes gnaw'd upon;
Wedges of gold, great anchors, heaps of pearl,
Inestimable stones, unvalued jewels,
All scatter'd on the bottom of the sea.
Some lay in dead men's sculls; and, in those holes
Where eyes did once inhabit, there were crept
(As 'twere in scorn of eyes) reflecting gems,
That woo'd the slimy bottom of the deep,
And mock'd the dead-bones that lay scatter'd by.
R. III. i. 4.

SEA   **Shakespearian Dictionary.**   SEC

SEA, PERILS OF THE (See also SHIPWRECK).
Our hint of woe
Is common: every day, some sailor's wife,
The masters of some merchant, and the merchant,
Have just our theme of woe.   *T.* ii. 1.

SEASONS.
The seasons alter; hoary-headed frosts
Fall in the fresh lap of the crimson rose;
And on old Hyems' chin, and icy crown,
An odorous chaplet of sweet summer buds
Is, as in mockery, set: The spring, the summer,
The childing autumn, angry winter, change
Their wonted liveries; and the mazed world,
By their increase, now knows not which is which.
    M. N. ii. 2.

SEASON.
               Every time
Serves for the matter that is then born in it.   *A.C.* ii. 2.

SEASONABLE.
The crow doth sing as sweetly as the lark,
When neither is attended; and, I think,
The nightingale, if she should sing by day,
When every goose is cackling, would be thought
No better a musician than the wren.
How many things by season season'd are,
To their right praise, and true perfection.   *M.V.* v. 1.

SECLUSION.
If Cæsar hide himself, shall they not whisper,
Lo, Cæsar is afraid?   *J.C.* ii. 2.

SECRECY.
Stall this in your bosom.   *A.W.* i. 3.
Masking the business from the common eye.   *M.* iii. 1.
When you have spoken it, 'tis dead, and I am the grave
of it.   *A.W.* iv. 3.
Give it an understanding, but no tongue.   *H.* i. 2.
       'Tis in my memory lock'd,
And you yourself shall keep the key of it.   *H.* i. 3.
Thou wilt not trust the air with secrets.   *Tit. And.* iv. 2.
Be thou assur'd, if words be made of breath,
And breath of life, I have no life to breathe
What thou hast said to me.   *H.* iii. 4.
I know you wise; but yet no further wise,
Than Harry Percy's wife; constant you are;

SECRECY,—*continued.*
But yet a woman: and for secrecy,
No lady closer; for I well believe,
Thou wilt not utter what thou dost not know;
And so far will I trust thee, gentle Kate.
H. IV. PT. I. ii. 3

But that I am forbid·
To tell the secrets of my prison-house,
I could a tale unfold, whose lightest word
Would harrow up thy soul. *H.* i. 5.

This secret is so weighty, 'twill require
A strong faith to conceal it. *H. V. III.* ii. 1.

Two may keep counsel, putting one away. *R. J.* ii. 4.

A juggling trick to be secretly open. *T. C.* v. 2.

SECURITY.
Whole as the marble, founded as the rock;
As broad and general as the casing air. *M.* iii. 4.

Shut doors after you: Fast bind, fast find;
A proverb never stale in thrifty mind. *M. V.* ii. 5.

But yet I'll make assurance doubly sure,
And take a bond of fate. *M.* iv. 1.

I look'd he should have sent me two-and-twenty yards of satin, as I am a true knight, and he sends me,—security.
H. IV. PT. II. i. 2.

A rascally, yea-forsooth knave! to bear a gentleman in hand, and then stand upon security! *H. IV.* PT. II. i. 2.

SEDITION.
Here do we make his friends
Blush, that the world goes well; who rather had
Though they themselves did suffer by't, behold
Dissentious numbers pestering streets, than see
Our tradesmen singing in their shops, and going
About their functions friendly. *C.* iv. 6.

These things, indeed, you have articulated,
Proclaim'd at market crosses, read in churches;
To face the garment of rebellion
With some fine colour, that may please the eye
Of fickle changelings, and poor discontents,
Which gape, and rub the elbow, at the news
Of hurly-burly innovation:
And never yet did insurrection want
Such water-colours to impaint his cause;
Nor moody beggars, starving for a time,
Of pell-mell havoc and confusion. *H. IV.* PT. I. v. 1

SEDITION,—*continued.*
The spinsters, carders, fullers, weavers, who,
Unfit for other life, compell'd by hunger
And lack of other means, in desperate manner
Daring the event to th' teeth, are all in uproar,
And danger serves among them.   *H. VIII.* i. 2.

SEDUCTION.
        Then if he says he loves you;
It fits your wisdom so far to believe it,
As he, in his particular act and place,
May give his saying deed; which is no further,
Than the main voice of Denmark goes withal.
Then weigh what loss your honour may sustain,
If with too credent ear you list his songs;
Or lose your heart; or your chaste treasure open
To his unmaster'd importunity.   *H.* i. 3.
        Ay, so you serve us,
Till we serve you: but when you have our roses,
You barely leave our thorns to prick ourselves,
And mock us with our bareness.   *A. W.* iv. 2.
This man hath witch'd the bosom of my child:
Thou, thou, Lysander, thou hast given her rhymes,
And interchang'd love tokens with my child:
Thou hast by moonlight at her window sung,
With feigning voice, verses of feigning love;
And stol'n th' impression of her phantasy
With bracelets of thy hair, rings, gawds, conceits,
Knacks, trifles, nosegays, sweetmeats; messengers
Of strong prevailment in unharden'd youth:
With cunning hast thou filch'd my daughter's heart,
Turn'd her obedience, which is due to me,
To stubborn harshness.   *M. N.* i. 1.
O cunning enemy, that to catch a saint,
With saints doth bait thy hook!   *M. M.* ii. 2.
  Many a maid hath been seduced by them; and the misery is, example, that so terribly shows in the wreck of maidenhood, cannot for all that dissuade succession, but that they are lim'd with the twigs that threaten them.
                        A. W. iii. 5.
Devils soonest tempt, resembling spirits of light.
                        L. L. iv. 3.

Beguiles him, as the mournful crocodile
With sorrow snares relenting passengers;
Or as the snake, roll'd in a flowering bank,
With shining checker'd slough, doth sting a child,
That, for the beauty, thinks it excellent.   *H. VI.* PT. II. iii. 1.

SEE   Shakespearian Dictionary.   SEN

SEEING.
I have a good eye, uncle: I can see a church by day-light.
M. A. ii. 1.

SEEMING.
Out on thy seeming! I will write against it:
You seem to me as Dian in her orb;
As chaste as is the bud ere it be blown;
But you are more intemperate in your blood
Than Venus, or those pamper'd animals
That rage in savage sensuality.   *M. A.* iv. 1.

SELF-CONCEITED.
The best persuaded of himself, so crammed, as he thinks,
with excellencies, that it is his ground of faith, that all, that
look on him, love him.   *T. N.* ii. 3.
Look, how imagination blows him.   *T. N.* ii. 5.

SELF-DENIAL.
The greatest virtue of which wise men boast,
Is to abstain from ill, when pleasing most.   *Poems.*

SELF-GOVERNMENT.
Virtue? a fig! 'Tis in ourselves that we are thus, or thus.
Our bodies are our gardens, to the which our wills are gardeners: so that if we will plant nettles, or sow lettuce; set hyssop, and weed up thyme; supply it with one gender of herbs, or distract it with many; either to have it steril with idleness, or manured with industry; why, the power and corrigible authority of this lies in our own wills.
O. i. 3.

SELFISHNESS.
Torches are made to burn; jewels to wear;
Things growing to themselves are growth's abuse.   *Poems.*

SELF-LOVE.
         Self-love is not so vile a sin
As self-neglecting.   *H. V.* ii. 4.
O villanous! I have lived upon the world four times seven years; and since I could distinguish between a benefit and an injury, I never found a man that knew not how to love himself.   *O.* i. 3.

SENATORS.
         These old fellows
Have their ingratitude in them hereditary:
Their blood is cak'd, tis cold, it seldom flows;
'Tis lack of kindly warmth, they are not kind;
And nature, as it grows again towards earth,
Is fashioned for the journey, dull, and heavy.   *T. A.* ii. 2.

SENTENTIOUS.
    By my faith he is very swift and sententious. *A. Y.* v. 4.

SEPULCHRE.
    The sacred storehouse of his predecessors,
    And guardian of their bones. *M.* ii. 4.

SERVANT, UNPROFITABLE.
    The patch is kind enough, but a huge feeder,
    Snail-slow in profit. *M. V.* ii. 5.

SET PHRASES.
    O! never will I trust to speeches penn'd,
        Nor to the motion of a school-boy's tongue;
    Nor never come in visor to my friend;
        Nor woo in rhyme, like a blind harper's song;
    Taffata phrases, silken terms precise,
        Three-pil'd hyperboles, spruce affectation,
    Figures pedantical; these summer flies
        Have blown me full of maggot ostentation:
    I do forswear them. *L. L.* v. 2.

SEVERITY.
    Tear-falling pity dwells not in this eye. *R. III.* iv. 2.

SHAME.
    Heaven stops the nose at it, and the moon winks:
    The bawdy wind, that kisses all it meets,
    Is hush'd within the hollow mine of earth,
    And will not hear it. *O.* iv. 2.
    Shame enough to shame thee, wert thou not shameless.
        H. VI. PT. III. i. 4.
    A sovereign shame so elbows him. *K. L.* iv. 3.
    O shame! where is thy blush? *H.* iii. 4.
    The shame itself doth speak for instant remedy. *K. L.* i. 4.
    He is unqualitied with very shame. *A. C.* iii. 9.
        Heaven's face doth glow;
    Yea, this solidity and compound mass,
    With tristful visage, as against the doom,
    Is thought-sick at the act. *H.* iii. 4.
        He was not born to shame;
    Upon his brow shame is asham'd to sit;
    For 'tis a throne where honour may be crown'd
    Sole monarch of the universal earth. *R. J.* iii. 2.
        Fie, fie, they are
    Not to be nam'd, my lord, not to be spoke of;
    There is not chastity enough in language,
    Without offence to utter them. *M. A.* iv. 1

SHE Shakesperian Dictionary. SHI

SHEPHERD'S PHILOSOPHY.
I know, the more one sickens, the worse at ease he is; and that he that wants money, means, and content, is without three good friends:—That the property of rain is to wet, and fire to burn: That good pasture makes fat sheep; and that a great cause of the night, is lack of the sun: That he, that hath learned no wit by nature, nor art, may complain of good breeding, or comes of a very dull kindred. *A. Y.* iii. 2.

SHERIFF'S OFFICER.
One, whose hard heart is button'd up with steel;
A fiend, a fairy, pitiless and rough;
A wolf, nay worse, a fellow all in buff;
A back-friend, a shoulder-clapper, one that countermands
The passages of alleys, creeks, and narrow lands;
A hound that runs counter, and yet draws dry-foot well;
One that, before judgment, carries poor souls to hell.
C. E. iv. 2.

SHIPWRECKS (See also SEA).
The king's son, Ferdinand,
With hair up-staring, (then like reeds, not hair,)
Was the first man that leap'd; cried, *Hell is empty,
And all the devils are here.* *T.* i. 2

Not a soul
But felt a fever of the mad, and play'd
Some tricks of desperation. *T.* i. 2

In few, they hurried us aboard the bark;
Bore us some leagues to sea; where they prepar'd
A rotten carcase of a boat, not rigg'd,
Nor tackle, sail, nor mast; the very rats
Instinctively had quit it: there they hoist us,
To cry to the sea that roar'd to us; to sigh
To the winds, whose pity, sighing back again,
Did us but loving wrong. *T.* i. 2.

To comfort you with chance,
Assure yourself, after our ship did split,
When you, and that poor number sav'd with you,
Hung on our driving boat, I saw your brother,
Most provident in peril, bind himself
(Courage and hope both teaching him the practice)
To a strong mast, that liv'd upon the sea,
Where, like Arion on the dolphin's back,
I saw him hold acquaintance with the waves,
So long as I could see. *T. N.* i. 2.

And not one vessel 'scape the dreadful touch
Of merchant-marring rocks. *M. V.* iii. 2.

SHIPWRECK,—*continued.*
Yet the incessant weepings of my wife,
Weeping before for what she knew must come.
And piteous plaining of the pretty babes,
That mourn'd for fashion, ignorant what to fear,
Forc'd me to seek delays for them and me. *C. E.* i. 1.

———— DESCRIBED BY A CLOWN.
I would, you did but see how it chafes, how it rages, how it takes up the shore! but that's not to the point: O, the most piteous cry of the poor souls! sometimes to see 'em and not to see 'em: now the ship boring the moon with her main-mast; and anon swallowed with yeast and froth, as you'd thrust a cork into a hogshead. And then for the land service,—To see how the bear tore out his shoulder-bone; how he cried to'me for help, and said his name was Antigonus, a nobleman:—But to make an end o' the ship: to see how the sea flap-dragon'd it:—but, first, how the poor souls roar'd, and the sea mock'd them;—and how the poor gentleman roar'd, and the bear mock'd him, both roaring louder than the sea, or weather. *W. T.* iii. 3.

SICK.
Zounds! how has he the leisure to be sick
In such a justling time? *H. IV.* PT. I. iv. 1

SIEGE (See also CANNONADE)
Tell us, shall your city call us lord,
In that behalf which we have challeng'd it,
Or shall we give the signal to our rage,
And stalk in blood to our possession? *K. J.* ii. 1.

Girdled with a waist of iron,
And hemm'd about with grim destruction. *H. VI.* PT. I. iv. 3.

These flags of France, that are advanced here,
Before the eye and prospect of your town,
Have hither march'd to your endamagement:
The cannons have their bowels full of wrath;
And ready mounted are they to spit forth
Their iron indignation 'gainst your walls. *K. J.* ii. 1.

SIFTING.
See you now:
Your bait of falsehood takes this carp of truth;
And thus do we of wisdom and of reach,
With windlaces, and with assays of bias,
By indirections find directions out. *H.* ii. 1.

SIGHS.
He rais'd a sigh, so piteous and profound,

SIGHS,—*continued.*
As it did seem to shatter all his bulk,
And end his being. *H.* ii. 1.
Blood-drinking sighs. *H. VI.* PT. II. iii. 2.
Blood-sucking sighs. *H. VI.* PT. III. iv. 4.
Her sighs will make a battery in his breast;
Her tears will pierce into a marble heart;
The tiger will be mild while she doth mourn;
And Nero will be tainted with remorse,
To hear, and see, her plaints. *H. VI.* PT. III. iii. 1.
    For heaven shall hear our prayers;
Or with our sighs we'll breathe the welkin dim,
And stain the sun with fog, as sometimes clouds,
When they do hug him in their melting bosoms.
Tit. And. iii. 1.
Blood-consuming sighs. *H. VI.* PT. II. iii. 2.
I could drive the boat with my sighs. *T. G.* ii. 3.
Heart-sore sighs. *T. G.* ii. 4.
Cooling the air with sighs. *T.* i. 2.

SIGNS OF THE TIMES.
And in such indexes, although small pricks
To their subséquent volumes, there is seen
The baby figure of the giant mass
Of things to come at large. *T. C.* i. 3.

SILENCE.
Hear his speech, but say thou nought. *M.* iv. 1.
With silence, nephew, be thou politic. *H. VI.* PT. I. ii. 5.
    Silence only is commendable
In a neat's tongue dried, and a maid not vendible.
M. V. i. 1.
I like your silence, it the more shows off
Your wonder. *W. T.* v. 3

——— PERSUASIVE.
The silence, often, of pure innocence,
Persuades, when speaking fails. *W. T.* ii. 2.
    See, see, your silence,
Cunning in dumbness, from my weakness draws
My very soul of counsel. *T. C.* iii. 2.
There was speech in their dumbness. *W. T.* v. 2.

SIMILIES.
A good swift similie, but something currish. *T. S.* v. 2.
Thou hast the most unsavoury similies. *H. IV.* PT. I. i. 2

SIMPLICITY.
    It is silly sooth.   *W. T.* iv. 3.
    By the pattern of mine own thougths, I cut out
    The purity of his.   *W. T.* iv. 3.
    How green are you, and fresh in this old world!   *K. J.* iii. 4.

SIN.
    Few love to hear the sins they love to act.   *P. P.* i. 1.
    O, 'tis the cunning livery of hell,
    The damned'st body to invest and cover
    In princely guards.   *M. M.* iii. 1.

SINCERITY.
    Believe me, I speak as my understanding instructs me,
    and as mine honesty puts it to utterance.   *W. T.* i. 1.

SINFUL.
    Smacking of every sin that has a name.   *M.* iv. 3.

SINGING.
    She will sing the savageness out of a bear.   *O.* iv. 1.

—— **BAD.**
    An he had been a dog that should have howled thus,
    they would have hanged him; and I pray God his bad
    voice bode no mischief.   *M. A.* ii. 3.
        Tax not so bad a voice
    To slander music any more than once.   *M. A.* ii. 3.

SINGULARITY.
    Methinks you prescribe to yourself very preposterously.
         M. W. ii. 2.

SINNERS, REFINED.
    Some of all professions, that go the primrose way to the
    everlasting bonfire.   *M.* ii. 3.

SLANDER (See also CALUMNY).
    No might nor greatness in mortality
    Can censure 'scape; back-wounding calumny
    The whitest virtue strikes.   *M. M.* iii. 2.
        For haply, slander,
    Whose whisper o'er the earth's diameter,
    As level as the cannon to his blank,
    Transports his poison'd shot, may miss our name,
    And hit the woundless air,   *H.* iv. 1.
        One doth not know,
    How much an ill word may empoison liking.   *M.A.* iii. 1
    I see, the jewel, best enamelled,
    Will lose his beauty: and though gold 'bides still,

SLANDER,—*continued.*
That others touch, yet often touching will
Wear gold: and no man, that hath a name,
But falsehood and corruption doth it shame, *C. E.* ii. 1.
'Tis slander;
Whose edge is sharper than the sword; whose tongue
Out-venoms all the worms of Nile; whose breath
Rides on the posting wind, and doth belie
All corners of the world; kings, queens, and states,
Maids, matrons, nay, the secrets of the grave
This viperous slander enters. *Cym.* iii. 4.

Many worthy and chaste dames even thus (all guiltless)
meet reproach. *O.* iv. 1.

Calumny will sear virtue itself. *W.T.* ii. 1.

I will be hang'd, if some eternal villain,
Some busy and insinuating rogue,
Some cogging cozening slave, to get some office,
Have not devis'd this slander. *O.* iv. 2.

For he
The sacred honour of himself, his queen's,
His hopeful son's, his babe's, betrays to slander,
Whose sting is sharper than the sword's. *W.T.* ii. 3.

Abus'd by some most villanous knave!
Some base notorious knave, some scurvy fellow:
O, heaven, that such companions thoud'st unfold;
And put in every honest hand a whip
To lash the rascal naked through the world! *O.* iv. 2.

So thou be good, slander doth but approve. *Poems.*

If thou dost slander her, and torture me,
Never pray more: abandon all remorse;
On horror's head horrors accumulate:
Do deeds to make heaven weep, all earth amaz'd,
For nothing canst thou to damnation add,
Greater than that. *O.* iii. 3.

A slave, whose gall coins slanders like a mint. *T.C.* i. 2.

SLANDERERS.
That dare as well answer a man, indeed,
As I dare take a serpent by the tongue:
Boys, apes, braggarts, jacks, milksops? *M.A.* v. 1.

Smiling pickthanks and base newsmongers.
H. IV. PT. I. iii. 2.

SLAVE AT LARGE.
I am trusted with a muzzle, and enfranchised with a clog.
M.A. i. 3.

SLAVISHNESS.

      Milk-liver'd man!
That bear'st a cheek for blows, a head for wrongs,
Who hast not in thy brows an eye discerning
Thine honour from thy suffering; that not know'st
Fools do those villains pity, who are punish'd
Ere they have done their mischief.   *K. L.* iv. 2.
How this lord's follow'd!   *T. A.* i. 1.
With plumed helm thy slayer begins threats;
Whilst thou, a moral fool, sit'st still, and cry'st,
Alack! Why does he so?   *K. L.* iv. 2.
     O, behold,
How pomp is follow'd.   *A. C.* v. 2.
Seeking sweet savours for this hateful fool. *M. N.* iv. 1.
To flatter Cæsar, would you mingle eyes
With one that ties his points?   *A. C.* iii. 2.
  To say *ay,* and *no,* to every thing I said! Ay and no too,
was no good divinity.   *K. L.* iv. 6

SLEEP.

      The innocent sleep:
Sleep, that knits up the ravell'd sleave of care,
The death of each day's life, sore labour's bath,
Balm of hurt minds, great Nature's second course,
Chief nourisher in life's feast.   *M.* ii. 2
    Please you, Sir,
Do not omit the heavy offer of it:
It seldom visits sorrow; when it doth,
It is a comforter.   *T.* ii. 1.
     Weariness
Can snore upon the flint, when restive sloth
Finds the down pillow hard.   *Cym.* iii. 6
How many thousands of my poorest subjects
Are at this hour asleep! O sleep, O gentle sleep,
Nature's soft nurse, how have I frighted thee,
That thou no more wilt weigh mine eye-lids down,
And steep my senses in forgetfulness?
Why rather, sleep, liest thou in smoky cribs,
Upon uneasy pallets stretching thee,
And hush'd with buzzing night-flies, to thy slumber;
Than in the perfum'd chambers of the great,
Under the canopies of costly state,
And lull'd with sounds of sweetest melody?
O thou dull god, why liest thou with the vile,
In loathsome beds; and leav'st the kingly couch,
A watch-case, or a common 'larum bell?

SLEEP,—*continued.*
    Wilt thou, upon the high and giddy mast,
Seal up the ship-boy's eyes, and rock his brains,
In cradle of the rude imperious surge;
And in the visitation of the winds,
Who take the ruffian billows by the top,
Curling their monstrous heads, and hanging them
With deaf'ning clamours in the slippery clouds,
That, with the hurly, death itself awakes?
Canst thou, O partial sleep! give thy repose
To the wet sea-boy, in an hour so rude:
And, in the calmest, and most stillest night,
With all appliances and means to boot,
Deny it to a king? Then, happy low, lie down!
Uneasy lies the head that wears a crown.
                                  H. IV. PT. II. iii. 1.
The deep of night is crept upon our talk,
And Nature must obey necessity.   *J. Œ.* iv. 3.
Till o'er their brows death-counterfeiting sleep
With leaden legs and batty wings doth creep.   *M. N.* iii. 2.
Care keeps his watch in every old man's eye,
And where care lodges, sleep will never lie.   *R. J.* ii. 3.
To bed, to bed: Sleep kill those pretty eyes,
And give as soft attachment to thy senses,
As infants empty of all thought.   *T. C.* iv. 2.
           Fast asleep? It is no matter;
Enjoy the honey-heavy dew of slumber;
Thou hast no figures, nor no fantasies,
Which busy care draws in the brains of men;
Therefore thou sleep'st so sound.   *J.C.* ii. 1.
    Sleep, that sometimes shuts up sorrow's eye,
Steal me awhile from mine own company.   *M. N.* iii. 2.
So sorrow's heaviness doth heavier grow,
For debt that bankrupt sleep doth sorrow owe. *M. N.* iii. 2.
O sleep, thou ape of death, lie dull upon her. *Cym.* ii. 2.

SLOTH.
    What pleasure, Sir, find we in life, to lock it from action
and adventure?   *Cym.* iv. 4.
    Sleeping neglection doth betray to loss. *H. IV.* PT. I. iv. 3.

SMELL.
    What have we here? a man or a fish? Dead or alive?
A fish: he smells like a fish; a very antient and fish-like
smell.   *T.* ii. 2.
    Master Brook, there was the rankest compound of villanous smells, that ever offended nostril.   *M. W.* iii. 5.

SMILES.
When time shall serve, there shall be smiles. *H. V.* ii. 1.
Some, that smile, have in their hearts, I fear,
Millions of mischief. *J. C.* iv. 1.

———— AND TEARS.
Patience and sorrow strove
Who should express her goodliest. You have seen
Sunshine and rain at once: her smiles and tears
Were like a better day: Those happy smiles,
That play'd on her ripe lip, seem'd not to know
What guests were in her eyes; which parted thence,
As pearls from diamonds dropp'd. In brief, sorrow
Would be a rarity most belov'd, if all
Could so become it. *K. L.* iv. 3.

SMITTEN.
I am pepper'd, I warrant, for this world. *R. J.* iii. 1.

SMOOTHNESS.
Smooth as monumental alabaster. *O.* v. 2.

SNAIL.
Though he comes slowly, he carries his house on his head, and brings his destiny with him, his horns; he comes armed in his fortune, and prevents the slander of his wife. *A. Y.* iv. 1.

SNORING.
Thou dost snore distinctly;
There's meaning in thy snores. *T.* ii. 1.

SOCIETY.
Society is no comfort
To one not sociable. *Cym.* iv. 2.

SOLDIER.
A try'd and valiant soldier. *J. C.* iv. 1.
Soldiers should brook as little wrongs, as gods. *T. A.* iii. 5.
Consider this: He hath been bred i' the wars
Since he could draw a sword, and is ill-school'd
In boulted language; meal and bran together
He throws without distinction. *C.* iii. 3.
He that is truly dedicate to war, hath no self-love.
H. VI. pt. ii. v. 2.
Consider further,
That when he speaks not like a citizen,
You find him like a soldier: Do not take
His rougher accents for malicious sounds,
But, as I say, such as become a soldier. *C.* iii. 3.

SOLDIER,—*continued.*
The armipotent soldier. *A.W.* iv. 3
'Tis the soldiers' life
To have their balmy slumbers wak'd with strife. *O.* ii. 3
'Tis much he dares;
And, to the dauntless temper of his mind,
He hath a wisdom that doth guide his valour
To act in safety. *M.* iii. 1.

A braver soldier never couched lance,
A gentler heart did never sway in court. *H.VI.* PT. I. iii. 2.

I am a soldier; and unapt to weep,
Or to exclaim on fortune's fickleness. *H.VI.* PT. I. v. 3.

Fye, my lord, fye! a soldier and afraid? *M.* v. 1.
Trailest thou the puissant pike? *H.V.* iv. 1.

Go to the wars, would you? where a man may serve seven years for the loss of a leg, and have not money enough at the end to buy him a wooden one? *P.P.* iv. 6.

Faith, Sir, he has led the drum before the English tragedians,—to belie him I will not,—and more of his soldiership I know not; except, in that country, he had the honour to be the officer at a place there called Mile End, to instruct for the doubling of files: I would do the man what honour I can, but of this I am not certain. *A.W.* iv. 3.

All furnish'd, all in arms,
All plum'd like estridges that wing the wind;
Bated like eagles having lately bath'd;
Glittering in golden coats, like images;
As full of spirit as the month of May,
And gorgeous as the sun at midsummer;
Wanton as youthful goats, wild as young bulls.
H.IV. PT. I. iv. 1.

Tut, tut; good enough to toss; food for powder, food for powder; they'll find a pit as well as better.
H.IV. PT. I. iv. 2.

———————— IN LOVE.
I look'd upon her with a soldier's eye,
That lik'd, but had a rougher task in hand
Than to drive liking to the name of love:
But now I am return'd, and that war-thoughts
Have left their places vacant, in their rooms
Come thronging soft and delicate desires. *M.A.* i. 1.

May that soldier a mere recreant prove,
That means not, hath not, or is not in love *T.C.* i. 3.

SOLDIER'S DEATH.
Your son, my lord, has paid a soldier's debt:
He only liv'd but till he was a man;
The which no sooner had his prowess confirm'd,
In the unshrinking station where he fought,
But like a man he died. *M.* v. 7.

They say he parted well, and paid his score;
So God be with him, *M.* v. 7

        I pray you, bear me hence
From forth the noise and rumour of the field;
Where I may think the remnant of my thoughts
In peace, and part this body and my soul
With contemplation and devout desires. *K. J.* v. 5.

So underneath the belly of their steeds,
That stain'd their fetlocks in his smoking blood,
The noble gentleman gave up the ghost. *H. VI.* PT. III. ii. 3.

        Why then, God's soldier be he!
Had I as many sons as I have hairs,
I would not wish them to a fairer death:
And so his knell is knoll'd. *M.* v. 7.

SOLDIER, A PASSIVE INSTRUMENT.
        To be tender-minded
Does not become a sword:—Thy great employment
Will not bear question. *K. L.* v. 3.

It fits thee not to ask the reason why,
Because we bid it. *P. P.* i. 1.

———— UNPRACTISED.
That never set a squadron in the field,
Nor the division of a battle knows
More than a spinster. *O.* i. 1

        Mere prattle without pactice,
Is all his soldiership. *O.* i. 1

SOLICITATION.
        Frame yourself
To orderly solicits; and be friended
With aptness of the season. *Cym.* ii. 3.

SOLITUDE.
How use doth breed a habit in a man!
This shadowy desert, unfrequented woods,
I better brook than flourishing peopled towns:
Here can I sit alone, unseen of any,
And, to the nightingale's complaining notes,
Tune my distresses, and record my woes. *T. G.* v. 4.

Shakesperian Dictionary.

SOMNAMBULISM.
A great perturbation in nature, to receive at once the benefit of sleep, and to do the effects of watching. *M.* v. 1.

SONG.
I can suck melancholy out of a song, as a weasel sucks eggs: More, I pr'ythee, more. *A. Y.* ii. 5.

My mother had a maid call'd Barbara;
She was in love; and he she lov'd prov'd mad,
And did forsake her: she had a song of *Willow*,
An old thing 'twas, but it express'd her fortune,
And she died singing it. *O.* iv. 3.

                She bids you
Upon the wanton rushes lay you down,
And rest your gentle head upon her lap,
And she will sing the song that pleaseth you,
And on your eye-lids crown the god of sleep,
Charming your blood with pleasing heaviness,
Making such difference 'twixt wake and sleep,
As is the difference betwixt day and night,
The hour before the heavenly-harnessed team
Begins his golden progress in the east. *H. IV.* PT. I. iii. 1.

'Fore heaven, an excellent song. *O.* ii. 3.

Why, this is a more exquisite song than the other. *O.* ii. 3.

Now, good Cesario, but that piece of song.
That old and antique song we heard last night;
Methought it did relieve my passion much;
More than light airs and recollected terms,
Of these most brisk and giddy-paced times. *T. N.* ii. 4.

It hath been sung at festivals,
On ember eves and holy ales;
And lords and ladies of their lives
Have read it for restoratives. *P. P.* i. *chorus*.

Mark it, Cesario; it is old, and plain;
The spinsters, and the knitters in the sun,
And the free maids that weave their thread with bones,
Do use to chant it; it is silly sooth,
And dallies with the innocence of love,
Like the old age. *T. N.* ii. 4.

SONG, POPULAR.
No hearing, no feeling, but my Sir's song; and admiring the nothing of it. *W. T.* iv. 3.

There's scarce a maid westward but she sings it: 'tis in request, I can tell you. *W. T.* iv. 3.

SONG-BOOK.
I had rather than forty shillings, I had my book of songs
and sonnets here. *M. W.* i. 1.

SONGSTERS, NOCTURNAL.
Shall we rouse the night owl in a catch? *T. N.* ii. 3.

SORROW (See GRIEF, LAMENTATION, TEARS).
Sorrow breaks seasons, and reposing hours,
Makes the night morning, and the noon-tide night.
R. III. i. 4.
Go, count thy way with sighs;—I mine with groans.
R. II. v. 1
When sorrows come, they come, not single spies,
But in battalions. *H.* iv. 5.
One sorrow never comes, but brings an heir,
That may succeed as his inheritor. *P. P.* i. 4.
'Tis one of those odd tricks which sorrow shoots
Out of the mind. *A. C.* iv. 2.
       A cypress, not a bosom,
Hides my poor heart. *T. N.* iii. 1.
O, if you teach me to believe this sorrow,
Teach thou this sorrow how to make me die.
And let belief and life encounter so,
As doth the fury of two desperate men,
Which, in their very meeting, fall, and die. *K. J.* iii. 1.
How ill all's here about my heart! *H.* v. 2.

I will instruct my sorrows to be proud;
For grief is proud, and makes his owner stout.
To me, and to the state of my great grief,
Let kings assemble; for my grief's so great,
That no supporter but the huge firm earth
Can hold it up; here I and sorrow sit;
Here is my throne, bid kings come bow to it. *K. J.* iii. 1.
       Cure her of that:
Canst thou not minister to a mind diseas'd;
Pluck from the memory a rooted sorrow;
Raze out the written troubles of the brain;
And with some sweet oblivious antidote,
Cleanse the foul bosom of that perilous stuff,
Which weighs upon the heart? *M.* v. 3.
Impatience waiteth on true sorrow. *H. VI.* PT. III. iii. 3.
For gnarled sorrow hath less power to bite
The man that mocks at it, and sets it light. *R. II.* i. 3
Sorrow ends not when it seemeth done. *R. II.* i. 2

SORROW,—*continued.*
All strange and terrible events are welcome,
But comforts we despise; our size of sorrrow,
Proportion'd to our cause must be as great,
As that which makes it. *A. C.* iv. 13.

    Weep I cannot,
But my heart bleeds. *W. T.* iii. 3.

    This she delivered in the most bitter touch of sorrow, that e'er I heard virgin exclaim in. *A. W.* i. 3.

Down, thou climbing sorrow, thy element's below.
K. L. ii. 4.

But sorrow, that is couch'd in seeming gladness,
Is like that mirth fate turns to sudden sadness. *T. C.* i. 1.

    This sorrow's heavenly,
It strikes where it doth love. *O.* v. 2.

And now and then an ample tear trill'd down
Her delicate cheek; it seem'd, she was a queen
Over her passion; who, most rebel-like,
Sought to be king o'er her. *K. L.* iv. 3.

    Her nature became as a prey to her grief; in fine, made a groan of her last breath, and now she sings in heaven.
A. W. iv. 3.

——— PARENTAL.
    My grief
Stretches itself beyond the hour of death;
The blood weeps from my heart, when I do shape,
In forms imaginary, the unguided days,
And rotten times that you shall look upon
When I am sleeping with my ancestors. *H. IV.* PT. II. iv. 5.

——— MANLY.
    One, whose subdu'd eyes,
Albeit unused to the melting mood,
Drop tears as fast as the Arabian trees,
Their medicinal gum. *O.* v. 2

——— MOCKED.
These miseries are more than may be borne!
To weep with them that weep doth ease some deal,
But sorrow flouted at his double death. *Tit. And.* iii. 1.

——— UNCALLED FOR.
The tears live in an onion that should water this sorrow.
A. C. i. 2.

SOUL.
Though that be sick it dies not. *H. IV.* PT. II. ii. 2.

SOUL,—*continued.*
    Every subject's duty is the king's, but every subject's
soul is his own. *H. V.* iv. 1.
Mount, mount, my soul, thy seat is up on high. *R. II.* v. 5.
Were souls do couch on flowers, we'll hand in hand,
And with our sprightly sport, make the ghosts gaze.
A. C. iv. 12.
Since thou hast far to go, bear not along
.The clogging burden of a guilty soul. *R. II.* i. 3.
Swift-wing'd souls. *R. III.* ii. 3.

SOUR LOOKS.
    How tartly that gentleman looks! I never can see him
but I am heart-burned an hour after. *M. A.* ii. 1.

SPARE FIGURE.
He was the very genius of famine. *H. IV.* PT. II. iii. 4.
    You might have truss'd him, and all his apparel, into an
eel-skin; the case of a treble hautboy was a mansion for
him, a court; and now has he land and bees.
H. IV. PT. II. iii. 2.

SPEECH (See also RECITATION).
Before we proceed any further, hear me speak. *C.* i. 1.
His speech sticks in my heart. *A. C.* i. 5.
    I would be loath to cast away my speech; for, besides
that it is excellently well penn'd, I have taken great pains
to con it. *T. N.* i. 5.
            'Tis well said again;
And 'tis a kind of good deed, to say well:
And yet words are no deeds. *H. VIII.* iii. 2.
Spoke like a spriteful noble gentleman. *K. J.* iv. 2.

———— DISORDERED.
            And when he speaks
'Tis like a chime a mending; with terms unsquar'd,
Which, from the tongue of roaring Typhon dropt,
Would seem hyperboles. *T. C.* i. 3

SPEED.
O, I am scalded with my violent motion
And spleen of speed to see your majesty. *K. J.* v. 7.
Bloody with spurring; fiery red with haste. *R. II.* ii. 3.

SPIRITS (See also APPARITIONS, GHOSTS, ELVES, FAIRIES).
    Why, now I see there's mettle in thee; and even, from
this instant, do build on thee a better opinion than ever
before. *O.* iv. 2.

SPIRITS,—*continued.*
Forth at your eyes, your spirits wildly peep. *H.* iii. 4.
That gallant spirit hath aspir'd the clouds. *R. J.* iii. 1.
The spirit of the time shall teach me speed. *K. J.* iii. 4.

——— INFERNAL.
Black spirits and white,
Red spirits and grey;
Mingle, mingle, mingle,
You that mingle may. *M.* iv. 1.
Now, ye familiar spirits, that are cull'd
Out of the powerful regions under earth,
Help me this once. *H. VI.* PT. I. v. 3.
Glendower.—I can call spirits from the vasty deep.
Hotspur.—Why, so can I; or so can any man:
But will they come when you do call for them?
H. IV. PT. I. iii. 1.
Show his eyes, and grieve his heart;
Come like shadows, so depart. *M.* iv. 1.
Infected be the air whereon they ride,
And damn'd all those that trust them. *M.* iv. 1.

SPIRITING.
Pardon, master:
I will be correspondent to command,
And do my spiriting gently. *T.* i. 2.

SPITE.
'Sfoot, I'll learn to conjure and raise devils, but I'll see some issue of my spiteful execrations. *T. C.* ii. 3.

SPLEEN.
Out, you mad-headed ape!
A weasel hath not such a deal of spleen
As you are toss'd with. *H. IV.* PT. I. ii. 3.
With the spleen of all the under fiends. *C.* iv. 1.

SPLENDOR.
As gorgeous as the sun at midsummer. *H. IV.* PT. I. iv. 1.
It stuck upon him, as the sun
In the grey vault of heaven. *H. IV.* PT. II. ii. 3.

SPORT.
Sport royal, I warrant you. *T. N.* ii. 3.
Nay, I'll come; if I lose a scruple of this sport, let me be boiled to death with melancholy. *T. N.* ii. 5.
Very reverend sport, truly; and done in the testimony of a good conscience. *L. L.* iv. 2.

SPORT,—*continued.*
>That sport best pleases, that doth least know how:
>Where zeal strives to content, and the contents
>Die in the zeal of them which it presents,
>Their form confounded makes most form in mirth;
>When great things labouring perish in their birth.
>*L. L.* v. 2.

>It is admirable pleasures and fery honest knaveries.
>*M. W.* iv. 4.

>There's no such sport, as sport by sport o'erthrown:
>To make theirs ours, and ours none but our own:
>So shall we stay, mocking intended game,
>And they, well mock'd, depart away with shame.
>*L. L.* v. 2.

>I'll make one in a dance, or so; or I will play on the tabor to the worthies, and let them dance the hay. *L. L.* v. 1.

—— LADIES.
>Thus men may grow wiser every day! it is the first time that ever I heard, breaking of ribs was sport for ladies.
>*A. Y.* i. 2.

SPOT (See also BLOT, STAIN).
>With a spot I damn him. *J. C.* iv. 1.

SPRING.
>When daisies pied, and violets blue,
>And lady-smocks all silver-white,
>And cuckoo-buds of yellow hue,
> Do paint the meadows with delight,
>   The cuckoo then, on every tree,
>   Mocks married men, for thus sings he,
>   Cuckoo, cuckoo, cuckoo. O word of fear,
>   Unpleasing to a married ear!

>When shepherds pipe on oaten straws,
>And merry larks are ploughmen's clocks,
>When turtles tread, and rooks, and daws,
> And maidens bleach their summer smocks.
>   The cuckoo then, &c. *L. L.* v. 2.

>When well-apparell'd April on the heel
>Of limping winter treads. *R. J.* i. 2.

SPRING FLOWERS.
>   O Proserpina,
>For the flowers now, that, frighted, thou let'st fall
>From Dis's waggon! daffodils
>That come before the swallow dares, and take
>The winds of March with beauty; violets, dim,
>But sweeter than the lids of Juno's eyes,

Shakespearian Dictionary.

SPRING,—*continued.*
Or Cytherea's breath; pale primroses,
That die unmarried, ere they can behold
Bright Phœbus in his strength, a malady
Most incident to maids; bold oxlips, and
The crown imperial; lilies of all kinds,
The flower-de-luce being one. *W.T.* iv. 3.

STAIN (See also BLOT, SPOT).
Out, damned spot: out, I say. *M.* v. 1.
All the perfumes of Arabia will not sweaten this little hand.
M. v. 1.
      It doth confirm
Another stain, as big as hell can hold. *Cym.* ii. 4.
    The more fair and crystal is the sky,
The uglier seem the clouds that in it fly. *R. II.* i. 1.

STALKING.
    I shall stalk about her door,
Like a strange soul upon the Stygian banks,
Staying for waftage. *T.C.* iii. 2.

STARE.
Now he'll outstare the lightning. *A.C.* iii. 11.

STARS (See also PLANETARY INFLUENCE).
The stars above us govern our condition. *K.L.* iv. 3.
Diana's waiting women. *T.C.* v. 2.

STEALING.
Convey, the wise it call: Steal! foh; a fico for the phrase.
M.W. i. 3.

——————— AWAY.
      Therefore, to horse;
And let us not be dainty of leave-taking,
But shift away: There's warrant in that theft,
Which steals itself, when there's no mercy left. *M.* ii. 3.

STRANGE OCCURRENCE.
If this were played upon a stage now, I could condemn it
as an improbable fiction. *T.N.* iii. 4.

STRATAGEM.
Saint Dennis bless this happy stratagem.
H.VI. PT. I. iii. 2.

STRENGTH.
      O, it is excellent
To have a giant's strength; but it is tyrannous
To use it like a giant. *M.M.* ii. 2.

STRIPLINGS, Military.
    Worthy fellows; and like to prove most sinewy swordsmen.
                                                           A. W. ii. 1.

STRIKING.
    This cuff was but to knock at your ear, and beseech listening.   *T. S.* iv. 1.

STUDY (See also Light).
    Study is like the heaven's glorious sun,
      That will not be deep search'd with saucy looks;
    Small have continual plodders ever won,
      Save base authority, from others' books.   *L. L.* i. 1.

    Why, universal plodding prisons up
    The nimble spirits in the arteries;
    As motion, and long-during action, tires
    The sinewy vigour of the traveller.   *L. L.* iv. 3.

    So study evermore is overshot;
    While it doth study to have what it would,
    It doth forget to do the thing it should:
    And when it hath the thing it hunteth most,
    'Tis won, as towns with fire; so won, so lost.   *L. L.* i. 1.

    Biron.—What is the end of study?
    King.—Why, that to know, which else we should not know.
    Biron.—Things hid and barr'd, you mean, from common sense?
    King.—Ay, that is study's god-like recompense.
                                                            L.L. i. 1.

STUPEFACTION.
        I have drugg'd their possets
    That death and nature do contend about them
    Whether they live or die.   *M.* ii. 2.

        How runs the stream?
    Or I am mad, or else this is a dream.   *T. N.* iv. 1.

STYLE.
    Why, 'tis a boisterous and cruel style,
    A style for challengers.   *A. Y.* iv. 3.

SUBJECTION.
                Condition!
    What good condition can a treaty find
    I' the part that is at mercy?   *C.* i. 10.

    Why this it is, when men are rul'd by women.   *R. III.* i. 1.

SUB   Shakespearian Dictionary.   SUI

SUBMISSION.
    You shall be as a father to my youth;
My voice shall sound as you do prompt mine ear;
And I will stoop and humble my intents
To your well-practis'd, wise directions.   *H. IV.* PT. II. V. 2.
    My other self, my counsel's consistory,
My oracle, my prophet!—My dear cousin,
I, as a child, will go by thy directions.   *R. III.* ii. 2.

—————— TO THE LAWS.
               If the deed were ill,
Be you contented, wearing now the garland,
To have a son set your decrees at nought;
To pluck down justice from your awful bench;
To trip the course of law, and blunt the sword
That guards the peace and safety of your person:
Nay, more; to spurn at your most royal image,
And mock your workings in a second body.
Question your royal thoughts, make the case yours;
Be now the father, and propose a son:
Hear your own dignity so much profan'd;
See your most dreadful laws so loosely slighted,
Behold yourself so by a son disdain'd;
And then imagine me taking your part,
And, in your power, soft silencing your son.
                                      H.IV. PT. II. V. 2.

SUFFERANCE.
    Of sufferance comes ease.   *H. IV.* PT. II. V. 4.

SUFFERING, UNJUST.
               Upon such sacrifices, my Cordelia,
The gods themselves throw incense.   *K. L.* v. 3.
    Why should hard-favour'd grief be lodg'd in thee,
When triumph is become an ale-house guest?   *R. II.* v. 1.

SUICIDE (See also CONSCIENCE).
               Against self-slaughter
There is a prohibition so divine,
That cravens my weak hand.   *Cym.* iii. 4.
    To be, or not to be, that is the question:—
Whether 'tis nobler in the mind, to suffer
The stings and arrows of outrageous fortune;
Or, to take arms against a sea of troubles,
And, by opposing, end them? To die,—to sleep,—
No more;—and, by sleep, to say we end
The heart-ache, and the thousand natural shocks
That flesh is heir to,—'tis a consummation
Devoutly to be wish'd. To die;—to sleep;—

SUI   Shakesperian Dictionary.   SUI

SUICIDE,—*continued.*
   To sleep! perchance to dream; ay, there's the rub:
For in that sleep of death what dreams may come,
When we have shuffled off this mortal coil,
Must give us pause: there's the respect,
That makes calamity of so long life:
For who would bear the whips and scorns of time,
The oppressor's wrong, the proud man's contumely,
The pangs of despis'd love, the law's delay,
The insolence of office, and the spurns
That patient merit of the unworthy takes,
When he himself might his quietus make
With a bare bodkin? Who would fardels bear,
To groan and sweat under a weary life;
But that the dread of something after death,—
That undiscover'd country, from whose bourn
No traveller returns,—puzzles the will;
And makes us rather bear those ills we have,
Than fly to others, that we know not of?
Thus conscience does make cowards of us all;
And thus the native hue of resolution
Is sicklied o'er with the pale cast of thought;
And enterprises of great pith and moment,
With this regard their currents turn awry,
And lose the name of action.   *H.* iii. 1.

   Even by the rule of that philosophy,
By which I did blame Cato for the death
Which he did give himself:—I know not how,
But I do find it cowardly and vile,
For fear of what might fall, so to prevent
The time of life:—arming myself with patience,
To stay the providence of some high powers,
That govern us below.   *J.C.* v. 1

              He is dead:
Not by a public minister of justice,
Nor by a hired knife; but that self hand
Which writ his honour in the acts it did,
Hath, with the courage which the heart did lend it,
Splitted the heart.   *A.C.* v. 1.

           All's but naught;
Patience is sottish; and impatience does
Become a dog that's mad: Then is it sin,
To rush into the secret house of death,
Ere death dare come to us?   *A.C.* iv. 13.

   The more pity, that great folk should have countenance in this world to drown or hang themselves, more than their even Christian.   *H.* v. 1.

SUICIDE,—*continued.*
My desolation does begin to make
A better life: 'Tis paltry to be Cæsar;
Not being Fortune, he's but Fortune's knave,
A minister of her will: And it is great
To do that thing which ends all other deeds;
Which shackles accidents, and bolts up change.   *A. C.* v. 2.

Nor stony tower, nor walls of beaten brass,
Nor airless dungeon, nor strong links of iron,
Can be retentive to the strength of spirit;
But life, being weary of these worldly bars,
Never lacks power to dismiss itself.   *J. C.* i. 3.

    Every bondman in his own hand bears
The power to cancel his captivity.   *J. C.* i. 3.

SUN Setting.
The weary sun hath made a golden set,
And, by the bright track of his fiery car
Gives token of a goodly day to-morrow.   *R. III.* v. 3.

But even this night,—whose black contagious breath
Already smokes about the burning crest
Of the old, feeble, and day-wearied sun,—
Even this night your breathing shall expire.   *K. J.* v. 4.

SUPERFLUITY.
To gild refined gold, to paint the lily,
To throw a perfume on the violet,
To smooth the ice, or add another hue
Unto the rainbow, or with taper-light
To seek the beauteous eye of heaven to garnish,
Is wasteful and ridiculous excess.   *K. J.* iv. 2.

SUPERSCRIPTION.
To the snow-white hand of the most beautiful Lady Rosaline.
                                            L. L. iv. 2.

SUPERSTITION.
Look how the world's poor people are amaz'd
At apparitions, signs, and prodigies!   *Poems.*

The superstitious idle-headed eld
Receiv'd, and did deliver to our age,
This tale of Herne the hunter for a truth.   *M. W.* iv. 4.

SUPPLICATION.
A sea of melting pearl, which some call tears:
Those at her father's churlish feet she tender'd;
With them, upon her knees, her humble self,
Wringing her hands, whose whiteness so became them,
As if but now they waxed pale for woe.   *T. G.* iii. 1.

SURETYSHIP.
Is not this a lamentable thing, that of the skin of an innocent lamb should be made parchment? That parchment being scribbled o'er, should undo a man? Some say, the bee stings: but I say, 'tis the bee's wax: for I did but seal once to a thing, and I was never mine own man since.
H. VI. PT. II. iv. 2.

SURFEIT.
A surfeit of the sweetest things,
The deepest loathing to the stomach brings.   *M. N.* ii. 3.

SURGES.
The murmuring surge,
That on the unnumber'd idle pebbles chafes,
Cannot be heard so high.   *K. L.* iv. 6.

SURLY COUNTENANCE.
The image of a wicked heinous fault
Lives in his eye.   *K. J.* iv. 2.

SUSPICION.
Suspicion always haunts the guilty mind.
H. VI. PT. III. v. 6.

Indeed! ay, indeed: Discern'st thou aught in that?
Is he not honest?   *O.* iii. 3.

It is a damned ghost that we have seen;
And my imaginations are as foul
As Vulcan's stithy.   *H.* iii. 2.
Shall be all stuck full of eyes.   *H. IV.* PT. I. v. 2.

I, perchance, am vicious in my guess,
As, I confess, it is my nature's plague
To spy into abuses; and, oft, my jealousy
Shapes faults that are not.   *O.* iii. 3.
Foul whisperings are abroad.   *M.* v. 1.

SWEARING.
For it comes to pass oft, that a terrible oath, with a swaggering accent sharply twanged off, gives manhood more approbation than ever proof itself would have earned him.
T. N. iii. 4.

When a gentleman is disposed to swear, it is not for any standers by to curtail his oaths.   *Cym.* ii. 1.

And then a whoreson jackanapes must take me up for swearing; as if I borrowed mine oaths of him, and might not spend them at my pleasure.   *Cym.* ii. 1.

I'll swear upon that bottle to be thy true subject, for the liquor is not earthly.   *T.* ii. 2.

Shakespearian Dictionary.

SWEETNESS.
Your words, they rob the Hybla bees,
And leave them honeyless. *J.C.* v. 1.
Things sweet to taste, prove in digestion sour. *R. II.* i. 3.

SWIMMING.
I saw him beat the surges under him,
And ride upon their backs; he trod the water,
Whose enmity he flung aside, and breasted
The surge most swoln that met him; his bold head
'Bove the contentious waves he kept, and oar'd
Himself with his good arms in lusty stroke
To the shore, that o'er his wave-worn basis bow'd,
As stooping to relieve him; I not doubt,
He came alive to land. *T.* ii. 1.
    Upon the word,
Accoutred as I was, I plunged in,
And bade him follow: so, indeed, he did.
The torrent roared; and we did buffet it
With lusty sinews; throwing it aside
And stemming it with hearts of controversy. *J.C.* i. 2.

SWORD.
A sword employ'd is perilous. *T. C.* ii. 2.
I have a sword, and it shall bite upon necessity. *M.W.* ii. 1.

SWORDSMEN.
Bodykins, master Page, though I now be old, and of the peace, if I see a sword out, my finger itches to make one: though we are justices, and doctors, and churchmen, master Page, we have some salt of our youth in us. *M.W.* ii. 3.

SYMPATHY.
You are merry, and so am I; Ha! ha! then there's more sympathy: you love sack, and so do I;—would you desire better sympathy? *M.W.* ii. 1.

Grief best is pleas'd with grief's society.
True sorrow then is feelingly surpris'd
When with like feeling it is sympathis'd. *Poems.*
Companionship in woe, doth woe assuage. *Poems.*
Sweets with sweets war not; joy delights in joy. *Poems.*

    Ay, sooth; so humbled,
That he hath left part of his grief with me;
I suffer with him. *O.* iii. 3.

Mine eyes, even sociable to the show of thine,
Fall followly drops. *T.* v. 1.

SYMPATHY,—*continued.*
     O I have suffer'd
With those that I saw suffer! a brave vessel
(Which had, no doubt, some noble creatures in her)
Dash'd all to pieces. O, the cry did knock
Against my very heart! Poor souls! they perish'd.
              T. i. 2
     Was this a face
To be expos'd against the warring winds?
To stand against the deep, dread-bolted thunder?
              K. L. iv. 7.
     And wast thou fain, poor father,
To hovel thee with swine, and rogues forlorn,
In short and musty straw? Alack! Alack!
'Tis wonder, that thy life, and wits, at once
Had not concluded all.   *K. L.* iv. 7.
     All bless'd secrets,
All you unpublish'd virtues of the earth
Spring with my tears! be aidant, and remediate,
In the good man's distress.   *K. L.* iv. 4.
   The mind much sufferance doth o'er-skip,
When grief hath mates.   *K. L.* iii. 6.
     That I am wretched,
Makes thee the happier: Heavens, deal so still!
Let the superfluous, and lust-dieted man,
That slaves your ordinance, that will not see
Because he doth not feel, feel your power quickly;
So distribution should undo excess,
And each man have enough.   *K. L.* iv. 1.
    If sorrow can admit society
Tell o'er your woes again by viewing mine. *R. III.* iv. 4.
Poor naked wretches, wheresoe'er you are,
That bide the pelting of this pitiless storm,
How shall your houseless heads, and unfed sides,
Your loop'd and window'd raggedness, defend you
From seasons such as these? O, I have ta'en
Too little care of this! Take physic, pomp;
Expose thyself to feel what wretches feel;
That thou may'st shake the superflux to them,
And show the heavens more just. *K. L.* iii. 4.

T.

TABLE TALK.
    Pray thee, let it serve for table talk;
Then, howsoe'er thou speak'st, 'mong other things
I shall digest it.   *M. V.* iii. 5.

TAILOR.
    O, monstrous arrogance! Thou liest, thou thread,
Thou thimble.
Thou yard, three-quarters, half-yard, quarter, nail,
Thou flea, thou nit, thou winter cricket thou:—
Brav'd in mine own house with a skein of thread!
Away, thou rag, thou quantity, thou remnant:
Or I shall so be-mete thee with thy yard,
As thou shalt think on prating whilst thou liv'st!
I tell thee, I, thou hast marr'd her gown.   *T. S.* iv. 3.

TAINT.
          The dram of base
Doth all the noble substance often dout
To his own scandal.   *H.* i. 4.

TALE.
          I shall tell you
A pretty tale.   *C.* i. 1.
I will a round unvarnish'd tale deliver.   *O.* i. 3.
I'll to thy closet; and go read with thee
Sad stories, chanced in the times of old.   *Tit. And.* iii. 2.
      A sad tale's best for winter:
I have one of sprites and goblins.
    *   *   *   *   *
I will tell it softly; yon crickets
Shall not hear it.   *W. T.* ii. 1.
    But it is true,—without any slips of prolixity, or crossing
the plain highway of talk.   *M. V.* iii. 1.
An honest tale speeds best, being plainly told. *R. III.* iv. 4.
Mark how a plain tale shall put you down.
    H. IV. PT. I. ii. 4.

——— OF WOE
    Floods of tears will drown my oratory
And break my very utterance.   *Tit. And.* v. 3.
In winter's tedious nights sit by the fire
With good old folks; and let them tell thee tales
Of woeful ages, long ago betid;
And, ere thou bid good night, to quit their grief,

TAL   *Shakesperian Dictionary.*   TEA

TALE of Woe,—*continued.*
Tell them the lamentable fall of me,
And send the hearers weeping to their beds.   *R. II.* v. 1.

TALKER (See also Babbler).
Why, what a wasp-stung and impatient fool
Art thou, to break into this woman's mood;
Tying thine ear to no tongue but thine own! *H.IV.* pt. i. i. 3.

If you be not mad, be gone; if you have reason, be brief;
'tis not that time of the moon with me, to make one in so
skipping a dialogue.   *T. N.* i. 5.

A knave very voluble.   *O.* ii. 1.

TAPSTER.
Five years! by'r lady, a long lease for the clinking of
pewter.   *H. IV.* pt. i. ii. 4.

That ever this fellow should have fewer words than a
parrot, and yet the son of a woman! His industry is—up
stairs, and down stairs; and his eloquence, the parcel of a
reckoning.   *H. IV.* pt. i. ii. 4.

TAXATION.
We must not rend our subjects from our laws,
And stick them in our will. Sixth part of each?
A trembling contribution! Why, we take,
From every tree, lop, bark, and part o' the timber;
And, though we leave it with a root, thus hack'd,
The air will drink the sap.   *H. VIII.* i. 2.

Large-handed robbers your grave masters are,
And pill by law.   *T. A.* iv. 1.

By heaven, I had rather coin my heart,
And drop my blood by drachmas, than to wring
From the hard hands of peasants their vile trash,
By any indirection.   *J. C.* iv 3.

Come, there is no more tribute to be paid: our kingdom
is stronger than it was at that time; and, as I said, there
is no more such Cæsars: other of them may have crooked
noses; but, to owe such straight arms, none.   *Cym.* iii 1.

The commons hath he pill'd with grievous taxes,
And lost their hearts.   *R. II.* ii. 1.

If Cæsar can hide the sun from us with a blanket, or put
the moon in his pocket, we will pay him tribute for light.
   Cym. iii. 1.

TEARS (See also Grief, Lamentation, Sorrow).
Heaven-moving pearls.   *K. J.* ii. 1.

Let me wipe off this honourable dew,
That silverly doth progress on thy cheeks:

TEA   Shakesperian Dictionary.   TEA

TEARS,—*continued.*
My heart hath melted at a lady's tears,
Being an ordinary inundation;
But this effusion of such manly drops,
This shower, blown up by tempest of the soul,
Startles mine eyes, and makes me more amaz'd
Than had I seen the vaulty top of heaven
Figur'd quite o'er with burning meteors.   *K. J.* v. 2.

Silver-shedding tears.   *T. G.* iii. 1.

Those eyes of thine, from mine have drawn salt tears,
Sham'd their aspécts with store of childish drops.
R. III. i. 2.

My manly eyes did scorn an humble tear;
And what these sorrows could not thence exhale,
Thy beauty hath and made them blind with weeping.
R. III. i. 2.

Sad unhelpful tears.   *H. VI.* PT. II. iii. 1.

    I did not think to shed a tear
In all my miseries; but thou hast forc'd me,
Out of thy honest truth, to play the woman.   *H. VIII.* iii. 2.

And wet his grave with my repentant tears.   *R. III.* i. 2.

Thy heart is big; get thee apart and weep,
Passion, I see, is catching; for mine eyes,
Seeing those beads of sorrow stand in thine,
Begin to water.   *J. C.* iii. 1.

    See, see, what showers arise,
Blown with the windy tempest of my heart.
H. VI. PT. III. ii. 5.

The pretty and sweet manner of it forc'd
Those waters from me which I would have stopp'd;
But I had not so much of man in me,
But all my mother came into mine eyes,
And gave me up to tears.   *H. V.* iv. 6.

Raining the tears of lamentation.   *L. L.* v. 2.

    Friends, I owe more tears,
To this dead man, than you shall see me pay.   *J. C.* v. 3.

The best brine a maiden can season her praise in.
A. W. i. 1.

When I did name her brothers, then fresh tears
Stood on her cheeks; as doth the honey dew
Upon a gather'd lily almost wither'd.   *Tit. And.* iii. 1.

    And he, a marble to her tears, is washed by them, and
relents not.   *M. M.* iii. 1.

TEARS,—*continued.*
Trust not those cunning waters of his eyes,
For villany is not without such rheum;
And he, long traded in it, makes it seem
Like rivers of remorse and innocency. *K. J.* iv. 3.

——— OPTICAL ILLUSIONS OF.
Each substance of a grief hath twenty shadows,
Which show like grief itself, but are not so:
For sorrow's eye, glazed with blinding tears,
Divides one thing entire to many objects;
Like perspectives, which, rightly gaz'd upon,
Show nothing but confusion; ey'd awry,
Distinguish form: so your sweet majesty,
Looking awry upon your lord's departure,
Finds shapes of grief, more than himself, to wail;
Which, look'd on as it is, is nought but shadows
Of what is not. *R. II.* ii. 2.

Alas, poor man! grief hath so wrought on him,
He takes false shadows for true substances. *Tit. And.* iii. 2.

——— AND SIGHS.
The tide! Why, man, if the river were dry, I am able to fill it with my tears; if the wind were down, I could drive the boat with my sighs. *T. G.* ii. 3.

TEDIOUSNESS.
This will last out a night in Russia,
When nights are longest there: I'll take my leave,
And leave you to the hearing of the cause;
Hoping you'll find good cause to whip them all. *M. M.* ii. 1.

Neighbours, you are tedious. *M. A.* iii. 5.

But, truly, for mine own part, if I were as tedious as a king, I could find in my heart to bestow it all of your worship. *M. A.* iii. 5.

TEMPERANCE.
Ask God for temperance, that's the appliance only
Which your disease requires. *H. VIII.* i. 1.

TEMPERS.
Now, by two-headed Janus,
Nature hath form'd strange fellows in her time:
Some that will evermore peep through their eyes,
And laugh, like parrots, at a bagpiper;
And other of such vinegar aspect,
That they'll not show their teeth in way of smile,
Though Nestor swear the jest be laughable. *M. V.* i. 1.

Shakespearian Dictionary.

TEMPEST.

Methinks, the wind hath spoke aloud at land:
A fuller blast ne'er shook our battlements:
If it hath ruffian'd so upon the sea,
What ribs of oak, when mountains melt on them,
Can hold the mortise? *O.* ii. 1

The night has been unruly; where we lay,
Our chimneys were blown down: and, as they say,
Lamentings heard i' th' air:—some say the earth
Was feverous, and did shake. *M.* ii. 3.

     The wrathful skies
Gallow the very wanderers of the dark,
And make them keep their caves: since I was man,
Such sheets of fire, such bursts of horrid thunder,
Such groans of roaring wind and rain, I never
Remember to have heard. *K. L.* iii. 2.

Flam'd amazement. *T.* i. 2.

For do but stand upon the foaming shore,
The chiding billows seem to pelt the clouds;
The wind-shak'd surge, with high, and monstrous main,
Seems to cast water on the burning bear,
And quench the guards of the ever-fixed pole:
I never did like molestation view,
On the enchafed flood. *O.* ii. 1.

     The fire, and cracks
Of sulphurous roaring, the most mighty Neptune
Seem'd to besiege, and make his bold waves tremble,
Yea, his dread trident shake. *T.* i. 2.

Are not you mov'd, when all the sway of earth
Shakes, like a thing unfirm? O Cicero!
I have seen tempests, when the scolding winds
Have riv'd the knotty oaks; and I have seen
Th' ambitious ocean swell, and rage, and foam,
To be exalted with the threatening clouds;
But never till to night, never till now,
Did I go through a tempest dropping fire.
Either there is a civil strife in heaven;
Or else the world, too saucy with the gods,
Incenses them to send destruction. *J. C.* i. 3.

 I have seen two such sights, by sea, and by land;—but I am not to say, it is a sea, for it is now the sky; betwixt the firmament and it, you cannot thrust a bodkin's point.
W. T. iii. 3.

     Let the great gods
That keep this dreadful pother o'er our heads,
Find out their enemies now. Tremble, thou wretch,

Shakespearian Dictionary.

TEMPEST,—*continued.*
That hast within thee undivulged crimes,
Unwhipp'd of justice: Hide thee, thou bloody hand
That perjur'd, and thou simular man of virtue,
That art incestuous: Caitiff, to pieces shake,
That under covert and convenient seeming
Hast practis'd on man's life! Close pent-up guilts,
Rive your concealing continents, and cry
These dreadful summoners grace. I am a man,
More sinn'd against than sinning. *K. L.* iii. 2.

TEMPTATION.
There lurks a still and dumb-discoursive devil,
That tempts most cunningly. *T. C.* iv. 4.
'Tis one thing to be tempted, Escalus,
Another thing to fall. *M. M.* ii. 1.
     Most dangerous
Is that temptation, that doth goad us on
To sin in loving virtue. *M. M.* ii. 2.
Let but your honour know,
(Whom I believe to be most straight in virtue)
That, in the workings of your own affections,
Had time coher'd with place, or place with wishing,
Or that the resolute acting of your blood
Could have attain'd th' effect of your own purpose,
Whether you had not sometime in your life
Err'd in this point, which now you censure him,
And pull'd the law upon you. *M. M.* ii. 1.
 I am that way going to temptation,
Where prayers cross. *M. M.* ii. 2.
   Sometimes we are devils to ourselves,
When we will tempt the frailty of our powers,
Presuming on their changeful potency. *T. C.* iv. 4.

TERROR.
Alas! how is't with you?
That you do bend your eye on vacancy,
And with the incorporal air do hold discourse?
Forth at your eyes your spirits wildly peep,
And, as the sleeping soldiers in the alarm,
Your bedded hair, like life in excrements,
Starts up, and stands on end. *H.* iii. 4.
    Thrice he walk'd
By their oppress'd and fear suprised eyes,
Within his truncheon's length; whilst they, distill'd
Almost to jelly with the act of fear,
Stand dumb, and speak not to him. *H.* i. 2.

TERROR,—*continued.*
Take any shape but that, and my firm nerves
Shall never tremble.   *M.* iii. 3.

THANKS.
When a man thanks me heartily, methinks, I have given
him a penny, and he renders me the beggarly thanks.
A. Y. ii. 5.

        Often good turns
Are shuffled off with such uncurrent pay:
But, were my worth, as is my conscience, firm,
You should find better dealing.   *T. N.* iii. 3.
Evermore thanks, the exchequer of the poor;
Which, till my infant fortune come to years,
Stands for my bounty.   *R. II.* ii. 2.

THEME.
It would be argument for a week, laughter for a month,
and a good jest for ever.   *H. IV.* PT. I. ii. 2.

THIEF, THIEVERY.
He will steal, Sir, an egg out of a cloister.   *A. W.* iv. 3.
What simple thief brags of his own attaint?   *C. E.* iii. 2.
A plague upon't, when thieves cannot be true to one another!
H. IV. PT. I. ii. 2.

        Yet thanks I must you con,
That you are thieves profest; that you work not
In holier shapes: for there is boundless theft
In limited professions.   *T. A.* iv. 3.
        Rascal thieves,
Here's gold: Go, suck the subtle blood of the grape,
Till the high fever seeth your blood to froth,
And so 'scape hanging: trust not the physician;
His antidotes are poison, and he slays
More than you rob: take wealth and lives together;
Do villany, do, since you profess to do't,
Like workmen. I'll example you with thievery:
The sun's a thief, and with his great attraction
Robs the vast sea; the moon's an arrant thief,
And her pale fire she snatches from the sun:
The sea's a thief, whose liquid surge resolves
The moon into salt tears: the earth's a thief,
That feeds and breeds by a composture stolen
From general excrement: each thing's a thief,
The law's your curb and whip, in their rough power
Have uncheck'd theft. Love not yourselves; away;
Rob one another. There's more gold: Cut throats;
All that you meet are thieves: To Athens, go,

THIEF,—*continued.*
Break shops; nothing can you steal,
But thieves do lose it.   *T. A.* iv. 3.
            Master, be one of them;
It is an honourable kind of thievery.   *T.G.* iv. 1.

THORNY POINT.
O, that way madness lies; let me shun that;
No more of that.   *K. L.* iii. 4.

THOUGHT.
In the quick forge and working house of thought.
                                                                         H.V. v. *chorus.*

                Jumping o'er times;
Turning the accomplishment of many years
Into an hour-glass.   *H.V.* i. *chorus*
Sky-aspiring and ambitious thoughts.   *R. II.* i. 3.
A generation of still-breeding thoughts,
And these same thoughts people this little world;
In humours, like the people of this world,
For no thought is contented.   *R. II.* v. 5.

THOUGHTFULNESS.
Why, he stalks up and down like a peacock, a stride and a stand; ruminates, like an hostess that hath no arithmetic but her brain to set down her reckoning; bites his lip with a politic regard, as who should say,—there were wit in his head, an 'twould out; and so there is; but it lies as coldly in him as fire in a flint, which will not show without knocking.
                                                                            T.C. iii. 3.

                  My lord, we have
Stood here observing him; some strange commotion
Is in his brain; he bites his lip, and starts;
Stops on a sudden, looks upon the ground,
Then lays his finger on his temple; straight,
Springs out into fast gait, then, stops again,
Strikes his breast hard; and anon, he casts
His eye against the moon; in most strange postures
We have seen him set himself.   *H.VIII.* iii. 2
There is a mutiny in his mind.   *H.VIII.* iii. 2

THREAT.
Unmanner'd dog! stand thou when I command:
Advance thy halberd higher than my breast,
Or, by St. Paul, I'll strike tnee to my foot,
And spurn upon thee, beggar, for thy boldness. *R. III.* i. 2.
                Priest, beware your beard;
I mean to tug it, and to cuff you soundly:

Shakesperian Dictionary.

THREAT,—*continued.*

Under my feet I stamp thy cardinal's hat;
In spite of pope or dignities of church,
Here by the cheeks I'll drag thee up and down.
H. VI. PT. I. i. 2.

Unhand me, gentlemen;—
By heaven, I'll make a ghost of him that lets me. *H.* i. 4.

What say you? Hence,
Horrible villain! or I'll spurn thine eyes
Like balls before me; I'll unhair thy head;
Thou shalt be whipp'd with wire, and stew'd in brine,
Smarting in ling'ring pickle. *A. C.* ii. 5.

Therefore hence, begone:—
But if thou, jealous, dost return to pry
In what I further shall intend to do,
By heaven, I will tear thee, joint by joint,
And strew this hungry church-yard with thy limbs:
The time and my intents are savage wild;
More fierce, and more inexorable far,
Than empty tigers, or the roaring sea. *R. J.* v. 3.

By my soul,
Your long coat, priest, protects you; thou shoulds't feel
My sword i' the blood of thee else.—My lords,
Can ye endure to hear this arrogance?—
And from this fellow? *H. VIII.* iii. 2.

Why, how now, ho! from whence ariseth this?
Are we turn'd Turks; and to ourselves do that
Which heaven hath forbid the Ottomites?
For Christian shame, put by this barbarous brawl:
He that stirs next to carve for his own rage,
Holds his soul light; he dies upon his motion. *O.* ii. 3.

For your partaker, Poole, and you yourself,
I'll note you in my book of memory,
To scourge you for this apprehension.
Look to it well; and say you are well warn'd.
H. VI. PT. I. ii. 4.

That roars so loud and thunders in the index. *H.* iii. 4.

If thou neglect'st, or dost unwillingly
What I command, I'll rack thee with old cramps:
Fill all thy bones with achés, make thee roar,
That beasts shall tremble at thy din. *T.* i. 2.

And he that throws not up his cap for joy,
Shall for the fault make forfeit of his head.
H. VI. PT. III. ii. 1.

THREAT,—*continued.*
    If thou more murmur'st, I will rend an oak,
    And peg thee in his knotty entrails, till
    Thou hast howl'd away twelve winters.   *T.* i. 2.
    Well, go, muster men. But, hear you, leave behind
    Your son, George Stanley: look your heart be firm,
    Or else his head's assurance is but frail.   *R. III.* iv. 4.

THRIFT.
    This was a way to thrive, and he was blest;
    And thrift is blessing, if men steal it not.   *M. V.* i. 3.

THUNDER (See TEMPEST).

TIME (See also LIFE, MAN).
    I,—that please some, try all; both joy, and terror,
    Of good and bad; that make, and unfold error.
                                   W. T. iv. *chorus.*
    Cormorant devouring time.   *L. L.* i. 1.
    What's past, and what's to come, is strew'd with husks,
    And formless ruin of oblivion.   *T. C.* iv. 5.
                  Let me pass:—
    The same I am, ere antient order was,
    Or what is now receiv'd. I witness to
    The times that brought them in; so shall I do
    To the freshest things now reigning, and make stale
    The glistering of this present.   *W. T.* iv. *chorus.*
                 Beauty, wit,
    High birth, vigour of bone, desert in service,
    Love, friendship, charity, are subjects all
    To envious and calumniating time.   *T. C.* iii. 3.
              Come what come may,
    Time and the hour run through the roughest day. *M.* i. 3.
              It is in my power
    To o'erthrow law, and in one self-born hour,
    To plant and o'erwhelm custom.   *W. T.* iv. *chorus.*
    What's past is prologue.   *T.* ii. 1.
    Well, thus we play the fools with the time; and the
    spirits of the wise sit in the clouds and mock us.
                                 H. IV. PT. II. ii. 2.
    Let's take the instant by the forward top;
    For we are old, and on our quick'st decrees
    The inaudible and noiseless foot of time
    Steals ere we can effect them.   *A. W.* v. 3.
              It is ten o'clock;
    Thus may we see, quoth he, how the world wags:

TIME,—*continued.*
'Tis but an hour ago, since it was nine;
And after an hour more, 'twill be eleven;
And so, from hour to hour, we ripe and ripe,
And then, from hour to hour, we rot, and rot,
And thereby hangs a tale. *A. Y.* ii. 7.

O, the mad days that I have spent! and to see how many of mine old acquaintance are dead! *H. IV.* PT. II. iii. 2.

Time travels in divers paces with divers persons. He ambles with a priest that lacks Latin, and a rich man that hath not the gout: for the one sleeps easily, because he cannot study; and the other lives merrily, because he feels no pain: the one lacking the burden of lean and wasteful learning; the other knowing no burden of heavy tedious penury: These time ambles withal. He trots hard with a young maid, between the contract of her marriage, and the day it is solemnized: if the interim be but a se'nnight, time's pace is so hard, that it seems the length of seven years. He gallops with a thief to the gallows: for though he goes as softly as foot can fall, he thinks himself too soon there. He stays still with lawyers in the vacation: for they sleep between term and term, and then they perceive not how time moves. *A. Y.* iii 2.

She should have died hereafter;
There would have been a time for such a word.—
To-morrow, and to-morrow, and to-morrow,
Creeps in this petty pace from day to day,
To the last syllable of recorded time;
And all our yesterdays have lighted fools
The way to dusty death. Out, out, brief candle!
Life's but a walking shadow; a poor player,
That struts and frets his hour upon the stage,
And then is heard no more: it is a tale
Told by an idiot, full of sound and fury
Signifying nothing. *M.* v 5.

Time, that takes survey of all the world,
Must have a stop. *H. IV.* PT. I. v. 4.

Gallop apace, you fiery-footed steeds,
Towards Phœbus' mansion; such a waggoner
As Phaeton would whip you to the west,
And bring in cloudy night immediately. *R. J.* iii. 2.

Men must endure
Their going hence, even as their coming hither:
Ripeness is all. *K. L.* v. 2.

The extreme parts of time extremely form
All causes to the purpose of his speed;

375

TIME,—*continued.*
 And often, at his very loose, decides
That which long process could not arbitrate. *L. L.* v. 2.
Time shall unfold what plaited cunning hides. *K. L.* i. 1.
Old Time, the clock setter, that bald sexton, Time,
Is it as he will? *K. J.* iii. 1.
We are Time's subjects, and Time bids be gone.
          H. IV. PT. II. i. 3.
    Time is like a fashionable host,
That slightly shakes his parting guest by the hand;
And with his arms out-stretch'd, as he would fly,
Grasps in the corner: welcome ever smiles,
And farewell goes out sighing. *T. C.* iii. 3.
 Time is a very bankrupt, and owes more than he's worth
to season. *C. E.* iv. 2.
The clock upbraids me with the waste of time. *T. N.* iii. 1.
     How sour sweet music is
When time is broke, and no proportion kept!
So is it in the music of our lives. *R. II.* v. 5.

—— AND DECAY.
 The wrinkles which thy glass will truly show,
  Of mouthed graves will give thee memory,
Thou by thy dial's shady stealth maiest know,
  Time's thievish progress to eternity. *Poems.*
Not know my voice! O, time's extremity!
Hast thou so crack'd and splitted my poor tongue,
In seven short years, that here my only son
Knows not my feeble key of untun'd cares?
Though now this grained face of mine be hid
In sap-consuming winter's drizzled snow,
And all the conduits of my blood froze up;
Yet hath my night of life some memory,
My wasting lamp some fading glimmer left,
My dull deaf ears a little use to hear. *C. E.* v. 1.
I wasted time, and now doth time waste me. *R. II.* v. 5.
Oh, grief hath chang'd me since you saw me last,
And careful hours, with Time's deformed hand
Have written strange defeatures in my face. *C. E.* v. 1.

TIME SERVER.
 Sirrah, thou art said to have a stubborn soul,
That apprehends no farther than this world,
And squar'st thy life according. *M. M.* v. 1.
 The devil a puritan is he, or any thing constantly, but a
time-pleaser. *T. N.* ii. 3.

TIM   **Shakespearian Dictionary.**   TOO

TIME TRIES OFFENDERS.
Well, Time is the old justice that examines all such offenders, and let Time try.   *A. Y.* iv. 1.

TIMIDITY.
O, I could divide myself and go to buffets, for moving such a dish of skimm'd milk with so honourable an action!
                                               H. IV. PT. I. ii. 3.

Such a commodity of warm slaves, as had as lief hear the devil as a drum.   *H. IV.* PT. I. iv. 2.

TIMON'S GRAVE.
Timon hath made his everlasting mansion
Upon the beached verge of the salt flood;
Which, once a day with his embossed froth,
The turbulent surge shall cover; thither come,
And let my grave-stone be your oracle.   *T. A.* v. 3.

TITLES (See also HONOUR).
             That is honour's scorn,
Which challenges itself as honour's born,
And is not like the sire: Honours thrive,
When rather from our acts we them derive
Than our foregoers.   *A. W.* ii. 3.

Here's a silly stately style indeed!
The Turk, that two-and-fifty kingdoms hath,
Writes not such a tedious style as this:—
Him, that thou magnifiest with all those titles,
Stinking, and fly-blown, lies here at our feet.
                                        H. VI. PT. I. iv. 7.

TONGUE.
Many a man's tongue shakes out his master's undoing.
                                               A. W. ii. 4.
Be not thy tongue thy own shame's orator.   *C. E.* iii. 2.
My tongue, though not my heart, shall have his will.
                                                 C. E. iv. 2.

These fellows of infinite tongue, that can rhyme themselves into ladies' favours,—they do always reason themselves out again.   *H. V.* v. 2.

TOOL (See also PIPING).
It is a creature that I teach to fight,
To wind, to stop, to run directly on;
His corporal motion govern'd by my spirit.
And, in some taste, is Lepidus but so;
He must be taught, and train'd, and bid go forth;
A barren-spirited fellow; one that feeds
On objects, arts, and imitations;

TOOL,—*continued.*
Which, out of use, and stal'd by other men,
Begin his fashion: Do not talk of him,
But as a property.   *J. C.* iv. 1.
This is a slight unmeritable man,
Meet to be sent on errands.   *J. C.* iv. 1.
Octavius, I have seen more days than you;
And though we lay these honours on this man,
To ease ourselves of divers slanderous loads,
He shall but bear them as the ass bears gold:
To groan and sweat under the business,
Either led or driven, as we point the way;
And having brought our treasure where we will,
Then take we down his load, and turn him off,
Like to the empty ass, to shake his ears,
And graze in commons.   *J. C.* iv. 1.

             For all the rest,
They'll take suggestion, as a cat laps milk;
They'll tell the clock to any business that
We say befits the hour.   *T.* ii. 1.

TOUCH.
I will touch thee but with reverent hands. *H. VI.* PT. I. v. 3

TOWERS.
Air-braving towers.   *H. VI.* PT. I. iv. 2.

TRADES.
There's boundless theft in limited professions.   *T. A.* iv. 3.

TRAGEDIAN.
For I must talk of murders, rapes, and massacres,
Acts of black night, abominable deeds,
Complots of mischief, treason; villanies
Ruthful to hear, yet piteously perform'd.   *Tit. And.* v. 1.

   Begin, murderer;—leave thy damnable faces, and begin.
                                                              H. iii. 2.
What scene of death hath Roscius now to act?
                                                 H. VI. PT. III. v. 6.

TRAITOR
A kissing traitor.   *L. L.* v. 2.
To say the truth, so Judas kiss'd his master;
And cried—all hail! when as he meant—all harm.
                                                 H. VI. PT. III. v. 7.

             I protest,
Maugre thy strength, youth, place, and eminence,
Despite thy victor sword, and fire-new fortune,

TRAITOR,—*continued.*
Thy valour, and thy heart,—thou art a traitor:
False to thy gods, thy brother, and thy father;
Conspirant 'gainst this high illustrious prince;
And from the extremest upward of thy head,
To the descent and dust beneath thy feet,
A most toad-spotted traitor. *K. L.* v. 3.

  Some of you, with Pilate, wash your hands,
Showing an outward pity; yet you Pilates
Have here deliver'd me to my sour cross,
And water cannot wash away your sin. *R. II.* iv. 1.
O, passing traitor, perjur'd, and unjust. *H. VI.* PT. III. v. 1.
A giant traitor. *H. VIII.* i. 2.
  Thus do all traitors:
If their purgation did consist in words,
They are as innocent as grace itself. *A. Y.* i. 3.
  Though those that are betray'd
Do feel the treason sharply, yet the traitor
Stands in worse case of woe. *Cym.* iii. 4.

But cruel are the times, when we are traitors,
And do not know ourselves; when we hold rumour
From what we fear, yet know not what we fear;
But float upon a wild and violent sea,
Each way. *M.* iv. 2.
  Oh, let me live,
And all the secrets of our camp I'll show. *A. W.* iv. 1.

TRANSLATING.
  He hath studied her well, and translated her well; out of honesty into English. *M. W.* i. 3.

TRAP.
  Now is the woodcock near the gin. *T. N.* ii. 5.

TRAVELLING (See also HOME-BREEDING).
All places that the eye of heaven visits,
Are to the wise man ports and happy havens. *R. II.* i. 3
Home-keeping youth have ever homely wits
Wer't not affection chains thy tender days
To the sweet glances of thy honour'd love,
I rather would entreat thy company,
To see the wonders of the world abroad,
Than, living dully sluggardis'd at home,
Wear out thy youth with shapeless idleness. *T. G.* i. 1.
  I had rather have a fool to make me merry, than experience to make me sad; and to travel for it too. *A. Y.* iv. 1.

TRAVELLING,—*continued.*

A traveller! By my faith you have great reason to be sad: I fear, you have sold your own lands, to see other men's; then, to have seen much, and to have nothing, is to have rich eyes and poor hands. *A. Y.* iv. 1.

Thou didst make tolerable vent of thy travel. *A. W.* ii. 3.

Travellers ne'er did lie,
Though fools at home condemn them. *T.* iii. 3.

Farewell, monsieur traveller; Look, you lisp, and wear strange suits; disable all the benefits of your own country; be out of love with your nativity, and almost chide God for making you that countenance you are; or I will scarce think you have swam in a gondola. *A. Y.* iv. 1.

They have all hew legs, and lame ones; one would take it, That never saw them pace before, the spavin,
A spring-halt reign'd among them. *H. VIII.* i. 3.

As far as I see, all the good our English
Have got by the late voyage, is but merely
A fit or two o' the face; but they are shrewd ones;
For when they hold them, you would swear directly
Their very noses had been counsellors
To Pepin, or Clotharius, they keep state so. *H. VIII.* i. 3.

He did request me to importune you,
To let him spend his time no more at home,
Which would be great impeachment to his age,
In having known no travel in his youth. *T. G.* i. 3.

Ay, now am I in Arden: the more fool I; when I was at home, I was in a better place; but travellers must be content. *A. Y.* ii. 4.

Types of travel. *H. VIII.* i. 3.

TREACHERY.
O monstrous treachery! Can this be so;
That in alliance, amity, and oaths,
There should be found such false dissembling guile?
H. VI. PT. I. iv. 2.

As a wood-cock to my own springe, Osrick,
I am justly kill'd with mine own treachery. *H.* v. 2.

TREASON.
Suspicion shall be all stuck full of eyes:
For treason is but trusted like the fox;
Who, ne'er so tame, so cherish'd, and lock'd up,
Will have a wild trick of his ancestors.
Look how we can, or sad, or merrily,
Interpretation will misquote our looks;

TREASON,—*continued.*
And we shall feed like oxen at a stall,
The better cherish'd still the nearer death.
H. IV. PT. I. v. 2.
Some treason, masters; yet stand close. *M. A.* iii. 3.

TREPIDATION.
She does so blush, and fetches her wind so short, as if she was frayed with a sprite: I'll fetch her. It is the prettiest villain :—She fetches her breath as short as a new ta'en sparrow. *T. C.* iii. 2.

TRIALS.
Withhold thine indignation, mighty heaven,
And tempt us not to bear above our power! *K. J.* v. 6.

TRIAL-FIRE.
With trial-fire touch me his finger-end;
If he be chaste, the flame will back descend,
And turn him to no pain; but if he start,
It is the flesh of a corrupted heart. *M. W:* v. 5.

TRICKS.
My master hath been an honourable gentleman, tricks he hath had in him, as gentlemen have. *A. W.* v. 3.

Well; if I be served such another trick, I'll have my brains ta'en out, and buttered, and give them to a dog for a new year's gift. *M. W.* iii. 5.

TRIFLING, ILL-TIMED.
All solemn things
Should answer solemn accidents. The matter?
Triumphs for nothing, and lamenting toys,
Is jollity for apes, and grief for boys. *Cym.* iv. 2.
Pr'ythee, have done;
And do not play in wench-like words with that
Which is so serious. *Cym.* iv. 2.

TRINKETS.
Immoment toys, things of such dignity
As we greet modern friends withal. *A. C.* v. 2.

TROUBLES.
O, how full of briers is this working-day world! *A. Y.* i. 3.

As flies to wanton boys are we to the gods;
They kill us for their sport. *K. L.* iv. 1.

Thou seest we are not all alone unhappy;
This wide and universal theatre
Presents more woeful pageants than the scene
Wherein we play. *A. Y.* ii. 7.

TRUANT.
Myself have been an idle truant,
Omitting the sweet benefit of time,
To clothe mine age with angel-like perfection. *T.G.* ii. 4.

TRUMPET.
Trumpet, blow loud;
Send thy brass voice through all these lazy tents. *T.C.* i. 3.
Make all our trumpets speak; give them all breath;
Those clamorous harbingers of blood and death. *M.* v. 6.
Go to the rude ribs of that antient castle;
Through brazen trumpet send the breath of parle
Into his ruin'd ears, and thus deliver. *R. II.* iii. 3.
Give, with thy trumpet, a loud note to Troy,
Thou dreadful Ajax; that the apalled air
May pierce the head of the great combatant,
And hale him thither. *T.C.* iv. 5.
Thou, trumpet, there's my purse.
Now crack thy lungs, and split thy brazen pipe:
Blow, villain, till thy sphered bias cheek
Out-swell the cholic of puff'd Aquilon:
Come, stretch thy chest, and let thy eyes spout blood:
Thou blow'st for Hector.
T. C. iv. 5.
Trumpeters,
With brazen din, blast you the city's ear;
Make mingle with our rattling tabourines;
That heaven and earth may strike their sounds together,
Applauding our approach. *A.C.* iv. 8.
Sound, trumpets! Let our bloody colours wave!
And either victory, or else a grave. *H.VI.* PT. III. ii. 2.

TRUST.
Antony
Did tell me of you, bade me trust you; but
I do not greatly care to be deceiv'd,
That have no use for trusting. *A.C.* v. 2.

TRUTH.
Truth is truth
To the end of reckoning. *M. M.* v. 1.
Truth needs no colour,—beauty no pencil. *Poems.*
Alas, it is my vice, my fault:
While others fish with craft for great opinion,
I with great truth catch mere simplicity. *T.C.* iv. 4.
Tell truth, and shame the devil.
If thou have power to raise him, bring him hither,

TRUTH,—*continued.*
And I'll be sworn, I have power to shame him hence.
O, while you live, tell truth, and shame the devil.
H. IV. PT. I. iii. 1.
Hence, thou suborn'd informer! a true soul,
When most impeach't, stands least in thy controul. *Poems.*
If circumstances lead me, I will find
Where truth is hid, though it were hid indeed
Within the centre. *H.* ii. 2.
    Pr'ythee speak;
Falseness cannot come from thee, for thou look'st
Modest as justice, and thou seem'st a palace
For the crown'd truth to dwell in: I'll believe thee,
And make my senses credit thy relation,
To points that seem impossible; for thou look'st
Like one I lov'd indeed. *P. P.* v. 1.
I am as true as truth's simplicity,
And simpler than the infancy of truth. *T. C.* iii. 2.
Methinks, the truth should live from age to age,
As 'twere retail'd to all posterity,
Even to the general all-ending day. *R. III.* iii. 1.
    Never man
Sigh'd truer breath. *C.* iv. 5.
Truth loves open dealing. *H. VIII.* iii. 1.
    Would, half my wealth
Would buy this for a lie. *C.* iv. 6.
What, can the devil speak true *M.* i. 3.
That truth should be silent, I had almost forgot. *A. C.* ii. 2
 Truth's a dog that must to kennel: he must be whipped
out, when Lady the brach, may stand by the fire and stink.
K. L. i. 4.

— ——— AN UNWELCOME, RARELY TOLD.
Life-loving sick men, when their deaths are near,
No news but health from their physicians know. *Poems.*

·TYRANT.
    Our country sinks beneath the yoke;
It weeps, it bleeds; and each new day a gash
Is added to her wounds *M* iv. 3.
    I grant him bloody,
Luxurious, avaricious, false, deceitful,
Sudden, malicious, smacking of every sin
That has a name. *M.* iv. 3.
    He would
Have made them mules, silenc'd their pleaders, and

TYRANT,—continued.

Dispropertied their freedoms; holding them,
In human action and capacity,
Of no more soul, nor fitness for the world,
Than camels in their war; who have their provand
Only for bearing burdens, and sore blows
For sinking under them.   *C.* ii. 1.

Upon thy eye-balls murd'rous tyranny
Sits in grim majesty to fright the world. *H. VI.* PT. II. iii. 3.

   Bleed, bleed poor country!
Great tyranny, lay thou thy basis sure,
For goodness dares not check thee! wear thou thy wrongs,
Thy title is affeer'd.   *M.* iv. 3.

For what is he they follow? truly, gentlemen,
A bloody tyrant, and a homicide;
One rais'd in blood, and one in blood establish'd;
One that made means to come by what he hath,
And slaughter'd those that were the means to help him;
A base foul stone, made precious by the foil
Of England's chair, where he is falsely set,
One that hath ever been God's enemy:
Then, if you fight against God's enemy,
God will, in justice, ward you as his soldiers. *R. III.* v. 3.

   I'll not call you tyrant;
But this most cruel usage of your queen
(Not able to produce more accusation
Than your own weak-hing'd fancy,) something savours
Of tyranny, and will ignoble make you,
Yea, scandalous to the world.   *W. T.* ii.

Till now you have gone on, and fill'd the time
With all licentious measure, making your wills
The scope of justice; till now, myself, and such
As slept within the shadow of your power,
Have wander'd with our travers'd arms, and breath'd
Our sufferance vainly.   *T. A.* v. 5.

And why should Cæsar be a tyrant then?
Poor man! I know he would not be a wolf,
But that he sees the Romans are but sheep;
He were no lion, were not Romans hinds.
Those that with haste would make a migthy fire,
Begin it with weak straws: What trash is Rome,
What rubbish, and what offal, when it serves,
For the base matter to illuminate
So vile a thing as Cæsar?   *J. C.* i. 3.

This tyrant, whose sole name blisters our tongues.
Was once thought honest.   *M.* iv. 3.

TYR   *Shakesperian Dictionary.*   VAL

TYRANT,—*continued.*
                 His demand
Springs not from Edward's well-meant honest love,
But from deceit, bred by necessity;
For how can tyrants safely govern home,
Unless abroad they purchase great alliance?
H. VI. PT. III. iii. 3.
         O nation miserable,
With an untitled tyrant, bloody scepter'd,
When shalt thou see thy wholesome days again?   *M.* iv. 3.
Then live to be the show and gaze o' the time;
We'll have thee, as our rarer monsters are,
Painted upon a pole; and under writ,
Here may you see the tyrant.   *M.* v. 7.
'Tis time to fear, when tyrants seem to kiss.   *P. P.* i. 2.
         Tyrants' fears
Decrease not, but grow faster with their years.   *P. P.* i. 2.
Those he commands, move only in command,
Nothing in love.   *M.* v. 2.

U. U.

VACANCY.
                 The city cast
Her people out upon her, and Antony,
Enthroned in the market-place, did sit alone,
Whistling to the air; which, but for vacancy,
Had gone to gaze on Cleopatra too,
And made a gap in nature.   *A. C.* ii. 2.

VALOUR (See also COURAGE).
He's truly valiant, that can wisely suffer
The worst that man can breathe; and make his wrongs
His outsides; wear them, like his raiment, carelessly;
And ne'er prefer his injuries to his heart,
To bring it into danger.   *T. A.* iii. 5.
Here, there, and every where, he leaves and takes;
Dexterity so obeying appetite,
That what he will, he does; and does so much,
That proof is call'd impossibility.   *T. C.* v. 5.
Engaging and redeeming of himself,
With such a careless force, and forceless care,
As if that luck, in very spite of cunning,
Bade him win all.   *T. C.* v. 5.
                  It is held,
That valour is the chiefest virtue, and

VALOUR,—*continued.*

Most dignifies the haver: if it be,
The man I speak of cannot in the world
Be singly counterpois'd.   *C.* ii. 2.

His valour shown upon our crests to-day,
Hath taught us how to cherish such high deeds,
Even in the bosom of our adversaries.   *H. IV.* PT. I. v. 5.

   O, this boy
Lends mettle to us all!   *H. IV.* PT. I. v. 4.

Methought he bore him in the thickest troop,
As doth a lion in a herd of neat:
Or as a bear encompass'd round with dogs,
Who, having pinch'd a few, and made them cry,
The rest stand all aloof and bark at him.
          H. VI. PT. III. ii. 1.

  When valour preys on reason,
It eats the sword it fights with.   *A. C.* iii. 11.

In a false quarrel their is no true valour.   *M. A.* v. 1.

I told you, Sir, they were red hot with drinking;
So full of valour, that they smote the air
For breathing in their faces; beat the ground
For kissing of their feet.   *T.* iv. 1.

 Plague on't; an I thought he had been valiant, and so cunning in fence, I'd have seen him damned ere I'd have challenged him.   *T. N.* ii. 4.

What valour were it, when a cur doth grin,
For one to thrust his hand between his teeth,
When he might spurn him with his foot away?
          H. VI. PT. III. i. 4.

The Douglas, and the Hotspur, both together,
Are confident against the world in arms. *H. IV.* PT. I. v. 1.

Disdaining fortune, with his brandish'd steel,
Which smok'd with bloody execution,
•Like valour's minion
Carv'd out his passage, till he fac'd the slave.   *M.* i. 1.

 The better part of valour is discretion; in the which better part I have saved my life.   *H. IV.* PT. I. v. 4.

 Why, thou knowest I'm as valiant as Hercules: but beware instinct; the lion will not touch the true prince. Instinct is a great matter; I was a coward on instinct. I shall think the better of myself and thee during my life; I, for a valiant lion, and thou, for a true prince   *H. IV.* PT. I. ii. 4.

VALUATION
    Their fortunes both are weigh'd:
In your lord's scale is nothing but himself,
And some few vanities that make him light. *R. H.* iii. 4.

VALUE.
 What is aught, but as 'tis valued? *T.C.* ii. 2.
But value dwells not in particular will;
It holds his estimate and dignity
As well wherein 'tis precious of itself
As in the prizer: 'tis mad idolatry.
To make the service greater than the god;
And the will dotes, that is attributive
To what infectiously itself affects,
Without some image of the affected merit. *T.C.* ii. 2.

VANITY.
    We are such stuff
As dreams are made of, and our little life
Is rounded with a sleep. *T.* iv. 1.
To worship shadows and adore false shapes. *T. G.* iv. 2.
Light vanity, insatiate cormorant,
Consuming means, soon preys upon itself. *R. II.* ii. 1
 By the strength of their illusion
Shall draw him on to his confusion. *M.* iii. 5.
Shine out, fair sun, till I have bought a glass,
That I may see my shadow as I pass. *R. III.* i. 2.

VENERATION.
    There is an old poor man,
Who after me hath many a weary step
Limp'd in pure love; till he be first suffic'd,
Oppress'd with two great evils, age and hunger,
I will not touch a bit. *A. Y.* ii. 7.
Let but the commons hear this testament,
(Which, pardon me, I do not mean to read,)
And they would go and kiss dead Cæsar's wounds,
And dip their napkins in his sacred blood
Yea, beg a hair of him for memory,
And, dying, mention it within their wills,
Bequeathing it, as a rich legacy,
Unto their issue. *J.C.* iii. 2.

VENETIAN WOMEN.
I know our country disposition well;
In Venice they do let heaven see the pranks
They dare not show their husbands; their best conscience
Is—not to leave undone, but keep unknown. *O.* iii. 3.

VENGEANCE.

Are there no stones in heaven
But what serve for the thunder? *O* v. 2.

Arise, black vengeance, from thy hollow cell!
Yield up, O love, thy crown and hearted throne,
To tyrannous hate! swell, bosom, with thy fraught,
For 'tis of aspics' tongues! *O.* iii. 3.

VERACITY.

If Jupiter
Should from yond' cloud speak divine things
And say, 'tis true, I'd not believe them more
Than thee, all noble Marcius. *C.* iv. 5.

VERBOSITY (See also WORDS).

He draweth out the thread of his verbosity finer than the staple of his agrument. *L.L.* v. 1.

Words, words, mere words, no matter from the heart.
T.C. v. 3.

Gratiano speaks an infinite deal of nothing, more than any man in all Venice: His reasons are as two grains of wheat hid in two bushels of chaff; you shall seek all day ere you find them, and when you have found them, they are not worth the search. *M.V.* i. 1.

VERILY.

Verily!
You put me off with limber vows: But I,
Though you would seek to unsphere the stars with oaths,
Should yet say, Sir, no going. Verily,
You shall not go; a lady's verily is
As potent as a lord's. *W.T.* i. 2.

VETERAN.

He did look far
Into the service of the time, and was
Discipled of the bravest; he lasted long;
But on us both did haggish age steal on,
And wore us out of act. *A.W.* i. 2.

VICE, PREVALENT.

All sects, all ages, smack of this vice. *M.M.* ii. 2

Yes, in good sooth, the vice is of a great kindred; it is well allied. *M.M.* iii. 2.

VICISSITUDE.

Yet better thus, and known to be contemn'd,
Than still contemn'd and flatter'd. To be worst,

VICISSITUDE,—*continued.*
The lowest, and most dejected thing of fortune,
Stands still in esperance, lives not in fear:
The lamentable change is from the best;
The worst rĕturns to laughter. Welcome then,
Thou unsubstantial air, that I embrace!
The wretch, that thou hast blown unto the worst,
Owes nothing to thy blasts.   *K. L.* iv. 1.

        World, world, O world!
But that thy strange mutations make us hate thee,
Life would not yield to age.   *K. L.* iv. 1.

VICTORY.
To whom God will, there be the victory.
                        H. VI. PT. III. ii. 5.

    A victory is twice itself, when the achiever brings home full numbers.   *M. A.* i. 1.

    Thus far our fortune keeps an upward course,
And we are grac'd with wreaths of victory.
                        H. VI. PT. III. v. 3.

        O, such a day,
So fought, so follow'd, and so fairly won,
Come not, till now, to dignify the times,
Since Cæsar's fortunes.   *H. IV.* PT. II. i. 1.

    Mine enemies are all knit up
In their distractions.   *T.* iii. 3.

VILLAIN (See also KNAVE, ROGUE).
        Slave, soulless villain, dog!
O rarely base!   *A. C.* v. 2.

    When rich villains have need of poor ones, poor ones may make what price they will.   *M. A.* iii. 3.

    He hath out-villained villany so far, that the rarity redeems him.   *A. W.* iv. 3.

    I like not fair terms, and a villain's mind.   *M. V.* i. 3.

    In this, though I cannot be said to be a flattering honest man, it must not be denied that I am a plain-dealing villain.
                        M. A. i. 3.

VIRAGO.
    I would not marry her, though she were endowed with all that Adam had left him before he transgressed: she would have made Hercules have turned spit; yea, and have cleft his club to make the fire too. * * I would to God

VIRAGO,—*continued.*
some scholar would conjure her; for, certainly, while she is here, a man may live as quiet in hell, as in a sanctuary.
M. A. ii. 1.

VIRGINITY.
Bless our poor virginity from underminers and blowers up. Is there no military policy, how virgins might blow up men? *A. W.* i. 1.

VIRTUE.
Virtue is bold, and goodness never fearful. *M. M.* iii. 1.

But virtue, as it never will be mov'd,
Though lewdness court it in a shape of heaven;
So lust, though to a radiant angel link'd,
Will sate itself in a celestial bed,
And prey on garbage. *H.* i. 5.

              Never could the strumpet,
With all her double vigour, art, and nature,
Once stir my temper; but this virtuous maid
Subdues me quite: Ever, till now,
When men were fond, I smil'd, and wonder'd how.
M. M. ii. 2.

Assume a virtue, if you have it not.
That monster, custom, who all sense doth eat
Of habit's devil, is angel yet in this;
That to the use of actions fair and good
He likewise gives a frock, or livery,
That aptly is put on. *H.* iii. 4.

Virtue is of so little regard in these costermonger times, that true valour is turned bear-herd. *H. IV.* PT. II. i. 2.

———— AND ABILITY.
        I held it ever,
Virtue and cunning were endowments greater
Than nobleness and riches: careless heirs
May the two latter darken and expend;
But immortality attends the former,
Making a man a god. *P. P.* iii. 2.

———— REWARDED.
Virtue preserv'd from fell destruction's blast,
Led on by heaven, and crown'd with joy at last.
P. P. v. *Ep.*

VITUPERATION (See also ABUSE).
What man of good temper could endure this tempest of exclamation? *H. IV.* PT. II. ii. 1.
The bitter clamour of two eager tongues. *R. II.* i. 1.

UNANIMITY.
I would we were all of one mind, and one mind, good:
O, there were desolation of jailers and gallowses. *Cym.* v. 4.

UNDERLINGS.
Shallow.—Use his men well, Davy; for they are arrant knaves, and will backbite.
Davy.—No worse than they are back-bitten, Sir; for they have marvellous foul linen. *H.IV.* PT. II. v. 1.

UNFITNESS.
There is but one puritan amonst them, and he sings psalms to hornpipes. *W.T.* iv. 2.

On old Hyems' chin, and icy crown,
An od'rous chaplet of sweet summer buds
Is, as in mockery, set. *M. N.* ii. 2.

UNFORTUNATE.
Thou, whom the heaven's plagues,
Have humbled to all strokes. *K. L.* iv. 1.

UNION. UNITY
So we grew together,
Like to a double cherry, seeming parted,
But yet a union in partition;
Two lovely berries moulded on one stem:
So, with two seeming bodies, but one heart;
Two of the first, like coats in heraldry,
Due but to one, and crowned with one crest. *M.N.* iii. 2.

The amity that wisdom knits not, folly may easily untie.
T.C. ii. 3.

Then you love us, we you, and we'll clasp hands:
When peers thus knit, a kingdom ever stands. *P. P.* ii. 4.

He, that parts us, shall bring a brand from heaven,
And fire us hence, like foxes. *K. L.* v. 3.

UNKINDNESS.
Is there any cause in nature that makes these hard hearts?
K. L. iii. 6.

UNMASKING.
Your leavy screens throw down,
And show like those you are. *M.* v. 6.

UNSOUNDNESS.
Something is rotten in the state of Denmark. *H.* i. 4.
Gilded tombs do worms infold. *M. V.* ii. 7.

Nay, not as one would say, healthy; but so sound, as things that are hollow. *M.M.* i. 2.

UNVEILED.
To the greedy touch
Of common-kissing Titan. *Cym.* iii. 4.

UNWORTHINESS.
You are not worth the dust which the rude wind
Blows in your face. *K. L.* iv. 2.

Thou wert dignified enough,
Even to the point of envy, if 'twere made
Comparative for your virtues to be styl'd
The under hangman of his kingdom, and hated
For being preferr'd so well. *Cym.* ii. 3.

VOCATION.
Why, Hal, 'tis my vocation, Hal; 'tis no sin for a man
to labour in his vocation. *H. IV.* PT. I. i. 2.

VOICE.
The shepherd knows not thunder from a tabor,
More than I know the sound of Marcius' tongue,
From every meaner man's. *C.* i. 6.

────── MELODIOUS.
Who starves the ears she feeds, and makes them hungry,
The more she gives them speech. *P. P.* v. 1.

VOWS (See also LOVERS' VOWS, OATHS).
Riotous madness,
To be entangled with those mouth-made vows
Which break themselves in swearing. *A. C.* i. 3.

The gods are deaf to hot and peevish vows
They are polluted offerings, more abhor'd
Than spotted livers in the sacrifice. *T. C.* v. 3.

Men's vows are women's traitors! All good seeming,
By thy revolt, O husband, shall be thought
Put on for villany; not born, wher't grows;
But worn, a bait for ladies. *Cym.* iii. 4.

It is the purpose that makes strong the vow;
But vows to every purpose must not hold. *T C.* v. 3.

Unheedful vows may heedfully be broken. *T. G.* ii. 6.

────── CONNUBIAL, FALSIFIED (See also INCONTINENCE).
Such an act,
That blurs the grace and blush of modesty;
Calls virtue, hypocrite; takes off the rose
From the fair forehead of an innocent love,
And sets a blister there; makes marriage vows
As false as dicers' oaths. *H.* iii. 4.

UPSTART.
A man, they say, that from very nothing, beyond the imagination of his neighbours, is grown into an unspeakable estate. *W. T.* iv. 1.

URGENCY.
The affair cries,—haste,
And speed must answer it. *O.* i. 3.

The time will not allow the compliment,
Which very manners urges. *K. L.* v. 3.

A horse! a horse! my kingdom for a horse! *R. III.* v. 4.

Her business looks in her
With an importing visage. *A. W.* v. 3.

USURY.
That use is not forbidden usury,
Which happies those that pay the willing loan. *Poems.*

Banish usury, that makes the senate ugly. *T. A.* iii. 5.

USURERS.
Poor rogues, and usurers' men! bawds between gold and want! *T. A.* ii. 2.

USURPER.
A sceptre snatch'd with an unruly hand,
Must be as boisterously maintain'd as gain'd:
And he that stands upon a slippery place,
Makes nice of no vile hold to stay him up. *K. J.* iii. 4.

In the name of God,
How comes it then, that thou art call'd a king,
When living blood doth in these temples beat,
Which owe the crown that thou o'ermasterest? *K. J.* ii. 1.

Those he commands, move only in command,
Nothing in love: now does he feel the title
Hang loose about him, like a giant's robe
Upon a dwarfish thief. *M.* v. 2.

A vice of kings;
A cut-purse of the empire and the rule;
That from a shelf the precious diadem stole
And put it in his pocket. *H.* iii. 4.

No hand of blood and bone
Can gripe the sacred handle of our sceptre,
Unless he do profane, steal, or usurp. *R. II.* iii. 3.

UTILITY AND DIGNITY.
A stirring dwarf we do allowance give
Before a sleeping giant. *T. C.* ii. 3.

W.

WAGER.
 Though't be a sportful combat,
Yet in the trial much opinion dwells. *T. C.* i. 3.
Nothing can seem foul to those that win. *H. IV.* pt. i. v. 1.

WAGGERY.
 A waggish courage;
Ready in gibes, quick-answer'd, saucy, and
As quarrelous as a weasel. *Cym.* iii. 4.

WANDERER.
He that commends me to mine own content,
Commends me to the thing I cannot get
I to the world am like a drop of water,
That in the ocean seeks another drop;
Who, falling there to find his fellow forth,
Unseen, inquisitive, confounds himself. *C. E.* i. 2.

WANT.
Where nothing wants, that want itself doth seek.
 L. L. iv. 3.

WANTON.
Your worship's a wanton. *M. W.* ii. 2.

WANTONNESS.
 The spirit of wantonness is, sure, scared out of him; if the devil have him not in fee simple, with fine and recovery, he will never, I think, in the way of waste, attempt us again. *M. W.* iv. 2.

WAR (See also BATTLE).
The storm is up, and all is on the hazard. *J. C.* v. 1.
 Slaves for pillage fighting,
Obdurate vassals, fell exploits effecting,
In bloody deaths and ravishments delighting;
 Nor children's tears, nor mothers' groans respecting.
 Poems.
Put armour on thine ears, and on thine eyes;
Whose proof, nor yells of mothers, maids, nor babes,
Nor sight of priests in holy vestments bleeding,
Shall pierce a jot. *T. A.* iv. 3.
The grappling vigour, and rough frown of war. *K. J.* iii. 1.
The imminent death of twenty thousand men,
That, for a fantasy, and trick of fame,
Go to their graves like beds; fight for a plot,

Shakesperian Dictionary.

WAR

WAR,—*continued.*

Whereon the numbers cannot try the cause;
Which is not tomb enough, and continent,
To hide the slain. *H.* iv. 4

Giving our holy virgins to the stain
Of contumelious, beastly, mad-brain'd war. *T. A.* v. 2.

      Let it not disgrace me,
If I demand, before this royal view,
What rub, or what impediment, there is,
Why that the naked, poor, and mangled peace,
Dear nurse of arts, plenties, and joyful births,
Should not, in this best garden of the world,
Our fertile France, put up her lovely visage?
Alas! she hath from France too long been chas'd:
And all her husbandry doth lie on heaps,
Corrupting in its own fertility.
Her vine, the merry cheerer of the heart,
Unpruned, dies: her hedges even-pleach'd, —
Like prisoners wildly overgrown with hair,
Put forth disorder'd twigs: her fallow leas
The darnel, hemlock, and rank fumitory,
Doth root upon; while that the coulter rusts,
That should deracinate such savagery:
The even mead, that erst brought sweetly forth
The freckled cowslip, burnet, and green clover,
Wanting the scythe, all uncorrected, rank,
Conceives by idleness; and nothing teems,
But hateful docks, rough thistles, kecksies, burs,
Losing both beauty and utility.
And as our vineyards, fallows, meads, and hedges,
Defective in their natures, grow to wildness;
Even so our houses, and ourselves, and children,
Have lost, or do not learn, for want of time,
The sciences that should become our country;
But grow, like savages,—as soldiers will,
That nothing do but meditate on blood,—
To swearing, and stern looks, diffus'd attire,
And every thing that seems unnatural. *H. V.* v. 2.

Now, for the bare-pick'd bone of majesty,
Doth dogged war bristle his angry crest,
And snarleth in the gentle eyes of peace:
Now powers from home, and discontents at home,
Meet in one line; and vast confusion waits
(As doth a raven on a sick-fall'n beast)
The imminent decay of wrested pomp.
Now happy he, whose cloak and cincture can
Hold out this tempest. *K. J.* iv. 3.

WAR,—*continued.*
Lean famine, quartering steel, and climbing fire.
H. VI. PT. I. iv. 2.
Now all the youth of Eugland are on fire,
And silken dalliance in the wardrobe lies;
Now thrive the armourers, and honour's thought
Reigns solely in the breast of every man:
They sell the pasture now to buy the horse;
Following the mirror of all Christian kings,
With winged heels, as English Mercuries. *H. V.* ii. *chorus.*

Accursed and unquiet wrangling days!
How many of you have mine eyes beheld!
My husband lost his life to get the crown;
And often up and down my sons were toss'd,
For me to joy, and weep, their gain and loss;
And, being seated, and domestic broils
Clean overblown, themselves, the conquerors
Make war upon themselves; brother to brother,
Blood to blood, self 'gainst self. O preposterous
And frantic outrage! end thy damned spleen;
Or let me die, to look on death no more! *R. III.* ii. 4.

Two thousand souls, and twenty thousand ducats,
Will not debate the question of this straw:
This is the imposthume of much wealth and peace;
That inward breaks, and shows no cause without,
Why the man dies. *H.* iv. 4.

The toil of the war,
A pain that only seems to seek out danger
I' the name of fame, and honour; which dies i' the search.
Cym. iii. 3.

Hence, therefore, thou nice crutch;
A scaly gauntlet now, with joints of steel,
Must glove this hand: And hence, thou sickly quoif;
Thou art a guard too wanton for the head,
Which princes, flesh'd with conquest, aim to hit.
H. IV. PT. II. i. 1.

The gates of mercy shall be all shut up;
And the flesh'd soldier,—rough and hard of heart,—
In liberty of bloody hand, shall range
With conscience wide as hell; mowing like grass
Your fresh fair virgins and your flow'ring infants.
H. V. iii. 3.

This churlish knot of all-abhorred war. *H. IV.* PT. I. v. 1.

O war, thou son of hell,
Whom angry heavens do make their minister,
Throw in the frozen bosoms of our parts

WAR,—*continued.*
Hot coals of vengeance! Let no soldier fly:
He that is truly dedicate to war,
Hath no self-love; nor he, that loves himself,
Hath not essentially, but by circumstance,
The name of valour. *H. VI.* PT. II. v. 2.
    In a moment, look to see
The blind and bloody soldier, with foul hand,
Defile the locks of your shrill-shrieking daughters;
Your fathers taken by the silver beards,
And their most reverend heads dash'd to the walls;
Your naked infants spitted upon pikes;
Whiles the mad mothers with their howls confus'd
Do break the clouds. *H. V.* iii. 3.
    The nimble gunner
With linstock now the devilish cannon touches.
            H. V. iii. *chorus.*
    See a siege:
Behold the ordnance on their carriages,
With fatal mouths gaping on girded Harfleur.
            H. V. iii. *chorus.*
    Follow thy drum;
With man's blood paint the ground, gules, gules:
Religious canons, civil laws, are cruel;
Then what should war be? *T. A.* iv. 3.
Mortal staring war. *R. III.* v. 3.
  God forgive the sins of all those souls,
That to their everlasting residence,
Before the dew of evening fall, shall fleet,
In dreadful trial of our kingdom's king. *K. J.* ii. 1.
  Why have they dar'd to march
So many miles upon her peaceful bosom;
Frighting her pale-fac'd villages with war,
And ostentation of despightful arms? *R. II.* ii. 3.

He is their god; he leads them like a thing,
Made by some other deity than nature,
That shapes man better; and they follow him,
Against us brats, with no less confidence,
Than boys pursuing summer butterflies,
Or butchers killing flies. *C.* iv. 6.

Sword, hold thy temper; heart, be wrathful still:
Priests pray for enemies, but princes kill. *H. VI.* PT. II. v. 2.
    Alas, poor country!
Almost afraid to know itself! It cannot
Be call'd our mother, but our grave: where nothing,

WAR   *Shakespearian Dictionary.*   **WAR**

WAR,—*continued.*

But who knows nothing, is once seen to smile;
Where sighs, and groans, and shrieks that rend the air,
Are made, not mark'd; where violent sorrow seems
A modern ecstacy; the dead man's knell,
Is there scarce ask'd, for who; and good men's lives
Expire before the flowers in their caps,
Dying, or ere they sicken.   *M.* iv. 3.

      Therefore, my Harry,
Be it thy course to busy giddy minds
With foreign quarrels; that action, hence borne out,
May waste the memory of the former days.
   H. IV. PT. II. iv. 4.

      Examples, gross as earth, exhort me:
Witness, this army of such mass, and charge,
Led by a delicate and tender prince;
Whose spirit, by divine ambition puff'd,
Makes mouths at the invisible event;
Exposing what is mortal, and unsure,
To all that fortune, death, and danger, dare,
Even for an egg-shell.   *H.* iv. 4.

England hath long been mad, and scarr'd herself;
The brother blindly shed the brother's blood,
The father rashly slaughter'd his own son,
The son, compell'd, been butcher to the sire.   *R. III* v. 4.

      He is come to ope
The purple testament of bleeding war;
But ere the crown he looks for live in peace,
Ten thousand bloody crowns of mothers' sons
Shall ill-become the flower of England's face;
Change the complexion of her maid-pale face,
To scarlet indignation, and bedew
Her pastures' grass with faithful English blood.
   R. II. iii. 3.

Ah, gracious lord, these days are dangerous!
Virtue is chok'd with foul ambition,
And charity chas'd hence by rancour's hand:
Foul subornation is predominant,
And equity exil'd your highness' land.   *H. VI.* PT. II. iii. 1.

Shall we go throw away our coats of steel,
And wrap our bodies in black mourning gowns,
Numb'ring our Ave-Maries with our beads?
Or shall we, on the helmets of our foes,
Tell our devotion with revengeful arms!
   H. VI. PT. III ii. 1.

WAR   **Shakesperian Dictionary.**   WAR

WAR,—*continued.*
I'll use the advantage of my power,
And lay the summer's dust with show'rs of blood,
Rain'd from the wounds of slaughter'd Englishmen.
R. II. iii. 3.
    Let confusion of one part, confirm
The other's peace ; till then, blows, blood, and death.
K. J. ii. 2.
    At this time,
We sweat and bleed : the friend hath lost his friend;
And the best quarrels, in the heat, are curs'd
By those that feel their sharpness.   *K. L.* v. 3.
    Your own ladies, and pale-visag'd maids,
Like Amazons, come tripping after drums ;
Their thimbles into armed guantlets change,
Their neelds to lances, and their gentle hearts
To fierce and bloody inclination.   *K. J.* v. 2.
It is war's prize to take all vantages,
And ten to one is no impeach of valour. *H. VI.* PT. III. i. 4.
    Thou know'st, great son,
The end of war's uncertain.   *C.* v. 3.
O, now doth death line his dead chaps with steel;
The swords of soldiers are his teeth, his fangs ;
And now he feasts, mouthing the flesh of men,
In undetermin'd differences of kings.   *K. J.* ii. 2.
    Let them come ;
They come like sacrifices in their trim,
And to the fire-ey'd maid of smoking war,
All hot and bleeding, will we offer them :
The mailed Mars shall on his altar sit,
Up to the ears in blood.   *H. IV.* PT. I. iv. 1.
Come, let us make a muster speedily :
Doomsday is near; die all, die merrily.   *H. IV.* PT. I. iv. 1.
    It may well serve
A nursery to our gentry, who are sick
For breathing and exploit.   *A. W.* i. 2.
    The gallant monarch is in arms ;
And like an eagle o'er his aiery towers,
To souse annoyance that comes near his nest.   *K. J.* v. 2.
Away, you trifler ! Love ? I love thee not,
I care not for thee, Kate ; this is no world,
To play with mammets, and to tilt with lips :
We must have bloody noses, and crack'd crowns,
And pass them current too :—Gods me, my horse !
H. IV. PT. I. ii. 3

WAR,—*continued.*
      I do believe,
Statist though I am none, nor like to be,
That this will prove a war.   *Cym* ii. 4.
  Let me have war, say I; it exceeds peace, as far as day does night; it's spritely, waking, audible, and full of vent.
                 C. iv. 5.
They shall have wars, and pay for their presumption.
             H.VI. PT. III. iv. 1.
  How now, lad? is the wind in that door, i' faith? must we all march?   *H.IV.* PT. I. iii. 3.
      O virtuous fight,
When right with right wars, who shall be most right.
                 T.C. iii. 2.
—— PROGNOSTICS OF.
The bay-trees in our country all are wither'd,
And meteors fright the fixed stars of heaven;
The pale-fac'd moon looks bloody on the earth,
And lean-look'd prophets whisper fearful change;
Rich men look sad, and ruffians dance and leap,
The one, in fear to lose what they enjoy,
The other, to enjoy by rage and war. *R. II.* ii. 4.

WASTE.
  To paint the lily is wasteful.   *K. J.* iv. 2.

WATCHMAN.
  Why, you speak like an antient and most quiet watchman; for I cannot see how sleeping should offend. *M. A.* iii. 3.

WEAKNESS.
  This milky gentleness, and course of yours,
Though I condemn it not, yet, under pardon,
You are much more attask'd for want of wisdom,
Than prais'd for harmful mildness. *K. L.* i. 4.
    I am weaker than a woman's tear,
Tamer than sleep, fonder than ignorance;
Less valiant than the virgin in the night,
And skilless as unpractis'd infancy. *T.C.* i. 1.

WEALTH.
  How i' the name of thrift doth he rake this together?
               H.VIII. iii. 2.
—— THE ASSUMED AND ASSIGNED PRIVILEGES OF.
  Faults that are rich, are fair.   *T.A.* i. 2.

WEEPING (See also GRIEF, LAMENTATION, SORROW, TEARS)
  Give me no help in lamentation,
I am not barren to bring forth laments:

WEEPING,—*continued.*
All springs reduce their currents to mine eyes,
That I, being govern'd by the wat'ry moon,
May send forth plenteous tears to drown the world!
R. III. ii. 2.
To weep is to make less the depth of grief.
H. VI. PT. III. ii. 1
And the remainder mourning over them,
Brim full of sorrow, and dismay; but chiefly,
Him you term'd, Sir, the good old lord Gonzalo;
His tears run down his beard, like winter's drops
From eaves of reeds. *T.* v. 1.
       No, I'll not weep:—
I have full cause of weeping; but this heart
Shall break into a hundred thousand flaws,
Or ere I'll weep. *K. L.* ii. 4.
I cannot weep: for all my body's moisture
Scarce serves to quench my furnace-burning heart.
H. VI. PT. III. ii. 1.
'Twill be this hour ere I have done weeping. *T. G.* ii. 3.

WELCOME.
A hundred thousand welcomes: I could weep,
And I could laugh; I am light, and heavy: welcome:
A curse begin at very root of his heart,
That is not glad to see thee! *C.* ii. 1.
Ah, Juliet, if the measure of thy joy
Be heap'd like mine, and that thy skill be more
To blazon it, then sweeten with thy breath
This neighbour air, and let rich music's tongue
Unfold the imagin'd happiness that both
Receive in either by this dear encounter. *R. J.* ii. 6.
Sir, you are very welcome to our house;
It must appear in other ways than words,
Therefore I scant this breathing courtesy. *M. V.* v. 1.

   I reckon this always,—that a man is never undone till he be hanged; nor never welcome to a place till some certain shot be paid, and the hostess say, welcome. *T. G.* ii. 5.

   If thou wantest any thing, and wilt not call, beshrew thy heart. *H. IV.* PT. II. v. 3.

WELL DOING.
        Things done well,
And with a care, exempt themselves from fear.
H. VIII. i. 2.
——————— THE DUTY OF. D
We are born to do benefits. *T. A.* i. 5

WELL Doing, the Duty of,—*continued*.
Heaven doth with us, as we with torches do;
Not light them for themselves: for if our virtues
Did not go forth of us, 'twere all alike
As if we had them not. Spirits are not finely touch'd,
But to fine issues: nor nature never lends
The smallest scruple of her excellence,
But, like a thrifty goddess, she determines
Herself the glory of a creditor,
Both thanks and use. *M. M.* i. 1

WELSH.
But I will never be a truant, love,
Till I have learn'd thy language; for thy tongue
Makes Welsh as sweet as ditties highly penn'd,
Sung by a fair queen, in a summer's bower,
With ravishing division to her lute. *H. IV.* pt. i. iii. 1.
Now I perceive the devil understands Welsh;
And 'tis no marvel he's so humorous. *H. IV.* pt. i. iii. 1

WHISPERERS.
Cannot a plain man live, and think no harm,
But thus his simple truth must be abus'd
By silken, sly, insinuating Jacks? *R. III.* i. 3.

WHITE.
Whiter than new snow on a raven's back. *R. J.* iii. 2.
      I take thy hand; this hand,
As soft as doves-down, and as white as it;
Or Ethiopian's tooth, or the fann'd snow,
That's bolted by the northern blasts twice o'er. *W. T.* iv. 3.

———— and Red.
If she be made of white and red,
  Her faults will ne'er be known,
For blushing cheeks by faults are bred,
  And fears by pale-white shown
Then, if she fear, or be to blame,
  By this you shall not know;
For still her cheeks possess the same,
  Which native she doth owe. *L. L.* i. 2.

WIFE (See also Espousal).
          My noble father,
I do perceive here a divided duty:
To you I am bound for life and education;
My life and education both do learn me
How to respect you; you are the lord of duty;
I am hitherto your daughter: But here's my husband;
And so much duty as my mother show'd

WIF   Shakespearian Dictionary.   WIF

WIFE,—*continued.*
To you, preferring you before her father,
So much I challenge that I may profess
Due to the Moor, my lord.   *O.* i. 3.

Within the bond of marriage, tell me, Brutus,
Is it excepted, I should know no secrets
That appertain to you? Am I yourself
But, as it were, on sort, or limitation;
To keep with you at meals, comfort your bed,
And talk to you sometimes? Dwell I but in the suburbs
Of your good pleasure? If it be no more,
Portia is Brutus' harlot, not his wife.   *J.C.* ii. 1.

Such duty as the subject owes the prince,
Even such a woman oweth to her husband:
And, when she's froward, peevish, sullen, sour,
And not obedient to his honest will,
What is she but a foul contending rebel,
And graceless traitor to her loving lord?   *T. S.* v. 2.

Thy husband is thy lord, thy life, thy keeper,
Thy head, thy sovereign; one that cares for thee,
And for thy maintenance: commits his body
To painful labour, both by sea and land;
To watch the night in storms, the day in cold,
While thou liest warm at home, secure and safe;
And craves no other tribute at thy hands,
But love, fair looks, and true obedience.   *T. S.* v. 2.

I will be master of what is mine own:
She is my goods, my chattels; she is my house,
My household-stuff, my field, my barn,
My horse, my ox, my ass, my anything;
And here she stands, touch her whoever dare;
I will bring mine action on the proudest he
That stops my way in Padua.   *T. S.* iii. 2.

                Go thy ways, Kate:
That man i' the world, who shall report he has
A better wife, let him in nought be trusted,
For speaking false in that: Thou art, alone,
(If thy rare qualities, sweet gentleness,
Thy meekness saint-like, wife-like government,—
Obeying in commanding,—and thy parts
Sovereign and pious else, could speak thee out,)
The queen of earthly queens.   *H. VIII.* ii. 4.

You are my true and honourable wife;
As dear to me, as are the ruddy drops,
That visit my sad heart.   *J.C.* ii. 1.

WIFE,—*continued*.

    O, ye gods,
Render me worthy of this noble wife! *J. C.* ii. 1.

I grant I am a woman; but, withal,
A woman that lord Brutus took to wife;
I grant I am a woman; but, withal,
A woman well reputed; Cato's daughter.
Think you, I am no stronger than my sex,
Being so father'd and so husbanded? *J. C.* ii. 1

    She is mine own;
And I as rich in having such a jewel,
As twenty seas, if all their sand were pearl,
The water nectar, and the rocks pure gold. *T. G.* ii. 4.

    Should all despair,
That have revolted wives, the tenth of mankind
Would hang themselves. Physic for't there is none:
It is a bawdy planet, that will strike
Where 'tis predominant. *W. T.* i. 2.

    As for my wife,
I would you had her spirit in such another;
The third 'o the world is yours: which, with a snaffle,
You may pace easy, but not such a wife. *A. C.* ii. 2.

    But the full sum of me
Is sum of something; which, to term in gross,
Is an unlesson'd girl, unschool'd, unpractis'd:
Happy in this, she is not yet so old
But she may learn; happier than this,
She is not bred so dull but she can learn;
Happiest of all, is, that her gentle spirit
Commits itself to yours, to be directed,
As from her lord, her governor, her king. *M. V.* iii. 2

I am asham'd, that women are so simple
To offer war where they should sue for peace;
Or seek for rule, supremacy, and sway,
When they are bound to serve, love, and obey. *T. S.* v. 2

Fye, fye, unknit that threat'ning unkind brow;
And dart not scornful glances from those eyes,
To wound thy lord, thy king, thy governor;
It blots thy beauty, as frosts bite the meads;
Confounds thy fame, as whirlwinds shake fair buds;
And in no sense is meet or amiable. *T. S.* v. 2.

  Would it not grieve a woman to be over-mastered by a piece of valiant dust? to make an account of her life to a clod of wayward marle? *M. A.* ii. 1.

Shakespearian Dictionary.

WIFE, SLIGHTED.
    Alas, poor lady!
'Tis a hard bondage, to become the wife
Of a detesting lord.   *A. W.* iii. 5.
    I do think, it is their husbands' faults,
If wives do fall; Say, that they slack their duties
And pour our treasures into foreign laps;
Or else break out in peevish jealousies,
Throwing restraint upon us; or, say, they strike us,
Or scant our former having in despight:
Why, we have galls; and, though we have some grace,
Yet have we some revenge. Let husbands know,
Their wives have sense like them: they see, and smell,
And have their palates both for sweet and sour,
As husbands have. What is it that they do,
When they change us for others? Is it sport?
I think it is: And doth affection breed it?
I think it doth; Is't frailty, that thus errs?
It is so too: And have not we affections?
Desires for sport? and frailty, as men have?
Then, let them use us well; else, let them know,
The ills we do, their ills instruct us to.   *O.* iv. 3.

WILFULNESS.
    O, Sir, to wilful men,
The injuries that they themselves procure
Must be their schoolmasters.   *K. L.* ii. 4.

WILL.
    For death remember'd, should be like a mirror,
Who tell us, life's but breath; to trust it, error.
I'll make my will then; and, as sick men do,
Who know the world, see heaven, but feeling woe,
Gripe not at earthly joys, as erst they did.   *P. P.* i. 1.
    Thou mak'st a testament
As worldlings do, giving thy sum of more
To that which had too much.   *A. Y.* ii. 1.

Fetch the will hither, and we shall determine
How to cut off some charge in legacies.   *J. C.* iv. 1.

Ay, who doubts that? a will! a wicked will;
A woman's will; a canker'd grandam's will.   *K. J.* ii. 1.

    My will? Od's heartlings, that's a pretty jest, indeed!
I ne'er made my will yet, I thank heaven; I am not such
a sickly creature, I give heaven praise.   *M. W.* iii. 4.

WIND.
    Ill blows the wind that profits nobody.   *H. VI.* PT. III. ii. 5

WINE (See also DRUNKARD).

Drunk! and speak parrot? and squabble? and swagger? and speak fustian with one's own shadow? O, thou invisible spirit of wine, if thou hast no name to be known by, let us call thee—devil! *O*. ii. 3.

Come, come; good wine is a good familiar creature, if it be well used; exclaim no more against it. *O*. ii. 3.

WINNING.

Winning would put any man into courage. *Cym*. ii. 3.

WINTER.

When icicles hang by the wall,
  And Dick the shepherd blows his nail,
And Tom bears logs into the hall,
  And milk comes frozen home in pail;
    When blood is nipt, and ways be foul,
    Then nightly sings the staring owl
    Tu-whit! to-who! a merry note,
    While greasy Joan doth keel the pot.

When all aloud the wind doth blow,
  And coughing drowns the parson's saw,
And birds sit brooding in the snow,
  And Marian's nose looks red and raw;
    When roasted crabs hiss in the bowl,
    Then nightly, &c. *L. L.* v. 2.

WISDOM.

Ay, marry; now unmuzzle your wisdom. *A. Y.* i. 2.

To wisdom he's a fool that will not yield. *P. P.* ii. 4.

WISHERS.

Wishers were ever fools. *A. C.* iv. 13.

WIT.

We will spare for no wit, I warrant you. *M. A.* iii. 5.

He uses his folly like a stalking horse, and under the presentation of that, he shoots his wit. *A. Y.* v. 4.

Odd quirks and remnants of wit. *M. A.* ii. 3.

Since the little wit that fools have, was silenced, the little foolery that wise men have, makes a great show. *A. Y.* i. 2.

            But a merrier man,
Within the limit of becoming mirth,
I never spent an hour's talk withal:
His eye begets occasion for his wit;

WIT   Shakespearian Dictionary.   WIT

WIT,—*continued.*
For every object that the one doth catch,
The other turns to a mirth-moving jest;
Which his fair tongue (conceit's expositor)
Delivers in such apt and gracious words,
That aged ears play truant at his tales,
And younger hearings are quite ravished,
So sweet and voluble is his discourse.   *L. L.* ii. 1.

A fellow of infinite jest, of most excellent fancy.   *H.* v. 1.

Muster your wits: stand on your defence;
Or hide your heads like cowards, and fly hence.   *L. L.* v. 2.

    Those wits that think they have thee, do very oft prove fools; and I, that am sure I lack thee, may pass for a wise man: for what says Quinapalus? Better a witty fool, than a foolish wit.   *T. N.* i. 5.

    I am not only witty in myself, but the cause that wit is in other men.   *H. IV.* PT. II. i. 2.

    It is no matter, if I do halt; I have the wars for my colour, and my pension shall seem the more reasonable: A good wit will make use of any thing; I will turn diseases to commodity.   *H. IV.* PT. II. i. 2.

    By my troth, we that have good wits, have much to answer for; we shall be flouting; we cannot hold. *A. Y.* v. 1.

Sir, your wit ambles well; it goes easily.   *M. A.* v. 1.

    Dart thy skill at me;
Bruise me with scorn, confound me with a flout;
Thrust thy sharp wit quite through my ignorance;
Cut me to pieces with thy keen conceit.   *L. L.* v. 2.

    You should then have accosted her; and with some excellent jest, fire-new from the mint, you should have banged the youth into dumbness.   *T. N.* iii. 2.

Have you not set mine honour at the stake,
And baited it with all the unmuzzled thoughts
That tyrannous heart can think?   *T. N.* iii. 1.

Lo, lo, lo, lo, what modicums of wit he utters!   *T. C.* ii. 1.

    O, she would laugh me
Out of myself, press me to death with wit.   *M. A.* iii. 1

He wants wit that wants resolved will.   *T. G.* ii. 6.

He doth, indeed, show some sparks that are like wit.
    M. A. ii 3.

WIT,—*continued.*
Good wits will be jangling; but, gentles, agree. *L. L.* ii. 1.

None are so surely caught when they are catch'd,
As wit turn'd fool: folly, in wisdom hatch'd,
Hath wisdom's warrant, and the help of school;
And wit's own grace to grace a learned fool. *L. L.* v. 2.

Folly in fools bears not so strong a note,
As foolery in the wise when wit doth dote;
Since all the power thereof it doth apply,
To prove, by wit, worth in simplicity. *L. L.* v. 2.

Are these the breed of wits so wondered at? *L. L.* v. 2.

Thou hast pared thy wit o' both sides, and left nothing in the middle. *K. L.* i. 4.

His wit is as thick as Tewkesbury mustard.
H. IV. PT. II. ii. 4.

Hector shall have a great catch, if he knock out either of your brains; 'a were as good crack a fusty nut with no kernel. *T. C.* ii. 1.

Are his wits safe? is he not light of brain? *O.* iv. 1.

See now, how wit may be made a Jack-a-lent, when 'tis upon ill employment. *M. W.* v. 5.

Well, better wits have worn plain statute caps. *L. L.* v. 2

When a man's verses cannot be understood, nor a man's good wit seconded by the forward child, understanding, it strikes a man more dead than a great reckoning in a little room. *A. Y.* iii. 3

God help me! how long have you profess'd apprehension?
M. A. iii. 4.

He'll but break a comparison or two on me; which, peradventure, not marked, or not laughed at, strikes him into melancholy; and then there's a partridge's wing saved, for the fool will eat no supper that night. *M. A.* ii. 1.

—— AN UNCONSCIOUS.
Nay, I shall ne'er be 'ware of mine own wit, till I break my shins against it. *A. Y.* ii. 4

WIT, REFLECTIONS ON THE SCULL OF A.
Where be your gibes now? your gambols? your songs? your flashes of merriment, that were wont to set the table in a roar? Not one now to mock your own grinning? quite

WIT   Shakespearian Dictionary.   WIT

WIT, REFLECTIONS ON THE SCULL OF A,—*continued.*
chap-fallen? Now get you to my lady's chamber, and tell
her, let her paint an inch thick, to this favour she must
come; make her laugh at that.   *H.* v. 1.

——, WOMEN'S.
Make the doors upon a woman's wit, and it will out at
the casement; shut that, and 'twill out at the key-hole:
stop that, 'twill fly with the smoke out at the chimney.
A. Y. iv. 1.

Upon her wit doth earthly honour wait,
And virtue stoops and trembles at her frown.
Tit. And. ii. 1.

WITLING.
This fellow pecks up wit, as pigeons, pease;
And utters it again when God doth please:
He is wit's pedlar; and retails his wares
At wakes, and wassails, meetings, markets, fairs;
And we that sell by the gross, the Lord doth know,
Have not the grace to grace it with such show. *L. L.* v. 2.

WITCHES.
What are these,
So wither'd, and so wild in their attire,
That look not like the inhabitants o' the earth,
And yet are on't? Live you? or are you aught
That man may question? You seem to understand me,
By each at once her choppy finger laying
Upon her skinny lips:—You should be women,
And yet your beards forbid me to interpret
That you are so.   *M.* i. 3.

I cónjure you, by that which you profess,
(Howe'er you come to know it,) answer me:
Though you untie the winds, and let them fight
Against the churches; though the yesty waves
Confound and swallow navigation up;
Though bladed corn be lodg'd, and trees blown down;
Though castles topple on their warder's heads;
Though palaces, and pyramids, do slope
Their heads to their foundations; though the treasure
Of nature's germins tumble altogether,
Ev'n till destruction sicken,—answer me
To what I ask.   *M.* iv. 1.

WITHDRAWING.
So to your pleasures;
am for other than for dancing measures.   *A. Y.* v. 4.

WOE.

O, what a sympathy of woe is this!
As far from help as limbo is from bliss!   *Tit. And.* iii. 1.

WOLSEY, CARDINAL.

    You are meek and humble mouth'd;
You sign your place, and calling, in full seeming,
With meekness and humility: but your heart
Is cramm'd with arrogancy, spleen, and pride.
You have, by fortune, and his highness' favours,
Gone slightly o'er low steps; and now are mounted,
Where powers are your retainers; and your words
(Domestics to you) serve your will as't please
Yourself pronounce their office. I must tell you,
You tender more your person's honour, than
Your high profession spiritual.   *H. VIII.* ii. 4.

    He was a man
Of an unbounded stomach, ever ranking
Himself with princes: one, that by suggestion
Tied all the kingdom: simony was fair play;
His own opinion was his law: I' the presence
He would say untruths; and be ever double,
Both in his words and meaning: He was never
(But where he meant to ruin) pitful:
His promises were, as he then was, mighty;
But his performance, as he is now, nothing.
Of his own body he was ill, and gave
The clergy ill example.   *H. VIII* iv. 2.

    This cardinal,
Though from an humble stock, undoubtedly
Was fashion'd to much honour. From his cradle
He was a scholar, and a ripe, and good one;
Exceeding wise, fair spoken, and persuading:
Lofty, and sour, to them that lov'd him not;
But, to those men that sought him, sweet as summer:
And though he were unsatisfied in getting,
(Which was a sin,) yet, in bestowing, Madam,
He was most princely. Ever witness for him
Those twins of learning, that he rais'd in you,
Ipswich, and Oxford: one of which fell with him,
Unwilling to outlive the good that did it.
The other, though unfinish'd, yet so famous,
So excellent in art, and still so rising,
That Christendom shall ever speak his virtue.
His overthrow heap'd happiness upon him;
For then, and not till then, he felt himself,
And found the blessedness of being little:

Shakesperian Dictionary.

WOLSEY,—*continued.*
And, to add greater honours to his age
Than man could give him, he died,
Fearing God. *H. VIII.* iv. 2.

WOMAN.

    Ah me! how weak a thing
The heart of woman is!   *J. C.* ii. 4.

    When maidens sue
Men give like gods; but when they weep and kneel,
All their petitions are as freely theirs
As they themselves would have them.   *M. M.* i. 5.

We cannot fight for love, as men may do;
We should be woo'd, and were not made to woo.
              M. N. ii. 2.

    Women are not
In their best fortunes, strong; but want will perjure
The ne'er touch'd vestal.   *A. C.* iii. 10.

These women are shrewd tempters with their tongues.
              H. VI. PT. I. i. 2.

    O most delicate fiend!
Who is't can read a woman?   *Cym.* v. 5.

She's beautiful; and therefore to be woo'd:
She is a woman; therefore to be won.   *H. VI.* PT. I. v. 3.

Come on, come on: You are pictures out of doors,
Bells in your parlours, wild cats in your kitchens,
Saints in your injuries, devils being offended,
Players in your housewifery, and housewives in your beds.
              O. ii. 1.

A woman mov'd, is like a fountain troubled,
Muddy, ill-seeming, thick, bereft of beauty;
And, while it is so, none so dry or thirsty,
Will deign to dip or touch one drop of it.   *T. S.* v. 2.

Can my sides hold, to think, that man,—who knows
By history, report, or his own proof,
What woman is, yea, what she cannot choose
But must be,—will his free hours languish for
Assured bondage?   *Cym.* i.

 The bountiful blind woman [Fortune] doth most mistn.
in her gifts to women. For those that she makes fair, she
scarce makes honest; and those that she makes honest, she
makes very ill-favouredly.   *A. Y.* i. 2.

WOMAN,—*continued.*
Ah! poor our sex! this fault in us I find,
The error of our eye directs our mind. *T. C.* v. 2.

That we can call these delicate creatures ours,
And not their appetites! *O.* iii. 3.

——— GENERAL INVECTIVE AGAINST.
Is there no way for men to be, but women
Must be half workers? We are bastards all:
And that most venerable man, which I
Did call my father, was I know not where
When I was stampt; some coiner with his tools
Made me a counterfeit: yet my mother seem'd
The Dian of that time: so doth my wife
The nonpareil of this. O vengeance! vengeance!
Me of my lawful pleasure she restrain'd,
And pray'd me, oft, forbearance; did it with
A pudency so rosy, the sweet view on't
Might well have warm'd old Saturn; that I thought her
As chaste as unsunn'd snow: O, all the devils!
Could I find out
The woman's part in me! For there's no motion
That tends to vice in man, but I affirm
It is the woman's part: Be it lying, note it,
The woman's; flattering, hers; deceiving, hers;
Lust and rank thoughts, hers, hers; revenges, hers;
Ambitions, covetings, change of prides, disdain,
Nice longings, slanders, mutability:
All faults that may be nam'd, nay, that hell knows,
Why, hers, in part, or all; but, rather, all:—
For even to vice
They are not constant, but are changing still
One vice, but of a minute old, for one
Not half so old as that. I'll write against them,
Detest them, curse them:—Yet 'tis greater skill,
In a true hate, to pray they have their will:
The very devils cannot plague them better. *Cym.* ii. 5.

WONDER.
Masters, I am to discourse wonders. *M. N.* iv. 2.

They spake not a word;
But, like dumb statues, or breathless stones,
Star'd on each other, and look'd deadly pale. *R. III.* iii. 7.

Can such things be,
And overcome us like a summer's cloud,
Without our special wonder? You make me strange,
Even to the disposition that I owe,

Shakespearian Dictionary.

WONDER,—*continued.*

When now I think you can behold such sights,
And keep the natural ruby of your cheeks,
While mine are blanch'd with fear. *M.* iii. 4.

For my part, I am so attir'd in wonder,
I know not what to say. *M. A.* iv. 1.

Why, 'tis the rarest argument of wonder, that hath shot out in our latter times. *A. W.* ii. 1.

One that excels the quirks of blazoning pens. *O.* ii. 1.

These are not natural events; they strengthen,
From strange to stranger. *T.* v. 1.

Bring in the admiration; that we with thee
May spend our wonder too, or take off thine,
By wond'ring how thou took'st it. *A. W.* ii. 1.

WOOING, WEDDING, AND REPENTING.

Wooing, wedding, and repenting, are as a Scotch jig, a measure, and a cinque pace: the first suit is hot and hasty, like a Scotch jig, and full as fantastical; the wedding, mannerly modest, as a measure full of state and ancientry; and then comes repentance, and, with his bad legs, falls into the cinque-pace faster and faster, till he sink into his grave. *M. A.* ii. 1.

WORDS (See also VERBOSITY).

A fine volley of words, gentlemen, and quickly shot off.
T. G. ii. 4.

And tire the hearer with a book of words. *M. A.* i. 1.

Good words are better than bad strokes. *J. C.* v. 1.

You have an exchequer of words, and, I think, no other treasure to give your followers; for it appears by their bare liveries, that they live by your bare words. *T. G.* ii. 4.

Words are very rascals since bonds disgraced them.
T. N. iii. 1.

Words are grown so false, I am loath to prove reason with them. *T. N.* iii. 1.

His plausive words
He scatter'd not in ears, but grafted them
To grow there, and to bear. *A. W.* i. 2.

I will maintain the word with my sword, to be a soldier-like word, and a word of exceeding good command.
H. IV. PT. II. iii. 2.

WORDS,—*continued.*
O, they have lived long in the alms-basket of words.
L. L. v. 1.

Let not his smoothing words
Bewitch your hearts; be wise, and circumspect.
H. VI. PT. II. i. 1.

—— AND BLOWS.
Brutus.—Sir, I hope,
My words disbench'd you not.
Coriolanus.—No, Sir; yet oft,
When blows have made me stay, I fled from words. *C.* ii. 2.

WORDS, MERETRICIOUS ABUSE OF.
They that dally nicely with words, may quickly make them wanton. *T. N.* iii. 1.

WORLD.
All the world's a stage,
And all the men and women, merely players:
They have their exits and their entrances;
And one man in his time plays many parts,
His acts being seven ages. At first, the infant;
Mewling and puking in the nurse's arms:
And then, the whining school-boy, with his satchel,
And shining morning face, creeping, like snail,
Unwillingly to school: And then, the lover;
Sighing like furnace, with a woful ballad
Made to his mistress' eye-brow: Then, a soldier;
Full of strange oaths, and bearded like the pard,
Jealous in honour, sudden and quick in quarrel,
Seeking the bubble reputation
Ev'n in the cannon's mouth: And then, the justice;
In fair round belly, with good capon lin'd,
With eyes severe, and beard of formal cut,
Full of wise saws, and modern instances,
And so he plays his part: The sixth age shifts
Into the lean and slipper'd pantaloon;
With spectacles on nose, and pouch on side;
His youthful hose, well sav'd, a world too wide
For his shrunk shank; and his big manly voice,
Turning again towards childish treble, pipes
And whistles in the sound: Last scene of all,
That ends this strange eventful history,
Is second childishness, and mere oblivion;
Sans teeth, sans eyes, sans taste, sans every thing.
A. Y. ii. 7.

Under the canopy. *C.* iv. 5.

WORLD,—*continued*.
 The varying shore o' the world. *A. C.* iv. 13.
  This wide and universal theatre
Presents more woful pageants, than the scene
Wherein we play. *A. Y.* ii. 7.
 O, world, thy slippery turns! Friends now fast sworn,
Whose double bosoms seem to wear one heart,
Whose hours, whose bed, whose meal, and exercise
Are still together: who twin, as 'twere, in love,
Unseparable, shall within this hour,
On a dissention of a doit, break out
To bitterest enmity: So, fellest foes,
Whose passions and whose plots have broke their sleep,
To take the one the other, by some chance,
Some trick not worth an egg, shall grow dear friends,
And interjoin their issues. *C.* iv. 4.

 A bad world, I say! I would, I were a weaver; I could sing all manner of songs. *H. IV.* PT. I. ii. 4.

     How you speak!
Did you but know the city's usuries,
And felt them knowingly: the art o' the court,
As hard to leave, as keep; whose top to climb
Is certain falling; or so slippery, that
The fear's as bad as falling: the toil of the war,
A pain that only seems to seek out danger
I' the name of fame, and honour, which dies i' the search;
And hath as oft a slanderous epitaph,
As record of fair act; nay, many times,
Doth ill deserve by doing well; what's worse,
Must court'sey at the censure:—O, boys, this story,
The world may read in me. *Cym.* iii. 5.

 A man may see how this world goes, with no eyes. Look with thine ears: See how yon' justice rails upon yon' simple thief. Hark, in thine ear: Change places; and, handy-dandy, which is the justice, which is the thief? *K. L.* iv. 6

It is a reeling world, indeed, my lord. *R. III.* iii. 2.

I hold the world but as the world, Gratiano,
A stage, where every man must play a part,
And mine a sad one. *M. V.* i. 1.

 Fie, fie, fie! Pah, pah! Give me an ounce of civet, good apothecary, to sweeten my imagination: there's money for thee. *K. L.* iv. 6.

O ruin'd piece of nature! This great world
Shall so wear out to nought. *K. L.* iv. 6.

WORLD,—*continued*.
                          Come, let's away to prison:
We two alone will sing like birds i' the cage:
When thou dost ask my blessing, I'll kneel down,
And ask of thee forgiveness: So we'll live,
And pray, and sing, and tell old tales, and laugh
At gilded butterflies, and hear poor rogues
Talk of court news; and we'll talk with them too,—
Who loses, and who wins; who's in, who's out;—
And take upon's the mystery of things,
As if we were God's spies: And we'll wear out,
In a wall'd prison, packs and sects of great ones,
That ebb and flow by the moon.   *K. L.* v. 3

Sweet prince, the untainted virtue of your years
Hath not yet div'd into the world's deceit:
No more can you distinguish of a man,
Than of his outward show, which, God he knows,
Seldom, or never, jumpeth with the heart. *R. III.* iii. 1.

I am in this earthly world; where, to do harm,
Is often laudable: to do good, sometimes
Accounted dangerous folly.   *M.* iv. 2.

You have too much respect upon the world:
They lose it that do buy it with much care. *M. V.* i. 1.

I am amaz'd, methinks; and lose my way
Among the thorns and dangers of this world. *K. J.* iv. 3.

——————'s REPORT.
             Noble madam,
Men's evil manners live in brass: their virtues
We write in water.   *H. VIII.* iv. 2.

The evil that men do lives after them;
The good is oft interred with their bones. *J. C.* iii. 2.

WORMS.
    Your worm is your only emperor for diet: we fat all creatures else to fat us; and we fat ourselves for maggots: your fat king, and your lean beggar, is but variable service; two dishes, but to one table; that's the end.
                                    H. iv. 3.

A man may fish with a worm that eat of a king, and eat of the fish that hath fed of that worm. *H* iv. 3.

WORST.
    O gods! who is't can say, I'm at the worst
I am worse than e'er I was.   *K. L* iv. 1.

         The worst is not,
So long as we can say,—This is the worst. *K. L.* iv. 1.

WOUND.
The private wound is deepest.   *T. G.* v. 4.

WOUNDED SPIRIT.
A discontented friend, grief-shot
With his unkindness.   *C.* v. 1

WRONGS.
If that the heavens do not their visible spirits
Send quickly down to tame these vile offences,
'Twill come,
Humanity must perforce prey on itself,
Like monsters of the deep.   *K. L.* iv. 2
O heavens, can you hear a good man groan,
And not relent, or not compassion in him?   *Tit. And.* iv. 1.
Broke oath on oath, committed wrong on wrong.
    H. IV. PT. I. iv. 3

Y.

YEOMEN.
    And you, good yeomen,
Whose limbs were made in England, show us here
The mettle of your pasture; let us swear
That you are worth your breeding, which I doubt not;
For there is none of you so mean and base,
That hath not noble lustre in your eyes.   *H. V.* iii. 1.

YOUTH.
A most acute juvenal; voluble and free of grace.
    L. L. iii. 1.

He capers, he dances, he has the eyes of youth, he writes verses, he speaks holyday, he smells April and May: he will carry't, he will carry't; 'tis in his buttons; he will carry't.   *M. W.* iii. 2.

A violet in the youth of primy nature.   *H.* i. 3.

    She is young, and apt;
Our own precedent passions do instruct us
What levity's in youth.   *T. A.* i. 1.

Young blood doth not obey an old decree.   *L. L.* iv. 3

    For in her youth
There is a prone and speechless dialect,
Such as moves men; besides, she hath prosperous art
When she will play with reason and discourse,
And well she can persuade.   *M. M.* i. 3.

YOUTH,—*continued.*
Briefly die their joys,
That place them on the truth of girls and boys. *Cym.* v. 5

We were, fair queen,
Two lads that thought there was no more behind,
But such a day to-morrow as to-day,
And to be boy eternal. *W.T.* i. 2

A proper stripling, and an amorous! *T.S.* i. 2.

YOUTH, MELANCHOLY.
He hears merry tales, and smiles not: I fear he will prove the weeping philosopher when he grows old, being so full of unmannerly sadness in his youth. *M.V.* i. 2.

———— UNRESTRAINED.
When his headstrong riot hath no curb,
When rage and hot blood are his counsellors,
When means and lavish manners meet together;
O, with what wings shall his affections fly
Towards fronting peril and oppos'd decay.
H. IV. PT. II. iv. 4.

Z.

ZANIES.
I protest, I take these wise men, that crow so at these set kind of fools, no better than the fools' zanies.
T. N. i. 5.

ZEAL DISREGARDED.
To whose ingrate and unauspicious altars,
My soul the faithfull'st offerings hath breath'd out,
That e'er devotion tender'd. *T. N.* v. 1.

ZED.
Thou unnecessary letter! *K. L.* ii. 2.

Finis.

www.ingramcontent.com/pod-product-compliance
Lightning Source LLC
Chambersburg PA
CBHW022104290426
44112CB00008B/541